CONTEMPORARY

ECONOMIC SYSTEMS

A Comparative View

CONTEMPORARY ECONOMIC SYSTEMS

A Comparative View

Gary M. Pickersgill

*Associate Professor of Economics, California State
University, Fullerton*

Joyce E. Pickersgill

*Associate Professor of Economics, California State
University, Fullerton*

PRENTICE-HALL, INC., Englewood Cliffs, New Jersey

Library of Congress Cataloging in Publication Data

Pickersgill, Joyce E.
    Contemporary economic systems: a comparative view.

    Includes bibliographies.
    1. Comparative economics. 2. Economic history—
1945- I.- Pickersgill, Gary M., joint
author. II.-Title.
HB90.P5   330.9'04   73-9510
ISBN 0-13-169342-5

© 1974 by Prentice-Hall, Inc.,
Englewood Cliffs, New Jersey

10 9 8 7 6 5 4 3 2 1

Printed in the United States of America

PRENTICE-HALL INTERNATIONAL, INC., *London.*
PRENTICE-HALL OF AUSTRALIA PTY. LTD., *Sydney*
PRENTICE-HALL OF CANADA, LTD., *Toronto*
PRENTICE-HALL OF INDIA PRIVATE LTD., *New Delhi*
PRENTICE-HALL OF JAPAN, INC., *Tokyo*

In Memory of Kay

Contents

Preface

Full employment, growth, price stability, the elimination of poverty, and a more equitable distribution of income are only a few of the problems facing most economies today. Political leaders of both Western and Communist nations are constantly searching for new economic policies and institutions within their ideological frameworks to achieve these diverse, often incompatible goals, and are even eyeing warily the methods of their traditional adversaries. Western economists and political leaders are interested in the possible benefits of planning, and Soviet and Eastern European leaders have grudgingly recognized the value of market institutions. What alternative methods of economic organization are available for solving economic problems? It is to this question that the authors address themselves in this text.

Commentators often array nations representing various economic systems along a spectrum, ranging from a heavy reliance on the market mechanism on one end, to the substantial use of the centrally-directed command principle on the other. This one-dimensional classification is misleading, because economies dissimilar in many aspects often wind up nestled together on the basis of one common characteristic, and a single economy may change position markedly in a short period of time because of war pressures or some other crisis.

An economic system has many dimensions. Accordingly, this book treats economic systems as bundles of characteristics that may be combined in many different ways. Although we recognize this multidimensional complexity, we have tried to avoid presenting such a welter of historic and institutional detail that the general pattern is lost in the particular. To give the reader a manageable framework within which to analyze a particular national economy, we have selected a few critical characteristics to define a system and have applied them uniformly in analyzing both economic models and representative national economies.

Part I, the theoretical section of the text, presents the method of classifying characteristics, as well as a set of criteria with which to judge the performance of both models and national economies. Part II defines and evaluates the model of perfectly competitive capitalism and examines the evolution of real-world, capitalist institutions. Part III introduces three mixed economies—France, Germany, and Britain—and analyzes their adaptations of capitalist institutions. A separate chapter is devoted to the international comparison of economic policies and performances. A survey of the Marxist critique of capitalism completes this section on capitalist/mixed economies and sets the stage for Part IV, which presents a theoretical model of central planning. The chapters on the Soviet Union illustrate these general principles and at the same time reveal the peculiar adaptations of planning to the needs of a Marxist political state superimposed on a centuries-old, authoritarian tradition. Part V introduces the theory of market socialism and examines its manifestation in the Yugoslavian economy. Finally, Part VI attempts to broaden the framework of analysis to include social, political, and cultural values.

The method of presenting and evaluating an economic system is necessarily influenced by the author's values. The authors of this text recognize this problem and have attempted to provide as value-free an analytic framework as possible for classifying and judging the performance of economic systems. The last chapter in the book explicitly departs from this norm, however, and we hope that this stimulates the reader to form his own judgments on the advantages and disadvantages of alternative systems.

The authors are indebted to Professor Marshall Goldman of Wellesley College, and Professors E. K. Hunt and Howard Sherman, Department of Economics, University of California at Riverside, for their helpful comments and criticisms in the preparation of the manuscript.

G. M. P.

J. E. P.

CONTEMPORARY ECONOMIC SYSTEMS

A Comparative View

I

SYSTEMS: CLASSIFICATION AND EVALUATION

1

The Study
of Comparative
Economic Systems

Introduction

Members of every society, individually and collectively, desire more goods and services than they currently produce. To those living in India, as well as to those living in the United States, there is an obvious "need" for more. It is a basic premise of economics that man has unlimited wants. No economy is in danger of reaching that utopian state in which goods must be given away to induce further consumption.

Individuals and societies attempt to satisfy their wants by producing goods and services. They produce goods and services by combining economic resources—land, labor, and capital. These resources are scarce because they do not exist in sufficient quantities to produce enough goods and services to satisfy all of man's wants. Scarcity necessitates choice. Man and societies must choose from an array of alternatives a particular combination of resources to produce that particular bundle of goods which will maximize their welfare over time. Many thorny problems lie hidden within that deceivingly simple statement. The necessity for choice is thrust on us because resources are scarce, and this results in a scarcity of goods.

Comparative economic systems is the study of alternative sets of institutions for making economic choices and for deciding among alternatives. We will define or label an economic system according to the mechanisms and institutions it uses in the process of economic decision-making and problem solving. Before considering how different systems solve economic problems, we will look at the nature of the problems themselves. The problems can be grouped into three major categories: 1) what should be produced, 2) how should production be organized, and 3) how should production be distributed among claimants.

ECONOMIC PROBLEMS CONFRONTING ALL SYSTEMS

What to Produce — Determinants of Supply

Regardless of the nature of the institutions making up an economic system, every system is faced with the problem of scarcity and the necessity of choice. The decision to produce more public goods implies the decision to produce less private goods. The decision to produce more plant and equipment must coincide with a decision to produce fewer consumer goods.

We can analyze the field of choice available to any economy by a *production possibilities curve,* illustrating the trade-off between two products. Every point on such a curve represents full employment of available resources, hence the limit of our "production possibilities."

Let us assume that our society has a limited amount of land, labor, and capital that it can allocate to the production of wheat and steel. If it allocates all its resources to the production of wheat, let us suppose that it can produce 500 tons of wheat. If it chooses to allocate all of its resources to steel, it can produce 400 tons of steel. In diagram 1.1 the curve connecting 500 tons of wheat and 400 tons of steel illustrates all the different combinations of wheat and steel this economy is capable of producing. This curve is called the production possibilities curve. It would be possible to choose a point lying within the production possibilities curve—say 250 tons of steel and 200 tons of wheat at point G—but this would imply that either some of the economy's resources are unemployed or that it is using its resources wastefully. It would be impossible to choose a point lying to the right of the production possibilities curve, like 325 tons of steel and 300 tons of wheat at point H, since there are not enough resources to produce both goods at this level.

The decision-makers in an economy, individually or collectively, attempt to pick the most desirable point on the production possibilities curve. They will be guided by their tastes and preferences, as well as by the rate of "trade-off" implied by the shape of the production possibilities curve. By trade-off we mean the rate at which we must sacrifice one good in order to obtain the other as we move along the curve. The curvature of the production possibilities curve illustrates this concept of trade-off or *"opportunity cost,"* that is, the amount of one good which must be sacrificed in order to gain a given amount of another good. In our illustration, wheat production must be lowered if additional steel is to be produced. This is accomplished by removing economic resources from the production of one good and allocating them to the production of the other good.

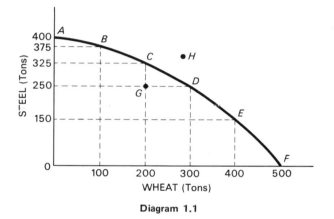

Diagram 1.1

Diagram 1.1 further illustrates the familiar principle of *"diminishing returns,"* or *increasing* opportunity costs. We see that as we move leftward along the PPC from point F to point E we sacrifice 100 tons of wheat and gain 150 tons of steel. The next sacrifice of 100 tons of wheat to point D earns us only 100 tons of steel. You can observe the continued decline of the steel payoff as the production combination shifts from D to C to B to A. These numbers illustrate "diminishing returns." Now move rightward along the curve from point A, retracing the moves just made. As we gain each additional 100 tons of wheat, we must sacrifice first 25 tons of steel to point B and a further 50 tons to point C, and 75 tons to point D, etc. These numbers illustrate the concept of "increasing opportunity costs."

We will discuss the problem of opportunity costs in more detail in the next chapter, but an important point must be made before we examine the next category of economic problems. The shape and position of the production possibilities curve is determined by the availability of resources and the level of technology in a particular society. The peculiar form of social or political arrangements of a society cannot alter either of these objective conditions. By this we mean that diminishing returns are as real in the steel mills and wheat lands of the Soviet Union as they are in the United States. More steel for spaceships and tanks means sacrifices of wheat (for this read "consumer goods") in any society.

To conclude, we have used only two goods, since we are restricted by the two-dimensional diagram to that number; but the principle is valid in the real world, where a vast multitude of goods are produced. With fully employed resources, increased output of any good will absolutely require a lowered output of some other good.

What to Produce — Determinants of Demand

The most desirable position on a production possibilities curve will depend upon a community's tastes as well as upon the rate of trade-off between the two goods involved.

It is possible to make some very simple statements about consumption behavior which will point to a solution of our problem of choosing what combination of goods to produce. First, more is preferable to less. This principle assures us that society will always prefer a point on the PPC of diagram 1.1 over some position inside the PPC like point G. At point G we can have the same amount of steel and 100 tons more of wheat by moving to point D. We can hold wheat constant and obtain 75 tons of steel by moving to point C. Note that this move is "costless" in the sense that nothing is given up or sacrificed to obtain more output. The tragedy of the Great Depression in the 1930s was that such a "costless" move was not made due to ignorance as to the means of accomplishing the necessary stimulation of demand.

Another reasonably intuitive statement about consumer behavior is that the more of a particular commodity a consumer has, the less satisfaction he gets out of additional amounts of this good. Diagram 1.1 illustrates that a consumer (or society) faced with choosing between bundle B of steel and wheat versus bundle C may prefer bundle C. When comparing bundle D with bundle C, the consumer must now consider that he has obtained 100 tons more of wheat, and he will be less keen on obtaining more. The consumer is now consuming 50 tons less steel, and the sacrifice of more steel will weigh heavier on his mind. These facts considered, on balance the consumer (or society) may still prefer bundle D. It is clear, however, that a point will ultimately be reached at which the loss of satisfaction from the sacrifice of steel will outweigh the gain from additional wheat, and the consumer will be content with that particular point reached on the PPC. We will deal more explicitly with this problem of marginal gains and sacrifices in the next chapter.

To summarize, the consumer or society, given its resources and techno-logical possibilities, will always prefer a point on the PPC to one inside. It will adjust its position along the curve until the gains of satisfaction from increasing the output of one good are balanced by the losses of satisfaction from sacrificing the other good.

Taken together, the principles of diminishing returns and diminishing marginal utility will jointly determine what goods should be produced and in what proportions.

How Should Production Be Organized?

Society faces another set of choices in addition to the selection of the bundle of goods and services to be produced and consumed. It must decide how it will produce each commodity. There is no unique way to produce a particular commodity, but rather a variety of alternatives. A farmer desiring to produce 10 tons of wheat must decide whether to use 40 acres of land and his own labor, or cultivate 20 acres intensively, requiring the help of a hired hand. He must also decide how much machinery and fertilizer to use, recognizing that it may be possible to substitute machinery for the hired hand, or fertilizer for both.

We can illustrate the choice of production techniques with a two-factor, one-product production function. A production function expresses the relationship between factor inputs and product output. Diagram 1.2, called an isoquant map, tells us that steel can be produced with varying amounts of capital and labor.

The word "isoquant" derives from the prefix "iso-" meaning equal and "quant" from quantity. Therefore each isoquant curve in diagram 1.2 shows the variety of combinations of capital and labor which will produce a constant quantity of steel, say 150 tons. By adding more labor and capital it is always possible to produce more steel, say 250 tons or 325 tons or anywhere in between. Each output level will have its own isoquant and every product, wheat, steel, autos, etc., will have its own production function and isoquant map.

The economic problem at this point is to choose the optimum combination of labor and capital (or any other input) in order to produce a given quantity of steel. Note that outputs of 150 tons, 250 tons, and 325 tons of steel correspond with points E, D, and C in diagram 1.1. If consumers had chosen point D (250 tons steel, 300 tons wheat) in preference to E or C, then the producers of steel would choose the center isoquant in diagram 1.2 and seek the best production combination of inputs. What will determine the specific combination of resources chosen by an economy in the production of any particular commodity? The curve tells us that substitution of factors is possible, but that they cannot always be substituted at the same rate.

If we begin production at point A in diagram 1.2 using a labor intensive method of production, we can substitute K for L. Moving from point A to point B along the 250 ton isoquant, we add 10 units of K, save 25 units of L, and leave output unchanged. Moving further from point B to point C, we again leave output unchanged; we have added another 10 units of K, but we have only saved 15 units of L. Further substitution of capital for labor along this 250 ton isoquant yields less and less labor savings.

If a unit of capital costs $10 and a unit of labor costs $5, then moving from point A to point B cost $100 in capital and saved $125 in labor, or a net saving of $25. A further move to point C would cost another $100 in capital costs but save only $75 in labor. The move to point C would not occur. A production com-

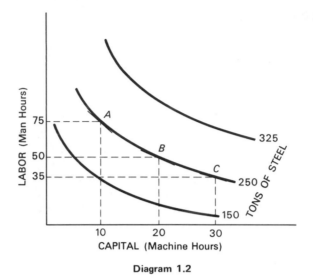

Diagram 1.2

bination around point B would be chosen, where the saving in labor would equal the costs of capital and vice versa. So the precise point on a production isoquant depends not only on the rate of curvature of the isoquant but on the price of capital and labor.

How Should Production Be Distributed Among Claimants?

Finally, the members of society must decide how production is to be divided among competing sectors of the economy. Output can be allocated to the production sector in the form of investment goods, to the consumer sector in the form of consumer goods, and to the government for investment purposes or to provide for collective consumption. Once these major divisions have been made, it remains to distribute the available consumer goods among households. Production is ultimately for the benefit of individual consumers, but which consumers? It is possible to imagine a society in which one individual household consumed the great majority of the output available while the remaining households lived at subsistence. At the other extreme, we can imagine an economy in which all of the member households received an equal share of total output. The distribution of output in most economies lies somewhere in between. The actual distribution of income and output prevailing in any particular economy will depend upon the economic institutions in operation, such as the wage and salary systems, the possibility of private ownership of property, the tax and subsidy system, and other redistributive devices. The development of these institutions, in turn, is influenced by the values of the members of the economy.

CLASSIFYING SYSTEMS

Solving these problems in a modern industrial nation is an extremely complex task. The so-called "developed" nations are characterized by extreme specialization of economic functions. No one in these societies is economically self-sufficient. Rather, each individual produces only a small fraction of the goods and services that he himself actually consumes. The worker bolting on door handles in a General Motors plant or the Soviet farmer producting flax must exchange the income he receives from his effort for the products of others. In order for each individual to survive, the activity of all individuals must be coordinated. Failure to coordinate these activities may have disastrous consequences in modern societies. Strikes by transportation or communications workers have occasionally crippled economies: wheat may rot in the fields because adequate provisions have not been made for storage or transportation. The price of specialization is interdependence and some degree of vulnerability, which may be perceived only at moments of crisis. Industrial societies have developed complex sets of institutions to solve the questions what, how, and for whom. These institutions attempt to insure the coordination of the millions of economic tasks being carried on daily in order to prevent economic paralysis. No two economies have identical solutions nor use identical institutions in the process of arriving at a solution. Through careful study, however, we can discern certain common features in the operation of economies that can be classified into systems.

There have been many "systems" in existence in the world—the feudal system, the caste system, the patriarchal system, the mercantilist system, the democratic system. Some of these systems are considered primarily political or social systems, others primarily religious or economic systems. But each system contains within it a great variety of characteristics which together have been given a particular label. Each system has political, social, economic, and religious characteristics regardless of its general nature. Thus it is extremely difficult to try to talk solely about political or economic systems because of the interaction of social, political, and economic influences. It is difficult to extract the economic content of feudalism from the complex social and political institutions upon which it is based. We are going to try, however, to conceptualize economic institutions as if they could exist independently of any particular set of social and political institutions. Each economic system is regarded as a bundle of characteristics. It is our belief that economic systems, like political and social systems, are multidimensional and cannot be characterized as points along a continuum representing varying degrees of intensity of a single characteristic, such as centralization of decision making. It is undesirable for analytical purposes, on the other hand, to try to completely catalogue all of the features of a system. To do so would be to have as many economic systems as there are national economies. Any particular set of characteristics singled out is bound to contain some elements of arbitrariness. The following classification scheme may enable us to distinguish the essential operational elements of an economic system without needless proliferation of categories.

Economic systems may be classified according to 1) who owns the means of production; 2) who makes the economic decisions of what, how, and for whom; and 3) what mechanisms are used to insure the carrying out of these decisions. Two possible variations for each characteristic will be defined. An economic system will be classified according to the bundle of characteristics it possesses.

Ownership of the factors of production can be classified as public or private. Private ownership exists if an individual or group of individuals has the right, subject to certain limitations, to possess, use, dispose of, and collect income from property. Private property implies that the owners are concerned solely with the use of property for the maximization of their own welfare. Public ownership implies that the state, rather than individuals, has these rights, and, furthermore, is interested in using property for some objective other than short-run profit maximization.

The distinction between private and public ownership, however, is often not clear-cut. There are many restrictions placed by government on the use of private property that limit the freedom of the owner and force him to consider objectives beyond the maximization of his personal welfare. Examples of these restrictions are zoning laws, noise and pollution control laws, etc. Privately held corporations are normally categorized as private property, but there is evidence to suggest that many firms, whether through public pressure or private conscience, look beyond their immediate gains to the effect of their activities on society as a whole. Certain institutions, such as the firm in Yugoslavia, have characteristics of both private and public property. Yugoslav workers have considerable latitude over the disposal of the firm's income, yet the freedom to sell, dismantle, or merge its assets is strictly controlled.

The difficulty of classifying property as private or public leads one to ask if it is meaningful to attempt such a classification. Is there any operational significance in such a dichotomy? It is our opinion that there is. First, the existence of private property may determine certain patterns of distribution of wealth, power, prestige, and influence different from those implied by public property. The existence of the possibility of accumulation of wealth and the investment of that wealth in capital will result in a different distribution of income in a society based on private property as compared with one based on public property. It is very likely that institutions will be developed and laws will be passed to protect those who have accumulated private wealth. It is also likely that the objectives of government policy will reflect the distribution of wealth and power. This is not to suggest that there will be no concentrations of power and influence in economies without private property, only that they will be different.

Secondly, the predominance of private or public property will have an effect on economic incentives. One would expect a different employment and savings pattern in a system under which the accumulation of savings and the investment of savings in income-earning property are possible. The expected rate of return on investment might be the same in an economy with private property as compared to one with public property. The possibility of extraordinarily profitable situations, whether through accident or intelligent design, may exist under either system of ownership. Under public property arrangements, society as a whole usually reaps the benefits of such a bonanza. Under private property, lucky or intelligent individuals seize the rewards. The possibility of catching the brass ring may drive men to exertions not justified by the overall expected profitability of commercial or industrial activity.

Turning to our second characteristic, we can classify economic decisions as individual or collective. Economic decisions can be made by individuals or groups acting independently in their own self-interest or by a collective authority, the state, acting on its own, or in what it presumes to be the interest of the public. The collective authority may be a democratically elected representative body or may coincide with a dictatorial political regime. In neither case are the state's preferences merely a summation of the preferences of its members. In both cases, certain decisions are no longer left to the individual, but are decided for all members of the economy by a group at the center. The objective of collective decision-making is to maximize the preference function of the state. In a democratically elected government the state preference function may be quite diverse. The state may satisfy everyone more or less, but no one in particular, and some not at all. States not organized on a democratic basis may have a state preference function which not only does not reflect the distribution of preferences of the population but no one *intends* that it should. In such a case, the state is like a super-household in its own right, with special powers like taxation and conscription to further press its desires on the population.

In both types of decision-making, conflicts among economic participants will arise. The resolution of these conflicts, however, will differ in the two cases. In a system of decentralized, individual decision-making, economic conflicts will tend to be resolved through the use of impersonal market forces. The winner will be the highest bidder. In a system of centralized, collective decision-making, other criteria, economic as well as non-economic, are likely to have considerable influence. The state may decide to award the use of a piece of land to a sportsmen's club as a hunting preserve rather than to a fertilizer factory as a site because of the lower pollution level of the former or because the club included big campaign contributors or high officials. The opposite might have resulted if the conflict had been resolved between the two contenders without the intervention of the state.

Finally, for our last characteristic let us consider how resources may be allocated once the basic economic decisions have been made. Resources may be allocated through markets or by directives from a central authority. In markets, prices serve as signaling devices to guide participants. Consumers compare the prices of various products, buying the mix of goods which gives them the maximum amount of satisfaction from the expenditure of their income. Producers produce that mix of outputs which maximizes their profits. Prices reflect both the intensity of consumer demand and the relative scarcity of factors of production.

An alternative form of economic organization is allocation by directive or command. Under this system, orders are given with reference to production and resource use to all producing units. Producing units do not independently determine what to produce and how to produce it in response to market signals; their actions are completely prescribed by directives.

Individual decision-making and market allocation are normally linked together in one system, as are collective decision-making and command. This need not be the case, however. As we shall see, the directives could reflect the decisions of individuals acting independently, or the market forces could be responding to the decisions of the state.

We have developed three sources of possible variations among economic systems: 1) property relations—public vs. private, 2) bases of decision-making—individual vs. collective, and 3) mechanisms for allocating resources and goods among competing uses—market vs. command. We will use these characteristics to analyze the functioning of certain basic traditional classifications of economic systems. These are capitalism, the socialist command economy, the mixed economy, and market socialism.

A very common failing of comparative economic systems analysis is to contrast the ideal form or model of one system with the actual functioning behavior of another. Avid proponents of capitalism contrast smoothly functioning, frictionless, spaceless, timeless market-clearing models with the bumbling, bottleneck-ridden, lethargic central planning experience of the Soviet-type economies. Marxists and socialists contrast their all-knowing, benevolent, efficient, and errorless central planning authority with an inequitable, anarchic, unjust, and merciless portrait of eighteenth-century capitalism. Comparison of traits and performance between rival economic and social systems inherently involves emotional issues and value judgments. For this reason it is essential for the remainder of the analysis of this chapter that our attention be focused on the "blueprint" or theoretical qualities of each of our systems. In later chapters we will contrast the actual performance of all the systems with their idealized models. We will consider the real world experience of actual national economies associated with each system.

Let us now turn to the economic systems we will be studying. We will examine each in terms of our three sets of characteristics. In the next chapter we will outline some criteria, devised to be as neutral as possible in terms of value judgments, by which the performance of economic systems can be judged.

The Capitalist Market Economy

The capitalist system is one characterized by the private ownership of the means of production, individual decision-making, and the use of the market mechanism to carry out the decisions of individual participants and facilitate the flow of goods and services. The capitalist economy is characterized by a voluntary exchange of goods and services in markets. This exchange can be illustrated with the use of a circular flow diagram depicting the interaction of households and firms in the exchange of finished commodities and factors of production.

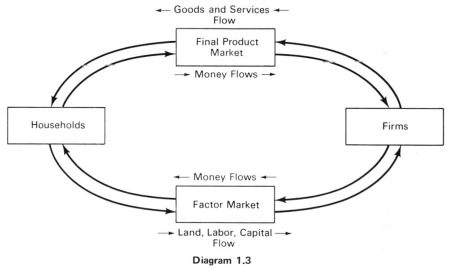

Diagram 1.3

In a capitalist economy, households and firms are the basic production units. Each individual household is the owner of productive factors. These factors include the household's own labor and may also include land, capital, and raw materials. Each household sells the services of its factors to the basic production unit, the firm. Private firms, organized by individuals, combine these productive factors to produce goods. The difference between revenues and costs constitutes profits, which then form the income of the firm's organizers. The income earned from the sale of a household's productive factors enables it to purchase the finished products of the firms. Those households in possession of larger holdings of productive resources will earn greater incomes. This will allow them to purchase a larger portion of the output of firms.

In a capitalist economy, each market participant, buyer or seller, is trying to buy cheap and sell dear. Each is interested in maximizing his own welfare. The consumer attempts to select that bundle of goods and services which will maximize his satisfaction with the least expenditure on his part. The firm attempts to select that combination of inputs that will produce a given quantity of output at the least possible cost. Both the consumer and firm are weighing benefits and costs, attempting to pick the optimum combination.

Each economic unit is guided by price in his selection of inputs and final outputs. Commodity prices are formed as a result of the aggregation of the demand and supply offers of market participants. If a product is in short supply relative to consumer demand, its price will rise. If one type of labor service is in excess supply relative to firms' demands, its price will fall. In a market system prices tend to reflect the relative availability of resources and the strength of consumer preferences. Prices provide the consumer and the firm with information with respect to the cost of alternatives. A change in consumer preferences or the availability of factors of production will initially be reflected in their price. The price change will signal to the buyer the fact that the cost of alternatives has changed and this will ultimately result in a change in the consumption and production patterns of the society.

The pure form of capitalism is the perfectly competitive market economy. Under the conditions of perfect competition, no individual unit is large enough to influence market price. Resources are homogeneous and perfectly mobile. Thus, firms do not discriminate among resource sellers, and resource sellers always seek out the highest bid. Under the conditions of perfect competition, each market participant is checked in his search for income and profits by the actions of his rivals. No firm can arbitrarily raise prices in an attempt to secure higher profits, for his competitors would undercut him and drive him out of business.

If the competitive market economy is functioning properly, government has no direct productive economic function. Intervention by government is regarded as having an unnecessarily disturbing influence on producers or consumers or both. The role of government is therefore limited to the establishment and enforcement of the rules of exchange. The government facilitates the exchange process by the protection of private property and the enforcement of contracts.

There are no economies in existence today, nor have any existed in the past, that meet the rigid requirements of perfect competition. The existence of monopoly power on the part of big business and organized labor, the immobility of resources, particularly labor, due to lack of knowledge and social and psychological barriers, and the "stickiness" of prices all contribute to substantial deviations of real behavior from ideal behavior. There are economies, the United States and West Germany for example, which contain many of the characteristics of a competitive market system and are singled out as examples of capitalism. We shall study these examples later in the text to analyze the complex interweaving of market and non-market economic institutions.

To sum up, the key feature of capitalism, whether of a perfect or imperfect variety, is the decentralization of decision-making. The choice of what to produce and how to produce it are made by thousands of individual consumers and firms according to their own self-interest. Prices, determined by the impersonal forces of supply and demand, provide the necessary information to the market which permits participants to choose among alternatives.

The Socialist Command Economy

An alternative economic system is the command economy. The command economy is characterized by public ownership of the means of production, collective determination of economic decisions, and the allocation of resources by commands issued by the planning elite.

Under this system all decisions with respect to production, investment, and distribution are made by the state planners. These decisions are formulated in a plan which forms the blueprint for the activity of individual economic units. The plan rather than the market coordinates the production of enterprises.

In order to formulate a plan, the economic leaders must have knowledge of the objective features of the economy, such as plant capacity, availability of raw materials, the size and composition of the labor force, and consumer preferences in order to select feasible production patterns. This information must flow from the producing units at the bottom to the planners at the top. Once decisions are made by the planners, they must be communicated to the enterprises.

In a "pure" command economy, individuals own no resources, are directed to their places of employment, and are assigned state-determined allotments of consumer goods. Firms or enterprises are publicly owned and operate in accord with state directives. They produce the quantity and assortment of goods specified in the plan using the quantity and combination of inputs also specified in the plan.

The primary feature of the command economy is the centralization of decision-making. There is no horizontal communication between producing and consuming units. All communication is vertical, i.e., between the individual economic unit and the planning agency.

No economy has ever existed which has been organized solely by the command principle. Even the Soviet economy under Stalin, considered the archetype of the command system, contained elements of private property (small private peasant plots), individual decision-making (in the allocation of labor among enterprises), and the use of the market (in the allocation of consumer goods). We will consider the operation of the Soviet economic system, however, as the best representative of a command system in practice.

In addition to the two "pure" models of economic organization, there are also economic systems which combine elements of both capitalism and the command economy. Two well-known examples are market socialism and the mixed economy. Both of those systems contain elements in common and can only be distinguished by the relative intensity of their reliance on markets, private property, and individual decision-making.

Market Socialism

Market socialism is characterized primarily by the public ownership of the means of production. Decisions with reference to the allocation of resources are made both collectively and by individual producing and consuming units. Prices and markets are the primary mechanisms used to facilitate the exchange of products. In this system, individual state-owned enterprises compete in a market setting for sales and inputs. They are free to determine what to produce and how to produce it and are guided by prices. Prices may be set in the market place by the impersonal forces of supply and demand or by a central planning board in response to observed shortages and surpluses.

The primary distinction between market socialism and the competitive market economy is the ownership of the means of production. Under market socialism individual households own and can freely dispose of only their own labor or liquid savings. They may not accumulate wealth in the form of earning property. The profits gained in production by firms will be distributed back to the members of the economy according to a state devised allocation scheme. The state may or may not play a significant role in the allocation of resources, but it has the residual power to influence resource allocation through its influence on prices through the central planning board and through its allocation of profits. The Yugoslav economy contains many of the elements of market socialism, although, as we shall see, it also is a unique blend of economic institutions.

The Mixed Economy

The mixed economy, as its name implies, also shares the characteristics of both capitalism and the command economy. The primary difference between the mixed economy and market socialism is the relatively greater importance of individual decision-making, private property, and the reliance on market determined prices to guide the allocation of resources. The mixed economy differs from competitive capitalism with respect to the share of collective decision-making in the economy.

In the mixed economy, many decisions are made by powerful economic groupings, such as organized labor, business, and the government, rather than by individual producing and consuming units. The impersonal clash of market forces leading to the formation of prices is reduced, while the role of pressure groups and combinations of firms and workers in price making is enhanced.

In this type of economy there is wide latitude for government participation. The government may function as a mediator between conflicting economic groups, as well as a consumer of the end-product of business and labor. Government may also attempt to guide the direction of the economy through the imposition of restrictions and granting of privileges to the private sector as well as by some form of planning.

Many economies, such as Great Britain and France, have been classified as mixed economies and are characterized by a large economic role for the state. The population of these countries has accepted the government's role in the economy as the guarantor of full employment and price stability, the redistributor of income, and the guiding force in determining the pace and direction of economic growth.

The state is not the only institution that has changed in the mixed economies. There has been a growing public acceptance of big business and large organized labor unions conferring in close contact with government. It is claimed that the objectives of a private productive sector have broadened beyond that of mere profit maximization to include a concern for the welfare of society as a whole. There is no longer complete confidence that the individual drive for profits, combined with the restraining influence of competitive market forces, will promote the best long-run interest of the economy. It is a commonly held opinion that although the market is an efficient device for the conveyance of information, it must be tempered by the state acting in consultation with private business and labor. We shall see that each mixed economy has chosen its own unique blend of market and command mechanisms to guide its economy toward the achievement of the shared goals of full employment, price stability, and rapid growth.

Alternative Systems

The above four systems certainly do not exhaust the possible combinations of economic characteristics described above. One could imagine an economy in which consumers fed their preferences and firms fed data on their productive capacities into a giant computer, which then matched preferences with opportunities. The computer would dictate production orders to enterprises and specify the distribution of production to consuming units. This would combine individual decision-making with the command principle. One could further imagine planners determining what to produce, how to produce, and for whom to produce, and then setting prices which led to the fulfillment of their plans as a result of the profit-maximizing behavior of individual enterprises. This would combine collective decision-making with the use of the market for allocating resources. These two possibilities have no counterparts in the real world today. There are many Soviet mathematicians and economists, however, who are experimenting with the use of computers into which planners' preferences and data on resource availability can be fed, and from which a feasible plan could be derived. Other Soviet mathematicians and economists are working equally hard to develop market institutions to carry out the broad wishes of the planners.

The remaining chapters of this text will be devoted to a more intensive study of the four major models of economic systems and a discussion of selected national economies. The national economies to be studied in this text fall primarily into one of our four systems, although no economy will be representative of pure capitalism or pure command. All economies are a mixture of the above characteristics, and thus it is often difficult to try to classify any particular national economy with its own unique institutions as one or the other. Classification, however, is not an end in itself, and is useful only if it helps us to understand the economic processes in action in any particular national context.

A final word is in order about the role of tradition in economic decision-making. There are certain areas in every economy in which none of the systems outlined above is relevant. In a capitalist system the owner of a firm may hire his son as manager, not because he will contribute more to profits than any other prospective employee, but because it is traditional. As an economy becomes more industrialized and specialization becomes important, tradition tends to play a smaller role. Since this book is concerned primarily with developed economies, it will concentrate on the role of market and command as allocation devices. The reader should be aware, however, of the persistence of elements of tradition in all the countries to be discussed.

QUESTIONS

1. What are the basic economic problems confronting all economic systems?
2. What essential economic characteristics can be used to distinguish economic systems?
3. How do you think economic decision-making will differ in an economy characterized primarily by private property compared to an economy characterized by public ownership?
4. According to the classification system developed in this chapter, what are the essential economic characteristics of capitalist and socialist command economies?
5. What are the differences between the mixed economy and market socialism?
6. In addition to the four economic systems discussed in the chapter, what other arrangements of economic institutions are possible for forming alternative economic systems?

2

The Performance
of Economic Systems

PERFORMANCE CRITERIA

Economic systems differ with respect to the problem solving institutions that have developed within each particular national context. Each system uses a different combination of individual and collective decision-making and of the market and command forms of organization to arrive at solutions to economic problems. The solutions as well as the institutions differ from one economic context to another. The task of this chapter is to develop a set of performance criteria by which to judge any particular economic system.

It is extremely difficult to agree upon a set of universally acceptable economic criteria because of the interrelationship between economic and social institutions and the possible conflict between economic and social values. It is difficult to assume that a country's welfare is solely dependent on the satisfaction of material wants, because of the possibility of a trade-off between economic and other forms of welfare. An economic system, for example, may be highly successful in providing material goods to its members, but this same system may include social and political institutions which are inimical to the welfare of the population.

In this chapter we will attempt to abstract certain criteria with which to judge the economic performance of different systems. Three criteria will be used in this context: static efficiency, dynamic efficiency, and equity. In a later chapter we will consider the relationships between the economic, social, and political environments.

Static Efficiency

Static efficiency is concerned with both the proper level of utilization of resources and with the optimum allocation of resources among competing uses. Full employment of resources is one requirement for the achievement of static efficiency. Clearly it is inefficient if an economy is allowing a part of its labor force and capital stock to sit idle because workers and owners of capital are unsuccessful in their search for employment. If the welfare of the members of an economy is dependent upon the level of production, welfare can be increased by employing these extra factors. Full employment does not imply, however, that all capital must be used twenty-four hours a day, that all labor must work the maximum physically possible, and that all raw materials be depleted. In defining full employment we must take into consideration the desire for leisure and the need for conservation. Full employment of the labor force is usually defined as the point at which all people who are willing to work at the going wage are currently employed. Thus, under this definition, one is not unemployed unless actively seeking a job and willing to accept current wage rates.

In order to achieve static efficiency, resources must also be optimally allocated. Optimal allocation ". . .is defined as a situation in which nobody can move to a position which he prefers without moving somebody else to a position which is less preferred. . ."[1] If products can be exchanged between individuals with an increase in the welfare of one without a decrease in the welfare of the other, or if factors can be reallocated to produce more of one product without sacrificing any alternative product, then the original allocation is not optimum. We can specify the requirements for an optimum allocation of resources more precisely in the following six efficiency conditions.

Condition No. 1 — *Optimum Exchange Among Consumers*

A classic case of an optimum exchange problem is the study of the exchange of consumption items within prisoner-of-war camps during World War II. The exact same situation is not unknown among college students living away

---

[1] Kenneth Boulding, "Welfare Economics" in B.F. Haley, *A Survey of Contemporary Economics* (Homewood, Illinois: Richard D. Irwin, Inc., 1952), II, 12.

from home in dorms or children at summer camp: the receipt of parcels and the consequent swap of relative undesirables for relative desirables. Let us examine a hypothetical situation which actually derives from such real experiences. Suppose we observe a prisoner-of-war camp containing American prisoners and let us further assume that each prisoner receives four parcels a year containing precisely 10 pounds of canned meat (M) and 10 pounds of chocolate (C) from the Red Cross.

In the camp some prisoners may find that they regularly exhaust their supply of chocolate before they run out of meat and others may find that just the opposite is true. This phenomenon develops because individuals' tastes differ, and it would be coincidental to find an individual who consumed the two goods in precisely the proportion fixed by the Red Cross. Ultimately, those individuals who run surpluses of chocolate will attempt to arrange barter swaps with others who are running surpluses of meat.

If we were to ask a prisoner, "Willy," what was the least amount of chocolate that would induce him to sacrifice a pound of meat, given that he had 10 pounds of meat to start with, he might respond 2 pounds. You would have established the worst deal he would accept, and that the pleasure (marginal utility) that the tenth pound of meat gave him was just about equal to the pleasure (again marginal utility) that an eleventh and twelfth pound of chocolate would give him. In other words, when this prisoner has 10 pounds of meat and 10 pounds of chocolate, 1 pound of meat is a close substitute for 2 pounds of chocolate. Very probably if you were to offer Willy a little more than half a pound of meat for a pound of chocolate, he would swap in the opposite direction. At the swap rate of close to 2C/1M he will trade either way depending on which way you shade the ratio. Therefore we can state that Willy has a "marginal rate of substitution" of 2C/1M.

Now suppose we query another prisoner, "Joe," holding his parcel of 10C, 10M. He responds that he is pretty much indifferent concerning meat and chocolate. Offer him a little more than a pound of chocolate for a pound of meat, and he will swap. On the other hand, offer a little more than a pound of meat for a pound of chocolate and he will trade in the other direction. Joe gets about as much pleasure (marginal utility) from the tenth pound of meat as he would from an eleventh pound of chocolate and vice versa. Therefore we can state that Joe's marginal rate of substitution is 1C/1M.

Let us bring Willy and Joe face to face. At a swap rate ratio of slightly less than 2C/1M Willy is inclined to barter not quite 2 pounds of his chocolate for an additional pound of meat, which he seems to value highly, as compared to Joe. He is better off because we have established that the worst deal he would accept would be 2C/1M. However, Joe will delightedly give up a pound of meat (a loss of utility) for about 2 pounds of chocolate (a gain almost twice that of the loss). Clearly Joe is the big gainer from the exchange, but an important thing to remember is that Willy was not a loser from the exchange.

On the other hand at a barter ratio of slightly more than 1C/1M, Joe is just barely induced to give up a pound of canned meat. Willy, who was prepared to accept the loss of close to 2 pounds of chocolate, now only has to give up a bit more than 1 to secure the desired pound tin of meat. The loss of satisfaction or negative marginal utility is almost half the anticipated loss. Willy is the chief gainer from this barter ratio, but Joe is not a loser or he would not have made the exchange.

The essence of a move toward optimality is that someone is better off and no one is worse off. The precise ratio of exchange is not as important as the principle that exchange will improve the welfare of all parties if the initial marginal rates of substitution for the bargainers are not the same. Let us say that some intermediate ratio of 1.5C/1M exists. At this ratio, Willy will trade chocolate for meat. Willy starts out with his 10C, 10M, and his marginal rate of substitution is 2C/1M. One trade later he has 8.5C, 11M. He has less chocolate and more meat and may no longer consider an additional pound of meat to be worth two pounds of chocolate. His MRS will have declined to say 1.75C/1M. Since Willy still only has to pay 1.50C for 1M, he will gain from still another trade. This trade will leave him with 7C,12M holdings of goods. At this point a further sacrifice of 1.5 will cost him more utility that he gains from the pound of meat. Willy loses all interest in further trade.

Joe is in the opposite situation. Remember that his MRS was 1C/1M when he had 10C/10M. The first trade left him with 11.5C,9M, at which point he values the ninth pound of meat more than he did the tenth, and 1.5 pounds more chocolate less than he did before. In other words, his MRS is rising above 1C/1M to say 1.3C/1M. A trade of 1M for 1.5C will still be desirable for him. Joe will continue trading until his MRS is 1.5C/1M. Notice that when both Willy and Joe stop trading their MRS's are equal to each other and both MRS's are equal to the barter price ratio. Obviously, enlarging this simple model to include other goods and other prisoners does not alter the fundamental conclusion— welfare will not be maximized unless you can show that further exchanges will not improve someone's position without hurting someone else's.

Summary conclusion: goods are optimally distributed when all consumers are willing to exchange them at the same rate. When different prices exist for different consumers, side deals are possible, which we may call "black" or "gray" markets, in which one person can gain advantage by buying cheap in some special market and selling dear in another. ("I can get it for you wholesale.") Every exchange should leave both parties satisfied.

Condition No. 2 — *The Optimum Degree of Specialization Among Producing Units*

The problem here is the situation in which you have a number of pro-ducing units such as assembly plants, farms, or colleges each producing several goods or services. General Motors has assembly plants in which cars or trucks or tractors may be assembled. The same is true for the Automotive Ministry of the Soviet Union. Textile plants may turn out cotton or woolen or synthetic, narrow or wide, plain, white or patterned cloth. Because of natural limitations of plant, equipment, or labor, not every producing unit will be able to produce every good or service as well or be able to switch lines as efficiently as some other firm. This being obviously true, it is possible that an arbitrary assignment of production ratios to various plants might lead to a less than optimum output.

Suppose that an automobile firm has two assembly plants, X and Y. The production possibilities for these plants are illustrated by the two curves in diagram 2.1.

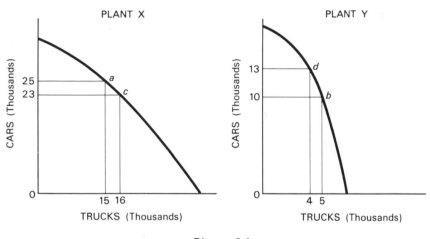

Diagram 2.1

Let us assume that Plant X has been arbitrarily assigned a quota of 25,000 cars and 15,000 trucks at point "a" on its PPC. Also, Plant Y has been assigned a quota of 10,000 cars and 5,000 trucks at point "b" on its PPC. Each plant is given the resources to produce its quota. However, utilizing these same resources each plant can actually produce *anywhere* on the two curves. Before proceeding, note that the automobile firm has provided the resources for both plants together to produce 35,000 cars and 20,000 trucks.

To make our point quickly, let us suppose that the two plants violate their quota assignments and shift resources internally in opposite directions. Plant X shifts its resources so that it produces at point "c" on its PPC and Plant Y shifts to point "d" on its PPC. Resources did not go from one plant to another. We observe that Plant X lowers its output of cars by 2,000 units and frees enough material and resources to produce a thousand more trucks. Plant Y cuts back its production of trucks by a thousand units and expands its production of cars by 3,000 units. Adding up the global results of the shifts we find that the combined output of trucks is still 20,000 but the production of cars is up to 36,000. A look at the curves will show you that a move the other way would worsen things and that further shifts in the first direction would eventually lead to no gains and finally to a loss.

Summary conclusion: as long as producing units differ in their internal marginal rates of transformation (MRT's), resources may be shifted internally so that the output of one good will rise without the output of any other falling. When the MRT's for every producing unit are the same, no gain is possible.

This conclusion is applied equally to different systems, since the rates of transformation depend on objective factors such as technology, capital, and skills. The problem of optimal allocation is as critical to the Soviet planner as it is to the capitalist manager.

Condition No. 3 — *Optimum Factor Allocation Between Producing Units*

This question is closely related to the previous one, but carries the logic a step further. If we can shift resources within producing units and get expanded output of one good and no less of the other, we should also be able to shift resources between units and observe the same thing—if the units are not equally efficient, of course.

Keeping the analysis as simple as possible, suppose Plants X and Y keep the production of trucks constant, but the automobile firm decides to take a million dollars in resources from Plant X and give them to Plant Y.

Diagram 2.2 shows that the production of autos fell by 1500 units in Plant X but rose by 2000 units in Plant Y when the resources were transferred. These numbers indicate, when divided, that the marginal cost of an auto was roughly

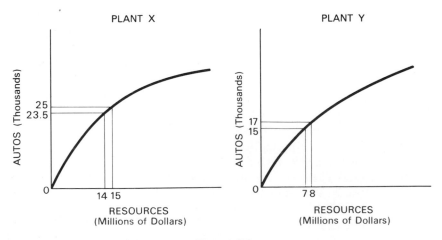

Diagram 2.2

$667 at Plant X and only $500 at Plant Y. If this transfer of resources were to continue, Plant Y would run into diminishing returns (the slope of the curve would become flatter and the pay-off in autos would become less). Plant X would be retreating along the curve enjoying increasing returns. Ultimately, the advantage of Plant Y over Plant X would be wiped out and resources taken from either plant would cause output to fall as much as it rose in the other. No transfer either way would be profitable and so things should remain at this point.

Summary conclusion: if plants do not transform resources into a good at the same rate, resources should be shifted from one producing unit to another until they do. At that point, no further gain is possible without adding more resources overall. Again observe that this conclusion is applicable to different systems. Anyone who works on the principle that more is preferable to less will make the shift, be he socialist or capitalist.

Condition No. 4 — *The Optimum Degree of Factor Substitution*

The production technique for most products is not absolutely unique. There is a surprisingly wide latitude for substituting capital for labor, and vice versa, in almost all products.

For example, rice is grown in Asia and California and Texas. Land is required in all cases, but the possibility for capital-labor substitution is remarkable. In Asia the rice is planted, cultivated, and harvested with the most rudimentary capital equipment imaginable and astronomical amounts of labor hours. In the United States, the seed may be sown from planes, weeded by chemicals sprayed from planes, fertilized from planes, and harvested with great machines with the harvest virtually untouched by human hands.

Consider two farms producing rice using labor and machinery. The first farm is using lavish amounts of labor and a small quantity of machinery, while the second is using a great deal of machinery but very little labor. If the first farm adds one more machine, it can produce the same quantity of rice and release 10 workers. If the second farm adds 5 workers it can produce the same output with one less machine. The marginal rate of substitution in the first case is 1M/10L and in the second 1M/5L. Surely it is desirable to arrange a swap between the two farms. If the first farm exchanges 10 workers for one machine with the second farm, the output of the first farm will be constant and that of the second will rise. As long as the MRS's of the two producers are unequal, total output can be increased as a result of a transfer of resources. As we move in from these extreme positions, the marginal productivity of labor rises and that of capital falls on the first farm, and the opposite occurs on the second.

Summary conclusion: if producers cannot substitute one factor for another at the same rate, resources should be transferred from one to another until the rates are equal. At this point it is impossible to increase the output of the good without providing additional resources, both labor and capital, for its production.

Condition No. 5 — *The Optimum Production Mix*

Consider Willy and Joe in the prisoner-of-war camp. After all exchanges had taken place each was willing to exchange chocolate for meat at the rate of 1.5C/1M. Suppose that a firm producing meat and chocolate was able, by transferring resources from the production of one good to the other, to produce 3 more pounds of chocolate if it produced 1 less pound of meat. Willy and Joe are willing to give up 1 pound of meat for only 1.5 pounds of chocolate. They would be delighted to get 3 pounds of chocolate for their sacrifice, and this is possible if the firm does produce more chocolate and less meat. Willy and Joe will be better off.

Recall, however, that the more chocolate each consumer has, the less he values an additional pound, and the less meat he has, the more he values an additional pound. The marginal rate of substitution of chocolate for meat will rise above 1.5C/1M, say to 2C/1M. As the firm produces more chocolate, its cost in terms of meat production will rise. Eventually the consumers' marginal rate of substitution will equal the firm's marginal rate of transformation.

Summary conclusion: whenever the relative value of goods in consumption differs from the relative cost of producing the goods, resources should be transferred until the relative values are equal to the relative costs.

Condition No. 6 — *Optimum Intensity of Factor Use*

Condition number six is concerned with the trade-off between output and income or leisure. Consider an individual selling his own labor for income. He can then use his income to purchase commodities. At the same time the producer can transform the labor time into output. Suppose the individual is willing to trade one hour of leisure for enough income to purchase two units of clothing. Thus his marginal rate of substitution (MRS) between leisure and output is one to two. Suppose further that a firm is able to utilize one hour of labor and produce three units of clothing with it. The firm's marginal rate of transformation (MRT) between labor and output is three to one, i.e., the marginal physical product of an hour of labor time is three. In this example, it will clearly pay for the individual to work an extra hour because he can be compensated by up to three extra units of clothing.

Again two trends will run counter to each other — diminishing returns in consumption and diminishing returns in production. As the individual surrenders more and more of his leisure, he will value each loss more and more, while the enjoyment of his income becomes less and less as he consumes more. A point will be reached eventually such that the loss of leisure utility exceeds the gain of income utility, and at this point further work and income are not desirable. Reinforcing this trend is the fact that additional work inputs are less and less effective due to diminishing returns. As the payoff from work effort falls, the worker will receive less for additional effort. With falling labor productivity and reduced pleasure from consuming income, optimum balance between work and leisure will be reached when the marginal rate of substitution of leisure for income is equal to the marginal rate of transformation of labor into output.

If there is some constraint placed on the individual so that he cannot choose the optimum amount of labor effort, then he is worse off, whether he wanted to work more or to work less. An example of this would be the traditional 40-hour week. Those workers who really prefer less income and more leisure will goldbrick on the job (leisure within the job), be absentees at the slightest excuse, and accept docks in their pay without a qualm. Those workers who want more income and less leisure will constantly press for overtime work or take second jobs (moonlighting).

Summary conclusion: the amount of work effort or factor intensity is best left to the individual concerned. Any external restraint can only leave him worse off. This conclusion rings true for any system—the Soviet Union has its share of goldbrickers, as any newspaper will inform you, but it also has its *Stakhanovites* or super-workers whose exploits on the job are a source of official pride (and fellow-worker irritation, no doubt).

Summary of Conditions 1 Through 6.

If any of the inequalities outlined above persist in an economy, unambiguous gains in welfare can be achieved by a reallocation of products and/or factors of production. We can summarize our efficiency conditions by the following statements:

1. The marginal rates of substitution in consumption must be equal for all consumers (Condition No. 1).
2. The marginal rates of transformation and substitution in production must be equal for all firms (Condition Nos. 2,3,4).
3. The marginal rate of substitution in consumption must equal the marginal rate of transformation in production (Condition No. 5 and No. 6).

We must be careful in our interpretation of the meaning of economic efficiency. According to our conditions, a situation is judged inefficient only if one person can move to a preferred position without moving another person to a less preferred position. Interpersonal comparisons of welfare are not taken into consideration. There can be many points of economic efficiency for a single economy, each one dependent upon the initial distribution of wealth. No one position can be preferred to another, because movement from one to another involves a transfer of income, and thus, losses for some and gains for others. This does not imply, however, that such value judgments cannot or should not be made, only that these judgments cannot be made on the basis of the criteria outlined above. We may decide that a situation with a more equal distribution of income but with some of the above conditions not fulfilled is superior to a position in which all of the conditions are fulfilled but large disparities in income exist. It would be difficult to argue, however, that some third position with all conditions fulfilled and with the same distribution of income as the first would not be superior to either the first or the second positions.

Growth and Social Welfare

We have seen in the preceding section of this chapter that scarcity can be reduced through a more efficient utilization of existing resources. Scarcity can also be reduced by the growth of real output over a period of time. An economy which is growing rapidly will be able to satisfy an increasing number of its members' wants and needs. Can we say, therefore, that an economy which is growing rapidly is superior to an economy which is experiencing a slower rate of increase of output? Before we establish growth as a criteria by which to judge the performance of economic systems, we must analyze what we mean by growth. Should we use as our measure of growth the yearly percentage increase in GNP? It would be foolish to state on *a priori* grounds that an economy growing at a rate of 6 percent per year is necessarily superior to another economy growing at a rate of 5 percent per year. Suppose the rapidly growing economy was investing 40 percent of its GNP every year, while the slower growing economy was investing only 20 percent of its GNP. Clearly the two economies are not making similar efforts in their attempts to increase the level of output over time. Further suppose the economy with the 5 percent growth rate had a rate of population increase of only 1 percent per year while the other economy's population was increasing at 3 percent per year. If we are concerned with the welfare of each individual, the higher growth rate of per capita income is superior. A better indicator of economic superiority might be the intertemporal transformation rate between investment and the growth of output in the two systems. For example, we might judge an economic system superior if it is able to increase its growth rate from 3 to 4 percent by a 20 percent increase in investment when we compare it to a second system which must increase investment by 25 percent to increase its growth rate from 3 to 4 percent. This measure also has some difficulties because it does not take into account what is happening to labor and other inputs. One economy might be experiencing large increases in output accompanied by relatively small increases in investment because it is extending the working day or utilizing newly discovered natural resources.

A commonly used measure of growth is the increases in productivity per man hour employed. Rising productivity implies that each worker is producing more with the same expenditure of effort. This measure does not take into account, however, the relative investment efforts of the economies being compared.

Thus, measurable growth rates *per se* are a crude measure of economic performance because they do not fully take into consideration the effort or sacrifice of the members of the economies involved. In order to distinguish between growth efforts it is useful to define two different types of growth — extensive and intensive. Extensive growth is the result of replication of the existing factors of production at previous levels of productivity. The sources of extensive growth are increases in the capital stock, growth of population, and the discovery of new lands and sources of raw materials. Extensive growth implies the absence of technological change. This type of growth is a common phenomenon in the underdeveloped world. The peasant economy expands as the peasant's sons essentially duplicate their father's household. They apply the same skills to similar plots of land and grow the same crops using the same techniques and equipment. The population is greater, output has risen, the capital and animal stock has expanded; by some measures of economic performance this would indicate progress. There is even a possibility, if there is a fixed supply of land, that per capita output may fall and the quality of life deteriorate.

The members of an economy can choose to increase the stock of resources through the process of savings and investment. By foregoing consumption in the present it is possible to transfer resources from the production of consumer goods to the production of investment goods. Then in the next period the stock of factors of production will be larger than in the initial period, and the capacity for the production of real output will increase.

Assuming a constant level of population, we see that continuous net investment (investment above and beyond that necessary for replacement due to depreciation) will result in increasing capital per man. Due to the principle of diminishing marginal returns in production, we would expect the additional output gained from each increment of investment to fall. The declining rate of return on capital would cause net investment to ultimately fall to zero. The per capita capital stock would reach a certain level and then stabilize. Extensive growth would cease. In order to maintain a given rate of extensive growth, the population must be increasing as fast or faster than the capital stock. In other words, the long-run rate of extensive growth is limited by the rate of population increase. If this is the case, extensive growth may result in a constant level of output per capita. It is a question of personal values as to whether this type of growth is to be considered desirable.

Intensive growth is the result of increases in the productivity of factors of production over time. Intensive growth will occur when it is possible to produce the same quantity and quality of output with a smaller quantity of all inputs. Intensive growth can be represented by a shift toward the origin of a set of isoquants. The primary causes of productivity increase are specialization and the division of labor, economies of scale, and technological change. The concept of "dynamic efficiency" is a useful way of considering an economy's effectiveness in achieving intensive growth. This term is used to describe the hypothetically possible increase in output achieved in two or more economies from identical increases in all resource inputs. Dynamic efficiency is a relative measure of an economy's ability to obtain increases in output from given increases in inputs. An economy may be more dynamically efficient if new technology is quickly diffused and if new investments are well coordinated.

There is no definitive theory of the nature and causes of technical progress. We can say with some assurance that the rate of technological change is dependent upon the rate of accumulation of physical and human capital, the rate of discovery of new production techniques, and the rate of dissemination of new knowledge and its application in industry, a learning process. There is much disagreement, however, on the significance of the level of investment in the process of applying new knowledge and the precise nature of the process of discovery and learning.

Let us consider the role of investment in the process of technological change. The existence of investment *per se* is not a sufficient condition for technical progress to occur. Investment may, as we have seen, merely involve the duplication of the existing capital stock. Investment may not be a sufficient condition, but is it a necessary condition? This question leads us to consider two complex ideas: 1) the interrelationship between the investment process and the application of new knowledge and 2) the necessity of the embodiment of a new invention in capital equipment and of retraining labor to deal with the new technology. Many economists believe that there is little or no connection between the rate of investment in an economy and the rate of progress or intensive growth. They argue that progress depends upon the elusive process of discovery and the application of new discoveries, which may be independent of the level of investment.

> The starting point of the system is invention. But invention also has its parameters: (1) in the degree to which those who possess creative capacities have been educated to a mastery of techniques and of the data of science, (2) in the pressures of social need and in the lures of industrial opportunity, (3) in the chance to experiment, (4) in the inducements to persevere in the inventive effort, and (5) in the organization and availability of the data of science and of other relevant bodies of information. [2]

[2] Robert Solo, *Economic Organizations and Social Systems* (New York: The Bobbs-Merrill Co., Inc., 1967), p. 120.

Once a new discovery takes place it must be applied to a production process before increases in output can be realized. It is argued that the rate of application of new knowledge is dependent upon the speed with which the information is disseminated throughout the economy and acted upon by those responsible for the transformation of production processes. Net investment is not necessary to obtain capital-embodied progress. Natural replacement of plant and equipment due to depreciation will allow the utilization of the new knowledge in new facilities even though the capital stock may not grow in an absolute sense.

We must bear in mind that this notion of the nature of technical progress can not be separated entirely from the process of savings and investment. Technical discoveries are not the result solely of flashes of insight, which are independent of the inventor's effort. Certainly many, if not most, of the technical advances made today are the result of organized research, and such research is a form of investment. The size of the research effort in an economy is dependent upon the amount of resources devoted to this area.

Another group of economists argue that the process of learning and the application of new discoveries are directly connected with the level of investment.

> Investment benefits productivity largely because it provides opportunities for learning new methods. ...The underlying notion is that technical progress has two elements: an exogenous increase in ideas, and the extension and exploitation of these ideas by learning. More investment permits the stock of ideas currently available to be more thoroughly explored and developed . . . [3]

Furthermore, if an innovation must be embodied in equipment before gains in productivity are realized, the rate of technological advance will be related to the level of investment.

Regardless of which side of the argument we support, the level of investment achieved by an economy will not, by itself, be a good predictor of the rate of productivity increase. Thus, it could be possible for an economy to make a smaller investment effort but achieve higher growth rates. This economy would be judged superior to a second economy which was growing slower with the same investment effort. The concept of dynamic efficiency allows us to take into consideration the increase in output achieved from a given effort.

No matter what measure of growth we accept as an indicator of economic performance, we are making the implicit assumption that increases in GNP per capita and the use of any method which results in increases in GNP per capita is coincident with an increase in economic welfare. The question we turn

[3] F. H. Hahn and R. C. O. Matthews, "The Theory of Economic Growth: A Survey," in *Surveys of Economic Theory* (New York: St. Martin's Press, 1967), p. 69.

to now concerns the relationship between growth and welfare, for what we are really after when we judge the performance of economic systems is their ability to increase the welfare of their members over time. There are many arguments that can be advanced to show that increases in GNP do not necessarily lead to increases in welfare and may, in fact, result in just the opposite.

GNP is supposed to represent the value of final goods and services produced in an economy in a year. We began Chapter I by saying that human wants were unlimited; therefore can we not conclude that increases in the quantity of final goods and services satisfy wants and result in improved welfare?[4] First, many goods we count as final goods and which enter into the GNP may not really be final goods at all. Freeways, rapid transit systems, home burglar alarm systems, and visits to the psychiatrist are some of the costs of the process of industrialization and urbanization. They are inputs into production not incurred directly by the producer but by society as a whole. Examples of these kinds of costs are in every newspaper—air pollution, water pollution, noise pollution. We cannot say that the production of $100 million worth of electricity used in private homes actually contributes $100 million to the GNP when it would be necessary to spend $25 million to clean up the air and water which is polluted by this production. Further, can we say that the production and sale of a $200 minibike contributes $200 to the GNP when its use results in the shattered nerves and shortened tempers of neighbors. What about the contribution of the automobile and the disposable can, which have made our cities intolerable and defaced our countryside? The quality of life is impossible to measure, but it is becoming increasingly clear to many that quantity and quality may be in conflict.

A third problem in the identification of growth with welfare is the question of just whose wants are being satisfied. Are people's wants formed independently or are they determined by dictators — dictators of fashion on Madison Avenue or dictators of taste in the Kremlin? Is the satisfaction of wants coincident with the improvement of welfare when these wants must be manufactured by the producers? It is impossible to determine the true nature and intensity of wants and to say that certain wants are genuine while others are created solely by advertising gimmicks. Yet it is disturbing that in a country such as the United States more is spent on advertising than on higher education.

Setting aside the question of advertising in the process of want creation, how can we compare the growth of an economy in which the direction of that growth is determined primarily by consumers with that of an economy in which the growth pattern is determined by a political elite? We must be concerned not only with the fact of growth but with the usefulness of the products which make up the growth statistics.

[4] For an excellent discussion of the relationship between welfare and growth see Ezra Mishan, *The Costs of Economic Growth* (New York: Frederick A. Praeger, 1967).

One final problem we should mention is the treatment of labor in the calculation of GNP. When we measure the cost of production we include labor along with capital and raw materials and assume that all labor effort results in disutility or a loss in welfare to the laborer. We also assume that the loss of welfare is dependent primarily on the number of hours worked. There may be some pleasure derived, however, in work itself, and the nature of this pleasure may depend upon the nature of the work arrangement. Increases in productivity that result from economies of scale and the specialization and division of labor may be partially offset by the greater frustration and alienation the worker experiences under the new conditions. A worker responsible for the production of a complete product may enjoy his work much more than one who adds one part on an assembly line.

From our discussion of the benefits of economic growth we have seen that a careful consideration must be given to all of the costs and benefits accruing to society from any increase in output before its net contribution can be assessed. Unfortunately, many of these factors cannot be measured. Many of them involve consideration of effects which are interdisciplinary in nature. But just because these effects are not easily analyzed or measured does not mean that they are negligible and can be ignored.

Equity

Equity is concerned with the way in which the final output of an economy is distributed among its members. There is no unique distribution of income which all men would agree is equitable. Equity, unlike static efficiency, is not an objective criterion, subject to measurement, but depends upon the subjective valuation of each individual.

Many standards of equity have been adopted by various groups in the past. People who are committed to capitalism as an ideology as well as a way of organizing resources believe that equity exists where every member of an economy shares in its fruits according to his "contribution." Contribution is measured by the value assigned to an individual's economic resources in the market place. Thus, an individual's economic reward depends upon the quantity and quality of the economic resources he possesses and the scarcity of these resources with respect to market demand. It is possible, however, to question some aspects of this concept of equity.

Implicit in the institution of private property is the right to pass on and receive resources through inheritance. Thus, accidents of birth can have a crucial effect on the initial endowments of inherited wealth as well as inherited talents. Attitudes toward economic activity, as well as wealth and ability, may or may not be communicated through the environment of the family. For some time social scientists have debated the extent of the role of the "puritan ethic" in economic and social development. Recently there has been discussion about and evidence of a "culture of poverty." By this is meant a complex interaction of traditional attitudes, behavioral patterns, discrimination, and a deprived environment that effectively communicates from one generation to another a lack of economic achievement.

In sum, the chance circumstances of birth, inheritance, and environment can combine to produce a pattern of resource ownership in which individuals may truly receive in proportion to the value of their contribution, but one may seriously question whether this is the best of all possible alternatives. These problems can be mitigated to a great extent if there is equal access to education and training, a general enrichment of the social and cultural environment, and the opportunity to participate meaningfully in social, economic, and political life to the limit of one's capacity. This has become the stated objective of most capitalist democracies, but there is a considerable and lamentable difference between objectives and achievements in most nations professing this ideal.

One can equalize incomes while retaining essentially a market economy by imposing a floor below which no one's income may fall. This can be accomplished by some form of negative income tax. Income distribution can also be shifted through the distribution of collective goods, that is, goods provided one by one by the state. A better measure of income equality is one which takes into account the distribution of private market income as well as the income in kind generated from the receipt of collective goods.

An alternative concept of equity is "equalitarianism." This may be defined as an equal share of output for all members of an economy without regard to an individual's contribution. A rationale for such a policy might be: given two individuals with similar tastes but with different incomes, it is only reasonable to believe that the added satisfaction, or the marginal utility, of the last dollar spent by the high income individual will be less than that of the last dollar spent by the low income individual simply because of the principle of diminishing returns in consumption. The historical power of the equalitarian ideal is based on the common, i.e., poor man's notion, that X dollars spent by someone better off would be better spent by himself and hardly missed by the other. While this concept has intuitive appeal, it is not possible to compare the intensity of satisfaction or utility of individuals so that a third party may make fine judgments about shifting income from one person to another.

Therefore, to summarize the case for the equalitarian concept of equity, we note that the more similar tastes and preferences are among individuals and the greater the differences in incomes, the more likely will an equalitarian redistribution of income lead to an overall increase in welfare. The high income individual will definitely lose satisfaction and the low income individual will gain satisfaction from an equal distribution of income. The only question is whether the gain is greater than the loss. It may be demonstrated that the probability is slightly better than one-half that total welfare would be increased.[5]

A third concept of equity is the Marxian notion, "from each according to his ability, to each according to his need." Under this scheme, income would not be evenly divided but distributed according to the needs of the individual members of the economy. Need, like contribution, is difficult to measure. If we let everyone be the judge of his own need, we may encounter the problem that the sum of the needs is greater than the supply of goods available. If someone other than the individual involved is to determine the need, we will be faced with the problem of establishing criteria to weigh one need against another.

Before we end our discussion of the measures of economic performance we should discuss the possibility of conflict among them. Regardless of the definition of equity chosen as "correct," that is, in accord with one's own value judgments, it is important to consider the trade-off between equity and other measures of economic performance. If income is extremely unequally distributed due to an unequal initial division of resources, talents, and access to opportunity, total production may be reduced. This may be the case because the great majority of the population will have no access to education and training, and thus their productivity and contribution to society will be reduced. A substantial redistribution of income from the rich to the poor, on the other hand, may also result in a reduction of total output. This may occur as a result of a disincentive effect on the part of wealthier groups if they feel that any extra effort is not worth the additional income after taxes. An equal distribution of income may result from equal pay for all economic tasks, but if this system is adopted there will be no incentive to undertake more difficult tasks. A more equal distribution may also result in a slower rate of growth due to the possibility that wealthier people save more of their income, which is then available for investment. An extremely unequal distribution of income, however, may mean that there are no mass markets for consumer goods, a situation which may discourage private investment. Many profess to have faith in the idea that distribution problems can be solved by economic growth. It is easier to divide a growing pie than a stable or shrinking one. It may be easier, but there is little evidence that it is being attempted in some of the faster growing areas of the world. The evidence seems to indicate that pockets of poverty do not participate in the overall growth of the economy even in good times. Special programs and training are needed to enable the inhabitants of poverty areas to participate in the economy on a productive basis at all. The gap between rich and poor seems

[5] For a full exposition of this point see A. P. Lerner, *The Economics of Control* (New York: The Macmillan Company, 1946).

to be widening rather than narrowing, although many have moved out of the "poverty" category.

An economist can merely suggest the nature of the conflicts involved. It is up to the individual, after weighing the costs of various distribution schemes, to pick the one which he believes to be most equitable.

Much has been written on the possible conflict between static efficiency and growth. It has been argued that an economy which may be using its resources efficiently at every moment of time may be inefficient in its use of resources over time. This may occur through poor timing of investment decisions due to a lack of knowledge about future prospects or through too small a devotion of effort to research and development because of attitudes toward risk. These same problems may arise, however, in an economy which is also using its resources inefficiently. It is difficult to understand the connection between the achievement of rapid growth and the failure to allocate resources efficiently at a point in time. Merely because an economy which has decided to devote vast quantities of resources to the achievement of growth is using resources wastefully does not prove that rapid growth and efficiency are necessarily in conflict. One may be willing to overlook misallocations if an economy is growing rapidly, but does this prove that the misallocations are a *cause* of the rapid growth? The notion of a conflict between the two implies that the requirements of static efficiency are not conducive to growth and vice versa.

Perhaps the economic leadership can devote its problem-solving ability to only one area of difficulty at a time. If growth policies are being developed and implemented, concern for the gains which a reallocation of resources can bring must suffer. This is an allegation which has yet to be proved. We will return to this in greater detail when we discuss the sources of the recent slowdown in Soviet economic growth.

QUESTIONS

1. Why is it desirable for any economy to attain a distribution of its output so that the marginal rate of substitution for all commodities is the same for all individuals in the economy?

2. Illustrate the loss to any economic system of allocating resources so that the marginal productivity of labor in one coal mine is twice that of labor in a second coal mine.

3. Do you agree that the achievement of static efficiency is a desirable objective for any economic system?

4. Why is economic growth an ambiguous criterion for judging the performance of economic systems?

5. What is dynamic efficiency and what factors determine if an economic system is dynamically efficient?

6. Which definition of equity presented in this chapter most closely agrees with your own values?

7. Are there other performance criteria which you think should be added to those discussed in this chapter?

BIBLIOGRAPHY

Balassa, Bela, "Success Criteria for Economic Systems," *The Hungarian Experience in Economic Planning.* New Haven, Conn.: Yale University Press, 1959, pp. 5-24.

Boulding, Kenneth, "Welfare Economics," *A Survey of Contemporary Economics,* ed. B. F. Haley. Homewood, Illinois: Richard D. Irwin, Inc., 1952, II, 1-34.

Grossman, Gregory, *Economic Systems.* Englewood Cliffs, N. J.: Prentice-Hall, Inc., 1967.

Knight, Frank, *The Economic Organization.* New York: Augustus M. Kelley, Inc., 1951.

Kohler, Heinz, *Welfare and Planning.* New York: John Wiley and Sons, Inc., 1966.

Mishan, Ezra, *The Costs of Economic Growth.* New York: Frederick A. Praeger, Inc., 1967.

Solo, Robert, *Economic Organizations and Social Systems.* New York: The Bobbs-Merrill Company, Inc., 1967.

II

CAPITALISM

3

The Model
of Perfect Competition

Introduction

In chapter one we briefly discussed the functioning of a capitalist economy. In this chapter we will analyze in greater depth one variant of capitalism—the perfectly competitive market economy. We will be concerned with how the decisions of individuals, acting as consumers and resource suppliers, and firms, acting as producers and resource users, determine what will be produced and for whom it will be produced.

Before we look at the behavior of individuals and firms, we must define the requirements for the functioning of a perfectly competitive market economy. A necessary condition for the existence of perfect competition is that each individual economic unit be so small in proportion to the total market that its behavior has no influence over market price. Since there is only one price for any particular commodity in the market at one time, no one will pay more than the going price, and no one can pay less. Some further requirments for the existence of a uniform price are the homogeneity or uniformity of all goods, the perfect mobility of all resources and all final products, and the possession of perfect knowledge on the part of consumers and firms with respect to price and quality.

THE CONSUMER AND THE FIRM

Behavior of the Individual as a Consumer

Each consumer tries to maximize his welfare by purchasing that particular bundle of goods and services which will give him the most satisfaction. He is limited in his choice by the size of his income and the prices of the products he faces in the marketplace. How should he allocate his income among the thousands of items available in the marketplace? It is unlikely that the consumer will concentrate all his spending on a particular item or even a particular class of items, like food. We have seen in the preceding chapter that consumers experience declining satisfaction from continued consumption of any good and switch their spending to another good to "get their money's worth." When the consumer has exhausted his income in the purchase of desirable commodities, we are certain that the pleasure he obtains from the last dollar's worth of each commodity is exactly the same. But how can we be so sure, since we can never get inside his head to make absolutely certain this is true. The logic of it is quite simple—if the consumer does *not* value equally the last dollar's worth of every good consumed, he will change his behavior until he does. He will cut back a dollar's spending on the good giving him relatively little satisfaction and transfer the dollar so released to spending on the good giving him greater satisfaction. In so doing the marginal utility of the former has been enhanced, and the marginal utility of the latter has diminished. The process will continue until the last dollar's worth of each good yields the same satisfaction. At this point the rate at which the consumer is willing to trade one good for another, i.e., his marginal rate of substitution, is equal to the rate at which he can trade one for the other in the marketplace, i.e., the ratio of their prices. Stated mathematically:

$$\frac{MU_x}{MU_y} \equiv MRS_{x,y} = \frac{P_x}{P_y}$$

As long as the behavior pattern outlined above remains constant, this consumer and every other consumer will put himself in a position of personal equilibrium and stay there. The consumer's tastes must remain constant, income be unchanged, and the price of every good remain the same. Should any of these change, then the individuals involved will alter their behavior and seek a position in which everything is in balance again. We will consider the effects of changes in consumer incomes and then of changes in price.

Consumer Response to Changes in Income

Suppose we start from a position of equilibrium where a consumer has allocated his income, balancing purchases of each good at the margin so that the last dollar spent on every good yields the same satisfaction. Now let us increase his income. Picking any good at random, he begins to spend the additional income. The very first purchase now pushes the entire original market basket of goods out of balance. Diminishing returns in consumption, or diminishing marginal utility, causes the consumer to obtain less satisfaction from the new purchase of the randomly selected good than he derived from the last purchase. He now proceeds to shift his new spending to the next good, where the same thing occurs, and to the next, and to the next, etc., until all the new income has been spent. When the new income has been allocated among all the goods and the consumer obtains the same satisfaction from the last dollar spent on every good, then he is back in equilibrium. Remember, "equilibrium" just means that he has reached a point at which, as long as his income remains at this level and prices don't change, he will continue to purchase the same mix of goods period after period.

By no means does the above analysis imply that the increase in purchases of every good will rise proportionately to the increase in income. Economists have developed terms to describe the possible consumption responses of consumers to changes in income. Should the consumer respond to a 10 percent increase in his income by increasing the consumption of a certain good or goods by an amount in excess of 10 percent, economists term these goods "income elastic." Obviously then, if the consumer raises his consumption level on some goods in excess of 10 percent, another good or other goods must suffer an increase in consumption of less than 10 percent. These goods are called "income inelastic." There are goods called "inferior goods" whose consumption actually declines absolutely as a result of increased incomes. Examples of inferior goods are cheap goods purchased by very low income households, like starchy foods, which with rising incomes are displaced by better quality items such as vegetables, fruits, and meats.

Consumer Response to Changes in Price

The consumer's response to a change in the price of a single good is a very subtle thing and will require close attention since we are avoiding the use in this chapter of the diagrammatics and algebra of utility theory.

The logic of this response is as follows: the consumer begins, as always, at a point at which his income is fully allocated and the satisfaction of the marginal dollar spent on every good is the same. Now let the price of a single good fall, perhaps to half of its former price. Should the consumer continue to allocate the same number of dollars to the lower priced good, he can now buy twice as much of it. If he should consume exactly the same bundle of goods as before, he would have money left over. Therefore, the solution to the problem is a subtle one—first, there is a "substitution" effect, that is, the purchase of additional quantities of the cheaper good. Second, there is an "income" effect, which derives from the fact that income may be released from the cheaper good without reducing overall consumption of the good. This analysis, of course, is the grossest of simplifications of much more sophisticated analyses. Many other effects, such as the interactions between substitutes and complements, will not be considered in this analysis. Hard on the heels of these conclusions, we can derive a fundamental tool in the economist's kit-bag—the demand curve. The demand curve encapsules the conclusions we have just reached; namely, that when the price of a good falls, the consumer will buy more of it and how much more depends on exceedingly complex interrelationsips between goods, none of which appear in the traditional demand curves shown here in diagram 3.1. Each consumer's demand curve shows only the complete and final adjustment to the change in price of the good shown. The market demand curve is derived by summing together the demand curves of all individual consumers. (see diagram 3.2).

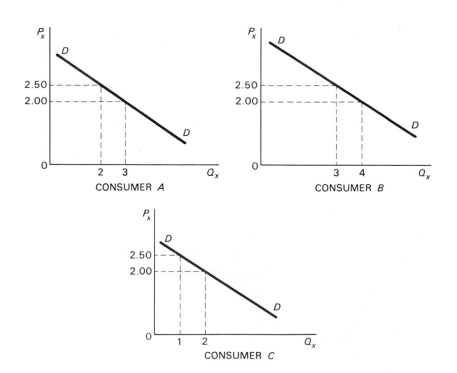

Diagram 3.1

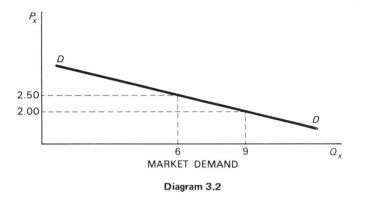

MARKET DEMAND

Diagram 3.2

Behavior of the Individual as a Resource Supplier—Labor Supply

Each individual must make certain decisions as a resource supplier. In this role he is concerned with maximizing the income from the sale of the services of the factors of production he owns. The individual must decide how much labor time he will offer on the market at various wage rates, how much land he will offer at various prices, and how much of his income he will save and make available to others for the process of capital formation.

Let's consider the decision to offer one's labor time in return for wages. Everyone has 24 hours a day which can be devoted to work and leisure. We will assume that leisure is pleasurable and that work is painful. Therefore, one must be compensated for giving up leisure.

The compensation is wages paid according to the valuation of one's services. These wages constitute the worker-consumer's command over commodities. The process of adjustment then is simple—the worker surrenders an hour of pleasurable leisure in return for an hour's worth of pleasurable commodities. The exchange will continue until the loss of leisure's pleasure weighs equally with the gain of material goods.

An increase in the wage rate will have the effect of increasing the terms of exchange between leisure and commodities and will encourage the worker-consumer to offer larger quantities of labor to the market. At high wage rates the possibility exists that leisure may become such a "superior" good that the worker may in effect "buy back" his leisure. It is widely observed that segments of the medical profession may have reached such heights of income. No such wage rates have materialized in the academic profession, so the case remains only a theoretical possibility for economists.

The Supply of Savings

Each individual household must also decide how to allocate its money income between consumption today and savings for future consumption. The distribution through time of a household's income is an optimizing problem that is of no conceivable concern to an outsider. The only impact of society on this individual decision should be to determine the terms of exchange between the future and the present, that is, the interest rate. Since both consumption in the present and in the future are pleasurable and both pleasures are limited by the available income, a choice, influenced by the interest rate, must be made as to which inter-temporal distribution is better.

Let us suppose a household receives $1,000 in income per year for two years. Let us further assume that the market rate of interest is 10 percent. The two years taken together represent $2,000 in consumption, considering of course that consumption deferred is not the same as consumption now. Let us examine the two extremes—a household may choose to consume nothing now and everything in the following year. The $1,000 saved is transformed by the capital market into $1,100, and next year's consumption will total $2,100. On the other hand, the household could have chosen to consume everything in the present and have nothing the next year. This is accomplished by borrowing enough money now (at 10 percent interest) so that the $1,000 next year will pay both principal and interest. The borrowed sum is $909 or $1,000 divided by 1.1. Total consumption today is $1909.

We have shown above that it is possible to switch spending back and forth between the present and the future through the capital market and that the interest rate determines the rate of exchange between the two periods no matter which way you go. While we have titled this section the "Supply of Savings" there is no necessity to assume that every household will always be saving at every moment in time. The household must simply examine its own tastes with respect to present versus future consumption and save (send money into the future plus interest) or borrow (bring future income back into the present minus interest). One is not "good" and the other "bad"; it is the household's business when it wants to consume and no one else's. The outside world sets the terms, however.

Suppose that at 10 percent interest more households decide to borrow for consumption. Consumer goods are not really brought back from the future— they are just transferred at each point in time from savers to borrowers and then back again in the next time period. Therefore the net savings of households taken as a whole is the sum of the positive savings of future-oriented consumers minus the dissavings of present-oriented consumers. As the interest rate rises, saving households are induced to save more and dissaving households to borrow less— therefore the market supply of savings is positively related to the interest rate even if a considerable number of households are net borrowers.

Now that we have surveyed the behavior of the individual as a consumer of goods and as a supplier of resources, we will examine the behavior of the firm as a producer of goods and a user of resources.

The Firm as a Producer

Assuming perfect competition, the owner or entrepreneur of each firm will produce the quantity of each product that maximizes his profits. He will produce to the point at which the cost of an additional unit is just equal to its addition to revenue, i.e., to the point at which MR=MC.

Let us assume that due to diminishing returns, marginal costs tend to rise with increasing output but that the firm is forced to accept whatever the going price is due to competition. Suppose a firm produces 40 thousand-yard bolts of cloth per day and that the cost of the fortieth bolt is $2000 (around $2.00 per yard). Other cost points may be listed: at a rate of 45 bolts per day the forty-fifth bolt will cost $2500 ($2.50 a yard); at a rate of 50 bolts per day the fiftieth bolt will cost $3000 ($3.00 a yard); at a rate of 55 bolts per day the fifty-fifth bolt will cost $3500 (or $3.50 per yard); unmentioned points in between are assumed to be progressively more expensive. If the price of cloth should be $2.50 a yard, production at a rate of 40 bolts per day is clearly not the best rate. The fortieth bolt costs $2000 and sells for $2500. The $500 margin for the fortieth bolt is profitable, but is this the *most* profitable point? No, because the forty-first bolt will cost more than $2000 but less than $2500, so some additional profit may be made by stepping up output. The opposite is true at a production rate of 50 bolts per day—the fiftieth bolt costs $3000 but sells for $2500. Production will be cut back until the last bolt pays for itself. The information about firm behavior we have just examined, given its costs and technology, is summarized in that classic economic tool that is the counterpart of the demand curve—the supply curve. If the market price is $3 a yard, the firm will produce 50 yards. If the price rises to $3.50 a yard, it will produce 55 yards. If the price falls to $2.50 the firm will cut output to 45. If it falls to $2 it will produce 40. If the price falls to the point that the firm cannot cover its production costs, it will ultimately cut its output to zero. We have derived four points on the firm's supply curve of cloth, which is basically a portion of the marginal cost curve. See diagram 3.3.

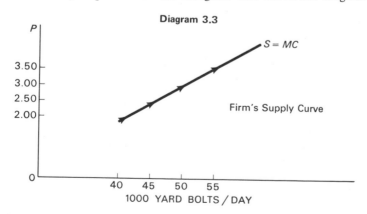

Diagram 3.3

We can sum the supply curves of all the firms in the industry to derive the market supply curve. Assuming there are one hundred identical firms producing in this industry, the market supply curve is graphed below.

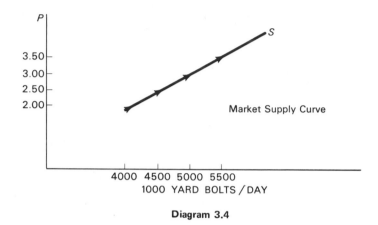

Diagram 3.4

We can combine the market supply curve with the market demand curve to determine what price will actually prevail in the market.

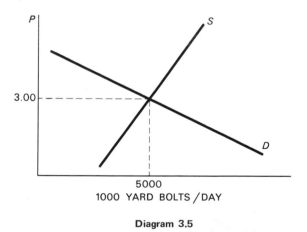

Diagram 3.5

At this price each individual firm is producing 50 bolts a day. Let us assume that each firm is making profits because the price is greater than the average cost of the *total* output. The existence of profits will attract new firms into the industry. Suppose ten new firms enter the industry. The supply curve will shift to the right, and market price will fall.

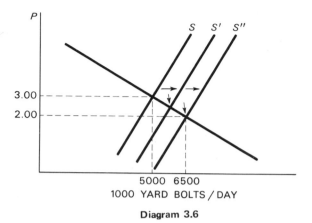

Diagram 3.6

New firms will continue to enter until profits disappear. Assume this will occur where average cost (or AC) equals price at $2.00. Two dollars is the long-run equilibrium price for this industry, because at this price there is no incentive for firms to change their output or for new firms to enter or leave the industry. Equilibrium can be disturbed, however, by a change in consumer tastes, by a change in factor prices, or by a change in technology.

Suppose that there is an increase in consumer demand for cloth. The demand curve will shift up to the right, from D to D'; price will rise, and the existing firms will increase their output by moving along their marginal cost or supply curves. At the higher price, higher profits are being earned. New firms will enter the industry, shifting the industry supply curve to the right (not shown) and pushing the price back toward $2.00. If the price of factors does not rise as industry output is expanded, the price will fall all the way back to $2.00.

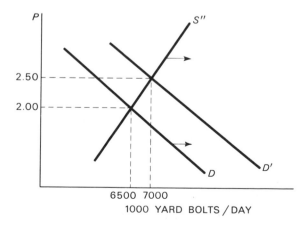

Diagram 3.7

We have seen an example of how prices provide information to market participants and guide them in their selection of alternatives. The increase in consumer demand was communicated to firms by the rise in the price of their product. Their response was to increase output. Other firms also responded to the higher price by moving from lower profit industries to this higher profit industry. Output responded to consumer preferences.

Consumers are also guided by price signals. Let us assume that the cost of producing the product increases. Each individual firm's cost of producing the product increases. Each individual firm's cost curves will shift up, and the industry supply curve will shift up and to the left. Firms will reduce their output and price will rise. At the new, higher price consumers will no longer want to buy as much. Thus, the higher price informs them that the cost of consuming this particular product relative to others has risen.

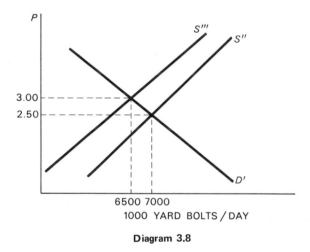

Diagram 3.8

They will now adjust their consumption patterns taking this new information into account.

The Firm as a Resource User

When the firm decides what output to produce it must also decide what level of inputs to use. The method of achieving maximum profit by balancing marginal cost with marginal revenue (MR=MC), as described above, can be applied to factor use. The firm will maximize its profit by using each resource to the point that one more of the resource units adds an equal amount to revenue and to costs. To produce each unit of output at the lowest possible cost, the firm will use the correct absolute amounts of all factors and also the correct combination of all factors. Consider a firm in our example above, producing 40 bolts of cloth a day at a price of $2000 a bolt, using two factors of production, labor and capital. The number of combinations may be infinitely varied—for our purposes we will single out three combinations of capital and labor which will produce 40 bolts of cloth per day as shown in table 3.1.

Table 3.1

	Capital			Labor	
A	600		A	600	
B	500	@ $100/machine day	B	1000	@ $20/man day
C	400		C	1600	

If you total the factor input costs and add the material costs of $10,000 ($250 per bolt) you find that Combination A totals $82,000, Combination B totals $80,000, and Combination C totals $82,000. The reason for this is that labor and capital are imperfect substitutes in production and using more of one instead of the other runs into diminishing returns *in both directions.* Some combination is bound to be least cost and that is the one the profit maximizing firm is bound to select. Firms are driven to do this by the market and their own technology. If a machine-day costs $100 and a man-day costs $20, the market exchanges them impersonally at a rate of 5 to 1. We can see from table 3.1 that in going from Combination A to Combination B, the firm dropped 100 machine-days and only had to add 400 man-days. The exchange then profited the firm because its internal exchange rate was less than the market's (saving the firm $2000). Going further to Combination C involved dropping another 100 machine-days but adding 600 man-days. Output is unchanged but the internal exchange rate of capital for labor is now *worse* than the market's and the firm is out an extra $2000. For small changes around Combination B, the internal exchange rate of machine-days for man-days is 5 to 1, or the same as the market's.

Now if the price of a machine-day should fall to $80, the market's ratio of value falls to 4 to 1. The three factor combinations now total $70,000, $70,000 and $74,000 respectively. You are indifferent between combinations A and B because the internal transformation rate is 4 to 1 between them and so is the market's. Should the price of a machine-day fall below $80, Combination A would be the least cost position. The student may work out for himself the situations in which the price of a man-day rises or falls or a machine-day rises or any combination of these.

Economic Aggregates—Output, Employment, and the Price Level

Up to this point only the microeconomic aspects of perfect competition have been analyzed. It is now necessary to determine what the aggregate effect of the individual behavior of consumers and firms will be on the total level of output, employment, and the price level. This determination will be made within the framework of a simple classical macroeconomic model in which all prices and wages are flexible and output is a function of the level of employment.

In order to determine the level of employment (N) it is necessary to consider the market demand and supply of labor. A market demand and supply function are plotted below in diagram 3.9. It is assumed that the demand for labor is an inverse function of the real wage rate, i.e., the nominal wage divided by the general price level. The supply of labor is a positive function of the real wage.

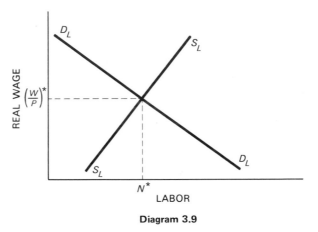

Diagram 3.9

The equilibrium level of employment is N*, and the equilibrium real wage rate is $(W/p)^*$. At this point everyone who is willing to work at the current wage is employed. At a wage greater than $(W/p)^*$ there will be a surplus of labor seeking employment, and the wage will be bid down. At a wage lower than $(W/p)^*$ there will be a shortage of labor, and the wage would be bid up.

The level of output (y) can be determined from the level of employment by the use of an aggregate production function. The production function drawn below shows the relationship between total output and the level of employment inputs. It is assumed that output is an increasing function of employment.

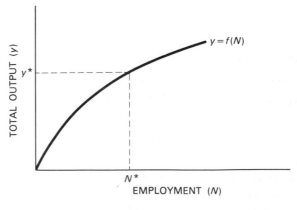

Diagram 3.10

It can be seen from the diagram that a level of employment of N* will result in a level of output y*. The equilibrium level of output is y*.

We can illustrate the automatic maintenance of full employment in this model with a specific example. It is assumed that the initial equilibrium real wage is $2.00 and the equilibrium level of employment is 100. Plugging the level of employment into the production function we generate a level of real output of 200. For simplicity let us assume that the level of output can be represented as equivalent to 200 bushels of wheat. Suppose that the supply of labor shifts to the right to S_L'. At the wage of $2.00 there is an excess supply of labor. The wage will be bid down until the surplus is eliminated and full employment is restored. This will occur when the wage is $1.75 and the level of employment is 110. At the higher level of employment real output increases to 240.

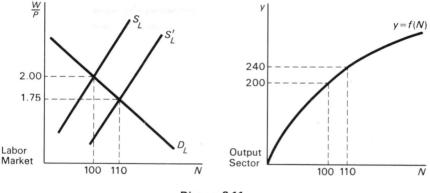

Diagram 3.11

Once the levels of employment and output have been determined, the general price level will be determined by the interaction of the money supply and the real variables. The larger the money supply, the greater the amount of purchasing power, and the higher the price level.

We have described how the competitive market model achieves equilibrium in product and labor markets. It remains for the next chapter to demonstrate whether this competitive equilibrium satisfies the efficiency and equity performance criteria.

QUESTIONS

1. What economic decisions confront the household in a market system?
2. What factors motivate the household in making these decisions?
3. What basic decisions confront the firm in a market system?
4. What factors motivate the firm in making these decisions?
5. Why is the equilibrium level of total output in the market model also the full employment level of output?

6. Who determines what goods and services will be produced in a market system?

7. What institutions or mechanisms communicate consumer preferences to producers in this system?

4

The Performance
of the Competitive
Market Economy

The Model Versus Reality

We have analyzed the economic processes in operation under the assumptions of perfect competition and have discussed the determinants of the pattern of resource allocation and the level of employment. We will now turn to the task of analyzing the performance of a competitive economy with respect to the criteria of static efficiency, dynamic efficiency, and equity. For all of the economic systems we will examine, significant deviations from the achievement of efficiency and equity may occur at the theoretical and operational levels. First, the model itself may be defective and fail to meet one or more of our performance criteria. Second, the necessary relaxations of the rigorous assumptions of the model in the transition from theory to practice may result in further deviations. Let us now evaluate the performance of the competitive market model.

THE COMPETITIVE MARKET MODEL

Static Efficiency

Recalling the requirements for static efficiency outlined in chapter two, we must now determine whether resources are fully and optimally employed. It has been shown that given flexible wages and prices, unemployment of resources in the competitive economy is only a temporary phenomenon, the length of which will depend upon the speed with which resources move from declining to advancing industries. Surpluses of labor, raw materials, land, or capital will result in a fall in their price, which will induce firms to make greater use of these relatively more abundant resources. Given price flexibility and resource mobility persistent unemployment is impossible.

Let us now turn to the question of the optimal allocation of scarce resources among competing uses. In the following section the allocation of resources in a perfectly competitive market economy will be compared with the optimal allocation defined by the six efficiency conditions. One of the primary virtues of a perfectly competitive economy is claimed to be the achievement of static efficiency. It will be assumed in the following section that all social costs are equal to private costs and social benefits are equal to private benefits, i.e., there are no externalities. We will discuss the problem of externalities in a later section of this chapter.

Condition No. 1—*Optimum Exchange Among Consumers*

We have seen in chapter two that if the marginal rate of substitution (MRS) of one good for another is equal for all consumers, no further exchanges of goods can improve anyone's welfare without reducing the welfare of a second party. The condition will hold under perfect competition as a result of the independent action of individual consumers. Recall from chapter three that each consumer allocates his income among goods and services in order to maximize his own satisfaction. Given his income, tastes, and preferences, and the prices of the products he buys, he will pick a particular combination of goods such that the satisfaction he enjoys from the last dollar spent on all goods is equal. Thus, when the consumer is in equilibrium, his marginal rate of substitution between any two goods will be equal to the ratio of their prices. Stated mathematically:

$$MRS_{x,y} = \frac{P_x}{P_y}$$

Since all consumers face the same market prices, it follows that their marginal rates of substitution are all equal. This analysis shows that the optimal allocation of goods, defined in condition one of chapter two, will hold in the competitive case described in chapter three.

Condition No. 2—*The Optimum Degree of Specialization Among Producing Units*

We have shown in chapter three that each firm maximizes its profit by producing each product to the point at which marginal revenue is equal to marginal cost, and for the perfectly competitive firm marginal revenue is equal to price. Thus, when each firm is maximizing its profits, the ratio of the marginal costs of all goods will be equal to the ratio of their prices. The ratio of marginal costs represents the rate at which the firm can exchange one good for another in production, i.e., the firm's marginal rate of transformation, MRT. Stated mathematically:

$$MRT_{x,y} = \frac{P_x}{P_y}$$

Since all firms face the same prices, in equilibrium the MRT's of all firms will be equal. We have seen in chapter two that when the MRT's are equal for all firms, additional output cannot be gained by transferring production from one firm to another. We have proven that the competitive market economy will achieve the optimum degree of specialization.

Condition No. 3—*Optimum Factor Allocation Between Producing Units*

In chapter three we saw that the firm maximizes its profits by using both the correct absolute amounts of all factors and the correct combination of factors. The firm is using the profit maximizing amount of each factor when its contribution to revenue is just equal to its marginal cost or price. Since all firms face the same prices, the contribution to output of any particular factor, or the rate at which that factor can be transformed into a good will be the same for all users. Thus, factors will be allocated optimally among all producing units, and no gain from reallocation will be possible.

Condition No. 4—*The Optimum Degree of Factor Substitution*

In chapter three we saw that a firm is using the profit maximizing combination of factors when the rate at which it can exchange one factor for another in production is equal to the rate at which it can exchange one for the other in the market place, i.e., when the internal rate of substitution is equal to the external rate of exchange. Since all firms in a competitive market place face the same factor prices or external rate, it follows that their internal rates of transformation are also the same. Therefore it follows that output cannot be increased by a recombination of factors.

Condition No. 5—*The Optimum Production Mix*

In the competitive economy we have shown that the consumer is maximizing his satisfaction when the

$$MRS_{x,y} = \frac{P_x}{P_y}$$

and the firm is maximizing its profits when the

$$MRT_{x,y} = \frac{P_x}{P_y}$$

Since consumers and firms face the same prices, it follows that the

$$MRS_{x,y} = MRT_{x,y}$$

The rate at which the consumer is willing to substitute one good for another, the relative value of the two goods, is just equal to the rate at which the firm can transform one good into another, their relative cost of the two goods. The optimal mix of goods is thus produced.

Condition No. 6—*Optimum Intensity of Factor Use*

We saw in chapter three that the individual supplies labor to the point at which the loss of satisfaction from the reduction of leisure is just equal to the gain of material goods represented by his wage. The firm uses labor to the point at which its marginal contribution is equal to the wage. Therefore in a competitive system the loss of satisfaction from sacrificing the last unit of leisure is just equal to labor's contribution to output. Additional leisure or additional labor effort will reduce consumer welfare.

The attainment of static efficiency, illustrated by the satisfaction of the six optimality conditions, is commonly considered to be one of the major achievements of a perfectly competitive market economy. It is argued that without any form of central planning or guidance, resources will flow to the areas where they are most valued, and those products in the greatest demand will be produced with a minimum of resource expenditure.

Consumers may shift their consumption from one good to another to improve their welfare if market prices do not reflect relative values. Looking at the production side, firms are induced to produce more of one good and less of another when the price of the first rises and the price of the other falls. Even though diminishing returns mean that the cost of producing the first good is rising, the rising price indicates that these costs will be covered and normal profits can be earned.

Let us imagine a situation in which food and clothing would be produced and no one cared whether everything balanced or not. We will assume that a small amount of cloth was produced and a large amount of food. Consumers would find that the benefits of the last bit of food given them would be low since they had so much of it. The reverse would be true for cloth. Consumers as a group would use prices as a signalling device to indicate that they wanted less food and more clothing. Firms which produced small quantities of clothing would find that everything sold well and people were clamoring for more. Quantities of food would remain unsold, and firms would have to unload the stuff. It does not take a degree from Harvard Business School to detect the likely response of the densest manager. Shifting resources from food production to clothing production does involve increasing costs or diminishing returns in clothing, but the sales are there to more than compensate.

The process of resource transfer is self-limiting since diminishing returns takes its toll and eats away the extra returns from ever larger production of clothing. Also, consumers find that the marginal benefit from increasing amounts of clothing gets less and less. These two trends crash into each other where the consumers' falling preference for clothing over food runs into the producers' rising costs of transferring resources from food to clothing. At this point further transfers in production raise costs higher than consumers perceive the benefits to be, and they will not purchase additional clothing. The optimal amount of food and clothing is produced.

Prices also serve as signals to producers determining what combination of inputs to use. Since abundant labor leads to low wages and scarce capital results in high-cost loans and relatively expensive machinery and vice versa, the firm is thereby encouraged to utilize the abundant factor intensively and to economize on the scarce factor, an eminently rational result. Resources are allocated optimally among producing units.

When painting this rosy picture it must be recalled, however, that the exact production mix and the distribution of output among members of the economy will depend upon initial resource endowments. There is no unique efficient production pattern for a perfectly competitive economy. The pattern will vary with the distribution of wealth. Various patterns of output may be considered economically efficient, but, on non-economic grounds, not equally desirable.

It must also be remembered that though efficiency, as we have defined it, may be shown to exist in equilibrium under the assumptions of perfect competition, real world capitalist economies are probably not using their resources efficiently. The assumptions of perfect competition are so restrictive that no real world economies can qualify. In the next chapter we will discuss the implications of market imperfections for the achievement of static efficiency.

Having discussed the efficiency with which resources are allocated within a single market economy, let us turn to the question of the efficiency with which resources are allocated among several market economies.

Equilibrium in the Balance of Payments—The Gold Exchange Standard

Our analysis of the market system to this point has been confined to a single "closed" economy—that is, an economy without foreign trade. The introduction of the possibility of the exchange of goods and services between countries considerably complicates the formal theoretical analysis. The full demonstration of the compatibility of the domestic market system with an international market system is more appropriate to an economics text in International Trade Theory.[1] For our purposes the classical gold standard system will be presented in a shortened form.

First some simplifying assumptions are necessary to reduce the number of problems to be considered to manageable proportions. These are:

1. Assume there are only two economies in this world, both with perfectly competitive markets.
2. Transportation costs are ignored, i.e., assumed to be zero until it is appropriate to consider them explicitly.
3. The circulating medium of exchange, money, is gold bullion, or coin, or a paper currency backed by gold deposits in a fixed proportion, say 100 percent.
4. The classical quantity theory of money, and the interaction of money, employment, national income, and prices is assumed to be operative.
5. There is no government monetary policy or intervention in the form of trade barriers.

Now that the mechanisms and behavioral assumptions have been presented, let us observe our model world economy in action. Suppose that individuals in Country A and Country B trade a large number of products between themselves. Some goods may be cheaper in Country A and some may be cheaper in Country B, and these products will naturally tend to flow into trade between the two countries. For those goods that importers in Country B buy in Country A, they must pay so many ounces of gold. For those goods that Country A buys in Country B, it likewise must pay a certain amount of gold. Goods flow both ways, and gold debts and earnings flow both ways in response. Diagram 4.1 illustrates this process.

Country A exports 150 gold ounces worth of goods, and it imports in turn only 100 gold ounces worth of goods. This export surplus is usually termed a favorable balance of trade and involves the trade activity of a given period of time, usually a year. Obviously the reverse side of this coin is that Country B is running an unfavorable balance of trade of precisely the same amount. On the monetary side of the exchanges of goods, Country A is owed 150 ounces of gold

---

[1]For a more thorough treatment of international trade theory see H. Robert Heller, *International Trade: Theory and Empirical Evidence* (Englewood Cliffs, N.J.: Prentice Hall, 1970).

by Country B, and it in turn owes 100 ounces of gold to Country B. One hundred of the 150 ounces of Country A's gold earnings may be used to pay off or cancel its debts in Country B. The remaining 50 ounces of gold earnings may be taken physically out of Country B and transported to Country A, where the gold will become part of the circulating money supply. Country B then has lost 50 gold ounces from its money supply, and Country A has increased its money supply by the same amount. Only the *net* excess/ deficit of gold earnings/ debts will actually have to be transported from one country to the other.

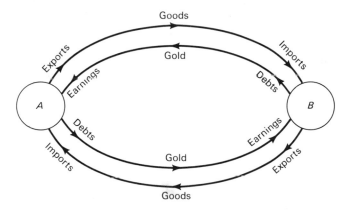

Diagram 4.1

We have observed that Country A enjoys an advantage in selling goods in Country B. This advantage presumably is caused by lower costs and prices in Country A. The resulting favorable balance of trade for Country A results in an inflow of gold, as we have seen. The increase in the gold money supply and the combination of increased domestic and foreign spending places pressures on an economy already running at full employment, and inflation results. Inexorably this inflation nibbles away at Country A's initial cost and price advantage.

The opposite is occuring in Country B. The loss of gold, hence decline in its money supply, together with the leakage of spending into foreign markets causes total spending to fall below the full employment level. Wages and costs begin to fall as some resources become unemployed and cut their asking price. Prices fall as inventories accumulate and output is curtailed. More and more of Country B's goods then begin to be more attractive in price to consumers in Country A.

The combination of rising prices and reduced advantage in Country A and falling prices and increased advantage (reduced disadvantage) in Country B causes the initial 50 net ounces of gold (A-surplus/B-deficit) to be reduced. This process will continue and with each additional round of trade the surplus/deficit will decline until it is completely eliminated. Once trade is balanced in value between the two countries, no gold need flow between them and their money stocks will stabilize. Total spending will also then stabilize in each country at the full employment level.

To summarize, the major conclusions to be drawn from this model are:

1. The system tends to eliminate imbalance in the trade between countries *automatically* with no need for governmental intervention.
2. The costs of adjustments, i.e., inflation in the surplus country and/or deflation and unemployment in the deficit country, are borne by both sides.
3. All the price systems of market economies are linked together by international markets for goods, services, and factors. Therefore the optimality and efficiency conditions, which can be demonstrated to hold for perfect competition in a single market economy, may now be generalized to the entire world economy.

The difficulties of this model world economy are that the initial assumptions we made may be in marked variance from real world experience. Differences between the workings and conclusions of our model and the actual functioning of the international economy will be discussed in the next section.

Dynamic Efficiency

Criterion No. 1—*Investment in Research, Invention, and Innovation*

We turn now to considering the dynamic efficiency of our model, perfectly competitive capitalism. In chapter two, we stated that economic progress, "intensive" growth, may be defined as an increase in per capita output, adjusted for increases in other inputs. To achieve intensive growth, an economic system must undertake a complex succession of activities resulting in technological change. These activities are scientific research, invention, and innovation. Since none of these activities is costless, an economic system must arrange its affairs so that adequate investments are made in each process. When the proper investments have been made, marginal social benefits are equal to marginal social costs of the investment.

Under perfectly competitive capitalism, any activity requiring investment must hold out the promise of rewards in proportion to the risks and efforts expended. Incentives must induce men and resources to turn their energies to the tasks of research, invention, and innovation. Unfortunately for the researcher, inventor, or innovator, facts and ideas once discovered become the common property of man and may be commercially exploited as much by the nimble imitator as by the creative initiator. Given a situation in which researchers can hope to capture only a fraction of the total social benefits derived from their discoveries, they will reduce their efforts proportionally. Pure decentralized capitalism, then, will tend to underinvest in fundamental research to a large degree, invention to a lesser extent, and innovation least of all. It must be remembered that we are considering a "pure" model of capitalism which does not admit the possibility of patent or copyright. These are monopolistic devices designed to circumvent precisely this difficulty.

To summarize, investment in research and invention in a decentralized market economy will not reach the point where marginal social benefits become equal to marginal social costs. The farther the process of research or invention is from direct production application and the more perfect is the transmission of new facts and ideas, the less likely is the original thinker to share in the fruits of his efforts and the riskier such investments become. Investment will be made only until marginal private benefits equal marginal private costs and these private benefits may be substantially less than the potential benefits to society of full exploitation of research and invention possibilities.

Setting aside for a moment the problem of investing adequately in basic research, invention, and innovation, competitive capitalism has some compensating features. For example, an invention, idea, or innovation once made is rapidly transmitted throughout the entire economic system. A firm may not be able to gain lasting advantage from its own invention or innovation, but equally, if it does not adopt other firm's innovations, it cannot survive. Decentralized capitalism thus maximizes the number of individuals with a direct economic interest in making or adopting innovations, provided only that risks, efforts, and rewards are in proper balance.

Criterion No. 2—*Investment in Human Capital*

In a capitalist market system, every worker has title to his stock of "human capital," i.e., the skills and knowledge he brings to any task. He may be expected to be compensated for supplying the services of his skills to the market. If these rewards are proportional to the effort necessary to acquire the skills, then the individual worker will voluntarily invest in himself to the proper degree. This being true, education, skills, and training may be provided by a private, profit-seeking system of technical and general educational schools. Individuals will make the sacrifices in the form of tuition and lost wages in order to obtain the skills offered by the school. Provided only that there are no external benefits derived by others from an individual's education, the amount of skills acquired (the rate of human capital formation) will be the optimum amount.

Criterion No. 3—*Investment in Physical Capital*

Investment in physical capital in the competitive model will take place until the marginal return on investment is equal to the marginal cost of the equipment. This rate of return on capital must also be equal to the marginal rate of substitution (MRS) between present and future consumption of income earners, or, in other words, their willingness to save. If the yield should be higher than the MRS, then individuals will be induced to save more. If lower, then they will save less. Providing there are no external benefits conferred on other entrepreneurs by someone's investments, the marginal compensation required to induce saving will be equal to capital's marginal productivity or ability to pay that compensation. This level of saving and investment is optimal.

Criterion No. 4—*Optimal Balance between the Forms of Investment*

The marginal return on investment in research, invention, and innovation; in human capital; and finally on physical capital must all be equal. If the yield differs between any of these areas, funds and then resources will flow from the low yield investment to the higher yield investment. The common yield will then be equal to the marginal rate of substitution between present and future consumption of income earners, as mentioned above. The rate of growth that results from this rate of saving and the equating of marginal yields on the various forms of investment must be considered optimum and efficient.

We conclude that due to the peculiar nature of the production and transfer of knowledge, even a perfectly competitive economy will be dynamically inefficient. Less than the optimal amount of investment in the production of new knowledge will take place.

Equity

Let us now look at the way in which output is distributed in a competitive market economy. One thing we can be fairly certain about is that output will not be equally divided among all the members of the economy. Those individuals who own large quantities of human and nonhuman resources will earn higher incomes than those less fortunately endowed. The quantity of resources one possesses, however, is not the sole determinant of one's income. These resources must also be scarce relative to the demand for them. Thus, one's income is influenced by the changing tastes of consumers and the discovery of new methods of production. The production of one item may become profitable, increasing the demand for the necessary resources and the income of the resource owners. The demand for other items may become less profitable, reducing the demand for the necessary resources and the income of the resource owners.

Equality of incomes, however, is not the only possible interpretation of the concept of equity. One may say that income is equitably distributed if individuals are receiving income in proportion to their contribution to the economy. This form of equity does exist in a perfectly competitive market economy. Each individual in the economy is earning in accord with the value of his contribution because each resource is paid the value of its marginal product. The forces of competition will ensure that each receives income in proportion to his contribution—no more and no less. The incomes of resources-owners may be volatile, however, as the value of their marginal product changes with shifts in consumer demands and the discovery of new technology and substitute resources.

The greater the mobility of resources and the easier the access to training and education, the more even will be the distribution of income in a market economy. If people and resources can flow quickly from low paying opportunities to high paying opportunities as tastes and technology change, larger income differentials will be reduced. The individual with few resources and little or no access to education has little prospect of sharing significantly in the output of the economy. Those unable to participate in the market process through illness, age, etc., will have to depend upon the private charity of others for their share.

There is a great incentive for those individuals with marketable resources to route these resources to high profit industries. The determination of rewards stimulates the efficient use of resources available. If some members of the economy, however, are so poor that they cannot invest in their own education and training, the distribution of rewards in the present may prevent the development of additional resources in the future.

THE CAPITALIST MARKET ECONOMY

The capitalist market economy is an imperfect copy of the competitive model. In all capitalist systems there are significant deviations from the assumptions of perfect competition. We will now discuss the nature of these deviations and their possible impact upon economic performance.

Static Efficiency Problems

Monopoly Power

One of the conditions of a perfectly competitive economy is small firm size relative to the size of the total market. Each firm must be so small that its actions as a producer and resource user do not affect price. Casual observation as well as more serious empirical investigation suggests that this is not the case for many industries operating in market economies today.[2] Firms which provide a

[2]See Richard Caves, *American Industry: Structure, Conduct, Performance,* 2nd ed. (Englewood Cliffs, N.J.: Prentice Hall, Inc., 1967).

significant share of the total market for their product have a degree of monopoly power. They are able to influence price by their actions. They maximize profits by producing to the point at which marginal cost equals marginal revenue, but marginal revenue does not equal price. The existence of monopoly power in a product market thus results in a divergence between product price, on the one hand, and marginal revenue and marginal cost on the other. The monopolist will restrict output and raise price above marginal cost.

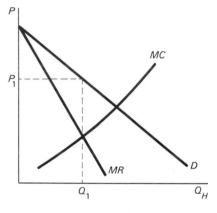

Diagram 4.2

Consider a firm whose market possibilities are represented by the demand and marginal revenue curves in diagram 4.2. The firm will produce Q_1 and market it at a price equal to P_1. This behavior violates the static efficiency conditions outlined in chapter two. Consider Condition 5, which requires that the $MRT_{x,y}$ in production equal the $MRS_{x,y}$ in consumption. Firms with monopoly power produce to the point at which the marginal cost of each good is equal to its marginal revenue. Since marginal revenue is not equal to price, we cannot conclude that the rate at which the firm can transform one good into another is equal to the rate at which the consumer desires to substitute one good for another. There will be a tendency for the output of products produced under monopoly conditions to lie below the level required for efficiency. The opposite is true for output produced under competitive conditions. An increase in welfare is possible by expanding the output of some products and contracting the output of others. The underproduction of the monopolist can be explained by comparing the value to the consumer of the last unit of a good x represented by its price (P) to the cost of producing the last unit of x, represented by its marginal cost. In diagram 4.2 it can be seen that the price of x is well above the MC. Consumers are willing to pay the cost of expanding the output of x, but given the monopoly power of the producer, no expansion will occur.

Monopoly power, therefore, results in a misallocation of resources and a loss in welfare. A possible solution to this problem is the elimination of monopoly power by antitrust actions. Perhaps competition can be restored by breaking up large, multi-plant concerns into small, independent firms. The use of antitrust to achieve competition will be feasible for those industries which have gained monopoly power by collusion, advertising, or special government treatment in the past. If there are natural monopolies due to substantial economies of scale, however, it will be impossible for many small firms to operate efficiently. If a single plant can supply one-third of a market before cost per unit begins to rise, the only alternative to monopoly will be high cost, inefficient firms. The dilemma facing capitalist economies in this case is the achievement of low cost, efficient methods of production without the exercise of monopoly power. Two possible solutions to this dilemma which we shall examine in the next chapter are government regulation of private monopoly and nationalization.

Externalities

Up to this point we have been assuming that all costs of production are borne by the firm and are represented by the cost of the resource inputs. We have also been assuming that the total benefits resulting from consumption are captured by the individual purchaser. Thus, when each firm produces to the point at which price is equal to marginal cost, the value to society of the last unit of a particular commodity is just equal to the cost society is willing to pay. Suppose, however, that there are costs of production which society must bear that the firm does not have to pay. Then the cost of production to the firm is less than the cost to society. The firm will expand output to the point at which marginal *private* cost equals price. At this point marginal *social* cost will be above price, and output will have expanded to a level beyond that required for efficiency. These costs to society which the firm does not bear are called external diseconomies. Examples abound. They include air pollution, water pollution, noise pollution. All of these are examples of costs of production which society must bear which do not enter into the profit calculations of the firm. Failure to consider these costs results in overproduction and a waste of scarce resources. The purely competitive market economy has no mechanisms that enable it to make these costs explicit. Society certainly pays the total cost of production. These costs are not specifically charged to any individual firm and are not accurately weighed against the benefits derived from production.

Inefficiency in the allocation of resources will also occur in a competitive economy when the private gain derived from consumption is not equal to the total social gain. We mentioned earlier that there will tend to be underinvestment in the production of new knowledge because the social gains exceed the private gains. Many believe that the benefits resulting from such goods as education and medical care accrue to society as a whole as well as to the individual consumer. It is claimed that the marginal social benefit of these goods exceeds the marginal private benefit. The production of these goods involves external economies. Left to themselves, people will consume too few of these goods. Gains in welfare are possible by a reallocation of resources towards the production of these goods. There are no mechanisms in a competitive economy, however, that will cause this reallocation to take place. Thus, we can conclude that in a perfectly competitive market economy there will be overproduction of goods with external diseconomies and underproduction of goods involving external economies.

Collective Consumption

The market system will only engage in the production of goods which can be marketed in definable units where the benefits of consumption can be limited to the purchaser. There are many commodities, however, where the benefits cannot be so limited. A classic example of a collective good is national defense. Once a defense system is established it is impossible to exclude a resident from protection. If he cannot be excluded from its benefits, it will be impossible to provide this good through the market. Other goods which have some collective aspects include police and fire protection, immunization programs and city parks. Non-market mechanisms must be used in the production and allocation of such goods.

Consumer Ignorance

One of the persistent criticisms of capitalism is the assumption of consumer knowledge and rational behavior. Does the consumer possess a reasonable amount of knowledge about the alternative products available in the market place and the alternative job opportunities? Does he use this knowledge to make rational decisions concerning the allocation of his income and the choice of his occupation? Or does he make decisions primarily on the basis of a momentary whim or on the pressure of a major advertising campaign? These questions raise serious doubts about the motivation of the consumer and the source of consumer wants. Critics of capitalism argue that many wants do not originate with the consumer himself but are manufactured by the producer through massive advertising. It is difficult to deal with these arguments because of the subjective nature of the issues involved. Who is to decide which consumer wants are legitimate and which are not?

It is possible to improve the decision-making power of the individual without questioning his right to make decisions by providing him with better information on the properties of commodities and on employment opportunities. Consumer education combined with the enforcement of minimum quality and safety standards can protect the consumer from major errors in judgment.

Further Problems

The market system may have difficulty in coping with major resource reallocations resulting from significant changes in national priorities. Governments of capitalist economies have felt it necessary to partially supplant the market with some degree of planning during wartime. War involves a reallocation of resources from consumer goods to producer goods and war-related materials. The government can bid up the price of these products in the market and wait for resources to flow into the new, high profit industries. This is not usually felt to be desirable because of the delays that may be involved and because of the high profits which would be earned for those firms lucky enough to be in the right place at the right time. It is argued that government must step in at such time because the market system is designed to accommodate and coordinate small or marginal changes in the allocation of resources.

Economic analysts of the market system have been criticized for undue concern with the benefits of marginal adjustments at the expense of attention to the merits and failures of the system as a whole. Radical critics argue that economists should turn their attention toward the benefits which may be gained from a major overhaul of present economic institutions. Piecemeal and uncoordinated reforms of an inferior economic system may not prevent the accumulation of social and economic ills.

This is a valid criticism of economists in any economic environment— planned or market oriented—and should not be leveled exclusively at economists in capitalist countries. Certainly it is always easier to conceive of and implement minor improvements in allocation efficiency than to destroy the foundations of the system and build anew. Radical critics of capitalist economies too often fall into the trap of recommending such a momentous task on the basis of incomplete information. They tend to compare the present system, with all of its faults, to some imagined, ideal system and to calculate the benefits of the transformation to the ideal society while ignoring the costs.

The Persistence of Unemployment

The maintenance of full employment in a competitive economy depends upon the flexibility of prices and wages and on a rapid adjustment process which will restore full employment whenever changes in demand and supply conditions result in reduced employment. Suppose there is a decrease in the demand for commodities and an increase in the demand for money. Consumers will reduce their purchases of commodities in an attempt to add to their holding of cash balances. Firms will find their inventories piling up. Prices and wages must fall to restore employment. If they do not respond rapidly, the firm will find it necessary to cut back on its orders for new stock, production will fall, and workers will be laid off. The readjustment process may be long and painful. Real resources, manpower and capital, are being wasted. Recurring periods of unemployment have been a common phenomenon in capitalist countries. We will see in the next section that the governments of capitalist economies have found it necessary and desirable to intervene in the economy to maintain full employment.

International Disequilibrium

The international exchange of goods, services, and factors of production was seen in the previous section to lead to a satisfaction of the static efficiency conditions between, as well as within, capitalist market economies. However, for a variety of reasons, some of them only marginally valid, a nation's government may choose to restrict the flow of goods, services, and resources. Sometimes a government may wish to reduce the output of a good in which it has an export monopoly; it may defend a powerful established industry or protect an "infant" industry; it may wish to induce a capital inflow or prevent a capital outflow.

As a rule, benefits acquired by a nation or groups within a nation through the use of restrictions on free trade must be at the expense of foreigners or other groups in the restricting country. The inevitable retaliation from stung trading partners does not lead to a restoration of the initial optimum but to a further departure from it. With each new round of restrictions and trade barriers, welfare is shifted back and forth with substantial net loss to all parties.

The gold standard "rules of the game," (i.e., increase or decrease of the money supply, hence rise or fall of the price level as a result of surplus or deficit in the balance of payments) may be violated in pursuit of narrow national economic policy goals. Given a disequilibrium situation in the balance of payments, each country, whether in surplus or deficit, may attempt to place the burden of adjustment on the other party. This can only result in a major and disrupting devaluation of the deficit country's currency. To the extent that the surplus country blithely ignores its obligation to adjust, the burden of adjustment is totally thrust on the deficit country, redoubling its difficulties.

We may conclude that one unfortunate consequence of the pursuit of "national" economic policies in an international setting is that the system as a whole may tremble on the brink of chaos occasionally and be in difficulty somewhere virtually all of the time.

Dynamic Efficiency Problems

Criterion No. 1—*Research, Invention, and Innovation*

In the previous section we noted that the model of perfectly competitive capitalism was seriously flawed with respect to our criteria of dynamic efficiency, specifically the probability of under-investment in research, invention, and innovation. Attention will now be turned to the evaluation of further growth problems encountered by a capitalist market economy.

Investment in Research, Invention, and Innovation

In the model of competitive capitalism, an assumption of perfect information would ensure that the particulars of any new knowledge, invention, or innovation would be freely transmitted to the entire society. Individuals or firms engaged in these activities could never capture enough of the total gains from their efforts to make it worth the personal costs and risks. Therefore, investment in research and invention would never be pushed to the point at which marginal social benefits would become equal to marginal social costs. In the real world, competitive capitalism and even some primitive systems have come to grips with this thorny practical problem. Among the devices which have been adopted to reward creative activity more in proportion to the benefits derived by society are:

1. Special awards, rewards, or bounties for creative and inventive acts.
2. Legal monopolies such as patents or copyrights on creative, inventive, or innovative acts.
3. Informal monopolies through secrecy or collusion.

One problem with inventive bounties or other *ad hoc* rewards is that they are awarded after the fact and may or may not be in proportion to marginal social benefits derived or the risks and sacrifices that were borne through the creative period. Another problem is how to properly evaluate a piece of research or invention when its true value may be realized only in conjunction with some other and later research or invention. A reward to the original researcher may be very late in arriving with no guarantee that it will arrive at all. In general then, we must conclude that a bounty-reward system for creative activity may be clumsy, arbitrary, unfair, and probably unworkable.

Patents and copyrights, by restricting the use of ideas or processes, enable an originator to capture some of the benefits which otherwise would be scattered freely throughout the system. To the extent that such creative rewards become marginal "costs" of production and the price of the product thereby rises, consumption and total benefits will be reduced. It is most difficult to distinguish between and weigh the costs and benefits of a patent system. On the one hand, the rewards of patent control promote research and inventive efforts; on the other hand, monopoly power, once granted legal cover, may be hard to limit or control.

The definition of a patentable creative act, processing of claims, and the awarding of monopoly rights, together with the problem of adjudicating rival or parallel claims, has proven to be cumbersome, frequently unfair and arbitrary, and all too often a tactic to throttle competition. A large firm may spin a web of patents around an area of research and pounce with massive and expensive legal maneuvers on any competitor who should buzz into the same area. This can only serve to discourage investment in original research and invention and promote "sewing-up" the frontiers of knowledge rather than exploiting them.

Secrecy and/or collusion among producers may serve to protect special advantages obtained through research, invention, or innovation. Again, the enhanced rewards encourage more intense creative efforts but at the expense of monopoly restrictions on output and consumption. In addition, considerable efforts must be made to guarantee the security of secret knowledge. To counter this secrecy, large investments may be made in an industrial espionage system to breach the walls of commercial secrecy. Investments in security and espionage tend to counter and cancel each other, thus constituting a drain on society's resources. It is a moot point whether or not benefits of secrecy-induced creative efforts are even positive.

In implicit recognition of the flaws of the several devices we have discussed, society (government) has intervened to promote investment in research and invention by an imposing and imaginative array of direct and indirect subsidies to industrial research. In the next chapter we will discuss the specific methods contemporary market economies have developed to promote research, invention, and innovation.

Criterion No. 2—*Investment in Human Capital*

If individuals Smith and Jones benefit in some way from individual Brown's investment in education without having to pay for it, then there clearly exists a situation in which Smith and Jones should be almost as interested in Brown's decision to "buy" education as Brown is. Furthermore, if Brown and Smith benefit from Jones' education without paying for it, and if Brown and Jones benefit from Smith's education without paying for it, then something must be done to make everybody pay a little more to support everyone else. The effect is to raise the total amount of investment in education all around. One practical way to do this is to retain the private school system and subsidize the tuition to lower the cost and encourage the purchase of education by the student. Another method is to have society (government) provide the service out of tax revenues and give it free or at low cost to whomever wants it. The latter is most frequently done, although both have their proponents and opponents.

Criterion No.3—*Physical Capital*

There are several sources of potential deviation from the optimal level of physical investment. Three are listed below.

1. Investments may have external effects.
2. Uncertainty and risks may affect investors' perceptions.
3. Inadequate savings may result from savers' short-sightedness.

The possibility that there may be external effects, either good or bad, from certain investments is already familiar to us from previous discussions. Pollution from public or private projects, spillover benefits from education, flood control and recreation from public or private dams, etc., all contribute to over- or under-investment in certain activities. Intelligent and vigilant social action or investment may prevent the worst abuses. Whether an *optimum* point will or can be reached is problematical.

Uncertainty as to future economic prospects may lead to substantial under-investment unless individuals are enabled to spread their risks. Large, lumpy, and risky investments may offer an individual a choice between disaster and high profits. Such a "lady or the tiger" prospect can deter all but the hardiest of plungers. In point of fact, contemporary capitalism offers a multitude of devices whereby an investor may place his eggs in many baskets—from stocks to bonds to banks and insurance companies (which spread his dollars around in thousands of projects). To a large extent then, an investor today may shop around and select precisely the proportions of riskiness and yield that suit his taste. Only deceit, fraud, unusually bad information, or stupidity can cause an investor to be "surprised" by the result of his investments.

Equity Problems

It has been pointed out that the perfectly competitive economy guarantees an "equitable" division of output in the sense that each resource is paid in accordance with its contribution. This equality between contribution and reward may be destroyed by the monopoly power of the resource buyer or the resource supplier. If the firm hiring resources is a major purchaser, the quantity of the resource it chooses to hire will affect its price. The marginal cost of hiring one extra unit of the factor will be above its price. The firm will hire to the point that marginal factor price is equal to the value of the marginal product. Resources will be paid less than the value of their contribution to output.

Strong employee organizations such as unions or the American Medical Association may have a degree of monopoly power over the supply of their resources. They may succeed in bidding up the wage of their members but only at the expense of increased unemployment. "Successful" unions are successful because they are able to restrict supply. Above-equilibrium wages are obtained for working members while potential entrants into the field are forced into other less well-organized occupations, usually causing wage declines in these areas. Strong employee organizations redistribute income from unorganized employees to organized employees.

As we mentioned earlier the distribution of income in a competitive economy may be quite volatile due to sudden shifts in demand or new technological innovations. Many feel that the rewards and penalties resulting from such changes are "unfair." War profiteers are examples of lucky individuals who own scarce resources which are critically needed. Many feel it is only just to relieve them of the extraordinary profits they chanced to be in a position to earn.

Finally, let us briefly consider the effect which the distribution scheme of a competitive economy has upon the motivations of its members. According to Robert Solo, the individual qualities which result in the accumulation of wealth may have undesirable social consequences. "Skill in fraud, deceit, bluff, and legal maneuver also yield the gains of power and leadership."[3] Furthermore, once wealth and power have been achieved, they become allies in the struggle to achieve greater wealth. Those in possession of economic power may be successful in gaining the political power to alter the rules of the game to their advantage. The oil depletion allowance is a good case in point. Once economic institutions have been readjusted in a way which favors the wealthy and discriminates against the poor, the motivation of the poor to succeed by working within the system may be destroyed. A growing feeling of frustration and despair may result in substantial economic losses as well as in serious social instability.

In no sense have we completed an evaluation of the capitalist market system with this chapter. Rather we have pointed out at both a theoretical and a practical level where we may well expect a capitalist economy to have major problems. Whether or not a specific capitalist national economy will violate this or that performance criteria and to what extent depends on the complex interaction of social, cultural, and economic factors relatively unique to each country.

---

[3] Robert Solo, *Economic Organizations and Social Systems* (Indianapolis, Ind.: Bobbs-Merrill Company, Inc., 1967), p. 38.

QUESTIONS

1. How does the behavior of consumers and producers ensure the achievement of static efficiency in the competitive market model?
2. It is sometimes said that a market system is extremely efficient at transmitting information, yet there are no formal institutions designed for this purpose. How is information communicated accurately and cheaply?
3. Why will there tend to be insufficient amounts of research, invention, and innovation in a market system?
4. Is income "equitably" distributed in a competitive market system?
5. What do you consider to be the most serious problems preventing real world market economies from achieving static efficiency?
6. What policies can be implemented in market economies to increase dynamic efficiency?
7. Discuss the ways in which an unequal distribution of income can perpetuate itself in a market system.

5

A Search
for New Solutions

The Evolution of the Market Economy

Introduction

World War II may be considered to be the great divide in the evolution of the role of government in contemporary market economies. Certainly there had been extensive governmental intervention and activity prior to this great conflict, particularly in Europe but also in the United States in the form of the New Deal of the Roosevelt era. However, in retrospect the depth of intervention and variety of controls developed during the war and the immediate postwar years makes the interwar years seem comparatively an age of innocence.

The marshalling of energies and absorption of national resources achieved through the agency of the government during World War II were unprecedented in the history of mankind. During the period of the war, the extraordinary intensity of governmental activity was justified, rightly or wrongly, as an attempt to save civilization from barbarism. On the other hand, victory of the Allied nations over the Axis powers did not produce a substantial reduction of governmental activity. Governments did not relax their efforts nor substantially restrict the range of their activities; in some cases government extended its functions into entirely new areas of activity such as "common markets" and other international or regional multi-national agencies. In the main, the focus of governments' attention shifted from the necessity of national self-preservation to that of national economic reconstruction.

After World War II, most economies of Western Europe were distorted by years of under-investment and under-maintenance of capital equipment and plant, direct physical allocation of strategic raw materials, rationing of consumer goods at prices unrelated to supply and demand, and rigidly controlled international trade. The United States had made large war loans to its allies, who were in no condition to repay either principal or interest. There was a great proliferation of new nations and prospects of more as the overseas empires of most European nations were liquidated. The problems were not irreconcilable, fortunately. The United States possessed great productive capacity untouched by war; Europe had great potential once its skilled labor force had equipment and materials to work with, and the less developed nations had resources and raw materials requiring only markets for their disposition. What was needed was for some agency to bring all these elements—the equipment of the United States and the resources of the less developed world—to Europe, where the goods to repay these nations would be fabricated. The United States made huge loans of equipment and resources to Europe, and recovery proceeded.

Nations could choose among several routes to recovery, depending on their unique political or economic situation and history. One route was for the government to make all the international contacts necessary to obtain the loans and resources from the United States or international agencies. However, the resources once received would be allocated internally according to the market mechanism. The government would not determine priority allocation of resources except perhaps in cases of health or hazardous situations. The short-run gyrations in prices as the distorted price structure was freed might have been quite large, but given stable monetary conditions and confidence in the political authorities, there was no reason to expect destructive tendencies to explode. Of course, stable monetary and/or political conditions might just be the rarest commodity of all in a country recovering from a war.

A second course of action might have followed from conditions that were less than ideal or from different circumstances. A nation might have decided to retain both macro and microeconomic controls over the economy. The extent of the distortion of the economy could have been great and the authorities might have felt that the loosening of the controls would cause large and inequitable burdens to be placed on certain groups or institutions. In this case the government would continue to allocate resources on a "priorities" basis until supply and demand conditions returned to something thought to be "normal." Then the government would bow out of its monitoring business and return to more customary "social" business. In other words, massive government controls and interventions in the economy are viewed in this instance as responses to extraordinary conditions and are to be liquidated upon a return to normalcy.

A third possibility, depending on particular circumstances, was for the government to find itself entangled in the economy in many ways. It had fulfilled so many vital functions for so many people with no feasible private alternatives that the government might have in effect been transformed into an altogether different economic factor or agent, retaining however the broad "capitalist" basis of the economy. Many postwar European governments found themselves not only managing their economies at both the macro and microeconomic levels, but also owning a variety of firms and occasionally possessing a commanding position in particular industries. After the war Britain nationalized a number of critical (and ailing) industries including the Bank of England, steel, coal, and most forms of transportation. As a result of nationalization both before and after the war France had obtained a substantial interest in the financial sector, communications, and automobiles through confiscation and nationalization. Germany was heir to Volkswagen and maintained state control over communications and rail transportation. The Italian government had inherited a vast and diversified economic empire from the previous regime and had developed a variety of management innovations including autonomous state corporations and holding companies.

Despite this substantial increase in social ownership of industry and finance, the enlargement of social welfare programs, and the vigorous use of government policies to promote a fuller utilization of resources, there was no doubt that democratic Europe intended to remain predominantly capitalist and that the market system was to be strengthened and adapted to the new social environment rather than scrapped.

EFFORTS TO IMPROVE THE FUNCTIONING OF MARKETS

As has been mentioned, governments of capitalist, private enterprise economies may choose among a variety of institutions and economic agents to exercise control over the direction of the national economy. The government may intervene to a greater or lesser degree, depending on national tastes or needs, without threatening in any major way the capitalist basis of the economy. One low cost, high yielding, and unthreatening activity of government is providing economic information.

Government and Economic Information

Historians assert that one of the most important functions of the ancient Egyptian state was to predict the coming of the annual flood of the Nile so that all the necessary preliminary work could be done and all would be in readiness. Economies have become incredibly more complex in the intervening centuries hence the importance of information about natural and man-made events has become proportionally greater.

The immediate concern of participants in the exchange process is information about current price, quality, and market conditions. The greatest part of this information has traditionally been received from other face-to-face participants to an exchange—other buyers, other sellers, their agents and salesmen, and trade associations, where such exist. Each economic agent also wishes to intelligently project present trends into the future and to modify long-run behavior in the light of these educated guesses. As the economy grows more complex, the need to project farther and farther into the future becomes more acute. However, projections into the future must take into account the effects of ever-larger circles of decision-makers who are also seeking information about the future. The process could break down in a morass of mutual indecision because no individual person or corporation, however large, could possibly afford to seek out and query all of the other individuals who will make decisions and thus affect everyone else. Therefore, in recent years customary face-to-face exchanges of information have been supplemented by a great variety of governmental information generated and supplied by agencies and commissions, planning bodies at all levels of government, international and national agencies of the United Nations, World Bank, or International Monetary Fund, and regional associations like the Common Market of Europe.

These public bodies query individuals and businesses and ask them what they are doing and what they intend doing in the immediate future. This information is then processed, analyzed, and disseminated free to all. Each individual may then observe his little place in the big picture. There are many problems at this point, such as what the individual does when he discovers that his place in the big picture is not what he thought it was when he filled out the questionnaire. We will discuss these problems later in the section on planning.

There can be a serious drawback to this vast expansion of information accumulation. Few people are really experts on statistics. This makes it possible for individuals or groups competing for your dollar, your vote, or just your attention to selectively define and pick and choose among the data, to distort it through "corrections and adjustments," or simply make things up when the occasion suits. These abuses can have a numbing effect. Faced with confusing and contradictory "facts," users could fall back on the old "rule of thumb" techniques of the past, and the money spent on information research would all be wasted. Fortunately we have not reached this point yet. Every day thousands of individuals and businesses utilize information supplied by the government. Among the uses are:

1. Business enterprises forecast sales, productivity, and resource costs.
2. Farmers forecast weather, fertility, and the need for fertilizers, likelihood of insects, and yields of various crops.
3. Government itself forecasts expenditures and demand for services, tax yields, and balance of payments.
4. Individuals try to forecast their incomes, chances for employment, price changes, career opportunities, draft odds, weather for picnics, etc.

The existence of more and better information supplied by government is probably a key element in the postwar acceleration of the pace of economic development in modern capitalist economies of Europe, the Americas, and Asia.

Government and Competitive Policies

Monopoly, oligopoly, or limited competition of one sort or another may arise from illegal conspiracy, legal cooperation, or the inherent nature of the market. Governments may respond in a great variety of ways to such limitations on free competition. Where conspiracy to limit competition exists and competition is a viable alternative, the damaged parties may seek legal recourse and demand compensation. For this policy to be effective in the long run, there must be a consensus among the economic actors of society that true competition is a desirable goal. Otherwise the legal process will be an on again-off again operation and therefore unfair and damaging to both business and consumer interests.

Certain non-competitive business practices may be legally tolerated, such as research done by industry-wide laboratories, or trade association "informational" surveys on costs, prices, and market shares, or cooperation in export ventures. Implicitly the nation has judged the benefits to exceed the costs of such actual or potential limitations on free competition. Such judgments, when the facts are known and properly analyzed and weighed, are a legitimate function of government. An unfortunate fact of the real world is that "cooperation" permitted in a limited context can rarely be prevented from spilling into other areas. Perhaps Adam Smith phrased it as well as it will ever be done when he alleged that, "People of the same trade seldom meet together, even for merriment and diversion, but the conversation ends in a conspiracy against the public or in some contrivance to raise prices."[1]

Finally, limited competition may arise from the nature of the product market. An optimal economic capacity may be such a large fraction of the entire market that splitting the market among competing firms can only raise costs and prices to the consumer. Regulation of the optimum number of firms or actual social ownership of the firms are alternative governmental policies. Both have advantages and disadvantages, so the choice may largely be one of taste, politics, expediency, or national experience.

Competitive Policy in the United States

The postwar record shows mixed competitive trends in the United States. Conspiracies to restrict trade have met some monumental legal defeats in the courts. However, many agreements to restrict competition have been left

---

[1] Adam Smith, *The Wealth of Nations* (New York: The Modern Library, 1937), p.128.

untouched. Nevertheless, cooperation in export marketing is under fire and "Fair Trade" laws have been defeated or ignored in many states. Competition between marketing and producing giants like Safeway, A. & P., Sears, and Montgomery Ward have threatened or cajoled discounts from the industrial giants. Conglomeration, or the bundling together of unrelated or loosely related firms, is itself a mixed trend. The threat of one industrial giant to enter the domain of another industrial giant through purchase or entry may be as effective in fostering competitive results as if competition existed. On the other hand, the market power of a giant combine covering many fields may accumulate so many advantages as to stifle competition even though its apparent market position may not appear too threatening in any single area. In any event, if defensive ability is any measure of of market power, the recession of 1970-71, during which many glamorous conglomerates of the 1960s came unglued, indicates that the conglomerate phenomenon may be here to stay but that they may not be the long-run threat some people believed.

European Competitive Policy

In postwar Europe, the tolerance of great cartels, traditional European industrial institutions, was looked on with some disfavor. This was largely political, stemming from the history in Germany, Italy, and France of cartel support of right-wing political causes. In many cases large industrial combines were broken up or nationalized. In some cases, they were allowed to partially re-form, but through the 1950s, most countries accumulated anti-monopoly legislation and regulations in what was becoming a new-found consensus that the market worked and the freer the market, the better it worked. Policy-makers discovered that national goals and projects could still be undertaken and at less cost, if the market could be permitted to allocate resources once the decisions had been made.

The competitive implications of the creation of the Common Market had also been thought through to their logical conclusions. National cartels supported by the state would not be tolerated in an enlarged economic community. National monopolies could not function when the productive potential of six or seven industrial nations were meshed together. As an example of this, Krupp steel works has a solid third of the West German steel capacity, but is only a tenth of the European Iron and Steel Community, a far smaller share of the market than U.S. Steel has in the American market. Thus it is possible that the free flow of goods and services between nations may be the most effective means of fostering the development of a free competitive market system in the domestic economy as well.

Government and Stabilization Policies

Any discussion of the stabilization functions of governments of modern capitalist economies ought logically to be preceded by a survey of the need for stability, or more accurately, the costs of instability.

First let us define our terms. By stability or instability we are referring to movements of macroeconomic variables such as gross national product, personal incomes, consumption, investment, prices, or interest rates. For example, if price, income, or interest rate changes are zero or low and in one direction they may be termed "stable," whereas if prices, incomes, or interest rates fluctuate up and down they may be termed stable or unstable depending on the magnitude of the swings. The definition need not be symmetrical or consistent and may depend on the point of view of the beholder. A steady 3 percent rise in income may be called stability while a 3 percent steady decline in income would be termed instability by many. A 5 percent rate of inflation is called instability in a country like the United States, which enjoyed negligible inflation for a number of years. On the other hand, several Latin American countries would look at 5 percent inflation as relative stability in contrast with their experience of rates in excess of 50 percent per year.

Now what are the costs of instability of macroeconomic activity? There are two kinds of costs—short-run or immediate costs and longer-run costs. The short-run costs of instability are experienced immediately and are not at all subtle—unemployment, inflation, bankrupt businesses, careers ruined or foreshortened, high welfare costs, foreclosures, and other disruptive events. Longer-run costs are more subtle but no less devastating in their cumulative effects.

In market economies the long-run trends of income and productivity depend on decisions made by a myriad of individuals determining the proper amount of investment in education or human capital and also business investment in plant, equipment, and research and development. No one orders these individuals to do anything; they get their signals from the environment and behave correspondingly. No amount of optimistic projections from official or unofficial sources will affect private decisions if these rosy predictions are consistently at variance with the reality that touches decision-makers. The subtle long-run effects of untamed economic cycles of boom and bust appear when decision-makers, in self-defense, add an extra allowance for risk in all their investment calculations. Businesses will not invest unless the yield is high enough to cover the usual costs, risks, and profits plus the extra risk of unpredictable market recessions. Individuals will not take on additional training and education if they are just exposing themselves to greater potential income loss. The aggregate effect of these decisions is to lower the rate of accumulation of physical capital, plant and equipment, and human capital, education and training.

The battery of weapons to counter economic instability and its costs are varied and complex but may be placed in four broad categories. The government may:

1. Manipulate the level of its expenditures to stimulate or suppress the level of output and incomes directly.
2. Raise or lower taxes to put income into or take it out of consumers' or investors' pockets.
3. Increase or decrease the money supply to decrease or increase interest rates and affect investors' or consumers' behavior.
4. Impose controls over various sectors of the economy.

The necessity for the government to utilize these instruments of stabilization depends on several things—the extent of the instability and the effectiveness of the policies. In modern times, there is growing evidence that the policies developed to solve problems of substantial unemployment or runaway inflation may be ill-adapted to contemporary economic problems. Modern economies optimally are poised on the knife-edge of full-employment and mild inflation—a bit more employment means a bit more inflation, a lowered rate of inflation means a rise in the unemployment figures. Fiscal policies and monetary policy may be imprecise or take long and varying periods of time to take hold. If the instability is slight and occurs randomly, then governments may actually disturb matters when they intervene actively in the economy. It is possible to be too pessimistic on this score, but the American experience of the late sixties and early seventies is not comforting to economic advisors close to the throne.

Government and Income Policies

Most modern mixed capitalist economies have adopted some measures which may loosely be termed an "incomes policy." By this is meant the control in some fashion by the government, or even some combination of private interests in concert with the government, of the level or distribution of incomes in society.

Governments have always disturbed the levels of incomes with their taxes and altered the distribution of incomes with discriminatory tax structures and/or benefits distribution. However, now they must be much more sensitive to the effects of their actions. People are more aware of their relative positions and in democracies have an occasional opportunity to redress their grievances. Governments are asked to perform a greater variety of functions today; hence, they are much larger and more disturbing in overall influence than in the past. Most developed economies are very delicate and interrelated. A government that did not think out the implications of its actions could be like the proverbial bull in the china shop.

A public or cooperative incomes policy can do three things. First, it can attempt to suppress the total claims against the national output to prevent inflation. Second, it can alter the structure of the claims by selectively suppressing or elevating private consumption, private investment, or public activity. Third, it can alter the distribution of factor incomes, as between labor and capital or even within each of these sectors.

Let us first consider the problem of inflation. It is the view of many economists, particularly of the emerging monetarist school, that persistent inflation cannot be sustained in the long run unless expansionary fiscal and monetary policies are supporting it. It is the monetarist position that all continuing inflations are the result of increases in the rate of expansion of the money supply, creating an excess supply of money and consequently an excess demand for commodities. So-called "cost-push" inflation can be interpreted not as a cause of inflation but as a result of past inflation, as workers attempt to restore the real wages lost during the previous round of inflation and begin to anticipate future inflation in their wage demands. A governmental incomes policy which denies wage increases on the one hand to suppress inflation and on the other pursues expansionary monetary and fiscal policies is irrational. A private voluntary wage slowdown will inevitably break down under the pressure of excess demand for labor as employers bid against each other. Some union somewhere will not be able to resist the temptation to break the wage front and then all will. In either case the government is basically at fault; it can slow the inflation any time it is willing to pay the short-run price of unemployment and closed factories. Broad governmentally imposed wage freezes are no substitute for restrictive monetary and fiscal policies but may supplement them for short periods during the transition from a high rate of inflation to a lower one.

Monopoly firms and unions may have the power to bid up prices and wages in the face of stable or declining demand at least in the short run, but their power would have to be continuously increasing to be responsible for long-run inflationary trends. It is argued that an incomes policy that suppresses the overall level of wages or prices could serve as a surrogate for truly competitive markets. Arthur F. Burns has stated that an incomes policy might be appropriate for the United States, which has experienced in recent years all the ills of inflation and recession simultaneously. President Nixon adopted a type of incomes policy in the fall of 1971 with a price freeze and the establishment of the Pay Board and Price Commission. It has been the task of these agencies to moderate the wage demands of labor and the price increases of business to reduce the overall rate of inflation. However, in any dynamic economy, the wages of some groups will rise and fall against the average as a result of natural economic forces. It would be an exceedingly difficult chore for the government to sort all the facts and permit one group to advance against another and assure perfect fairness and equity. It would be even more difficult for private interests to meet together and decide on measures to prevent monopoly abuses of power.

A bureaucracy much larger than the membership of the Pay Board and Price Commission would be necessary to determine which price increases were appropriate and which were not. Incorrect price and wage policies or those not supplemented by the appropriate monetary and fiscal policies will lead to "quasi-legal" methods of price adjustments such as quality deterioration and the expansion of non-monetary fringe benefits.

Another possible use of an incomes policy would be to alter the structure of claims against the national product. Potential claimants for the goods and services produced by the economy are: (1) consumers, (2) business investments and inventories, (3) public consumption (defense, government services), (4) public investments (roads, buildings, dams, schools, equipment, etc.), (5) exports (to pay for imports). It is difficult for government to calculate the priorities to be associated with each of the claimants. People always want to consume more, but if they want to expand their consumption, they must save and invest in new capital. It is a big step for government to say that people *ought to* save or invest more and consume less, and then do something about it. This action implies that somehow government knows better than the people themselves what their best interests are. You can go down that road a long way. Public consumption and public investment are easier decisions. There are definite political channels through which the public can express a desire for these goods and services; taxes constitute the price they pay. Democratic solutions are perhaps not always optimal, but no one has suggested an alternative that isn't a variation of "Daddy knows best." To return to the question, an incomes policy that discourages consumption and encourages private investment in plant and equipment has been very popular in Europe as a way of improving the productivity of industry and exports particularly, thus raising the growth rate overall. The government may be absolutely right that more investment is just what the doctor ordered for lagging economies. However, one has to ask the disturbing question, "Why did profit maximizing capitalists require governmental prodding to make investments that proved to be very profitable?" If it was so obvious to government planners, why wasn't it even more obvious to the parties directly involved? The only explanation is that the government may possess knowledge not available to the individual firm.

A third purpose of an incomes policy could be to redistribute income from labor to capital, from capital to labor, or from both to government. Also, a natural drift of income from one sector to another could be permitted to occur through inaction. Why would the government want to shift income from one group to another or to permit a shift to occur? One reason might be the political persuasion of the political forces in control of the government. One party might feel itself to be labor-oriented and therefore might place a high priority on an "equitable" distribution of income, which would translate to a policy of shifting income from capital to labor. Another political party might feel that the long-run interests of labor are best served by a high rate of investment and the growth this makes possible. Their policy could be to shift income from labor to capital. Higher growth of incomes would presumably compensate labor for their involuntary sacrifices in the short run.

It is possible to accomplish the shift of claims against output suggested above without directly attacking incomes. For example, the government could change the terms of installment purchases (larger down payment or a shorter payoff period) and make low interest loans to business. Another way to accomplish much the same shift of claims against output would be to actually shift the incomes of the respective economic agents by altering the tax and transfer structure of the economy.

The principal instruments of an incomes policy are: (1) the government's power to set tax rates and the structure of taxes; (2) the government's power as a direct purchaser of labor, goods, and services; (3) the government's power as a source of capital, credit, and determiner of interest rates, (4) the government's persuasive power, i.e., the credibility of its threat to take direct action if private forces do not cooperate; (5) the government's provision of negotiating machinery through which private bargains may be struck. This machinery may be neutral, or it may include the input of spokesmen for the "national interest." Outside this formal framework of governmental incomes policy instruments lies the possibility that a national bargain may be struck by large labor and business confederations, with the government adopting a hands-off policy. In the United States we have large national labor and business groups, but the bargaining is still done on an industry-wide basis. In Sweden, however, a national bargain is settled on a national basis, and it remains only for the details to be sorted out and rationalized afterwards, industry by industry. Such a national private incomes policy may be workable and is certainly preferable to a government fiat that nobody likes. However, it is critically important that the government maintain a balanced monetary and fiscal policy for reasons we have mentioned. Some monopoly of labor or capital will be tempted to exert its power and break the bargain if the government has permitted excess purchasing power to come into existence.

Government and the Mobility of Resources

The resources we are concerned with in this section are labor and capital, not raw materials or other goods and services. The movement of workers and factories is a sticky phenomenon which may not always occur in directions and magnitudes large enough to meet the demands of an evolving economy. If this is true, then it is possible that depressed regions can exist for extended periods of time within a prosperous overall economy. Examples of depressed regions abound. In the United States, the South was depressed for several generations after the Civil War and to this day has a lower average level of development and income. There are pockets within this region of abject poverty. Southern Italy has been depressed relative to the North since the state of Italy was formed in 1861. Most other countries have their pockets of relative backwardness.

The characteristics of such depressed regions are frequently very similar. Most have a higher proportion of agricultural production; unemployment rates are higher; existing industry pays low wages and utilizes smaller amounts of capital per worker; skills of workers are lower; and the population growth rate is usually higher than average. An economist might state that natural forces should bring things into balance. Labor should move from the low wage region to the high wage region, raising wages in the former and lowering them in the latter. Industry should move from the high wage area to the low wage area to secure higher profits. However, things don't always work out that way, not because the theory is bad but because there are other things to consider.

Labor may not move from the low wage area to the high wage area because they do not have the skills required to get jobs there. In other words, the higher wages may actually be a function of higher productivity of labor rather than a deficit of labor in the high wage area. Costs of migration may be high and also there may be cultural differences that prevent workers from leaving their familiar surroundings. It may be difficult to secure housing at various destinations. All in all, there may be a number of perfectly good reasons why labor does not move to other regions.

Capital also may not move to the depressed regions, no matter how low the wages may seem to be, for a number of very valid reasons. As we have seen, low wages can indicate low skills. What good does it do to pay half the wages if the productivity is one-third in the retarded region? Many other things are also lacking in these areas. Frequently the transportation system is not as good or slightly inconvenient. The tax system may be poor or discriminatory. Government services may be non-existent, poor, or surrounded by corruption and delays. The low incomes of the region may not make markets large enough to justify the investment.

For these and other reasons, labor and capital may not flow in amounts that the government thinks is necessary to produce a "balanced" economy. What can it do about it? First, it can attempt to make it easier for people to move out of the depressed areas. It can provide housing and help migrants to ease the expenses of finding jobs and permanent quarters. It can provide information on job opportunities so that workers are more confident in their willingness to take the risks of migration to a new area. At the extreme, the government could provide transportation, housing, and jobs and hope that someday the individual would integrate himself into the private economy.

The most common policy of government, however, is to attempt to influence the flow of capital between regions. The number of devices it may use is fairly numerous. Governments can give contracts to firms that promise to locate new plants in underdeveloped regions. It can subsidize the interest rate on borrowed funds to locate plants there. It can build plants and lease them at advantageous rates to industry. It can provide tax incentives like accelerated depreciation on capital invested in these regions. Finally, at the extreme, the government can build plants and operate them as state-owned industry, absorbing any losses within the state budget. The proper long-run strategy of government ought to be, whatever it does in the short run, to isolate the root causes of private industry's reluctance to move to these areas and then work to eliminate these causes. Long-run subsidies are unlikely to provide good long-run solutions.

Minimum wage legislation can have an adverse effect on mobility policies. Workers may be forced to sit idle if their marginal product is below the minimum wage, and no amount of information or government subsidization of moving expenses will create jobs for them in private industry. Minimum wage legislation may also affect the mobility of capital. Northern United States senators have lobbied in favor of higher minimum wages, not primarily to increase the income of their constituents, but to make lower skilled Southern workers less attractive to Northern firms contemplating moves to the South.

EFFORTS TO CORRECT MARKET DEFECTS

There are a number of areas in which market economies cannot function optimally or in which political or moral judgments are superimposed on "correct" market solutions. A market system cannot be expected to produce optimal solutions when there are external effects from consumption or production. Likewise, natural monopolies due to significant economies of scale produce results similar to man-made monopolies—high prices—since there is no alternative, such as breaking up the monopoly. Societies may determine that the structure of incomes is not socially or morally acceptable and may intervene to change the distribution of income.

Government and the Provision of Collective Goods

In any market system there will be insufficient production of collective or public goods. Government must provide for the production of purely public goods such as defense, since it is impossible to exclude anyone from consuming the good once it has been produced. Society may determine that the social value of certain goods or services is greater than individuals are separately able or willing to pay for, due to the existence of positive externalities associated with their consumption. The government acting as agent for society may boost the consumption of such goods in several ways. It may partially or completely subsidize the production of the favored good or service, permitting the market price to fall far enough to stimulate the proper amount of consumption, or it can produce the good itself and distribute it free or at low cost. It makes little difference whether the government produces the good itself or merely subsidizes the private production of it, unless there is a difference between public and private managerial proficiency.

Products which fall in this category are usually associated with health, culture, education, and recreation. Obviously, one man's health is linked to another's in cases of infectious diseases. Government appears as the dispenser of low-cost or free diagnoses and innoculations. Governmental promotion of culture, the arts, and literature is a sensitive area since governments may dispense or deny subsidies according to priorities unrelated to the intrinsic worth of the offerings. Nevertheless, certain reasonably neutral forms of subsidies, such as for the construction and support of museums and theatres, is felt to be acceptable. Many countries support "national" groups involved in the performing arts, such as ballet companies, orchestras, theatre groups, dance groups, writers and composers retreats, etc. The interaction of educated people with themselves, society, their children, and the work environment contains so many external benefits that societies universally have provided free or subsidized education.

It is extremely difficult, however, to estimate the value of the externalities involved. It is very tempting for those who enjoy cultural events which cannot pay for themselves to stress the benefits accruing from them to society. What may actually result is that government subsidizes the production of a good whose marginal social cost exceeds its social benefits. It is often argued that the provision of recreational as well as cultural facilities has positive externalities and should be subsidized. When the argument is examined more carefully, what many people are saying is that access to certain goods should not be dependent upon one's income. The poor have a "right" to beaches, campsites, and play-grounds, and they would be excluded if the price of these facilities was set to equate supply and demand. Oddly enough, the same people who argue in this fashion about campsites do not seem to feel the poor are equally entitled to subsidized food, clothing, or shelter. If one is truly concerned about the income of the poor, it would seem more appropriate to provide them with increased income and then let them choose the goods and services they prefer to consume.

Government and the Redistribution of Income

Society may disagree with the distribution of income that results from the spontaneous working of a market economy. This is rarely an economic judg-ment, although a case may be made occasionally. Usually, the judgment is that a group *ought* to have more or less income because they "deserve" it in some sense. Pressures for such judgments exist in any system in which the political weight of an individual (one man, one vote) differs from his economic weight (one dollar, one claim—a million dollars, a million economic claims). Since the political process can redistribute economic claims or dollars in many ways, it is inevitable that groups will jostle for the favors that governments can dispense.

Redistribution of income can occur in many ways. As mentioned above governments can provide to select groups special goods and/or services such as public tennis courts, public housing, food stamps, public health facilities, public golf courses, parks, and schools. There may also be private provision of these goods for those individuals that can afford extra quality or convenience.

Another technique is to discriminate between taxpayers with loopholes, deductions, exemptions, write-offs, and progressive or regressive rate schedules. The use of tax devices is an extremely complex and subtle process since the "burden" of the taxes may be shifted from one group to another until it is hard to determine on balance whether or not you have hurt or helped the target group.

Governments can redistribute income by use of minimum wages, welfare programs, granting of partial monopolies, tariffs, agricultural subsidies, and scores of other ways. To make a summarizing point about most redistributional schemes of governments, rarely is it possible to favor one group over another without triggering ripples of effects that partially or completely neutralize the original purpose. Minimum wage legislation designed to increase incomes will result in the unemployment of low-skilled or marginal workers. Minorities, teenagers, and the elderly have suffered increased amounts of unemployment with each increase in the minimum wage.

Government and the Regulation of Natural Monopolies

As we have noted above, natural monopolies exist where a single firm produces most economically at a level at which it supplies most of the market. Two or more firms could divide the market but at increased per unit costs. The market cannot provide a desirable solution since the "optimum" firm is one, but one firm would not price optimally. Governments have responded to this dilemma by forming public monopolies that provide the service and price it at the socially optimal level. Another solution is to permit private ownership but to regulate prices. There is formally no difference, unless governments are poor businessmen or businessmen are good politicians. In the former case the public utility would have higher costs and prices; in the latter the private utility would obtain higher rates and monopoly profits. Ideally, whether dealing with a public or private firm, one would wish to set price equal to marginal cost. If the firm is operating in the stage at which average cost is still declining, however, it will be necessary to provide the firm with a subsidy if it is to cover its costs and earn a normal rate of return on its investment.

Government and the Determination of the Savings Rate

The savings of a nation, and therefore its capacity to invest, depend largely on the distribution of income, the level of income, risk, and the earnings of savings. There is no reason for the government to intervene in the private calculations of savers as between the future and the present unless it wants to change the rate of investment. Should the government decide that the spontaneous provision for the future is inadequate, then it will intervene to increase savings, but how?

As we have seen, the government may redistribute income from low income spenders to high income savers. This policy, however, may run directly counter to political and moral judgments. Such a situation is a common dilemma of democratically governed, under-developed nations. In addition the amount of private savings generated by such government intervention may be small and channelled into "incorrect" areas.

Another possibility, that of generating savings through increased national income, is limited by the capacity of the economy, which is the object of the government efforts in the first place. Little hope rests here in the short run.

To encourage saving the government may do much to reduce the apparent risk to savers. It may "insure" savings deposits (actually by insuring the savings institutions). The government may create its own savings institutions such as postal savings accounts, bonds, special banks, social security funds, etc. A saver considers his savings to be as secure as the government (a cause for alarm in some cases) and presumably will save more. The government can pass on the savings to investors through regular investment channels such as private banks or public banks or may undertake investments of its own. The actual total risk involved in the investments is not fundamentally altered; only the attitude of savers toward their *share* of the risk is altered through the agency of the state. For all this to be meaningful, one must assume that the government is indeed correct in asserting that spontaneous saving is inadequate.

One additional source of saving is for the government to tax more than it spends and channel the "forced saving" into public or private investment. There is no limit to this process other than the taxing capacity of the fiscal system. The magnitude of the difference between private savers' aggregate provision for the future and the government's forced rate of provision for the future may diverge substantially if this form of savings is used.

One last aspect of social intervention in the savings process is that the investment funds channelled through the government may be allocated according to its calculation of "social" productivity rather than direct profitability. The government may feel that it knows better than the market where funds ought to go to insure the proper balanced development of the economy. This process will be discussed in the section on planning.

ECONOMIC PLANNING IN A MARKET CONTEXT

Why Planning?

Since World War II, many governments of developed Western economies have adopted various forms of planning in the attempt to improve the functioning of their economy over time. The notion that the development and implementation of policies to influence the economy constitutes a legitimate area of governmental activity was already fairly widespread in most market systems by the late 1940s. The attempts of governments to cope with the economic problems inherited from World War II and its aftermath forced governments to actively intervene in the economic process. Many economists and political leaders began to develop the idea that government would be a more effective economic participant if its decisions and actions were coordinated both internally and with the decisions and actions of the private sector.

Belief in the efficacy of coordinated governmental and private decision-making in a market context was particularly relevant to the widespread desire to increase post-war growth rates and maintain full employment. The primary aim of many Western leaders was to increase the growth rate beyond what it would have been in the absence of government intervention, and many felt that some sort of planning was the appropriate method for achieving this objective. One must be careful at this point to distinguish between types of planning. Certainly central planning of the sort described in connection with the command economy in chapter one was not believed by many to represent an improvement over the market economy. Rather, the notion of planning to aid rather than supplant market forces grew in popularity. We can define planning in the broadest sense as the "systematic management of one's assets."[2] Planning may take place at all levels of economic activity—from the individual private firm to the national government. If we recognize that it is the responsibility of the national government to preserve the value of our physical and human resources, then it seems logical that governmental activities in this area should be coordinated or planned. In many Western countries the government has taken the responsibility for maintaining an adequate rate of economic growth and full employment, recognizing that it is constrained in its actions by a reasonable degree of price stability and balance of payments equilibrium. It is concerned, however, not only with the rate of growth but also with the composition of output measured by the growth statistics. There is an expressed desire for an optimal allocation of goods among sectors. It is commonly agreed that the pursuit of these objectives requires economic planning, and some form of "indicative planning" has been adopted by most Western economies. Indicative planning has been defined as an

[2] For a more complete discussion of this idea see Neil Chamberlain, *Private and Public Planning* (New York: McGraw-Hill, 1965), p. 4.

attempt to promote stable, balanced growth by pooling the opinions and forecasts of the numerous small decision-makers in a market economy. The
collection and dissemination of this information provides better, more accurate
information for the future economic decisions of all sectors of the economy.]

Although the desire for economic growth and full employment provided a
strong impetus for the development and use of indicative planning, there were
other common problems which many felt could not be left to the free market
for solution. The recognition of the problem of externalities, the need for the
provision of collective goods, the desire for greater income and regional
equality—all pointed to the necessity of coordinated government action. At the
same time the apparent success of Soviet bloc planning in achieving high growth
rates spurred the Western capitalist economies to experiment with planning
techniques.

Let us examine the argument advanced for experimentation and against
the return to *laissez faire* capitalism. The major criticism of the growth potential
of capitalism deals with the inability under this system to coordinate the
investment plans of many small firms. The decision to invest depends upon the
expected future profitability of a project. The private entrepreneur must make
his estimates with limited knowledge of the future prices of both his output and
his inputs and the decisions of his competitors and his suppliers. Further, the
private entrepreneur makes his profit calculations solely upon the basis of
private costs and benefits, which may or may not be equal to the total social
costs and benefits of the project. It is argued that uncertainty about the future
leads to decisions which are less than optimal. The firm makes decisions to
reduce risk such as using labor intensive methods of production and starting
numerous small projects, which can limit the growth possibilities of the economy
over time.[3] Investment projects which involve the construction of long-lived
plant and equipment and the training of a skilled labor force are avoided by the
small firm, even though such investment programs may be in the best long-run
interest of the economy.

It is argued, therefore, that some form of governmental planning is
necessary to reduce risk and uncertainty in order to ensure the balanced
growth of the economy. But what is the nature of planning in a market context?
The two concepts, plan and market, have often been considered opposites, yet
all economic actors in a market system must "plan" their activities to some
extent. In the most limited sense planning implies the awareness of the time
dimension of economic activity—the realization that the nature of the economy
tomorrow will be a function of decisions and actions taken today. Planning for
the future involves knowledge about the interaction between the economic
participant and his environment, about how his actions affect his welfare, and
finally about the probability which he must attach to each projection of the
future of his environment. Planning implies both awareness and action. Seeking,

---

[3] J. Black, "The Theory of Indicative Planning," *Oxford Economic Papers,* vol. 20,
no.3 (Nov. 1968), pp. 303-320.

acquiring, and evaluating information are costly and are not undertaken lightly. The intention is to alter behavior based on better information so as to optimize welfare over time. Planning thus consists of the collection and analysis of information, and action based upon this information, designed to alter the future economic environment.

The government is a data gatherer and a data disseminator. It collects information on consumers' spending plans, incomes, holdings of consumer durables, enterprise investment plans, capacity, and costs. It processes this primary data, aggregates it, and feeds it back to the economic participants. This better, cheaper, and more reliable information causes a number of people to alter their plans and thereby changes the product and incomes mix of the economy. The government also acts as an externalities calculator. Part of the information which it gathers includes estimates of the impact of one producer or consumer on another, data not measured in the market place. The government may then manipulate the environment so as to cause these external effects to be internalized in its own accounts.

The primary purpose of data collection and dissemination is to optimize the sequence of investment in order to increase the growth rate, given any particular saving rate. Indicative planning promotes higher growth rates in three primary ways. First, planners try to raise demand expectations by making private and public decision-makers aware of the future growth of the economy. It is argued that if firms believe that the government is going to act to prevent slumps and stimulate the economy, they will be more optimistic about the future and make their investment decisions accordingly. The expectation of growth thus is a major force in the attainment of growth—it becomes a self-fulfilling prophecy. Second, and closely connected with the raising of demand expectations, is the reduction of uncertainty. If the planners can make the firm aware of the growing market for his product and the adequacy of the suppliers of his inputs as well as the direction his competitors are taking, he will be less hesitant to expand his capacity to meet future needs. A third task of the planners is the prevention of bottlenecks by removing constraints on the supply side. It is their job to spot shortages of critical raw materials and specialized types of labor and to redirect resources to eliminate them. The planners may also attempt to improve the quality of inputs through the sponsorship of research and development programs and the support of education and training.[4]

Let us now turn to the question of how the planners accomplish these three tasks through the procedure of indicative planning. Before we begin, however, it is necessary to caution the reader that there are as many styles of planning as there are countries engaged in planning. Plans differ as to their scope, the time period covered, and the types of controls adopted to enforce them.

---

[4]See Malcom MacLennan, Murray Forsyth, and Geoffrey Denton, *Economic Planning and Policies in Britain, France, and Germany* (New York: Frederick A. Praeger, 1968), pp. 133-154.

Most planning procedures, however, do involve some type of forecast as to the state of the economy in some future period and provide for the use of some governmental controls if there is a significant divergence between reality and the forecast. We will divide our description of the planning process into two parts. First we will discuss the process of plan construction, and second we will discuss the possible techniques of enforcement and control. In the following chapters we will look at the planning process in particular national contexts.

Plan Construction

Plan construction begins with the gathering of information about the present state of the economy, which includes such variables as existing capacity, rate of population growth, rate of productivity increase, and the situation in important world markets. The planning agency uses this information to develop a plan which outlines the nature of the economy in some future time period. A short-term plan may cover only one year, while a long-term plan may make projections five, ten, or even twenty-five years into the future. The nature of the future state of the economy is dependent upon decisions made by private and public policy-makers today. Normally several variants of the future state of the economy are discussed. A forecast of the future which involves no change in present policies may be developed and analyzed. If this picture of the future is not the desired one, new forecasts can be developed which incorporate alternative policies. The planning agency thus assesses the feasibility and consequences of several possible variants and the means of achieving them.[5]

There are two basic procedures used by planning agencies to develop consistent plans. One, which we will label the input-output method of plan development, involves the balancing of supply and demand for major sectors of the economy through the use of an input-output table. Using a simple econometric model of the economy, planners estimate the major components of GNP at several alternative growth rates.[6] Once one rate has been chosen, it is the task of the planners to work out the implications and consequences of this rate of growth for the major sectors of the economy. The necessary allocations of investment and employment are determined by sector as the planners attempt to achieve a supply-demand balance of inputs and outputs by major sectors. Imbalances are analyzed as to source and possible methods of alleviation. The correction of imbalances may result in the creation of imbalances in other sectors, which must then be re-examined.[7]

[5]See Jan Tinbergen, *Central Planning* (New Haven, Conn.: Yale University Press, 1964), pp. 3-42.

[6]For a more thorough discussion of this process see Neil Chamberlain, *Private and Public Planning* p. 147.

[7]For a discussion of the input-output technique see the Appendix in Chapter Ten.

In developing the plan and in attempting to achieve balance, planners may consult various public and private decision-makers with respect to their plans for the future. Their answers are then incorporated into the projections. If the projections involve inconsistencies, the planners may return to the decision-makers with this knowledge, and their action may result in altered private intentions. This type of planning is an iterative process, which involves many stages as planners attempt to eliminate inconsistencies. The final plan consists of a sketch of the economy in some future time period, which involves varying degrees of detail where the plan is broken down by sector and by region.

An alternative procedure for developing a forecast of the economy involves the use of an econometric model to test the feasibility of several variants. It is possible to make simultaneous forecasts of all the sectors of the economy using a macroeconomic model that takes into account the technical interrelations between the sectors of the economy. The model is usually specified at a high level of aggregation. It consists of an equal number of equations and unknowns where the unknowns are the target variables.[8] The knowns are the exogenous data, such as population trends, and government policy variables. A highly simplified macroeconomic model of the economy is presented below.[9]

1. $C = 20 + 0.7(Y-T)$
2. $I = 2 + 0.1\ Y_{t-1}$
3. $T = .2Y$
4. $Y = C + I + G$

The model consists of four equations and four unknowns, C (consumption), Y (income), I (investment), and T (taxes). The policy variables are G (government expenditures), and the tax rate, which is .2. The equations are solved for a set of values for the policy variables. Several variants can be drawn up and presented for consideration. Needless to say, the plan constructed with this procedure is only as reliable as the relationships expressed in the model. Outside data, however, may be substituted for one of the unknowns, such as investment, if it is believed the incorporation of this data will make the estimate more accurate.

Plan Implementation

Once the plan is constructed it is normally submitted for approval to the legislature, and once approved, can be implemented. It is extremely difficult to

[8] Daniel Suits, "Forecasting and Analysis with an Econometric Model," in *Readings in Economic Statistics and Econometrics,* ed. Arnold Zellner (Boston: Little, Brown and Co., 1968), pp. 583-611.

[9] *Ibid.,* p. 585.

generalize about the implementation process, which may vary all the way from mere verbal support by the government to the use of a wide variety of micro and macro controls to insure compliance with the plan.

Some advocates of indicative planning argue that a well-developed, consistent plan implements itself. When private firms and other public agencies see how they fit into this consistent projection of the future, they realize that it would be foolish for them to act counter to the plan. Why produce in excess of the projected rate since markets will be inadequate; why plan to expand capacity when there will be a shortage of skilled labor? One problem in this approach to implementation is that the plan is not specified in such detail that a particular firm can find his place in it. He may reason that his rate of development should be greater than the average, and he may be right. This problem will be reduced depending upon the degree of consultation and mutual interaction between the planner and the firm during the construction phase of the plan.

No forecast, however, will be perfect, and deviations between the forecast and reality are bound to develop. The action which the government takes at this time depends upon its ability to assess the economic situation clearly and quickly in order to recognize deviations and its philosophy toward governmental intervention in the private economy. All Western planners stress that their plans are indicative rather than imperative. They are a guide to the future and are not legally binding on anyone. The extent to which they are implemented, or actions are taken when variations develop, depends upon the willingness and ability of the government to "induce" the appropriate behavior in the private sector and to manipulate those areas under its direct control. What areas are directly under the government's control and what inducements it has to offer vary widely from one country to another. We will briefly discuss three types of implementing action: macro controls, micro controls, and the operation of the nationalized sector.

Macro Controls

The broadest controls used by all Western economies, regardless of the nature of planning practiced, are the fiscal and monetary policies discussed earlier in this chapter. These tools are designed primarily to influence the general level of economic activity rather than to direct resources toward particular sectors of the economy. These tools can be coordinated and used in order to ensure a level of economic activity consistent with the planned overall rate of growth of capacity, while at the same time preventing excessive spending which may lead to inflation and balance of payment disequilibrium. Incomes policies discussed earlier are often used in a planning context to avoid inflation by reducing wage and profit demands through the mutual cooperation and inter-action of labor, management, and the government during plan construction.

Micro Controls

A variety of microeconomic controls have been developed by Western economies to influence behavior related to the fulfillment of plan objectives. One group of micro controls that are commonly employed involve controlling the access to capital markets. If the government is able to screen loan applicants either through the operation of its own credit institutions or through government control over private sources of credit, it can discriminate among borrowers. Those firms which are behaving in accord with plan objectives will obtain easier access to credit than those firms which are not. To the extent that the private sector is dependent upon publicly owned or controlled sources of credit, this can be a powerful tool for plan implementation. A second set of micro tools commonly used in plan implementation involves the granting of privileges and favors for behavior appropriate to the plan. These privileges include tax exemptions and favorable tax rates, increased depreciation allowances, and subsidies for such activities as research and development and the location of new plants in the underdeveloped regions of the economy. The government may also attempt to improve the flow of needed resources, particularly labor, to priority areas by providing information on employment opportunities, as well as offering inducements for mobility such as moving allowances and subsidizing on-the-job training.

The Nationalized Sector

It may seem logical to assume that the planners will have the greatest control over the nationalized sector of the economy, but this is not always the case. The amount of control depends critically upon the historical development of the nationalized industries, which often preceded the development of the planning institutions. Many nationalized industries are loosely controlled by government and essentially have an independent existence. Independent public managers may have different ideas about the development of their industries from those held by the planners. Sometimes it is more difficult for the planners to induce the appropriate behavior in public enterprises than in private enterprises. To the extent that various governmental agencies and activities are coordinated, however, the operation of the nationalized sector can be an important aid in plan implementation.

The Performance of the Planners

Up to this point the benefits of coordinating governmental economic decisions and actions have been stressed. The question arises as to how the performance of government can be judged. One of the primary objectives of coordinated activity has been to achieve a more rapid rate of economic growth, while at the same time securing a more optimal production mix. If governmental performance is to be evaluated, we must ask: more rapid and more optimal than what? What standard is being used to evaluate the impact and effectiveness of indicative planning? We have demonstrated in an earlier chapter that the ideal, perfectly competitive market economy does not exist because the conditions necessary for its operation do not hold. What does exist is some imperfect version of a competitive market economy, retaining some of its advantages but also possessing many disadvantages. The same is true of planning in a market context. It cannot be assumed that the process of plan construction and plan implementation will be frictionless.[10]

> Exaggerated ideas of the omniscience of the government could always be found among theoretical economists. But in the 1930's and 1940's the abstract models based on the government as a perfect economic calculator become ever more widely accepted as a description of potential reality. Unchecked by confrontation with experience, the literature on planning flourished. In general this literature was characterized by the implicit assumptions that the objectives of the society were agreed upon; that the central collection and processing of economic information involved no major difficulties; that the government possessed unusual powers to foresee the future; that governmental personnel were disinterested automatons more 'rational' in their decision-making than private individuals and seeking only to maximize the social welfare; that economic calculation and politics could be kept in separate compartments.[11]

There are many inherent defects in the processes of plan construction and implementation, which may significantly reduce or perhaps entirely eliminate the improvements in economic performance attributed to indicative planning. We can divide our discussion of the problems inherent in governmental economic planning into two parts. The first is concerned with those problems which reduce the efficiency of governmental activity and lead to non-optimal decisions. The second deals with the possible conflict between planning activities and democracy.

INHERENT DEFECTS IN THE GOVERNMENTAL DECISION-MAKING PROCESS

Our discussion here is concerned not with the technical difficulties involved with plan construction, such as the development of more accurate forecasting techniques, but with certain basic problems which would still remain

[10] The following analysis follows the lines of the excellent discussion of the inherent problems involved in the participation of government in the economy in Gerald Sirkin, *The Visible Hand: The Fundamentals of Economic Planning* (New York: McGraw-Hill, 1968). See in particular chapters four and eight.

[11]*Ibid.,* pp. 169-170.

if all of the technical problems of plan construction and implementation could be solved. First, it is not at all clear how economic objectives are to be determined. If the development of the economy is no longer to follow from the individual decisions of private firms responding to and anticipating the wants of consumers, what or who is to determine its development, and on the basis of what criteria? It is one thing to say that the direction resulting from private activity is not optimal and another, much more difficult, problem to agree upon what is the optimal direction. Public policy-makers do not have an infallible guide leading them to optimal decisions concerning the rate of growth and mix of private and public goods. Although trained economists may be able to indicate feasible, consistent plans for the future and to state the nature of the trade-offs involved in the selection of alternative feasible growth paths, they do not make the final decisions. Consistent plans may not be politically desirable plans. A full, open discussion of the nature of politically unpopular trade-offs may be suppressed. The final policy may be the result of a bargaining process, and the nature of the decision dependent not upon rational economic calculation but upon the relative political strengths of the compromisers.[12]

A second problem involves the evaluation of public policies and projects. It is impossible to turn back the clock and try a second alternative solution to an economic problem. How can the success of the first one be judged? The profit criterion applied to business activity is often not applicable to governmental activity, which frequently involves externalities and long range benefits and costs that are difficult to measure today. Since there is no necessity to show an immediate profit, it is easy to ascribe large, long-run, unmeasurable benefits to all government projects. Policies are judged successful if the stated objective is reached without precipitating "serious" side effects at the same time. Governmental activity is judged appropriate or correct if its results are within certain tolerance limits with respect to such variables as inflation, unemployment, and balance of payments disequilibrium. Unlike private enterprise, government enterprises' mistakes are not limited by the necessity of showing a profit even over the long-run. Government can and has continued policies which have had disastrous long-run consequences on the economy. Given the ability of government to gain revenue by taxing or deficit-financing, it can continue to pursue bad policies far longer than a private firm with its inherently limited ability to secure capital.

Whenever power is centralized, schemes must be devised and boundaries established for subordinating the activities and decisions of lower levels to that of higher levels. To the extent that planners influence the decisions of private firms and other government agencies, rules must be established to guide the local decision-maker. The planner will not have the time or the staff to consider the unique circumstances of each firm. The guidelines must be appropriate for the

[12] *Ibid.*, p. 59.

"average" firm, but no firm is the "average" firm. Thus the rules will not lead to the optimal decisions by any firm. Firms that wish to deviate from the plans for their industry or sector may be discouraged from doing so by the threat of governmental reprisals in the form of harder access to credit. The firm may have been prevented from making a bad decision, but innovative behavior may at the same time have been stifled.

Finally we must not forget that the concentration of power in the government and its ability to dispense economic favors must inevitably result in a certain amount of corruption. Leaders of industry and labor as well as the heads of public agencies will all be trying to convince government that their interests are meritorious, coincident with the interest of the nation as a whole, and deserving of special attention. The individual and the consumer may be under-represented in vital economic and political decision-making in advanced capitalist economies today.

Let us consider this question of the conflict between planning and democracy. There is reason to believe that the nature of the behavior required for successful planning reduces the power of the legislative representatives of the people and enhances the power of the executive. We will briefly touch upon three arguments supporting this belief. First, there is the question of speed. The plan is not a perfect, static document which, once approved by the legislature, will implement itself. Rather it is an imperfect document based upon incomplete and sometimes unreliable information. Plan implementation must be flexible, capable of coping with changing circumstances. Decisions must be made today to influence events one, two, or five years from today. Legislative bodies have not proved able to make these rapid adjustments, and thus power has had to be entrusted to the executive.

> Who controls the planners? It is not just a matter of getting parliamentary approval for the broad outline of a scheme for raising the standard of living of a nation by a certain amount over a stated period of years. A plan is a living body of economic policy, adapting itself constantly to changing circumstances, sometimes undergoing drastic alteration in its component parts in order to secure particular objectives which come in time to acquire a new order of priority. The traditional Western parliament, a nonexpert body, by instinct non-interventionist unless there is some manifest abuse or need for legislation, is hardly equipped for the job of supervising the systematic intervention which planning implies. [13]

Second, it is argued that planning in a market economy fosters corporatism. Planners will find it easier to deal with and coordinate the decisions of a few large firms rather than many small ones. It may seem to the planner that the

[13] Andrew Shonfield, *Modern Capitalism* (London: Oxford University Press, 1969), p. 230.

advantages of competition are outweighed by the ease of working with the cooperative industrial giants. Economic decisions may be increasingly made by a few powerful firms aligned with government.

Finally, we turn to the question of how democratic control can be exercised in the planning process. The plan is a complex, technical document whose worth depends upon the consistency of its parts. A legislator who is asked to approve the plan in its final form is not really able to exercise his judgment concerning the nature of this particular plan. He is probably not a trained economist or statistician and thus does not completely understand the methodology of plan construction. Even if he does possess this understanding, it will be too late to significantly alter the plan at this stage. The experts will plead that the plan is a consistent, coherent whole and that none of its parts can be touched without upsetting the balance. All the legislator can do is specify in broad terms the desired development path and perhaps choose among certain alternatives if the nature of the trade-off is clearly specified. Meaningful legislative participation must take place *early* in the planning process; it cannot take place during the ceremony of formal plan approval.

In the previous chapters the economic problem was developed in detail. How the perfectly competitive market system produces the optimum solution was shown; defects of the market system were pointed out; and this chapter has shown how governments try to correct for these defects. The following chapters will examine the workings of a number of actual mixed economies and compare and contrast individual approaches to economic problems.

QUESTIONS

1. How can you explain the rapid rise in government participation in the economies of Western nations in the post World War II period?
2. How do economic policies designed to improve the functioning of markets differ from those policies designed to correct inherent market defects?
3. Which particular policies do you think have been most successful and least successful in improving the postwar performance of capitalist economies?
4. What functions can planning perform in the context of a market system?
5. What is the difference between a forecast, an indicative plan, and an imperative plan?
6. How can governments enforce indicative plans?
7. Does indicative planning improve the performance of a capitalist economy?

BIBLIOGRAPHY

Brennan, Michael J. *Theory of Economic Statistics, 2nd ed.* Englewood Cliffs, New Jersey: Prentice-Hall, Inc., 1970.

Chamberlain, Neil. *Private and Public Planning.* New York: McGraw-Hill, 1965.

Friedman, Milton. *Capitalism and Freedom.* Chicago: University of Chicago Press, 1962.

Galbraith, J. K. *The Affluent Society.* Boston: Houghton Mifflin, 1958.

Heilbroner, R. L. *The Economic Problem.* Englewood Cliffs, New Jersey: Prentice-Hall, 1968.

Sirkin, Gerald. *The Visibile Hand; The Fundamentals of Economic Planning.* New York: McGraw-Hill, 1968.

Solo, Robert. *Economic Organizations and Social Systems.* The Bobbs-Merrill Company, Inc., 1967.

Tinbergen, Jan. *Central Planning.* New Haven: Yale University Press, 1964.

III

THE MIXED
ECONOMY

6

The French Economy

Introduction

The French economy has been singled out by many authors as an example of a modern mixed economy. It is a unique blend of economic institutions. Applying the classification scheme developed in chapter one it would be classified as a mixed economy according to all three criteria. First, consider the issue of public versus private ownership of the means of production. In France private ownership is predominant; i.e., the great majority of firms operating in the areas of agriculture, industry, and services are privately owned. The public sector by the standards of the United States, however, is quite large. Public utilities, including electricity and gas, are state owned. All of the railroads and a major portion of the airlines are state operated. The state owns the coal mines and has a major interest in the petroleum industry. The state is also engaged in the production of automobiles and aircraft. The Bank of France and the four major deposit banks, as well as a large segment of the insurance industry, are nationalized. Approximately 20 percent of the gross national product flows through the budget of the central government, including expenditures on goods and services and transfer payments. Investment by public enterprises counts for 25 percent of gross fixed investments.[1] Much of the nationalization took place immediately after World War II, however, and the nationalized sector has not been extended significantly since that period.

The second criterion used in the classification scheme concerns the question of the locus of decision-making power. Economic power in France resides both in the individual consumer and private firm as well as in the state. The private decision-maker is free to choose his employment and his consumption pattern. The private firm is free to determine its output and input mix. Collective decision-making does have a powerful influence, however, on the nature of the private decisions made. The state, through a variety of techniques which will be discussed later in the chapter, is able to modify many of the parameters entering into the private decision-making process, and thus is able to modify the decisions themselves. Collective decision-making in the operation of the nationalized sector also has an important influence on the direction of the entire economy.

The state further influences the allocation of resources through its extensive redistribution measures. Social Security expenditures have run approximately 13 percent of French gross national product.[2] The French operate a family allowance scheme financed by a tax on employees, and a comprehensive social security system providing sickness insurance, maternity and pension benefits, and unemployment compensation, financed by taxes on employers and employees.

Turning to the third criterion, the mechanism used to allocate resources among competing uses, it is clear that France has predominantly a market system, and market signals are the dominant influence on resource allocation decisions. Despite extensive government influence in the economy and the existence of a national plan, few economic actions are the result of a direct order from the government. The government may intervene in the economy, altering supply and demand conditions, but this intervention will be reflected in the changing costs of doing business and will influence the profit prospects of private enterprise.

There has been widespread interest in the French blend of economic institutions, due in large part to the remarkable performance of the economy in the post-war period, particularly when this performance is contrasted to France's pre-war growth experience. France has achieved high rates of growth in the post-war period with what appears to be a judicious use of limited inputs. Gross national product, measured in constant prices, increased at an average annual rate of 4.8 percent from 1951 to 1965.[3] By the middle of the 1960s France's

[1] Bent Hansen, *Fiscal Policy in Seven Countries 1955-65*. Organization for European Cooperation and Development, (March 1969), pp. 149-152.

[2] *Ibid.*, p. 191.

[3] Vera Lutz, *Central Planning for the Market Economy* (London: Longmans, Green and Co. Ltd., 1969), p. 6.

GNP per capita was comparable to those of Great Britain and West Germany. The interesting feature of this achievement is that growth was accomplished with a nearly constant labor force and a relatively low rate of investment.

The French post-war experience, however, is not universally judged a complete success. The French have achieved full employment and high stable growth rates, but have not permanently managed to control inflation, which has been a persistent problem often threatening to block expansion programs. France also appears to have been less successful in the division of output among economic claimants, a difficult task in a complex industrial economy. Social tensions have developed and occasionally erupted into violence despite the strong performance of economic aggregates.

The remainder of this chapter is devoted to the study of the interaction of the public and the private sectors in the French economy in an attempt to better understand the nature and functioning of a modern mixed economy. Although French history and institutions are unique to France, they provide a fascinating illustration of an eclectic approach to the solution of economic problems within the basic framework of a market economy.[4]

Tradition and the Role of the State in the French Economy

French economic history prior to World War II is a history of state intervention in a protected, noncompetitive, private economy with a slow rate of economic growth. It can be argued that France was not really a capitalist economy in the tradition of the United States or Great Britain. Mercantilist practices continued into the twentieth century, protecting private enterprise from foreign and domestic competition. The state aided the development of private industry through the use of tariffs, subsidies, and tax privileges designed to reduce the risk and uncertainty associated with private enterprise. There was a common mistrust of the workings of the market and a belief in the need for state guidance in the direction of the economy.

Although France was a wealthy agricultural nation in the eighteenth and early nineteenth centuries, by 1914 she ranked behind the United States, Russia, Germany, Austria-Hungary, and Great Britain in industrial development. The poor performance of the French economy has been attributed to its low rate of population increases, its uneven distribution of wealth, the peasant problem, and the nature of French entrepreneurship. It is estimated that between 1815 and 1914 the French population increased only 35 percent and that 10 percent of the population owned 87 percent of the income producing property. The government protected the agricultural sector through subsidies and retarded the movement of population from rural to urban areas, thereby reducing the

---

[4]A more detailed statistical analysis of French economic performance and a comparison of the French economy with that of other mixed economies will be presented in chapter nine.

potential supply of industrial labor. The development of the corporation as a form of business was exceedingly slow in France. The typical French business was, and to a great extent continues to be, a small family firm, more concerned with secure rather than profitable markets. French firms have been protected from failure, and entry of new firms has been difficult.

After World War II there was general agreement that the state must play a dominant role in the reconstruction of the French economy. The war had seriously damaged the economy, resulting in critical shortages of labor, capital, and raw materials. There was a need for significant amounts of investment in transportation and housing. The state had powerful tools at its disposal to guide the development of the economy. It controlled a large nationalized sector and the major credit sources in the economy. The study of the French economy in the post-war period is in large part a study of the changing pattern of inter-relationships between the public and the private sectors. The state has had a major influence on economic affairs throughout the post-war years, but the institutions through which its influence is felt and the methods of control it uses are in a continual process of evolution. The one institution which has captured the interest of many observers of the French economy is planning. In the next section of the chapter we will examine the philosophy underlying planning, the process of planning as incorporated in the five year plans, and the achievements of planning.

The French Experiment with Indicative Planning

Planning in France began shortly after World War II with the adoption of the first plan in 1947. From the beginning the stated aim of French planners has been to supplement, not supplant, the market system. Planning has been indicative rather than imperative. The purpose of planning has been to improve the efficiency with which the economy operates and raise the overall rate of economic growth. This was to be accomplished by improving the information available for private decision-makers. Many advocates of planning believed that the mere existence of a plan indicating the future direction of the economy would provide businessmen with the confidence to invest for the future expansion of output. Thus planning would reduce uncertainty and extend the time horizon of the private firm. The plan would also make future bottlenecks visible, thus allowing for timely action and increasing the long-run rate of growth. The function of the planners was to assess alternative rates of economic growth, the means of achieving them, and the consequences associated with the selection of a particular growth rate. At no time did the planners intend for the plan to be imperative or binding upon any segment of the economy. It was merely to provide a guide to the future development of the economy, although we shall see that the government has many tools to enforce its particular view of the future upon other sectors of the economy.

The Process of Planning

Planning Organizations

The Planning Commission (*Commissariat au Plan*), headed by the Planning Commissioner (*Commissair au Plan*), is the agency responsible for the construction of the plan. The Commission employs a professional staff of thirty to thirty-five people, who are responsible for supervising the work involved in planning. Much of the substantive staff work is done by traditional government agencies and made available to the Planning Commission. Beneath the Commission are six "horizontal" modernization commissions and twenty-six "vertical" modernization commissions. The "horizontal" commissions are concerned with interpreting the implications of the plan on a cross-sectional basis, including the areas of finance, manpower, and research. The "vertical" commissions are concerned with the impact of the plan on specific sectors and industries such as agriculture, chemicals, and general manufacturing.

The Planning Cycle

In the formal process of plan preparation the planning commission prepares several preliminary forecasts of the economic situation in the terminal year of the plan. These forecasts are based upon projected rates of growth in major sectors of the economy and are presumed to be compatible with a stable price level and full employment. These variants are then presented to the government and Parliament, who choose among them. The variant selected then goes to the vertical modernization commissions where the plan is disaggregated by industry and more detailed supply plans are constructed. The plan is also sent to the horizontal commissions to check for overall consistency with the resource constraints of the economy. The plan is then reviewed by the Economic and Social Council and both houses of Parliament, and is, upon adoption by the latter, published by the government. The plan, although officially adopted, does not represent a firm commitment by the government and is not legally binding upon the industries included in it.

In the actual practice of plan preparation the Planning Commission prepares the plan variant with the aid of the statistical section of the Ministry of Finance, and the second stage of the plan involves complex bargaining between the Planning Commission and the Ministry of Finance. The two agencies do not always have the same economic objectives. The Planning Commission has consistently lobbied for growth-inducing programs, while the Ministry of Finance has often opted for price stability and balance of payments equilibrium over economic growth. Thus, the major decisions with regard to the future direction of the economy are the result of complex negotiations between the Planning Commission, the Ministry of Finance, and the government. In practice Parliament has had little influence upon the plan and has merely ratified the final document, having little or no role in its formulation.

When the plan is completed, it consists of an outline of the overall growth of the economy as well as the direction of the future development of various sectors such as agriculture, commerce, and industry. The plan is concerned primarily with supply conditions in physical terms, while sectoral and subsectoral demand is forecast but not planned. The key element of supply is productive capacity, and the amount and types of investment needed to achieve the planned growth of output are estimated. The means of financing these investments and the availability of inputs, such as labor, are also calculated.

One of the unique features of French planning is the role of the modernization commissions. It is the task of these commissions to work out the detailed implications of the overall objectives for their particular industries. The membership of the planning commissions includes representatives of management, labor, and government, but the commissions are frequently dominated by business. It is in the commissions that businessmen actively participate in the planning process. The responsibility of the commission is to choose the growth rate and modernization objectives of the industries under it and to divide forecasted output and investment among firms in those industries. In more concentrated industries representatives of the most powerful firms sitting on the modernization commissions bargain with other firms in the industry for their share of future markets. In less concentrated industries the planners bargain with trade associations representing large numbers of firms.

In summary, one can view planning in France as a process in which broad economic objectives are determined by the government at the top and broken down by sector and by industry in the vertical modernization commissions under the supervision of the Planning Commission. The detailed industry and sector plans are then aggregated by the horizontal commissions in an attempt to achieve a coherent plan in which all markets are cleared. The planning process in theory involves a concerted effort by all segments of the economy, although labor and Parliament have often contributed to the plan in a perfunctory way, having little real influence on the economic choices embodied in it.

The Changing Nature of Economic Objectives

The scope and the objectives of planning have changed considerably since the introduction of the First French Plan in 1947 (the Monnet Plan). Planning became more and more detailed and covered a larger portion of the economy in the Second and Third plans. It now appears, however, that planners are backing off from the prospect of continued detailed microeconomic planning; they have been more concerned with planning economic aggregates in the Fifth and Sixth plans. The methods of plan implementation have varied from plan to plan and will be discussed in the following section.

The Monnet Plan was a response to the immediate post-war situation, an attempt to rebuild key industries and to coordinate Marshall Plan aid to assure its most effective use. The plan was comprised of a series of investment and modernization programs covering coal, electricity, steel, cement, mechanized agriculture, and transportation. In 1953 the plan was extended two more years and enlarged to cover petroleum, basic chemicals, synthetic fibers, shipbuilding, and synthetic fertilizers.

The First Plan did not attempt to coordinate all sectors of the economy but merely to channel resources into industries whose reconstruction and development were believed to be crucial for the future growth of the economy. The techniques used in preparing the plan were quite crude, involving no input output analysis or formal consideration of the opportunity cost of the resources being diverted to the planned sectors. The planners were successful in diverting resources to the priority areas in large part due to their control over the flows of capital in a capital-short economy.

Although the plan was considered a success, problems which were to recur in future plans began to appear. Perhaps the most serious and persistent problem was inflation. The planners were committed to expansion programs and the long-run development of French economic potential even if this policy might result in significant amounts of inflation. In the early plans, when French markets were protected from foreign competition, the effects of inflation could be minimized. The balance of payments was protected from the effects of domestic inflation through the use of import controls and export subsidies. After entering the Common Market, macroeconomic considerations became more important since domestic inflation would reduce the competitiveness of French exports. A second problem which appeared at this time and has continued to plague French planners, is one of priorities. Investment needs of heavy industry, light industry, education, housing, and other social services all competed for limited amounts of resources. The planners, concerned with the long-run growth of the economy, consistently opted for investment in heavy industry whenever mounting pressure on resources necessitated difficult choices. Although lip service has been given to the importance of investment in housing and education, they remained until recently at the bottom of the priority list. The reconstruction of the industrial sector proceeded on schedule, but the provision of social goods and services lagged far behind.

The coverage of the Second and Third plans (1954-57 and 1957-1961) was extended to include the entire economy in aggregate terms. Attention was shifted from the key sectors of the First Plan to programs for the improvement of productivity throughout the economy. Productivity was to be increased by a "rationalization" of the economic structure. State protection of private industry was reduced and firms were encouraged to regroup to achieve a more efficient size. Rationalization was also to be achieved by capital-deepening investments and the development and implementation of new technology. The planners felt that French industrial efficiency suffered from the operation of large numbers of small-scale firms. They favored mergers to achieve large-scale, specialized production, thereby lowering costs and making French products more competitive.[5] Taxes were selectively lowered to promote desirable mergers, and a value-added tax was substituted for the sales tax which had been levied at every stage of production. It was hoped that the new tax would encourage specialization and the use of more capital-intensive techniques.

Methods of plan construction became more sophisticated. In the Third Plan sectoral demand projections were arranged in an input-output table with input coefficients used to estimate intermediate demands. The coefficients represented the technical relationships observed between industries in previous years after adjustments had been made for innovations resulting in productivity increases. Given the final demand for various types of output, the coefficients were used to calculate the total output needed to satisfy both intermediate and final uses. These calculations were then checked for consistency with the economy's supply constraints to see if the growth targets were feasible.

Despite the use of more sophisticated planning techniques, the results of the Second and Third plans were mixed. There was a continuation of the conflict between inflation and expansion, and the high rate of inflation which was allowed to develop in the Second Plan resulted in a foreign exchange crisis. The problem of inflation and balance of payments disequilibrium necessitated the scrapping of the Third Plan and the substitution of an interim plan in 1959. Targets had to be revised downward, and the planners tried to maintain the level of investment spending while restricting consumption. The spirit of cooperation between government, labor, and business showed signs of strain. Business was no longer as dependent upon government for needed capital and felt freer to ignore the plan if they felt it was to their advantage. Labor had become disenchanted with the aims of planning, which they felt were to promote the profits of big business rather than the welfare of the workers. They refused to participate in the construction of the Second and Third plans.

The Fourth Plan (1962-65) marks a movement away from detailed sectoral planning toward a more aggregative approach. In 1959 a projection of the economy to 1975 was made which formed the background for the preparation of the Fourth and Fifth (1966-70) plans. Long term trends in population, productivity, consumption, and technical developments were examined. More detailed interim estimates were made for 1965, the terminal year of the Fourth Plan. The planners analyzed the impact of three different rates of economic

[5]Stephen Cohen, *Modern Capitalist Planning: The French Model* (Cambridge, Massachusetts: Harvard University Press, 1969), pp. 137-145.

expansion—3, 4.5 and 6 percent—and presented these alternatives to the Economic and Social Council for their consideration. The planners attempted to conform to the spirit of a democratic discussion of economic alternatives prior to the preparation of the detailed plan.

Inflation threatened the objectives of the Fourth Plan. The Stabilization Plan of 1963, developed by the Ministry of Finance, was adopted to curb inflationary pressure. The adoption of the Stabilization Plan again necessitated a choice between the retention of investment programs and social welfare programs. The planners again chose to maintain the level of investment while abandoning many social welfare programs in the areas of housing and education. During the preparation of the Fifth Plan the planners tried to prevent a similar recurrence by coordinating long-run expansion programs with short-term stabilization policies. Three major innovations were introduced in the Fifth Plan. First, planning was done in value terms as well as in physical terms, and physical output objectives for individual industries were de-emphasized and labeled forecasts rather than firm targets to be achieved. Thus, the planning emphasis shifted from output and supply considerations to broad financial aggregates— prices, incomes, foreign exchange, gross national product, investment, and savings.

The second major innovation involved the introduction of a set of warning signals to indicate the development of a conflict between growth objectives and stabilization. A safe range was determined for the general price level and balance of trade. If the figures exceeded this range, an inflation warning was sounded, triggering corrective measures or explicit changes in plan goals. Similar warning devices were attached to production, investment, and employment to signal a recession.

The third innovation involved the development of an incomes policy to help control inflation. The Fifth Plan regarded as acceptable a 2.8 to 4 percent increase in per capita wages, depending upon skill category. The government received little cooperation from labor, however, and has not worked out methods of implementing its incomes policy.

Despite the innovations involved in the construction and implementation of the Fifth Plan, there was a tremendous amount of hostility expressed toward the government's priorities. France almost had a revolution in 1968, due in large part to the government's failure to provide for social needs of the population including better schools, housing, and medical facilities. The Sixth Plan (1971-1975) stresses the need to improve working conditions, to increase living standards, and to protect the environment. The average work week has been reduced 1½ hours. Investments are being made in job training programs and the objective is to double the number of students in post-school job training programs between 1970-1975. The number of students in higher education is to rise from 647,000 in 1971 to between 750,000 and 800,000 in 1976. Consumption per capita is to increase 4.5 percent per year. The number of new housing units called for is 510,000, and 250,000 renovated units are projected—a 20 percent increase over the Fifth Plan. Social Security benefits are to be substantially increased.[6] At this time it appears that more emphasis will be placed on the consumer, but it is too early to tell if the stated plan objectives signify a true reordering of priorities, particularly if the government is faced with new inflationary pressures.

Plan Implementation and Government Intervention in the Economy

The first thing one must be aware of in a discussion of plan implementation is the lack of formal coordination among a variety of government agencies actively engaged in work which directly affects the economy. The Planning Commission is only one agency with economic power, and we shall see that it has surprisingly few tools under its direct control. France has traditionally had a powerful state bureaucracy comprised of many agencies often pursuing conflicting objectives while attempting to maintain or increase their spheres of influence. Among the more important agencies in determining economic policy are the staff and agencies attached to the offices of the President and Prime Minister. These include the personal staff of the Prime Minister, the permanent staff or secretariat of the Prime Minister, and service agencies such as the General Organization for Technical and Social Research and the National Planning Commission.

Perhaps the most important economic policy-maker is the Ministry of Economic Affairs and Finance, which controls a variety of tools for influencing economic behavior. The Ministry is divided into five functional units: the Department of the Budget, which resolves disputes with other government departments over budget allocations and studies and analyzes budget requests; the Treasury, which is responsible for monetary and financial policies, exercising control over the credit system; the Economic and Social Development Fund, which examines public and private investment programs; the Office of Price Controls; and the Forecasting Department, added in 1968.

In short, much governmental activity is carried on in widely dispersed government agencies for the express purpose of influencing economic activity. It is not clear, however, how much of this action is consistent with or in conflict with the objectives of the plan. To a large extent this depends upon the relationships established between the Planning Commissioner and the other agencies and the commitment of the government to the achievement of plan objectives. Certainly these various agencies are aware of the plan, but whether they regard

[6]Ambassade de France, Service de Presse et d' Information, *The Options of the Sixth Plan,* (June 18, 1970); and *Domestic Policy* (April 20, 1971).

activity designed to implement it as having a high priority is an open question. Before passing judgment on the success of plan implementation, let us look at the variety of techniques available for implementation purposes.

The Operation of the State Sector and the Nationalized Industries

Due to the large percentage of the gross national product channeled through the state budget, the government can exercise considerable direct influence on the economy. The state is a significant employer and buyer and seller of resources as well as final products. It can use its purchasing power to stimulate expansion in priority areas, to encourage the introduction of new techniques and products, and to promote the rationalization of various industries.

The operation of and investment in the nationalized industries can also be used to achieve plan objectives. Each nationalized industry is managed by a public board composed of representatives of labor, management, and consumers. Each industry falls under the jurisdiction of the appropriate ministry. The planners influence the behavior of nationalized industries primarily through their control of finances. The Economic and Social Development Fund controls state-supplied investment funds and requires the nationalized industries to prepare operating plans. If the industries have surplus funds, however, they can avoid the controls.

Some of the nationalized industries have been extremely aggressive and eager to modernize and expand their markets. The state railroad system has been a leader in the development of econometric techniques for use in pricing, traffic, and inventory decisions. The electricity industry has used a sophisticated concept of marginal cost pricing for its pricing and production policies. Although many state-owned enterprises have been progressive, they have not always operated in accordance with the plan. Renault, in a successful attempt to capture export markets, developed its production facilities far in excess of plan. The coal-mining industry is being phased out at a slower rate than that envisaged by the planners due to the political problems caused by worker unrest in coal producing areas. There is a general consensus that nationalized firms have, in fact, escaped many of the controls of government agencies, often acting more independently than large private firms.

Monetary and Credit Controls

The most important influence the state has had over business activity is the control of major sources of credit. The traditionally weak private capital market in France has forced the government to finance a large part of public and private investment. The government has been able to perform this task as a result of its control over the banking industry and the most important specialized financial institutions and insurance companies. In a tight capital market, such as prevailed in the years after World War II, access to credit at favorable rates had a powerful influence on private investment decisions.

The government exercises its control through a number of institutions. The major savings bank (*Caisse des Depots*) is state-owned and holds all funds accumulated in local savings banks, pension funds of nationalized industries, and unspent tax revenues. It transforms short-term funds into medium-term credit for industry. The *Credit Nationale* is a semi-public bank which supervises the granting of medium-term credit and can guarantee private banks loans up to five years. The *Credit Nationale* also has the power to discount commercial bank paper, and, thus, private banks have an incentive to check with it before making loans. The Economic and Social Development Fund can grant long-term loans at reduced interest rates and subsidize part of the interest charges on bonds issued by public enterprises and large private firms or groups of firms.

Although borrowing is controlled by agencies of the government it is not under the direct control of the Planning Commission. The power of the Commission depends upon its advisory role to the major credit institutions. While short- and medium-term loans are made primarily by private commercial banks and are free from government control, long-term loans have been channeled through public institutions which pass loan applications on to the Planning Commission for scrutiny before they are approved.

The government also has had a significant influence over external capital generated by the sale of securities on the private market. From the end of 1946 to 1959 the Minister of Finance could control the issue of shares of fixed interest securities. It also controlled the amount, timing, rate, and conditions pertaining to each new issue of bonds and stocks sold publicly.

The gradual loosening up of the capital market has weakened government control over credit sources. By 1952 approximately 45 percent of private investment was self-financed, and this percentage has continued to grow. Firms that wish to expand by more than the amount perceived compatible with planned investment in that sector can often circumvent the government and finance internally.

Tax Policies

France collects nearly 40 percent of national income in taxes. Direct taxes account for a smaller percentage and indirect taxes for a larger percentage than in most Western developed countries. In 1963 indirect taxes accounted for 80 percent of total taxes.[7] Tax relief has been an important tool used by government to promote desired business behavior. Subsidies in the form of lower taxes and accelerated depreciation allowances have been used to discriminate in favor of certain types of investment, export- and import-competing industries, industrial regroupings, and certain sites for new plants.

A variety of tax laws have been enacted since the introduction of planning. A special relief-on-profits tax amounting to ten percent of the value of new capital purchases was granted to encourage capital-intensive investment. A reduction in taxes on transfers of lands and buildings was allowed to promote the reorganization of firms.[8]

A study for the years 1963-1964 indicates that the use of special tax privileges was widespread. An average of one hundred firms benefited in each year from partial tax relief on dividends on new shares, an additional one hundred from relief of taxes on changes in legal form, and between five hundred and one thousand from aids such as loans and grants and relief from property taxes.[9] What is not clear from this study is the rationale for granting this aid, which was not bestowed at the prerogative of the Planning Commission. In the following section on the effectiveness of planning we shall examine this question.

Price and Wage Controls
and the Development of an Incomes Policy

Inflation has been a continuing problem in France threatening the expansion programs of the Planning Commission and causing periodic balance of payments crises. There have been periodic freezes on prices and wages since 1950, but as table 6.1 indicates, they have not been very successful in preventing inflation. Credit has been extended to finance investment despite the continuing pressure on available resources, particularly on labor. Price and wage freezes were an unsuccessful attempt to prevent the economy from feeling the consequences of expansionary fiscal and monetary policies. Beginning in the 1960s, however, less emphasis has been placed on direct controls and more emphasis is being placed on controlling aggregate demand by the use of appropriate monetary and fiscal policies. Except for 1962 and 1963 prices were reasonably stable from 1960 through 1967, but inflation has been more rapid since 1968.

Price controls reappeared in the Fifth Plan in the form of an incomes policy. The plan specified its targets in value terms as well as physical terms, indicating a concern for balance between aggregate demand and supply. Rates of

[7]Cited in John H. McArthur and Bruce R. Scott, *Industrial Planning in France,* Division of Research, Graduate School of Business Administration, Harvard University (Boston: 1969), p. 285.

[8]Vera Lutz, *Central Planning,* pp. 41-44.

[9]*Ibid.,* p. 48.

Table 6.1
The Consumer Price Index
Annual Percentage Change, 1951-1971*

	Annual % Change		Annual % Change
1951	16.92	1961	3.29
1952	11.82	1962	4.84
1953	−1.19	1963	4.82
1954	−0.30	1964	3.40
1955	1.10	1965	2.51
1956	1.95	1966	2.74
1957	2.06	1967	2.66
1958	15.75	1968	4.56
1959	6.12	1969	6.42
1960	3.65	1970	5.23
		1971	5.40

Source: Organization for European Cooperation and Development (OECD), Main Economic Indicators, 1950-60, 1957-66, 1967-71.

growth for different categories of income and expenditures compatible with a 1½ to 2 percent overall rate of inflation were calculated. Permissible increases in wages and income were calculated:[10]

2.87% per capita for wages with no upgrading of skills

3.3% per capita for wages with upgrading of skills

3.3% for gross incomes of individual nonfarm entrepreneurs

4.8% for farm incomes

Machinery for the implementation of the incomes policy has not been established, and labor has lent little support to the program. The government has relied on more traditional deflationary fiscal and monetary policies to control inflation.

The government did introduce in the Fifth and Sixth plans a regime of program contracts designed to supervise price increases. In 1965 and 1966 two types of "quasi-contracts" were initiated. These involved, first, agreements between government and private firms allowing firms to raise prices on some items in return for holding prices on others; and second, allowing firms to set prices if they agreed to discuss their investment, production, import, and export plans with the government, and accept earnings guidelines. This appears to be

[10]Ambassade de France, Service de Presse et d' Information, *The Fifth Plan* (April 1967), p. 8.

the first attempt made to link price controls to the achievement of plan objectives. The contract amounts to the use of an incomes policy with respect to business earnings.

The government introduced some novel wage agreements in the Sixth Plan for the nationalized industries, designed to prevent workers from getting additional wage increases in anticipation of inflation. Railway workers were granted a 6 percent wage increase in 1971 plus a cost of living increase if consumer prices rose by more than 4 percent in 1971. Wage increases in the electric utility industry were linked to increases in the growth of nominal GNP and productivity.

The Effectiveness of Plan Implementation and the Contribution of Planning to the French Economy

The French have a plan, and the French government has powerful tools at its disposal to influence economic behavior. This does not imply, however, that the tools are always, or even usually, used to foster plan objectives. In this section we will examine the relationship between targets and achievements and present some explanations of the divergence between the two.[11]

Beginning with the Second Plan, which was the first attempt at comprehensive planning for the entire economy, there is certainly a lack of precision in meeting plan targets. The target for gross domestic output was exceeded, industrial output growing much faster than forecast while agricultural output grew more slowly. Although targets and realized output may correspond in the aggregate, there is little relationship between targeted and realized levels of production within any particular sector. A similar pattern develops for the Third Plan, which was officially dropped in 1960 and an interim plan substituted due to inflationary pressures. In fact, even though the goals of the interim plan were significantly lower than the original, the original aggregate targets were nearly achieved due to the continued high rate of investment. Again, although the aggregate targets were almost reached, there is a great discrepancy between prediction and achievement by sector.

Although the Fourth Plan was not officially abandoned, its targets too were threatened by inflation and a stabilization plan implemented in 1963. The aggregate targets of the Fourth Plan indeed were met, but the plan predicted poorly when more detailed targets are considered. The rate of foreign trade turnover and the supply of labor were particularly poorly forecast. The Fifth

[11]The analysis of the divergence between targets and realized outputs is drawn from the study of Vera Lutz, *Central Planning*, pp. 67-107.

Plan attached less importance to detailed sectoral targets and gave more emphasis to the calculation and projection of aggregates and the means of achieving them.

Our brief survey of plan achievements indicates only partial success, particularly at the sectoral and industry level. We will now consider the reasons for this phenomenon.[12] The government influences four levels of the economy—the economy as a whole, all industry, individual industries or branches, and individual companies or projects—in an attempt to achieve plan objectives. It can influence these levels by actions which directly influence resource allocation by giving rewards and penalties for desired and undesired behavior, by changing the rules of the game, and by altering the underlying structure of any level. To effectively implement the plan, the government must have a strategy linking its actions with its objectives. Are corporate decisions influenced or altered by government activity, and is this activity consistent with the plan? The answer to the first question is an unqualified yes, but the answer to the second is extremely uncertain. Much of the explanation for this phenomenon is the widespread role of a multitude of government agencies in the French economy, combined with imprecise sectoral targets, and the lack of any guidelines to determine whether particular types of behavior are or are not compatible with the plan. It appears to be very difficult to translate plan objectives in precise enough terms to judge the appropriateness of individual firms' requests for loans or tax subsidies and privileges. The complexity of planning increases as the priorities become less clear, making it more difficult to distinguish between desirable and undesirable behavior. Furthermore, it becomes more difficult to prevent undesirable behavior as firms grow independent of government and can rely on internal financing for investment.

An overriding objective of French planning has been the achievement of "balance." New investment has been deemed consistent with plan objectives if it added to capacity in a critical bottleneck area. As the economy has become more complex, however, bottlenecks are more difficult to identify, and no one segment of the economy has a clear priority. Further, as France has developed a satisfactory balance of payments position, it has been found that shortages can be met by importing, which at times may be the most economical source of a particular commodity in short supply.

It can be argued then that once France had accomplished the reconstruction outlined in the first plans, setting detailed targets in physical terms was no longer a useful exercise because of the lack of any relevant criteria to guide resource allocation decisions. This point is summarized in the following quote from the study by McArthur and Scott.

> Far from aiming for near self-sufficiency via coherence among sectors, the new problem was to aim for selective employment of resources in the industries and products where investment had the highest potential return.

[12] The following analysis is drawn from the work of John McArthur and Bruce Scott, *Industrial Planning.*

Selectivity rather than coherence had become the basic problem at the industry, branch and company levels.[13]

Faced with the need for a comparative analysis of strengths and weaknesses, and particularly with a need for estimates of revenues, costs, and profits, industrial planners—whether employed by the state, an industry association, or a company—found that no such analysis had been developed within the national planning process.[14]

A related problem of plan implementation concerns the cooperative effort involved in the planning process. French planners have argued that they engage in concensus planning. All segments of the economy—management, labor, government—participate in plan construction, and differences or conflicts are settled by compromise. This approach may be satisfactory when there are no sharp differences of opinion and all can agree upon broad planning objectives which allow for the expansion of all. For planning to be effective after the initial reconstruction phase, however, certain interests will have to be promoted at the expense of others, and the planners have no effective means of dealing with the conflicts that inevitably arise. For example, one objective of the Fourth and Fifth plans was a restructuring of French industry. Assuming this to be a desirable objective, the government had to use its power to promote mergers. This action implied that the power of some would be enhanced while that of others would be diminished. Since the Planning Commission did not have the means to resolve these kinds of conflicts, it lost some of its influence on business behavior.

One alarming finding of the McArthur and Scott study was the lack of interest in planning and the ritualistic nature of the private firm's role in plan formulation.[15] Businessmen regarded the later plans as working documents designed for political purposes rather than as blueprints for their future decisions. They were not concerned with the possibility of government action if their behavior was inconsistent with the plan. Evidence of their disinterest was the practice of sending lower-level management to the Modernization Commission meetings as spokesmen for the firm. There is even evidence that meetings of the Modernization Commissions were used as opportunities for business executives to get together to divide up the market for their product and avoid competition.[16]

Other Governmental Programs to Aid the Economy

Planning has not been the only economic activity engaged in by the French government. Two additional activities which merit attention are social welfare measures and regional development. We will briefly discuss each in turn.

[13]John H. McArthur and Bruce R. Scott, *Industrial Planning*, p. 494.

[14]*Ibid*, p. 497.

[15]*Ibid.*, p. 428.

[16]*Ibid.*, p. 429.

Social Welfare

After World War II the French government adopted and implemented a series of social welfare programs considered at the time to be among the most progressive in Western Europe. The government's stated intention was to develop a series of programs to protect the population from catastrophic losses due to illness, unemployment, and disability. The government was also concerned with aiding those whose incomes placed them at the bottom of the socioeconomic ladder.

Family allowances were instituted, and direct payments were made to families in accordance with the number of children. These payments formed a significant part of the income of poorer families in the 1950s but have declined steadily since then. Income splitting is allowed not only for husband and wife but is extended to include children, with each child counting as one-half.

An extensive health insurance program was established which covers over 85 percent of the population. The individual is reimbursed for his expenditures up to 100 percent for hospital bills, 75 percent for doctor's bills, and 70 percent for drugs. Four out of five doctors have joined the program, and their fees are determined by negotiations between regional medical groups and health insurance officials. Like most medical programs in Western Europe, costs are rising rapidly. The government, concerned with controlling the rise, is attempting to reduce the proportion of medical bills covered by the program but is meeting resistance from the population.

In addition to family allowances and health insurance, the government administers a social security program providing for old age pensions, disability, and sick pay. These programs are financed by a payroll tax which has tended to increase labor costs, resulting in increased prices paid by the consumer. Almost 25 percent of GNP is transferred from one segment of the population to another through these programs. The transfer does not represent, however, an income transfer from the rich to the poor, since programs are not financed by progressive taxes.

Regional Planning

Two major regional or structural problems have hindered French economic development—the large number of small, inefficient farms and the increasing industrial density of the Paris region. Small farmers have long been protected by tariffs and price support programs which have prevented their migration to urban areas where there are more productive jobs. The government has stated many times that it wants to rationalize agriculture by reducing the number of farmers and increasing the size of their holdings. It has met with stiff resistance on the part of the farmers, and by and large has retained its program of price supports and export subsidies. The development of the Common Market, with its high protective tariffs to the outside world, has allowed inefficient French agriculture to find a market for its products within the Common Market countries. The government stated in the Fifth Plan that the percentage of the population engaged in agriculture will be reduced from 20 percent to 10 percent by 1980.

The government is attempting to cope with the regional difficulties in industrial development by making it more costly for firms to locate in the Paris area and subsidizing development in selected areas of potential growth. Regional plans were developed along with the Fifth National Plan. Ten regions were selected to receive 35 to 40 percent of the new industrial jobs created by 1970. It was decided to concentrate growth in a few areas rather than disperse investment funds throughout France. Firms locating in selected zones qualify for government subsidies covering up to 20 percent of total capital costs.

Summary and Conclusions

The recent history of the French economy is a continuation of the prominent role of the government in economic activity within the framework of a market system. The government has pursued policies with both a macro and microeconomic impact. It has lowered tariffs, reformed the tax structure, and engaged in periodic price and wage freezes in order to create a climate which is favorable to stable growth. It has also selectively intervened in the economy to influence micro decisions by offering easier access to credit, faster depreciation allowances, and tax subsidies in order to promote a variety of objectives, including investment, the development and application of new technology, and a restructuring of industry.

Upon casual observation, it appears that this activity has been a part of and guided by a comprehensive, detailed national plan. Upon closer examination, however, it is not clear that this has been the case. Major macroeconomic decisions such as entry into the Common Market and the stabilization plan of 1963 were made with little reference to the plan. The day-to-day operations of the government in its relation with the public and the private sector are widely dispersed among a variety of state agencies. Aids and subsidies to French industry, though plentiful, at many times do not seem to be coordinated with each other or with the plan itself.

French planners appear to have realized this problem, and perhaps this accounts for the changes in the scope and strategy of the Fifth Plan. In the early phases of French planning, when priorities were clearer, there was a consensus on appropriate policy, and private enterprise was dependent upon the state for credit. Under these circumstances planning in physical terms to achieve balance or coherence was appropriate. The employment of the same techniques to promote growth after recovery was less useful, and, indeed may even have been counterproductive as businessmen realized that the Planning Commission's influence had weakened. Due to French entry into the Common Market, the reliability of quantitative output projections for specific products was reduced. The Plan had to become more flexible with less importance attached to detailed branch targets, which were now labeled projections. More emphasis was placed on forecasting broad economic aggregates and achieving financial balance.

While many governments are studying the contribution of indicative planning in a market context, and examining the role of planning in France in particular, the nature of that contribution seems to be changing. Planning can be viewed as a political process, in which a variety of economic alternatives and their consequences and implications are spelled out for the government as well as the public.[17] An indicative plan is an excellent instrument for studying the implications of a contemplated shift in resources. It is not as effective an instrument for the detailed regulation of the economy.

It follows from this view that the usefulness of indicative planning depends upon democratic participation in evaluating and selecting from among the broad alternatives presented, particularly in regard to government budget decisions. Planning in France has been the province of the government and big business. Neither the trade unions nor Parliament have had an effective role in selecting from alternatives the growth path incorporated in the plan. Futhermore, once the plan was formally adopted, the government was often not committed to its implementation, and major changes in strategy were initiated by the government and reflected in budget policy without consultation with the Planning Commission. Although satisfactory growth rates have been maintained, there is a great deal of dissatisfaction in France regarding priorities or the composition of output. Housing, education, and social services have been neglected. A greater degree of democratization in the formulation of government economic policy might have resulted in a different set of priorities.

QUESTIONS

1. Why is France classified as a mixed economy?
2. Compare and contrast the nature of governmental participation in the prewar and postwar French economy.
3. How is the French national plan constructed?
4. What techniques does the government have available for the implementation of the plan?

[17]See Stephen Cohen, *Modern Capitalist Planning,* pp. 155-163, for an exposition of this view.

5. Why has the achievement of plan goals been continually threatened by inflation?

6. Why have the French placed more emphasis on macro planning rather than micro planning in recent years?

7. From your study of the French economy do you think indicative planning has been a useful exercise?

7

The West German Economy

Introduction

West Germany is often characterized as a capitalist economic system in contrast to the mixed systems of Britain and France. As is usually the case with generalizations, this one has a grain of truth but unfortunately conceals more about the structure and functioning of the German economy than it reveals. According to the classification scheme developed earlier in the text, Germany is also a mixed economy. First, although private property is predominant, the German government owns and runs a wide variety of enterprises including the railroads, the telegraph and telephone, and radio and television broadcasting. Ninety percent of all producers of electricity and 70 percent of the aluminum industry are state-owned. Volkswagen was totally government owned prior to 1960 and partially government-owned after 1960. The government holds up to 70 percent of the stock of the mining, steel, nonferrous metals, shipbuilding, oil refining, chemicals, and movie production industries.[1] In addition the government—

[1]Hans-Joachim Arndt, *West Germany, Politics of Non-Planning* (Syracuse: Syracuse University Press, 1966), pp. 92-93.

federal, state, and local—has a major interest in the banking industry. The state share in the credit business increased from 49 percent in 1950 to 55 percent in 1960.[2]

Turning to our second criterion, that involving the locus of decision-making power, Germany is again classified as a mixed economy. Although the great majority of economic decisions are made by individual consumers and firms, collective decision-making has a significant impact on the structure and direction of the economy. In addition to the influence of the state-owned sector, the government influences the economy through the operation of a large budget. In 1965 over 36 percent of GNP was collected in taxes by all levels of government, and the government's share of goods and services equalled 20 percent of GNP.[3] Between 1950 and 1964 the government, including the publically owned enterprises, accounted for over 30 percent of net capital formation.[4] The government also influences the allocation of resources through its housing, agricultural, and regional development programs, as well as through the operation of an extensive social security system.

Finally, the market mechanism is used to carry out most economic decisions, public as well as private. Although the state sector is large, most state-owned enterprises act independently and are concerned with their profitability. Government influence on the economy, although widespread, does not take the form of commands; instead, we shall see that the government indirectly influences the decisions of individual firms by altering the costs and benefits of certain private decisions.

The recovery of the German economy after World War II is often called a miracle. Between 1948 and 1964, industrial production increased nearly six times while real gross national product increased over threefold between 1950 and 1964. The growth rate of GNP averaged 9.93 percent from 1950-55, 5.3 percent from 1955-1962, and 3.2 percent from 1962-1967.[5] Unemployment was fairly high in the early stages of recovery, reaching 9.5 percent in 1951, but it was extremely low in the late 50s and early 60s, falling to .4 percent in 1965.[6]

German recovery has been labeled a miracle primarily due to the magnitude of the problems facing the economy immediately after the war. Due to the division of Germany into East and West, West Germany was separated from its former food-supplying areas at the same time that it was receiving large influxes

[2]*Ibid.*

[3]Bent Hansen, "Fiscal Policy in Seven Countries, 1955-1965," *Organization for Economic Cooperation and Development* (March 1969), pp. 209-210.

[4]Malcolm MacLennan, Murray Forsyth, and Geoffrey Denton, *Economic Planning and Policies in Britain, France and Germany* (New York: Frederic A. Praeger, 1968), p. 223.

[5]See chapter nine for a more detailed discussion of German growth rates.

[6]Gustov Stolper, et. al., *The German Economy 1870 to the Present* (New York: Harcourt, Brace and World, Inc., 1967), pp. 220-221.

of refugees needing food, shelter, and employment. Much of the capital stock had been damaged or destroyed by the war, and the transportation network was in need of vast repairs. Raw materials as well as finished goods were in short supply, and the economy was subject to a vast network of controls over prices, production, and imports.[7] Due to the rapid production of the German mark, inflation was a severe problem and the beginning of recovery was marked by a currency reform in which 100 old marks were exchangeable for 6.5 new marks. The reform and the much slower rate of increase of the new currency allowed controls gradually to be lifted and the market mechanism to begin functioning.

Many reasons can be cited to explain the post-war German growth rates. Although much of the capital stock needed to be replaced or repaired, the basic economic structure survived the war. Germany was not an underdeveloped economy seeking to construct an industrial sector, modernize agriculture, and educate a labor force. It possessed large quantities of skilled labor, including the refugees, and was able to replace the capital stock with new plant and equipment embodying the latest technology. Heavy taxes allowed the government to channel resources into investment. Expanding world markets provided an outlet for German production even though the domestic market was depressed.

After the war the Germany economy was a peculiar mixture of centralized and decentralized economic institutions. It was the official policy of the government to decentralize economic power, and large industrial firms and the banks were broken up. Despite these attempts Germany remained highly centralized. Industry was organized along hierarchical lines in industrial associations. The associations, headed by the Federation of German Industry, was closely connected with the government and performed some of the tasks of the modernization commissions in France.[8] Although industry and banking were quite centralized, there was a widespread belief in the role of the competitive market in Germany and a distrust of planning. Planning was identified with the period of hyperinflation following World War I and the Nazi period of the 1930s and 1940s. The rapid economic progress following the war was identified with liberalization of the economy and the increasing role of competitive market institutions.

German Economic Policy and the Philosophy of Neoliberalism

The view of neoliberal economists strongly influenced government policy-makers, particularly Ludwig Erhard, and became the cornerstone of future economic policy. Neoliberalism, as expounded by the German economist Walter Eucken, was thought to be a better solution to the problems of the second half of the twentieth century than either the laissez-faire philosophy of the pre-World

[7] Malcolm MacLennan, et. al., *Economic Planning,* pp. 50-51.

[8] Andrew Shonfield, *Modern Capitalism* (London: Oxford University Press, 1969) p. 245.

War I era, the total planning experiments of the Soviet bloc, or the partial planning adopted by some countries of Western Europe. Neoliberalism was based on the belief in the efficiency of a price system, combined with competition and monetary stability. The government had a significant but different role to play from that in most planned or semi-planned states. Competition did not have to be of the perfect variety discussed in chapter three but "workable" in the sense that all firms were striving to improve their performance. Neoliberalism differed from laissez-faire capitalism in the recognition of the need for government intervention in the economy. The primary responsibility of government was to promote competitive market forces by removing trade barriers and state controls and by dissolving economic power groups. The government was also responsible for the conduct of monetary policy to insure price stability. This philosophy was compatible with a wide range of government activities including income redistribution, social welfare measures, and pollution control.

The test of the appropriateness of government action was its effect on the price mechanism and the establishment of market equilibrium. Intervention was permissible if it hastened the movement toward a new equilibrium position necessitated by changes in technology or demand conditions. Countercyclical policy was compatible with the neoliberalist philosophy but would not ordinarily be needed. It was believed that in a competitive market economy monetary policy would be the most appropriate and neutral tool to promote stability. In contrast to France, Germany has chosen to follow the policy of neoliberalism rather than indicative planning to promote growth and stability. Many of the actual policies adopted by the German government, however, are similar to those used in France. In the following section we will examine the implementation and impact of neoliberal policies on the German economy.

The Implementation of Neoliberal Policies

The Germans have pursued three basic types of policies in an attempt to reduce economic concentration and promote competition: anti-monopoly policies, policies to encourage small and medium-size firms, and policies designed to redistribute wealth and encourage savings and the ownership of capital among as broad a spectrum of the population as possible. After several years of debate an anti-monopoly law, the Law Against Restraints of Competition, was passed in 1957 and amended in 1965. The law prohibits horizontal and vertical agreements in restraint of trade and can be viewed as a significant attempt by the government to curtail monopoly behavior. The effectiveness of the law is limited, however, by a number of exemptions, both of industries and practices. It was understood at the time of passage that the law did not apply to organized labor, banking, insurance, or the railroads. Further, many types of agreements covering areas such as rebates, uniform standards, exports and imports, as well as agreements necessitated by major structural changes, were exempt from the law.[9] Resale price maintenance agreements were also exempted from the law. The law provided the government with practically no control over mergers, which, if involving companies over a certain size, must merely be registered with the General Office.

In contrast to the purpose of the Law Against Restraints, several laws have been passed which act to prevent competition among German firms. Among these are the Shop Closing Act, establishing compulsory hours for all stores and shops, and the Artisan Charter passed in 1953 and revised in 1957, requiring proof of competence, expertness, and reliability for the issuance of craft licenses. Considering the diverse measures the government has taken affecting competitive behavior, it is not at all clear that there has been the significant reduction of economic power and concentration intended by the implementation of anti-monopoly policies. However, it has been the belief of many advocates of the competitive market system that Germany's entry into the Common Market and the exposure of German industry to international competition provides a substitute for the passage and enforcement of stronger anti-monopoly laws.

A second method in use to promote competition has been the official encouragement of small and middle-size firms, with an eye to enabling them to compete effectively with larger firms. The Middle Estate Policy, adopted in 1957, was designed to encourage small and middle-size firms through such measures as subsidization of their research and development, provision of vocational training, aid in the establishment of new firms, and preferential placement of government contracts.

A third set of German policies was designed to spread wealth and the ownership of capital. Denationalization was used for this purpose. The shares of the Prussian Mining and Smelting Company, Volkswagen, and the United Electricity and Mining Company were sold at a special discount to individuals earning less than a certain income with the provision that they be held by that individual for a stated period of time. The Savings Premium Act of 1959 paid a premium on private savings invested in a wide variety of assets, including savings and loans, for five years or more. The 1959 Small Company Reform Law aided managers of private companies in acquiring their company's stock shares in order to sell them at a favorable price to company employees. The 1961 Law for the Promotion of Capital Formation by Employed Persons provided that appropriate investments of up to 312 marks a year be tax exempt.[10] These laws can be considered an attempt to encourage the holding of wealth among lower and middle income families as well as an inducement to save and invest, thereby increasing the growth of the economy.

[9]Malcolm MacLennan, *Economic Planning*, p. 59.

[10]*Ibid.*, p. 67.

Monetary and Credit Policies

Since 1957 the *Bundesbank* has been the central bank, and its managing board has been nominated by the government for eight-year terms. The bank has the power to regulate the money supply through the use of discount policy, minimum reserve requirements, and open market operations. In addition, the federal and state governments must deposit their liquid funds at the *Bundesbank* unless they have the bank's permission to do otherwise. The primary aim of the *Bundesbank* has been to promote price stability even at the cost of considerable amounts of unemployment in the early years of reconstruction. Fortunately a growing world market for German products allowed German industry to expand despite the curtailment of domestic demand by tight monetary policies. Germany's favorable trade position resulted in a tremendous growth of monetary reserves due to the influx of foreign exchange earnings and short-term foreign capital. These reserves had to be neutralized to prevent domestic inflation.

In addition to controlling inflation, the German government was interested in promoting a high level of investment and influencing to a certain extent the direction of that investment. Laws were passed to encourage savings. The laws discussed in the previous section were concerned with encouraging savings in general, as well as spreading ownership. The Law of Encouragement of the Capital Market of 1952 exempted all or part of interest income from taxation to promote capital formation. To encourage investment in what were considered to be bottleneck industries the government passed the Investment Aid Law in 1952. At this time, coal, steel, electric power, gas, and transportation were still subject to price controls and short of funds for needed expansion. The government collected one billion marks in the form of extraordinary contributions from industries thought to be benefitting from the artificially low prices, and these industries received bonds of the debtor industries. The funds were redistributed and aided the bottleneck industries to double their investment in two years.[11] Finally, the Reconstruction Loan Corporation was established by the government to supplement investment funds by channeling public funds through private commercial banks. Initially the agency attempted to channel investment into high pay-off, bottleneck areas, but from the middle of the 1950s on, devoted its attention to the financing of government-supported regional development schemes.[12]

The purpose of this discussion has been to illustrate the government's role in the German capital market. The government has certainly influenced both the

[11]Gustov Stolper, *The German Economy*, p. 257.

[12]Andrew Shonfield, *Modern Capitalism*, pp. 276-279.

level and direction of investment. During the earlier phases of post-war recon-struction the German government pursued policies similar to those pursued under the Monnet Plan in France. In the later stages of recovery, however, the private capital market was freed of the bulk of government restrictions, such as interest rate controls, and has functioned successfully. In the more recent period the government has been less concerned with using credit policies to influence the direction of private investment, although it is still concerned with main-taining the level. It must be kept in mind, however, that the government is a large investor itself, given the size of the public sector, and uses tax policies and subsidies as well as credit policies to influence investment decisions. We will see in a later section of this chapter how fiscal policies are used to influence firms' decisions, as we look at the government's role in the construction of housing.

Although the government may not have made extensive use of credit policies to influence the direction of investment in the private sector, there is a great deal of evidence to support the view that the private banking industry has a considerable amount of economic power which it uses to systematically influence private investment decisions. German banks exercise power over the non-banking industry outside of the normal channels of the provision of credit. First, banks own outright a significant share of the stock of private companies. A report issued in 1964 indicated that in 138 companies, the banks had a minority holding of 25 percent or more, capable of blocking decisions, while they had a majority holding in 55 others.[13] In addition, the banks are able to gain control of additional shares of stock through the use of proxies. Bank depositors may entrust their proxies to their bank for extended periods of time. The 1964 report states that a sample of 425 joint-stock companies indicated that approximately 70 percent of the capital was held by the banks.[14] Banks are also able to trade proxies among themselves, enabling a single bank to gain a majority of a company's shares even though the bank and its depositors combined hold less than 50 percent of the shares. Further, approximately 70 percent of all shareholders' proxies held by banks were held by the three largest banks in Germany.[15] In 1965 a law was passed forcing the banks to notify their share-holding depositors of the agenda of a company meeting and request voting instructions. Finally, bank representatives sit on the supervisory boards of companies, which meet four times a year. Although no individual sits on the board of more than one company in a given or closely related industry, employees of the same bank do so.

It is difficult to analyze precisely the effect of these interlocking rela-tionships. It has been suggested that the banks play a role similar to the French modernization commissions. They spread modern business practices, attempt to

[13]Malcolm MacLennan, *Economic Planning,* p. 68.

[14]*Ibid.,* p. 69.

[15]Andrew Shonfield, *Modern Capitalism,* p. 250.

avoid company investment decisions that would lead to surplus capacity, promote mergers and firm cooperation to achieve greater efficiency, and try to forecast market demand. An interesting illustration of inter-firm agreements involves the steel industry. In the early 1960s firms agreed to pool orders for specialized products and take turns in producing them, sharing production facilities but maintaining individual ties with their own customers.[16]

Tax Policies and Investment Incentives

The German government has continuously used tax privileges and subsidies to stimulate the overall level of savings and investment as well as to encourage investment in specific sectors of the economy. As we mentioned earlier, savings deposited with insurance companies, building societies, savings and loans, and commercial banks can be deducted from taxable incomes. Privileges have been granted to industry in the form of accelerated depreciation allowances and tax exemption of retained earnings in order to increase investment. In the 1950s the incentives were designed to aid selected industries such as export-producing firms, basic industries such as steel, coal, iron ore, electric power plants, housing and shipping.

Due to the confusing variety of taxes and exemptions together with high tax rates, tax reform was proposed in 1953 but not implemented until 1958, when the income tax progression was smoothed out and tax rates lowered, so that the top bracket is 53 percent. The corporate income tax is levied on net profits of companies, with distributed profits taxed at a rate of 15 percent and undistributed profits at 51 percent.[17] In 1968 the turnover tax was replaced by a value-added tax of 11 percent. Discriminatory tax policies are not as important now as they were formerly, but we shall see in the next section that tax policies are used to regulate the overall level of expenditures.

Stabilization Policy

Until the middle 1950s the German government was reluctant to use expenditures and revenues as stabilization tools and was reluctant to accept the Keynesian view that planned budget deficits are a legitimate policy for combating unemployment. Primarily due to their previous experience with inflation, the government was more concerned with building up monetary reserves than fighting unemployment. Thus until the mid 1950s, rather stringent

[16]*Ibid.*, p. 255.

[17]Bent Hansen, "Fiscal Policy," p. 217.

budgetary policies were pursued, and budget surpluses amassed in the face of rather high levels of unemployment. By the mid 1950s, however, these revenues were being used to finance government programs, and the change of leadership at the Central Bank in 1957 marked a move away from the traditional financial orthodoxy and towards the use of fiscal policy as a stabilization tool.

Although the Constitution stipulates that budget estimates of receipts and expenditures must balance, it does not in fact preclude the government from pursuing a countercyclical fiscal policy. The definition of receipts and expenditures is not given, and receipts have been interpreted to include loans as well as tax revenues, with the restriction that loans may be used to cover capital expenditures but not current expenditures. There have been periods of slack demand, however, during which loans have been used to cover current expenditures. The government, in fact, has considerable flexibility in planning and adjusting its revenues and expenditures for countercyclical purposes. With the consent of a simple majority of Parliament the government may order by decree that the personal income tax be raised or lowered within a 10 percent range. Adjustments in the corporate income tax automatically follow. The government, with the consent of Parliament, may also introduce a 7.5 percent investment subsidy in periods of inadequate demand and may reduce certain special depreciation allowances during inflationary periods. The government also has flexibility with regard to the level and timing of expenditures. If there is excess demand, the government may direct the Minister of Finance to make the disposal of certain appropriations, the start of construction works, and the undertaking of future obligations dependent upon his consent. In periods of slack demand, the government may increase expenditures above that specified in the yearly budget if the expenditure appears in the five-year budget. When expenditures are reduced, funds are to be deposited in an account in the State Bank, and when above-budget expenditures are planned, revenue is to be drawn from this account.[18]

The government attempted to reduce the inflation which developed in the late 1960s through the active use of restrictive monetary and fiscal policy. In 1970 the government temporarily blocked the expenditure of DM 2.5 billion, enacted a temporary 10 percent surcharge on corporate and personal income, and suspended the accelerated depreciation allowances on investment goods ordered between July 1970 and January 1971. These taxes were lowered again in 1971, although DM .8 billion of government expenditures remained blocked.

Labor and the Development of an Incomes Policy

Germany was able to reconstruct its economy after the war without many of the labor problems faced by Britain and France. In the early phases of

[18]*Ibid.,* pp. 223-224.

development, prior to 1955, there was a substantial amount of unemployment, and wages grew at a slower rate than productivity. Even after 1955, when unemployment disappeared and the pace of wage increases quickened, inflation was still not a serious problem. Germany also benefited from the fact that there were far fewer man-hours lost due to strikes and lockouts than in France or Britain. This phenomenon has been attributed by some to the weakness of the German labor union movement but has been attributed by others to the sensitivity of all Germans to the dangers of inflation. In the 1960s, however, labor conflicts grew more frequent in what was essentially an overfull-employment economy, and fear of a wage-price spiral grew.

The Council of Economic Experts recommended the use of wage guidelines based on productivity advances in 1964, 1965, and 1966, but these recommendations were largely ignored by government. In December 1966 the government endorsed the Council's recommendation and sponsored meetings between government, industry, and labor to discuss wage policies. Guidelines for acceptable wage increases have been established, and in 1971 average wages and earnings were to rise at a 7 to 8 percent annual rate, which was supposed to be compatible with a 3 percent increase in consumer prices. Lack of enforcement machinery, combined with high-demand pressure and extreme labor shortages (five vacant jobs for every person unemployed), have made the incomes policy fairly ineffective. Wage settlements have been negotiated at rates well above 8 percent and, in addition, profit-sharing, year-end bonuses, and increased vacation benefits have been used to circumvent the guidelines. Inflation has been considerably above the goal of 3 percent.

One unique aspect of German labor policy is co-determination. In 1951 an act was passed that gave labor 50 percent of the seats on the supervisory boards of the mining, iron, and steel industries. Labor members were also added to management boards. In 1952 the Act Concerning Industrial Constitution was passed, which stated that one-third of all the members of supervisory boards in all stock companies would be labor representatives. This extension strengthened labor's voice in management decisions. Labor is still a minority on the boards, however, and is influential primarily in management policies directly concerned with labor. It is believed that the policy of co-determination has been helpful in mitigating labors' wage demands and has contributed to price stability.

Budgetary Planning

The government collects more than 30 percent of the GNP in taxes and accounts for more than 30 percent of net capital formation. Thus the effect of government budgetary policies on the economy is very large. By the early 1960s there was much interest in budgetary planning and in forecasting national economic trends, although the government stated explicitly that it was not interested in comprehensive planning along French lines. In 1963 the Council of

Economic Experts, referred to in the previous section, was established to prepare an annual survey of current economic conditions and to forecast the economic situation in the following year. The task of the committee was to offer alternative choices based upon different economic assumptions about priorities and trends but not to make policy recommendations. The committee was also to indicate what it believed were dangerous trends in the economy which might endanger price stability, full employment, growth, or external equilibrium. Specific growth targets were not included in the forecast. The government was required to react to the report and submit the report and its reaction to the Bundestag (legislature) within eight weeks of its receipt.

The Social Democrats, a socialist party, replaced the Christian Democrats in 1966 but retained most of the economic policies and programs developed by the previous government. In fact, due to rising public expenditures, growing government deficits, and the threat of inflation the new government reduced spending and raised taxes in 1967. When the economy later showed signs of recession, special public investment programs and depreciation allowances were introduced. The Stabilization Law of June 1967 enhanced the role of the Council of Economic Experts and the concept of budgetary planning. The annual federal budget is now drawn up within the framework of a moving five-year financial plan prepared by the Ministry of Finance and designed to forecast expenditures and revenues over a five-year period. The law requires the federal government to submit an annual report to the Bundestag containing its reaction to the report of the Council of Economic Experts as well as a description of its economic goals in quantitative terms and its policies for the current year. Every two years the government must account for all of the subsidies it grants. Finally, the Council of Economic Experts, in addition to its annual report, is to issue additional reports whenever the goals of the government are in danger. Thus, a structure and a set of institutions have been established for limited planning purposes. These purposes, however, are quite different from those of French planning in that detailed sectoral targets are not the government's concern. Rather, the reports and forecasts are designed to provide greater coordination of budgetary policies so that the budget will be a more useful countercyclical weapon. It is argued that the new procedures are consistent with the German neoliberal philosophy and are legitimate techniques within the context of a mixed economy. The government is concerned not with determining the direction of the private sector but with projections of overall economic patterns, forecasting the effect of specific economic policy measures, and planning the government-operated sectors of the economy.[19]

Social Welfare

Germany has traditionally had an advanced social welfare program, being one of the first nations to introduce a form of social security in the nineteenth-

---

[19]Hans-Joachim Arndt, *West Germany*, p. 119.

century. After the war the government rebuilt the social security system and then continued to extend its coverage and add benefits. The social security program includes old age, disability and survivors' insurance, health and maternity insurance, unemployment insurance, workmen's compensation, and child allowances. The program is financed by payroll taxes shared equally by employers and employees. Contributions run approximately 10 percent of wages and salaries for health and maternity; 14 percent for disability, old age, and survivors; and 1.3 percent for unemployment insurance. Thus, total contributions average 25 percent of total wages and salaries, although there are ceilings on the absolute amount paid.[20] After 1957 retirement benefits were automatically linked to earnings at the time of retirement and periodically revised upward according to a formula measuring wage and productivity advances.

In addition to direct social welfare measures, the government's housing policy has promoted the construction of low-and middle-income housing, which was in chronic shortage in most European nations after the war. The German housing policies are often portrayed by the government as an example of government activity designed to foster market equilibrium rather than promote permanent disequilibrium in the form of housing shortages as has been the case in many other countries. The government faced two difficult housing problems after the war, the need to control rents, which would have been extremely high due to the acute shortage of housing, and the need to increase the long-run supply of housing. Rent control policies alone often result in prolonging a housing shortage, for they remove the incentives for private industry to expand the supply of housing. The government passed the first Housing Act in 1950. The Act provided for: (1) publicly-built housing with subsidized rents, (2) private housing construction aided by tax privileges, and (3) unaided privately financed housing. In the first category the government determined rents and limited occupancy to low-income groups. The government retained some control over the rents in the second class of housing, and none in the third. A total of one-third of capital invested in housing up to 1961 came from public sources.[21] The result was a significant increase in available housing. Between 1949 and 1964 approximately eight million units were added. Per capita, more units were built in West Germany than in any other Western country.[22] The particular policies adopted by Germany induced private enterprise to participate in construction while providing some protection for low-income families. They also allowed the government to gradually withdraw controls from the housing market as the shortage was eliminated.

Agricultural Subsidies and Regional Development

Germany faced the problem of economic disequilibrium in the agricultural sector after the Korean War, when agricultural prices fell and there was a surplus

[20]Bent Hansen, "Fiscal Policy," p. 219.

[21]Gustov Stolper, *The German Economy,* p. 281.

[22]*Ibid.*

of agricultural output. Again, the government's problem was twofold: one, to support sagging farm incomes; and two, to eliminate the surplus by reorganizing agriculture to reduce the number of small inefficient farms and consolidate the land into larger, more technically advanced production units. The Green Plan, started in 1955, resulted in the expenditure of several million marks devoted to subsidizing fertilizer production, consolidation of land, and resettlement. Low interest loans were made available to farmers, and their income was virtually tax-free. The plan resulted in a considerable increase in productivity due to consolidation and mechanization and a significant reduction of the number of people engaged in agriculture. Although agricultural incomes have risen, the government has been less successful in extricating itself from the agricultural sector. Subsidies and price support programs have continued and are regarded now by critics as permanent income subsidies to a powerful special interest group rather than attempts to correct market disequilibrium.

Although the formal responsibility for the administration of local regions is in the hands of the state governments, the federal government entered into the area of promoting regional development with the Regional Development Program of 1961. The aim of the government has been to equalize the income of the more backward regions with that of the more advanced. It has done this by establishing development areas and towns. Existing firms expanding there or new firms entering into these areas are eligible for low cost, long-term loans. Due to the development of new industry, the income of backward areas has been growing more rapidly than the national average.

Conclusion

Germany has developed a unique set of economic institutions within the framework of a market system. Less reliance has been placed on direct controls than in France, and less enthusiasm has been displayed for the benefits of planning than in either France or Britain. Although the German government has been an active participant in the economy, it has been less concerned with manipulating the private sector to influence the level or direction of growth. Perhaps the German faith in the benefits of a free market economy are as much a result as a cause of her successful economic performance in the areas of growth, price stability, full employment, and her strong balance of payment position.

Despite its neoliberal philosophy, however, the German government has pursued many of the same programs for aiding investment, promoting stability, and providing social welfare services as has France. But detailed supervision of industry activity has been largely absent in Germany. Both Germany and France have been considered to be fast-growing, "successful" economies in the post-war period. We will now begin a discussion of another mixed economy, Britain, which is not clearly identified with active planning by government nor the neoliberal belief in the market system, and which is also the slowest-growing economy of Western Europe.

QUESTIONS

1. Why is Germany classified as a mixed rather than a capitalist economy?
2. What is neoliberalism, and how does it differ from *laissez-faire* capitalism?
3. What economic policies have been introduced into Germany to promote the philosophy of neoliberalism?
4. What economic policies have been adopted in Germany that are inconsistent with the philosophy of neoliberalism?
5. How does the private banking industry influence economic decisions in Germany?
6. What are the features adding to the flexibility of German fiscal policy?
7. To what extent is the German economy a "planned economy?"

8

The British Economy

Introduction

There is a popular misconception in America that Great Britain is some-how a "socialist" economy, in contrast to continental European "capitalist" nations like France or West Germany. The origins of this misconception derive jointly from the wave of social reforms and nationalizations that took place in Britain following World War II and the peculiar sensitivity of Americans to developments in their linguistic and cultural homeland. Certainly the public sector in Britain is larger than that of the United States, but not so much larger as to suggest a different species. It is more the structure of this public sector that differentiates Britain from the United States or West Germany.

Like France, Britain has a large nationalized sector and has socialized its medical services to a large degree. The overall percentage of the GNP that passes through the government's accounts in Britain, however, is actually very similar to other Western European economies. However, in Britain the nationalized industries show up in the government's accounts. These socially owned industries both sell to and purchase from the private sector, are large employers, and undertake a substantial fraction of total national investment. On the other hand, the British social security system, unemployment compensation, and welfare and retirement programs are much less comprehensive than those of many other developed nations including West Germany. The overall size of the "public sector" is then an imperfect measure of the extent and nature of the government's role and of its ability to influence or guide the economy. But before we go too far into the particulars of the British economy, let us evaluate it on the basis of our classification criteria, the first of which is the balance between public and private ownership of the means of production.

In the financial sector, Britain nationalized the Bank of England after World War II. This act only brought British practice into line with the practice of the rest of the world including the United States, where the Central Bank is publicly owned and operated in the national interest. Further nationalizations in the financial sector did not take place, leaving the remainder of the British capital market in private hands. In communications, the BBC, a state-owned communications monopoly, was established as far back as 1927 and made responsible for a national broadcasting system. Private radio and television broadcasting is now also permitted and enjoys considerable commercial success. In civil aviation, several public corporations dominate national and international service and an Airports Authority controls ground facilities. The Transport Act of 1947 placed many passenger and freight haulage facilities under a single public body, the British Transport Commission. Long distance road haulage has been partly nationalized, partly denationalized, but remains largely in private hands. The fuel and power industry—coal mining, electrical generating and distributional facilities—and the steel industry are either completely or preponderantly socialized. Public authorities, principally local building societies subsidized by the central government, have built more than half the new housing units constructed since 1945. Having inventoried the state's presence in British industry, one can be impressed by the degree of social intervention, at least by American standards, or on reflection, equally impressed by the vast areas of enterprise, trade, and commerce into which the state has not intruded. The great preponderance of industries, firms, and shops that do not have to contend with direct state intervention may be viewed alternatively by planners as the anarchic element which has made their plans unworkable or by antiplanners as the last healthy elements of a mismanaged, over-managed economy.

The second criterion of the classification system concerns the location of centers of decision-making power in the economy. Power may reside in differing degrees with the consumer, the firm, or some social collective—local, regional, or national government. As in most democratic nations, the economic implications of British democracy are the rights of an individual to freely choose his employment and what he wishes to consume. Private firms are free to determine their output and input mix in pursuit of maximum profit. Governments at all levels, however, have a variety of levers which can alter the evnironment within which private decision-makers operate. By manipulating tax levels and structures, subsidies, and tariffs governments can influence what remains nevertheless a *private* decision by a worker-consumer or firm. Practical and legal limitations on the power of government to alter these decisions do exist. Certain policies can be pushed just so far, and then diminishing returns of various sorts appear. Problems of this sort will be discussed below.

The state, of course, has a sector—the nationalized industries—in which it theoretically should not have to wheedle or pussyfoot to get results. Yet even here limitations to its power exist. The British government may impose its will on socially owned industry and force it to do something "unprofitable" in a strictly accounting sense. This may produce socially desirable results (less pollution, better location, more investment, more employment, etc.), but the government must be prepared to pay the price in terms of direct subsidies to the "loss-making" industry.

The government may also impose social welfare programs in areas that could theoretically be left to private decision-making. These programs involve the area of personal "rainy-day" risks, wherein the individual could carry private reserves to protect himself in situations such as illness, unemployment, or retirement. Any rational person would set something aside to meet such contingencies, so the question then becomes whether the individual has properly judged the amount of risk which exists. Public programs in this area implicitly represent a social judgment that universal minimum coverage is socially desirable or that individuals are not adequate judges of the true social risks that exist. The extensive British social welfare, medical, and social security system is evidence of such a judgment. The National Health Service provides universal free or low cost medical attention, pharmaceuticals, and hospitalization services. The problem of queuing (excessive demand leading to long waiting periods) does exist and will always exist as long as no one is barred through price from seeking attention or until the supply of medical services is less restricted than at present. Extensive services for children's health and welfare as well as for the elderly and disabled are provided.

The third criterion for classifying an economic system is the mechanism for allocating resources—the market or command principle. As we have seen, Britain is predominantly a capitalist nation; the representative firm is small in most industries and buys or sells in essentially free and competitive markets. A substantial number of firms are large and diversified enough to have established an international reputation and a position in world markets as well as domestic ones. The socialized industry sector could be a serious qualification of the judgment that Britain is primarily a market economy but, as we shall see, even the nationalized firms are market-oriented.

The government does intervene in the economy, but as in the case of France, its intervention is usually limited to changing the environment of doing business and inducing people to do things rather than forcing them to. To summarize, Britain has a capitalist economy with a strategic sector of socially owned industry. The locus of decision-making is principally private and decentralized, with a number of social programs run directly by or subsidized by several levels of government. Market signals direct the activities of most economic actors, with even the socially owned industries responding to market forces and dealing through markets with the private sector.

Let us now turn our attention to a broad outline of the development of the British economy, institutions, and economic history since World War II. By way of example some commentators have contrasted the British economy with the French, German, or Italian economies and have alleged that the principal theme of post-war British performance has been failure. Failure of workers to work, managers to manage, institutions to stabilize, and government to govern. Where things have been done, they have been wrong or carried too far. The proper actions have been delayed to a point in time when, if applied, they may be no longer appropriate. Productive investment has been too little and/or in the wrong things. The economy has been jerked forward and back in response to short-run problems until a new term, "stop-go," was coined to describe these policies. Some of these allegations are objectively true and others are tinged with condescension and partisan value judgments. An ostensibly "successfully" managed economy may have hidden political and social tensions which can surge to the surface and rip it apart, as Charles de Gaulle discovered at the close of his career. A nation, "unsuccessful" in many indicators such as growth of GNP or personal incomes or exports, may be pursuing policies of social development and democratic reform which are incompatible in the short run with these narrow economic goals. This line of argument can be effective in countering some of the criticism of Britain, since it is obvious that the British people are progressive, democratic, and dynamic in many ways. Nevertheless, one can point to many things that could have been done differently without substantial infringement upon their democratic heritage or cultural achievements.

FACTORS INFLUENCING THE BASIC STRUCTURE OF THE BRITISH ECONOMY

One cannot read far in the literature of the British economy without running into the recurrent theme of the balance of payments. We will begin this survey of the highlights of the British economy with a statement on the importance of the foreign trade sector.

Once the first flush of industrialization was past, Britain found that she needed to import large quantities of foodstuffs for her large urban working class, which had deserted the land. She also needed to import industrial raw materials because Britain has few natural resources beyond her coal and iron ore deposits. To pay for all these imports, Britain has found it necessary to set aside a portion of her industrial output for export. Since market forces dominate the economy, individuals must freely and spontaneously seek out foreigners and sell them satisfactory merchandise at a good price. The summed value of their sales must be in rough balance with the value of the food and materials that other individuals are spontaneously purchasing abroad. The forces and events that influence exporters are not necessarily those that influence importers, hence the balance of trade may be out of balance for periods of time. Such imbalances can be fundamentally corrected by a spontaneous reversal of trends, or a change in the value of the currency through a devaluation, or by government policy to slow down the economy so as to stimulate exports and reduce imports.

Over and over again in postwar Britain a little scenario of events has occurred. When later we are examining the new institutions, planning boards, and councils, and the great hopes and strategies pursued by successive British governments, we will find the grand theme of the balance of payments intruding at the most delicate moments. The dreary collapse of prosperity, growth, and governments follows shortly. Let us sketch the balance of payments scenario abstracted from the events of any particular crisis.

Let us say the economy has been moving along a middling course, with a moderate amount of unemployment, and a rate of inflation no faster than anyone else's. Either spontaneously or stimulated by the government, the economy may begin to speed up. First one, then another, industry begins to squeeze up toward full capacity. Imported resources rise in price, so importers buy more to build up their depleted inventories and to anticipate further rises in prices. Export industries find they can sell all their output in domestic markets, so don't bother to put out the extra effort to seek foreign markets for their goods. To cover rising costs, firms begin to raise prices. Labor unions respond to rising profits and prices by demanding higher wages and striking to obtain them. Strikes of transportation workers prevent goods from moving abroad. The decline of exports, rising prices, and rising imports all combine to produce a substantial deficit in the balance of payments. Speculators or businessmen, anticipating a devaluation of the currency, begin to take their money out of Britain, which of course puts the currency under even more pressure in the same downward direction—a form of self-fulfilling prophecy.

The government, finding things are getting out of hand and observing their reserves of gold and foreign currencies melting away, may do several things:

Option A: The government may alter the value of the currency through devaluation. This is readily done with a few telephone calls. Now the importers and exporters have a whole new ball game. All imports are more expensive and so their consumption will fall. Exports are less expensive to foreigners, and they should respond favorably. With a little time to sort things out, the balance of trade should move back toward equilibrium. If none of the fundamental conditions causing the initial disequilibrium have been eliminated, the movement toward equilibrium will be halted. The balance of payments will then drift back toward a deficit position again. The devaluation will have to be repeated.

Why have the British governments of the past so consistently delayed a devaluation which could buy time to make more fundamental adjustments? First and probably most important, the government has felt an obligation to preserve the value of foreign-owned capital invested in Britain or pound-sterling held for trading purposes. Second, over the years the value of the pound has taken on domestic political significance, as the last symbol of the great economic power that England once wielded. No politician has wanted to represent the party that devalued the pound. Changing the value of the currency has become less of a political trauma in recent years, but since Britain has entered the European Economic Community (the Common Market), the exchange rate will become critical for various Communitywide pricing agreements mandated by the EEC.

Option B: If the authorities are indeed determined to hold the value of the currency at some fixed value and reserves or credit are exhausted, the government must deflate the economy with contractionary fiscal policies and tight money. Less output means less imported materials. Lower labor incomes means less money spent on imported consumer goods. Excess capacity of capital means lower prices and an inducement for firms to seek out foreign business. Unemployment means less pressure for wage increases and hence price increases. Most of these tendencies in the economy would lead toward an improvement in the balance of payments. Unfortunately, there are considerable short-run costs imposed on large sectors of the economy. Unemployment, falling profits, high interest rates, and higher taxes to support increased welfare and unemployment payments are burdens that must be borne by some individuals or groups of individuals.

After some time, the dose of deflation should bring the balance of payments into a reasonably healthy condition at the expense of an unhealthy underemployed economy. Impending parliamentary elections could spell disaster for the government if the unpopular recession extended into the campaign. A new government or a defensive old government could try to improve its position through stimulating the economy. Should this occur before a full recovery of the balance of payments, the whole cycle will start over again. It is this cycle of overstimulation leading to engineered recessions leading to more stimulation that has been termed "stop-go." Let us now observe the stages of development of the British economy and central government institutions since 1945 with this scenario in mind.

THE POSTWAR BRITISH ECONOMY—THE FAILURE OF PLANNING

Prelude to Planning

It is difficult to imagine worse circumstances in which to commence a policy of conscious social direction of an economy, ie., planning, than those existing in Britain in 1945. Housing was in extremely short supply. The capital plant and equipment of industry were physically worn out and economically obsolete. The labor force was trained to produce a menu of war material which was no longer appropriate. External commerce was thoroughly disrupted, the Commonwealth was strained, and a large fraction of pre-war foreign assets had been sold off to pay for war expenses. Shortages of everything existed, so it was felt that the wartime apparatus of controls could not be immediately dismantled. The magnitude of the national tasks of reconversion and reconstruction was staggering, but the ambitions and optimism of the planners were limitless. In 1945, even before the war was over, a Labour government was elected and took power with a mandate for extensive social and economic reforms. The goals of the Labour party planners were clear enough:

1. to promote a more equitable distribution of income and wealth
2. to ensure that aggregate demand was sufficient to absorb full employment output
3. to ensure a more appropriate proportion of social versus private goods
4. to reduce the personal risks borne by the average citizen.

The central government had to adapt the wartime administrative machinery to formulating peacetime national goals and plans to meet these goals. A strategic position in the economy was rapidly consolidated. In general, three types of industries were ticketed for nationalization: important basic industries such as fuels, power, transportation, and metals; monopolized industries; and finally, "sick" industries like coal mining and railroads. The constituent firms were bundled together into semi-autonomous public corporations and left to do business without day-to-day supervision of their affairs by government officials. Some of these public corporations required subsidies and massive injections of public capital, which was only to be expected since the capital equipment of most basic industries was pretty well run down through lack of maintenance during the war years. The hope was, of course, that following the initial costly re-equipment program, these industries would become self-supporting.

Planning in Britain—1945 to 1951

There are three vital elements necessary to make economic planning viable in a democratic society like Britain's. *First,* there must be a broad social consensus that public intervention is desirable or necessary. It need not be true in fact that such intervention is useful or necessary—only that most major interest groups accept the legitimacy of the attempt. The laissez faire or "hands off" tradition is a long and honorable one in Britain. The lessons and advantages of the free market have been learned and become the "instincts" of generations of businessmen and officials, in contrast to continental nations like France, which have a long history of state intervention. Therefore, economic planning starts with a substantial reservoir of skepticism from all social groups—from labor and capital alike and even from the government bureaucrats themselves. *Second,* the government, having secured its mandate to plan, must have some levers of economic power, some ways to alter private decisions in desired directions and in desired magnitudes. The means for manipulating the economy are manifold, from the most neutral of macroeconomic stimuli to the most discriminating of particular controls. Only the most extreme of socialist planners, on the one hand, or laissez faire entrepreneurs, on the other hand, could not find some array of tools which just suited his tastes and purposes.

Third and finally, after achieving the will to plan and the powers to influence, planners must accumulate the expertise and the experts, the data and the knowledge, the perspective and retrospective necessary to produce a coherent plan with some prospects for achievement. They must know how the economy works; what the consequences of actions and inactions are; the combinations of timing, cajolery, and compromise that will get the job done with the least undesirable side effects. Let us examine the record of the Labour government from 1945 to 1951, its first term of office, to see how well it put together these three ingredients to achieve its goals of substantial social and economic reform through democratic planning.

As we have mentioned, the Labour party achieved a resounding electoral victory in 1945 and held a commanding majority in Parliament. Its mandate for substantial social and economic change was unquestioned and was based on its comprehensive campaign document, "Let Us Face the Future." This document could not have been a clearer statement of the goals of the Labour party and what it hoped to achieve. Immediately on taking office the Labour government passed a number of laws designed to implement this blueprint for a new planned, but democratic, society. Nationalizations of iron and steel, railroads, coal, electricity, gas, and the Bank of England took place. This satisfied the initial goals of the Labour party. They now held the levers of economic power and influence through social ownership that they felt to be indispensable for planning. While Britain had been at war, half the nation's output flowed through the hands of the government. Years of experience at controlling a high pressure and war-warped economy had developed a skilled and competent economic bureaucracy. It remained to be seen if this bureaucracy could reverse its field and manage the economy as it swerved back from an overstrained position toward normalcy and a peacetime balance between supply and demand.

Reconstruction and Reconversion—1945 to 1947

The mixed results of the two immediate postwar years cannot be attributed to flaws in the planning structure since one cannot really say that "planning" existed for these years. We have mentioned the extreme shortages of raw materials, the permanent loss of some overseas markets and suppliers, the distortion of the productive apparatus, the misdirection of the labor force, and the problem of assimilating the returning armies. Knitting the economy together and re-meshing it with the international economy again would have been a Herculean task for any government, much less one dedicated to simultaneous and substantial social reforms—a disquieting experience in the best of times.

The reconstruction and reconversion of the economy in this period was relatively successful, considering that Marshall Plan aid had not commenced yet. An overriding weakness, however, was the inability of the British economy to pay its way in the international economy. There is no effective way to plan the foreign sector—the customers are not open to "persuasion" as in the domestic economy. Internally, the success of reconversion meant that many markets were coming into balance and the need for controls was no longer critical. The Labour government had no love of "controls for control's sake" and took the opportunity to drop some of the apparatus of controls when possible. However, the national government jealously guarded its powers to control local government expenditures and restrictive licensing of new construction and imports. Flotation of private capital issues was also controlled. Through these devices, the government could turn back other claimants to national output and advance its own projects or favor one private project over another. The purpose was to prevent excess bidding for limited resources. The government's direct powers were waning as its purchases of national output fell from the wartime level of 50 percent to only a fourth of national output—considerably reducing its leverage over prices and labor markets.

The planning apparatus for this period suffered from a lack of firm central control. An Official Steering Committee, consisting of representatives from the various ministries which had economic functions, had responsibility for formulating the short-run annual national plans. Planning with more perspective would have been a pointless exercise since there were so many national and international imponderables. Actually, it is fair to say that planning as it is commonly defined, say in France, did not take place from 1945-47. Rather the government pursued a number of short-run goals, trying to stay one step ahead of unexpected and unanticipated developments, and then it called this array of ad hoc policies (some contradictory) "planning."

The problem of having no effective central planning apparatus came to a head with the postwar raw materials crisis. The issue had been resolved for several years, it was thought, by a loan from the United States in 1946. The government's inability to keep consumer incomes and spending down, however, caused this loan to be frittered away more quickly than expected, leaving the economy naked before the wave of speculation against the pound that naturally resulted. One can detect the first playing out of the balance of payments scenario. During the winter of 1947, the planners had not built up adequate stocks of fuel for a hard winter, and a severe fuel shortage plagued household and industry alike. It is in this context that the government determined to revamp the central governmental economic planning machinery.

A new ministry, the Ministry of Economic Affairs, was created and took on many of the planning functions that had been decentralized among the various economic ministries. The Official Steering Committee referred to above was transformed into the Central Economic Planning Staff under authority of the Treasury; thus the lines of responsibility were considerably tightened. To further aid in formulating national goals so as to retain the "consensus" of 1945, a Central Planning Board was created in 1947 to bring together representatives of business, labor, the nationalized industries, and various governmental ministries.

At last the three vital ingredients for planning had come together in an operational sense. The nationalizations had been digested, though some nationalized industries were vast drains on the government's resources. Public corporations, with some managerial autonomy, were functioning. The economy, while not healthy, had, to all extents and purposes, been restored to a balance of supply and demand. The planners were gathered more or less under one roof and could begin to look into the future with some assurance.

Economic Recovery—1948 to 1951

During this period the government achieved more success in restraining the growth of consumption and import demands. The unions voluntarily restrained wage demands to the extent necessary to keep purchasing power constant. The government made this restraint more palatable by subsidizing imported and home-grown food-stuffs—although it ought to have been obvious that *somebody* had to pay for the subsidies. The wage restraint and attendant slowing of price increases greatly assisted a turnaround in the balance of payments.

In 1949 the Labour government was dealt a crushing political blow when it nevertheless was forced to devalue the pound from $4.03 to $2.80, a change of 30 percent. The reason for the devaluation was not that the export-import situation was unfavorable, for Britain actually achieved overall trade balance that year. However, Britain had a deficit with the *dollar* region, and speculative pressures from there drained the British reserves to the point that they were forced to devalue. This devaluation, together with the wage restraint, assured that the balance of payments would be favorable for a period of time. Tragically, the seeds of further inflation were contained within that devaluation. Imported foodstuffs now rose substantially in price, putting pressure on union wage demands. Imported raw materials were likewise more expensive, and the added costs had to be passed on in higher prices to domestic and foreign customers alike. It can be seen that this large devaluation was actually partially self-nullifying.

By 1951, the Labour government had reached the end of its five-year political mandate and had to return to the voters. Things had not gone well for the Labour party. The continuation of controls and rationing long after the end of the war had irritated a large portion of the electorate. The policy of wage restraint had reached its limit, as inflation began to accelerate after the devaluation of 1949. The nationalized industries had not had time to reap the full benefits of reorganization and refitting programs by 1951—many of them ran fairly substantial deficits during this period, the coal mines being particularly disappointing in the area of productivity. The devaluation had been an opportunity to establish a strong international trade position, but inflation and the soaring price of imported raw materials saw most of the advantage vanish. The Conservative party ran on a platform that promised to retain the principal features of the welfare state in health, education, and welfare while dismantling the system of controls, returning to a free market system, and denationalizing the iron and steel and road transport industries. The Conservatives won a majority of seventeen seats in Parliament but did not secure a majority of the votes cast. This anomaly occured because Labour's voters tend to be highly concentrated in working-class districts while the Conservative party's supporters are more generally distributed. Despite the clouded mandate, the Tories pressed for a reversal of economic policy and an end to controls and so-called planning.

What Went Wrong in Labour's Planning Efforts

A principal failure of government planning from 1947 to 1951 was the inability to formulate long-range goals to which the short-run annual plans could be linked consecutively. There was a complete gap in the use of modern econometric or input-output techniques and the information that these techniques imply. The use of these models is not an empty exercise. Whatever else one may think about their usefulness, they greedily demand more and better information of precisely the sort that planners require. Suffice it to say that if planners *cannot* produce an input-output table of the economy, they don't have the information it takes to plan that economy.

In addition to this technical failure of British planning, there were organizational failures. At first the planning process was divided up among a number of agencies and ministries, which functioned without reference to each other's efforts in many cases, and these efforts were coordinated by an interagency committee with no formal powers. After the abject failure of this form of "unplanning," planning activities were somewhat more centralized within the Treasury. This powerful institution, however, could be counted on to press its own policy prescriptions on the planners, who may or may not have had the capacity to resist. Generally speaking this can be a good thing if the planners are incompetent or overambitious. On the other hand, the purpose of planning is to take the long view of the total economic picture. The Treasury, by the very nature of the institution, is short-term in outlook and looks only to the accounting balance-sheets of government agencies.

The critical strategic failure of the Labour government was its lack of control over the aggregate level of demand for national output. The state cannot undertake massive investment programs and encourage private investment if consumers are also pressing claims on the same resources. The sum of their demands must inevitably exceed national output, resulting in inflation and rising imports. The Labour government simply did not have the political will to resist the clamour for higher incomes.

A fundamental question presents itself, "Is planning compatible with political democracy?" Can the planners do the proper things at the appropriate moments if their actions are politically unpopular and the moments are near election time? Can the planners resist the pressure to run an over-full employment economy when this can only spell inflation? Can they restrain wage or price demands when the demanders may be the ruling party's political constituents? Can they make long-range committments at the expense of some popular short-run achievements? The experience of Britain in 1947-1951 inclines one to pessimism on all counts.

CONSERVATIVE GOVERNMENT:
THE ATTEMPT TO DE-CONTROL—1951-1964

The new Conservative government, while ideologically committed to a return to the free market, did not have a mandate to dismantle the Welfare State. Some reforms, such as the National Health Service, the expansion of educational opportunities, and other social services, were too popular and firmly entrenched for the Tories to touch, even had they wanted to. They contented themselves with raising the nominal fees charged for health services in order to reduce the drain on the Treasury. The iron and steel industries and long-distance road haulage were denationalized. Controls over foreign exchange and investments abroad were retained but most of the internal direction of resources was eliminated. Rent controls were gradually to be eliminated and a free housing market was to take its place. The government cut off the subsidized grants and interest rates to the local housing authorities to facilitate the formation of a free market. Businesses were free to import raw materials from foreign markets, to float securities and build plants without licensing restrictions, and were free to export to the most profitable market they could find.

In general, there was a renewal of faith in the efficacy and efficiency of the free market allocation of resources, goods, and services, except in the highly sensitive areas of agriculture and foreign exchange.

The concern for British agriculture, given the overwhelming dominance of industry in the economy, may seem to be misplaced. For several reasons both Labour and Conservative governments have been concerned about the economic health of agriculture. First, a fairly substantial number of people still derive their income from the production and processing of agricultural products. Dislocations in this industry would upset the regional balance of population, contribute to unemployment, require large sums to care for and retrain the workers, and finally, would upset a large bloc of voters. Second, a decline in domestic agriculture would directly lead to imports of foodstuffs, already a large component of total imports. These imports would have to be paid for with further sacrifices of industrial goods set aside for foreigners.

The control of foreign exchange and foreign investment was particularly sensitive to the Tories because of their preoccupation with the balance of payments. The picture which emerges is that of a government which was positively anti-planning and pro-market and which had seized on one indicator as a measure of policy success. Sincere men may honestly differ over the extent, nature, and utility of governmental activity, but the final determination is results as most people perceive them—an increase in social and individual welfare.

What were the results of the retreat from planning to a more conventional management of economic affairs? The government managed a feat that had eluded the Labour planners—they reduced the share of private consumption by 4 percentage points, from over 70 percent to less than 66 percent of GNP. They were aided in this shift by the growth of incomes such that the absolute level of consumption did not decline. The devices used to accomplish the suppression of consumption were sales taxes and controls over the terms and timing of installment purchases. There was no exotic secret to this medicine; the Labour government simply had not dared politically to push restraint of incomes as far as the Tories did. The tax structure was altered to favor business investment, which increased from an average of 13 percent to over 15 percent of GNP. Expenditures on social services remained at about the same level, 17 percent of GNP, as under the Labour government.

Ultimately, the Conservatives were no more able to resist the political enticements of a full-employment economy than the Labourites were. The resulting tightness in the labor markets led to rapid wage increases and more inflation. Price disadvantages prevented the growth of British exports at the same rate as continental rivals. The stock of gold and foreign exchange could not rise to the point where the government would have breathing room to promote stable growth.

Throughout the decade of the fifties, the Tories learned that the workings of the free market could not guarantee full employment without inflation or a positive foreign trade balance any more than Labour's controls and planning could. The expansion of 1954-56 led the government to pursue tight money, raise sales taxes, and place controls on the flotation of new equity issues in order to slow inflation and reduce the balance of payments deficit. The economy ground to a halt by 1957 and slid into a recession through 1958 and 1959. The balance of payments improved but principally through a decline in imports due to decreased spending. This is the weakest way of improving the balance of payments, because the difficulty will return the instant the economy improves. The only fundamental improvement which could possibly result from an engineered recession would be an improved competitive price position of exports. To the dismay of the Conservative government, wage and price increases did not abate appreciably during the years of stagnation. A term was invented to describe this situation—"stagflation." The term would appear to be relevant for the experience of the early 1970s in the United States as well.

The British economy was lifted out of the recession in the early 1960s, but naturally imports immediately soared while exports had gained no advantage due to the steady advance of prices, in good times and bad. The recovery or "go" years, 1960-1963, had generated wage inflation and stagnant exports—the twin causes of the next "stop" period.

THE DEVELOPMENT OF CONSERVATIVE PLANNING—1962-1964

Two institutional changes in 1962 and a major cabinet shuffle heralded a rather radical shift in the views of the top leadership of the Conservative party in power. The first change was the replacement of the old Council on Prices, Productivity, and Incomes with the National Economic Development Council (NEDC, nicknamed "Neddy") and its professional staff, the National Economic Development Office (NEDO). The NEDC drew representation from the government, labor, business, and the public. In 1962 NEDC drew up a projection of the implications of a growth rate of 4 percent for the economy to 1966. This was an interesting and fruitful exercise for all concerned because it was really the first perspective "plan" the British had undertaken. Unfortunately, the practical impossibility of achieving the projected growth figure was bound to create credibility problems for the Council. Nothing is more deadly for planning and planning agencies than plan projections that are perceived to be unrealistic and therefore are discounted by "practical" men in business and labor.

A second institutional change was the reorganization of the Treasury. A separate National Economy Group was formed within the Treasury to examine in particular the effects of government activities on the real allocation of resources rather than just the financial balance sheets of agencies and ministries. Clearly this National Economy Group would serve as the technical nucleus for a planning agency should the government ever decide to move in that direction.

It would appear in retrospect that the two new organizations were operationally just window-dressing for the politicians. The NEDC projection to 1966 was patently unrealistic, and NEDC was powerless to effect changes which would be needed to implement their suggestions. Organizationally NEDC was outside the seats of power and had essentially only recommendatory authority. The professional staff in the NED Office was put to work on analyzing the incomes bargain with the unions for 1963-64. This injected the planners into the hurly-burly of dickering between interest groups—a nasty position for anyone, but especially for planning technicians.[1] The concentration on short-term tactics rather than long-run strategies was damaging to "Neddy's" institutional development and was to become a tradition for British-style planning.

As another turning point approached, the general elections of 1964, the two institutions of planning had not made any impact on the short- or long-run management of the economy. NEDC in particular had not put out the institutional roots it needed to make contact with the economic environment. Economic Development Committees ("little Neddies") were intended to serve a purpose similar to the modernization committees in France. They were to translate the general goals of the professional planning staff at the NED Office into meaningful industrial goals and to supply feedback on practical problems or unprojected changes to the planners. The "little Neddies" were slow to form and suffered from organizational weaknesses.

The record of the Conservative governments from 1951 to 1964, then, was similar to that of the Labour government of 1945 to 1951. The first approach was ideological in an enthusiastic pursuit of free markets and neutral, even blindfolded, government. This was analogous to Labour's enthusiastic nationalizations and Labour's naive optimism that new institutions and controls could solve all problems. Both parties were to see their hopes and aspirations founder on the shoals of the balance of payments. The final phase for each was to attempt a reorganization of central government responsibilities for economic management, searching for some successful combination of tools and institutions. The failure of the institutions to develop properly, more "stop-go" economic policies, and new elections culminated in each case in a defeat for the government. In 1964, the Labour party was returned to power with a majority of four seats, a razor-thin margin.

Labour and Planning: 1964-1968

Immediately on taking office in October 1964, the Labour Government created the Department of Economic Affairs (DEA). A new Ministry of Tech-

---

[1] Andrew Schonfield, *Modern Capitalism* (New York: Oxford University Press, 1965), p. 157.

nology was formed and charged with many responsibilities in the field of increasing industrial efficiency. The professional planning staff of NEDC was moved bodily into DEA while both DEA and the Ministry of Technology raided NEDO for personnel. The NEDC was retained as an institution which could express an independent view in counterpoint to the in-house views of DEA, which had also absorbed the National Economy Group of the Treasury.

The Department of Economic Affairs drew up a new National Plan projecting growth of the economy to 1970 and predicting an expansion of 25 percent in GNP, or 3.8 percent a year. It was obvious to most independent observers that the 3.8 percent figure could not be met except with the most favorable turn of events in the later years of the Plan. The actual rate of growth registered under the previous Conservative Plan had not been close to the target rate of 4 percent. Again the question arises: are the technical requirements of planning (i.e., realistic, believable, achievable targets) compatible with democratic political processes? The 25 percent figure for Labour's 1966-1970 National Plan was unrealistic and was an exercise in growthmanship—Labour felt it could not announce a perceptibly lower projected rate of growth than the Conservatives, even though the failure to achieve these rates would severely damage the credibility and thus the social acceptability of the planning process.

The drawing up of the 1966-1970 Plan was actually an interesting exercise in faulty methodology; in other words, it demonstrated how not to plan. The overall growth figure of 25 percent through 1970 was a political target selected before questionaires were sent out and any feedback at all became available. Firms and industrial trade associations were queried as to what they felt their situation would be if the economy grew at about a 4 percent annual rate up to 1970. What could the summed results possibly predict but that the economy would grow at something approximating 4 percent annually? This process is analogous to asking students to predict their grade point averages assuming that they attend all lectures, are unfailingly alert, study together with "A" students, and that the professor is in top form for every lecture.

If one views the Plan as a forecast of things to come, based on surveys of intentions, the 1966-1970 Plan was not merely flawed, it was positively mendacious. As an attempt to push the economy in desired directions, it was only slightly over-ambitious as far as the domestic economy was concerned. The defect of this plan was that it was not internally consistent. The weakest part of the Plan was the foreign sector targets. Once more the planners had left moderately realistic goals hanging from a slender thread of wildly optimistic balance of payments assumptions. Failure of the targets for export growth of 5.5 percent annually could inevitably lead to only one thing—restrictive monetary and fiscal policies designed to halt the economy in its tracks as had happened time and time again since the war.

The inevitable was not long delayed. The National Plan, published in September 1965, was formally abandoned in July 1966 when stringent restrictions were placed on the economy. The screws were tightened further in July of the following year. The debacle was capped by a devaluation in November 1967 following a massive, stubborn, expensive, and almost irresponsible defense of the pound.

GOVERNMENT POLICIES AND OBJECTIVES

British Incomes Policies

In Britain the principal public concern which led to a demand for an incomes policy was the persistent, almost inexorable, upward drift of wages, then costs, then prices. This sure chain of events would not be so certain if it were not that money wages consistently rise faster than productivity. The cure for this is, first, prevent or slow down the rate of wage increase, second, increase productivity up to the rate of wage advance, or both simultaneously. Slowing down the rate of inflation is certainly an important goal of an incomes policy, but there are others. The government has frequently wanted to suppress private consumption to make room for public consumption, public investment, exports, or private investment. The British economy is too open to foreign trade to be able to support the expanding demands of all five sectors.

Unfortunately, there are a limited number of policy variables at the disposal of the authorities, and it may prove to be impossible to fine-tune consumption, investment, government expenditures, and the foreign sector to desired optimum levels. Policies that depress consumption have a way of depressing investment expectations, which you may wish to encourage. Low interest rates to encourage investment will increase balance of payments deficits usually leading to new restrictive policies.

Many voices in postwar England have called for "voluntary" restraints on price and wage increases. To expect such restraint when the economy is overheated is economic naivete. Inflation-fed price and wage advances seem to move like the surge of a glacier—at a speed independent of efforts to chip away at it and push back at this point or that.

In 1961 a formal governmental call for voluntary wage restraint met with little success in the private sector, but salaries for government workers were frozen. There, at least, some restraint existed, but the question of equity appears—why should government workers bear the costs of society's problems? The pause period was followed by a period of wage guidelines during which total wage advance was linked to the average economy-wide productivity increase of 2.5 percent. Since this was to be the *average*, everyone claimed to be above average. Many settlements exceeded 2.5 percent and wages tended to drift higher than rates established in the negotiated settlements as firms competed for labor.

In 1965 the new Labour government established guidelines for wage increases at 3.5 percent and immediately got bogged down judging settlements in excess of that amount. Gradually a set of voluntary "early-warning" arrangements was made so that the government could register its opinion before the event rather than after it. Major unions opposed the arrangement and the Labour cabinet itself experienced differences of opinion. In July of 1966 a total freeze on wages went into effect. This lasted into 1967 when the total freeze was lifted, but during the freeze there were arrangements for increased wages if productivity increases were great enough. November 1967 culminated in a devaluation of the pound, which, of course, produced a number of price increases due to higher prices for imported goods and materials.

The dreary record of inflation, wage boosts, deflation, unemployment, inflation need not be detailed again here; the pattern is clear. For a variety of reasons (and we know more now about why this occurs) the British economy was very poorly managed throughout the postwar years. Inflation carries a certain momentum and takes time to work itself out even if the pressures are eliminated. The explanation for British inflation, good times or bad, is that the successive governments could never wait long enough for inflationary expectations to die down, hence muting wage demands and then price increases. Unemployment would reach politically sensitive levels, an election would loom, and the government would drop a package of stimulations into the economy. All the inflationary expectations would be confirmed, and off they would whirl, again and again. No amount of exhortations or controls can halt the tide of wage and price advances if there is fundamental excess aggregate demand. Legal barriers to price rises will set off quality deterioration. Wage freezes cause janitors to become "maintenance engineers" and secretaries to become "assistant office managers" for salary purposes with no change in work function.

Someone has remarked about the virtually universal record of the failure of incomes policies, "If you don't have fundamental macroeconomic balance, no incomes policy will work. If you have fundamental macroeconomic balance, you don't need an incomes policy." In the longer run this is certainly true, and more experience with the American incomes policy may confirm this.[2]

The pattern of development of a British incomes policy was fairly typical of the development of much of its other policy-making apparatus. First, there was only academic lip service to the idea of formulating a long-run incomes policy which would combine stability with equity and a sense of fair play

[2]The timing of the American incomes policy and the relative innocence of Americans in these matters may lead to better results than an incomes policy deserves. First, there had been a considerable period of restraint prior to August 1971. There were signs that inflation was slowing. However, it might have taken Americans quite some time to perceive this fact and stop demanding wage increases *anticipating* further inflation. President Nixon's Phase I and Phase II may have short-circuited this process to make people think inflation had slowed. The real crunch comes when the public finds out whether inflation has indeed slowed and the new expectations are true or false. Resurgent inflation will blow the lid off any controls system if the authorities attempt to reimpose a Phase I type freeze.

between competing income groups. Second, there was the familiar reliance on newly created institutions, born in optimism, to be neglected once the immediate crisis had faded, only to be reborn in another guise when the next crisis loomed. The British genius for pragmatic muddling-through, in this case, is a counterproductive tradition.

British Regional Development

Britain, like many countries including France and the United States, has long had problems of uneven regional development. These retarded regions were truly depressed between the two world wars, with unemployment rates in excess of 15 and 20 percent. Today the unemployment rate may run twice as high as the national average, but this really means 2 to 4 percent—which is hardly a crushing level of unemployment although a waste, nevertheless, if it could be avoided. Trying to beat down this level of regional unemployment by pressing aggregate demand to higher levels can only serve to set off inflationary wage boosts in the more developed regions which are relatively short of labor.

Policies to eliminate the regional differentials are theoretically quite simple—move the men to the jobs or the jobs to the men. The former is difficult to accomplish in a free society if the workers prefer not to move, and the latter is expensive. Workers cannot be expected to move voluntarily if there is a substantial nationwide housing shortage. Businessmen cannot be expected to make massive investments in depressed regions unless a trained work force and other productive services are available. Therefore, substantial social investments in transportation, housing, and education must be made before business can be induced to leave the developed areas. Recognizing this to be the case, the Labour government in 1946 passed a New Town Act, the first of a series of actions intended to redistribute the nation's working population.

The creation of New Towns is an audacious and ambitious concept. A New Town was to function as a sort of "spin-off" of surplus population from a major industrial center which had reached the limit of its ability to absorb industry and population and still preserve a livable environment. Development corporations were to be set up and given grants to develop facilities and induce firms to locate new plants. A successful and complete New Town could then be turned over to local authorities in stages.

New Towns were also designed to serve as "growth points" in the retarded regions. A growth point is a center of activity which, merely through its existence, will attract satellite suppliers and customers who in turn will attract their own circles of dependencies. As an example, a large automobile assembly plant in a New Town would attract a number of specialized metal-working and engineering industries, parts manufacturers, and various service firms, while the new work force would attract consumer goods and service industries which would require their own servicing firms. The only question is whether the seed capital initially invested by the government would not have been better invested in improving the congested conditions, housing, transportation, and environment of the existing urban areas where so many of the fixed costs of urbanization have already been made. There is no evidence that the calculations of the relative merits of the two alternatives were made.

One further approach to regional development was the definition of "development areas" which would be aided in other ways, such as giving special tax advantages to relocated firms, leasing publicly built plants at low rents, gifts of capital funds, subsidized loans, and other inducements to locate in the region. Given the British penchant for restless institutional change, these development areas would be alternately large (1934–4 Special Areas); smaller (1954–8 Development Areas); smaller yet (1960–165 Development Areas); and large again (1964–8 Planning Regions). However, no matter what the set-up at the particular moment, the British were consistently very concerned about regional development, and just as consistently, they refused to develop institutions with real responsibilities to accomplish the task.

The Labour government of 1964, its faith in planning restored, created regional Planning Boards and Councils, which were charged with planning regional resource utilization and integrating the regional economy into the goals of the National Plan. True to form, the Regional Councils were not given institutional roots or connections with the political process. Hence they were dependent on other levels of government for the actual initiatives and funds for regional development. The curiously ambivalent position of the regional planners is one more piece of evidence documenting the failure of successive British governments to establish a long-run view of where the economy ought to be headed. The lack of this long-term viewpoint at the very center of power and decision-making prevented the rational construction of effective policy-making institutions.

Agricultural Policy

British agriculture is highly protected and generally fairly specialized. Average food prices are kept down through purchases of certain agricultural products from lower cost Commonwealth sources. However, domestic food producers have been kept afloat by a variety of means, such as the familiar device of price supports. When the inevitable surpluses have accumulated, the government has enforced production cutbacks. The result is that the consumer pays high prices for products in the store and then pays taxes to finance the support payments.

In 1951 the Conservative government switched to a more rational program sometimes suggested for adoption in the United States. Products may be sold in the market for whatever they will fetch—then the government will make up the difference between that freely determined price and some negotiated "standard" price. The taxpayer is still stuck for the "deficiency" payments but at least has relatively cheap products in the market. Various subsidies are also granted to farmers to restructure their production or to improve their efficiency.

Summary and Conclusions

British economic policies and planning practices may appear jumbled, chaotic, and contradictory to someone who has studied the French planning system with its First through Sixth Plans and orderly organizational charts. This is because British policies and planning practices *are* jumbled, chaotic, and contradictory. Time and again the sympathetic analyst is left breathless by the apparent incompetence and irresponsibility of the Central government ministries and planners, Labour or Conservative. For a people known for their appreciation of stability and tradition, one cannot but be struck by the restless, rootless creation and destruction of institutions and agencies. Policy-making machinery has been created overnight, bureaucrats plucked from their career positions, voluminous reports issued and ignored, and then the agency destroyed, reshuffled, or juggled into a new organizational structure or put under another ministry. How many decades of this can occur before a moral fatigue and cynicism sets in among the circles of professionals who man the bureaucratic pyramids which have been torn down and restacked a half-dozen times?

Both opponents and proponents of economic planning can point to the British experience as bolstering their viewpoints. Opponents of planning and advocates of the market mechanism can point to decades of monumental errors, miscalculations, poor timing, political compromise, and waste of vast sums of money. Most of their criticisms are valid.

Proponents of economic planning can respond to the above criticisms by first granting that they are true, then establishing that the failures all demonstrate what can happen when you *don't* plan. Simply put, the British didn't plan at all, they merely *said* they were planning every time they created some ad hoc agency to draft a report to take the heat off the government. At every critical juncture—the unveiling of a new National Plan or creation of a new agency—it was obvious or quickly became obvious that no one had thought through the implications of the action. What happens if your goals are inconsistent? What is the probability of balance of payments difficulties? Is a fall-back position prepared if a balance of payments crisis occurs (July 1966) or will the Plan have to be ingloriously scrapped? What is the probability of inducing private individuals to respond to suggestions from official agencies which were created yesterday and will probably be disestablished tomorrow?

Can we point to any differences between Britain and France to explain their very different planning experiences? First, the political institutions made a vast difference in approach possible. It is true that French bureaucrats are more accustomed to making strategic decisions and having their authority accepted. The British civil service is far more accustomed to having the main activity occur in the marketplace, after which it tidies up the loose ends, deferring to the principle private interests.

On the other hand, another hypothesis supplements this one nicely. In the postwar years the very weakness of the French central government and lack of strong regional or local authorities left a power vacuum into which the professional bureaucrats could step to mold institutions into workable structures with defined tasks and goals and a division of labor. Institutional evolution could then occur without the disruption and confusing collapses of the decision-making machinery such as occurred in Britain.

In Britain, the strength and vitality of the democratic political process meant that ascendant parties and politicians had a mandate and the power to mold institutions in the way they saw fit. Unfortunately for the sake of consistent institutional development, a shift of a few percentage points in parliamentary elections could displace one mandate and replace it with its precise opposite.

QUESTIONS

1. Why is Britain classified as a mixed rather than a planned or socialist economy?
2. What is the significance of the balance of payments for the success or failure of British economic policies?
3. What were the causes of the failure of the Labour government's first attempt at planning?
4. What were the causes of the Conservative government's failure to solve Britain's economic problems by a return to the free market?
5. Why were both the Conservative and Labour governments' planning efforts in the 1960s so unsuccessful?
6. What were the aims and results of the British incomes policy?
7. Compare and contrast the British, French, and German approaches to planning.

9

The Performance
of the Mixed Economies

Introduction

In the previous chapters we have surveyed the economic institutions and policies
of three modern, industrial mixed economies in the postwar period. It is
useful now to compare and contrast their approaches to common problems
as well as their performance in the solution of these problems. In this chapter we
shall first consider the similarities and differences in the evolution of their
economic institutions and their use of policy tools. Second, we will contrast
their performance in the areas of static efficiency, dynamic efficiency, and
equity. And finally we will discuss the effects of the increasing integration of
their economies and the development of the Common Market.

PHILOSOPHIES, INSTITUTIONS, AND POLICIES

Britain, France, and Germany all emerged from World War II with
common problems and common objectives. Their capital stocks had been
severely depleted or destroyed. The housing shortage was acute, and their

economies were riddled with wartime controls. They each had a highly skilled labor force and the technical knowledge to operate a modern industrial economy. They each desired to improve the welfare of their populations by creating an atmosphere conducive to stable growth and full employment while providing certain welfare services that would raise the level of living of those at the bottom of the economic ladder and reduce the risk to the individual of the consequences of unemployment, illness, and disability.

All three economies rejected both laissez-faire capitalism and command planning as desirable or effective means of achieving their objectives. All retained market institutions as the primary mechanism by which to allocate resources, although governments' responsibility for economic affairs grew tremendously. From table 9.1 we can see that they met with varying degrees of success. It must be remarked first, however, that in contrast to their pre-war experiences each economy achieved a substantial degree of stability and prosperity. Growth was positive in nearly every year, and France and Germany were able to sustain extremely rapid growth rates throughout the 1950s and 1960s. The sources of this growth and the disappointing record of the British will be examined in a later section of the chapter. Despite its limited economic growth Britain was able, as well as the others, to avoid any but the mildest of recessions and to keep its labor force at high levels of employment. Compared to the distressing period of the 1930s, the 1950s and 1960s were prosperous years for all three economies. The United States was not so fortunate and grew more slowly, suffered longer and deeper recessions, and sustained higher rates of unemployment than these other nations.

From tables 9.2 and 9.3 we can see that the structure of the three economies is quite similar. France and Germany, however, have been able to devote a significantly larger share of GNP to investment than Britain, where the share of GNP devoted to private consumption is greater. The rapid growth of government's role in the economy in the post-war period is evidenced in the high proportion—over 30 percent in 1970—of GNP accounted for by government expenditures in all three economies and the United States. This figure may exaggerate the impact of the government on the economy, on the one hand, and understate it on the other. First, the government does not actually produce 30 percent of the goods and services comprising the GNP in any of the economies. Interest on the debt and current transfers represent the transfer of income from one segment of the private sector to another and not a claim on resources by government. Current expenditures on goods and services more closely reflects the government's claim, but even here most goods and services are purchased by the government from the private sector. The government's total influence on the economy is much larger, however, than these figures reflect. First, gross fixed asset formation does not include investments made by public corporations, i.e., the nationalized industries. Second, and more importantly, the data do not reflect at all the large indirect influences of the government on the private sector. We have seen that each economy has adopted a large number of policies

Table 9.1

Growth, Employment Prices

	FRANCE			GERMANY		
	(1) GNP (Annual average % change in constant prices)	(2) Unemployment (% of labor force unemployed)	(3) Prices (Annual % change Consumer Price Index)	(1) GNP (Annual average % change in constant prices)	(2) Unemployment (% of labor force unemployed)	(3) Prices (Annual % change Consumer Price Index)
1950	—	—	—	—	7.2	—
1951	6.0	—	16.9	10.9	6.4	7.8
1952	2.5	—	11.8	9.0	6.1	2.1
1953	3.1	—	−1.2	7.9	5.5	−1.8
1954	4.8	1.8	−0.3	7.1	5.2	.2
1955	5.8	1.6	1.1	11.8	3.9	1.6
1956	5.0	1.1	2.0	6.9	3.4	2.5
1957	6.0	.8	2.1	5.7	2.9	2.1
1958	2.6	.9	15.8	3.2	3.0	2.2
1959	2.9	1.3	6.1	7.0	2.1	1.0
1960	7.1	1.2	3.7	8.8	1.0	1.3
1961	5.4	1.0	3.3	5.4	.7	2.4
1962	6.8	1.2	4.8	4.0	.6	4.0
1963	5.8	1.4	4.8	3.5	.7	4.0
1964	6.6	1.1	3.4	6.7	.6	2.3
1965	4.7	1.3	2.5	5.6	.5	3.4
1966	5.6	1.4	2.7	2.9	.6	3.5
1967	4.7	1.8	2.7	−0.3	1.7	1.5
1968	4.8	2.1	4.6	7.2	1.2	1.8
1969	8.0	1.7	6.4	7.9	.7	2.7
1970	5.6	1.7	5.2	6.3	.5	3.9
1971	5.3	1.8	5.4	2.0	.6	5.1
1972	5.5	2.0	5.8	2.3	.9	5.7

Source: OECD, Main Economic Indicators, National Accounts of OECD Countries 1953-1969, and Economic Surveys.

Table 9.1 (cont)

Growth, Employment Prices

	BRITAIN			U.S.		
	(1) GNP (Annual average % change in constant prices)	(2) Unemployment (% of labor force unemployed)	(3) Prices (Annual % change Consumer Price Index)	(1) GNP (Annual average % change in constant prices)	(2) Unemployment (% of labor force unemployed)	(3) Prices (Annual % change Consumer Price Index)
1950	—	.2	—	—	—	—
1951	2.3	.9	8.9	8.1	—	6.4
1952	-.5	1.4	9.5	3.1	—	2.4
1953	4.7	1.3	3.1	4.4	—	1.2
1954	3.9	1.0	1.2	-1.3	—	0.0
1955	3.1	.8	4.5	7.6	—	2.3
1956	2.0	.9	4.9	1.8	4.0	3.4
1957	2.1	1.1	3.7	1.5	4.1	2.2
1958	.9	1.7	3.0	-.8	6.5	1.1
1959	3.7	1.7	.6	6.1	5.3	2.1
1960	4.8	1.3	1.0	2.4	5.3	1.0
1961	3.5	1.1	3.4	2.2	6.5	1.0
1962	1.3	1.6	4.3	6.4	5.3	1.0
1963	4.0	1.9	2.0	4.0	5.5	1.0
1964	5.4	1.4	3.3	5.4	5.0	2.0
1965	2.5	1.1	4.7	6.3	4.4	1.9
1966	2.1	1.1	3.9	6.6	3.6	3.8
1967	2.1	1.9	2.5	2.7	3.7	4.6
1968	2.9	2.1	4.7	4.8	3.4	5.3
1969	1.3	2.0	5.5	2.8	3.4	5.8
1970	1.6	2.5	6.4	-.7	5.9	5.8
1971	1.2	3.6	9.4	2.7	5.9	4.3
1972	0.0	—	7.0	6.4	5.6	3.2

Table 9.2

GNP by End Use

% of GNP	France			Germany		
	1955	*1965*	*1970*	*1955*	*1965*	*1970*
1. Private consumer expenditures	67	61	59	59	56	55
2. Government current expenditure	13	13	12	13	15	16
defense	5	4		3	4	3
civil	8	3		10	11	13
3. Gross domestic fixed asset formation	18	24	26	23	27	27
4. Change in stocks	0	1	3	3	2	1
5. Exports of goods and services	16	14	17	20	20	24
6. Less: imports of goods and services	14	13	16	18	20	22

Source: *OECD, National Accounts of OECD countries 1953-1969, Economic Surveys, and U.S. Department of Commerce, Survey of Current Business.

Table 9.3

Breakdown of Total Government Expenditures
As a % of GNP

	France			Germany		
	1955	*1965*	*1970*	*1955*	*1965*	*1970*
Current expenditure on goods and services	13.0	12.6	12.1	13.2	15.2	15.8
Subsidies	1.8	2.0	1.9	0.2	1.3	1.4
Interest on Public Debt	1.3	1.1	1.0	0.7	0.7	—
Current Transfers	13.1	16.1	16.7	11.4	12.8	12.6
Gross fixed asset formation	2.3	3.3	3.4	2.7	4.4	4.3
Total	31.5	35.1	35.1	28.2	34.4	39.5

Source: OECD, National Accounts of OECD Countries 1953-69; 1960-1970.

Table 9.2 (con't)

GNP by End Use

% of GNP	Britain			U.S.		
	1955	*1965*	*1970*	*1955*	*1965*	*1970*
1. Private consumer expenditures	67	64	62	63	62	63
2. Government current						
expenditure	17	17	18	17	18	22
defense	8	6	5	10	7	8
civil	9	11	13	7	11	14
3. Gross domestic						
fixed asset						
formation	15	18	18	18	17	14
4. Change in stocks	2	1	1	2	1	2
5. Exports of goods and						
services	25	21	22	5	6	6
6. Less: imports of goods and						
services	25	21	22	5	5	6

Table 9.3 (con't)

Breakdown of Total Government Expenditures
As a % of GNP

	Britain			United States		
	1955	*1965*	*1970*	*1955*	*1965*	*1970*
Current expenditure						
on goods and services	17.0	18.5	17.9	16.9	18.1	20.9
Subsidies	2.8	1.7	1.7	0.0	0.2	0.2
Interest on Public Debt	4.0	4.1	4.0	1.3	1.3	1.5
Current Transfers	5.4	7.9	8.8	3.8	5.1	7.4
Gross fixed asset						
formation	3.9	4.5	4.9	2.4	3.1	2.7
Total	33.1	36.7	37.3	24.0	27.8	32.7

and uses a wide variety of tools to stimulate or retard the economy as a whole as well as particular sectors of the economy. The subsidies recorded in table 9.3 include only formal subsidies paid to nationalized enterprises who cannot cover their costs with their revenue. They do not include the many tax and credit incentives devised by government to support the expansion of private industry. We will now briefly review the governmental policies in common use in these three mixed economies as well as in many other mixed economies.

Nationalization and the Welfare State

The two governmental activities which created widespread interest and some dismay after the war were nationalization of certain private industries and the development of the welfare state. The importance of these two programs and their effect on the future of market economies can be greatly exaggerated. In all three economies, public utilities, communications and transportation facilities, and a few basic, usually ailing, industries were nationalized in the period immediately following the war. Nationalization did not proceed further and in certain instances in Britain and Germany industries were denationalized or stock sold to private individuals. Nationalization, by itself, did not determine the performance of these industries. In most instances each nationalized industry was administered by a separate agency, and many behaved like private corporations, often displaying a great deal of independence from government control. Their performance varied all the way from the perpetually subsidized British coal industry to the progressive French electricity industry. Their success or failure depended to a great extent on the skill and ability of their managers and their freedom from political pressure.

All three economies have greatly expanded their welfare services in the post-war period. The provision of a social security package including sickness and unemployment benefits as well as old-age pensions is an accepted and established policy. Germany has moved the furthest in this direction of protecting the real income of the lower groups by tying pensions to a cost of living index. All three governments have stepped into the medical and housing industries in an attempt to provide low cost medical and housing facilities for all segments of the population. Britain chose to nationalize the health industry, while France and Germany provide comprehensive health insurance. Each has found that to improve the quality and quantity of health services and housing, resources must be channeled to these areas to increase the available supply, since the provision of "free" or "low cost" services tends to create greater demand for those services and thus aggravate a situation where there are shortages.

Stabilization Policies

The governments of all three economies have accepted responsibility for the maintenance of full employment stability and growth, and use a variety of fiscal and monetary tools to secure these ends. The economies differ, however, in their willingness to use these tools to intervene selectively in the private sector, although all use fiscal and monetary policy to control the level of aggregate demand. Germany was a late comer in the use of countercyclical fiscal policy, and France relied considerably on direct controls rather than tight fiscal and monetary policies to mitigate the effects of an overheated economy in the 1950s. Britain has attempted until recently to regulate the credit markets directly rather than indirectly through control of the money supply. All now

Table 9.4

Sources of Government Revenues

	(1) Total government revenue *(% of GNP)*	*(2)* Direct taxes on households *(% ot TGR)*	*(3)* Direct taxes on corporations *(% of TGR)*	*(4)* Indirect taxes *(% of TGR)*
		France		
1950	32.8	39.9	5.8	46.8
1955	33.2	41.4	5.7	50.6
1960	34.1	48.8	6.9	47.3
1965	37.6	48.4	5.2	44.5
1970	37.2	51.3	6.4	39.2
		Germany		
1950	31.5	43.7	9.1	42.6
1955	34.8	41.7	8.3	42.2
1960	35.5	45.8	8.9	40.4
1965	35.7	48.7	6.9	39.4
1970	37.5	55.8		35.5
		Britain		
1950	32.6	33.6	17.5	47.6
1955	30.1	32.6	15.7	46.1
1965	32.3	43.5	5.0	43.1
1970	40.8	52.6		40.6
		United States		
1950	23.9	39.2	25.8	34.7
1955	24.9	45.6	21.5	32.7
1965	27.2	49.5	16.6	31.7
1970	30.6	66.2		

Source: OECD: National Accounts of OECD Countries, 1953-69; 1960-70.

attempt to influence the level of aggregate demand through the use of discretionary monetary and budget policies.

Table 9.4 records the sources of government revenues of the three economies and the United States. Indirect taxes are a much more important source and corporate income taxes a much less important source of revenue in the three than in the United States. A widespread indirect tax used by Britain, France, and Germany, as well as many other Western economies, is the value-added tax. Many governments feel that it is impossible to raise substantial additional revenue from the personal income tax because rates are already quite high. They also believe that increasing the corporate income tax will reduce after-tax profits available for investment and thus reduce the long-run rate of growth. The value-added tax is similar to a national sales tax but is paid at each level of production only on the addition to value contributed at that stage. The value added by previous stages, recorded on invoices of purchased goods and services, is subtracted from the selling price of the good, and a tax is paid on the difference. Although there still is a great deal of debate over the consequences and impact of the value-added tax, it has become extremely popular. It is easy to collect and it allows the government to influence consumption expenditures by varying its rate. Since the value-added tax is a tax on consumption rather than income, it is argued that it will stimulate savings and free resources for investment. The level of demand can be reduced without reducing the level of investment. Opponents of the tax argue that it is regressive, but the European economies have tended to rely on extensive welfare programs rather than progressive income taxes to redistribute income toward the lower classes.

It is ironic, now that there is almost complete acceptance of the role of discretionary stabilization policy in Western governmental circles, that there is a growing doubt on the part of professional economists as to the usefulness of these policies, particularly if the attempts to manipulate taxes and government expenditures are for short-run countercyclical purposes. The long-run growth of an economy appears to depend more on the ability to increase aggregate supply through stimulation of productivity advances and removing bottlenecks than the skillful manipulation of aggregate demand. The nature and sources of economic growth in the three economies will be analyzed in more detail in the section on dynamic efficiency.

In our summary of stabilization policies a final word must be said about the widespread use of incomes policies as a substitute for the more traditional monetary and fiscal policies. There is a widely held belief among Western government leaders that the traditional policies are inadequate to control inflationary pressures in a world in which large corporations have the power to push up prices and powerful unions can bargain for large wage increases, thus pushing up prices even in recessionary periods. The three countries we have studied and many other Western economies, the United States among them, have adopted some form of incomes policy to set acceptable limits to price and wage increases. There still seems to be great faith in their eventual effectiveness despite the poor results displayed so far. Neither Britain, France, nor Germany have developed machinery or institutions to implement their guidelines, and it is not clear how they could do so given the lack of agreement over any method of determining the appropriate division of the overall increases in income among the multitude of competing claims in each economy.

Planning and Micro Controls

Perhaps the greatest divergence in philosophies and policies among the three economies occurs in the area of planning and the use of micro controls to selectively intervene in the economy. These differences seem to be narrowing and a consensus on the acceptability of certain limited types of planning is beginning to develop. In the 1950s France appeared to be headed toward comprehensive planning at the micro level, reinforced by government sanctions and controls, while Germany totally rejected the role of any type of government planning in a market context. Britain equivocated, fascinated at times with French planning techniques but reluctant to develop and use the controls necessary to implement the plan. By the middle 1960s there was a growing disenchantment with detailed sectoral planning and a growing belief in the need for a government to plan its own activities over a period of time longer than one year. France reduced the emphasis on sectoral targets in its plans whereas Germany adopted budgetary planning.

There still is a substantial difference in the approach to planning in the three economies. Germany considers its limited plan more of a forecast than an objective to be achieved through deliberate manipulation of policy tools. The preparation of the plan in Germany is quite different from this process in France. In the former, a body of impartial experts draws up the plan, which the government then presents to the Bundestag for approval. The government believes that democracy is better served through legislative control than consultation with interest groups in the preparation of the plan. British planning is still in a state of flux.

COMPARATIVE PERFORMANCE

Static Efficiency

We have seen in chapter two that static efficiency implies getting the most out of the available factors of production at a moment in time. In a democratic market system it implies the maximization of consumer welfare. In chapters three and four we observed that a perfectly competitive market economy may come close to the achievement of static efficiency, but that there are many impediments to its achievement in actual market or mixed economies. Certainly welfare is lost if one of the six efficiency conditions is not achieved, but how can we judge how much static inefficiency exists in any particular economy and how much welfare can be gained by the use of appropriate policies?

One can look at qualitative evidence which indicates that resources are allocated inefficiently in all three countries under consideration—subsidies to agriculture, high regional unemployment, and monopoly practices are examples. However, it is difficult to determine relative performance from a series of anecdotes pointing to glaring cases of waste and inefficiency. Britain is usually the most severely critized for its inefficient allocation of resources, with its antiquated and inefficient railroads, coal mines, and shipyards, its depressed regions with high unemployment rates, its endemic housing shortage, its fragmented unions ready to strike at a moment's notice, and its high defense expenditures. But will quantitative data support the view that Britain is indeed the most inefficient of the three?

Table 9.5

Measures of Static Efficiency (USA = 100 percent) *

| | National Income per Employed Worker[a] | |
	Based on foreign national price weights (1)	Based on U.S. price weights (2)
United States	100	100
Northwest Europe	44	56
France	43	55
Germany	43	55
United Kingdom	44	56

| | National Income per Unit of Combined Factor Inputs | |
	Based on foreign national price weights (1)	Based on U.S. price weights (2)
United States	100	100
Northwest Europe	50	63
France	49	62
Germany	52	63
United Kingdom	50	63

[a]In comparisons of Western Europe and the United States employment is calculated to allow for differences in annual hours, though not proportionately.

Source: Abram Bergson, Planning and Productivity, p. 22.

The ultimate objective of quantitative studies in this area is to measure the relative efficiency with which various economies use their resources to produce goods and services. Given a certain amount of land, labor, capital, and raw materials can Country A produce more than Country B? In practice it is very difficult to answer this question because different economies have different factor endowments and produce different bundles of goods. An attempt must be made to measure inputs and outputs in comparable units. One study, based on 1960 data, attempts to focus on the question of relative performance by calculating national income or output per worker and per unit of a composite of labor and capital taken together.[1] The results are reported in table 9.5. Two figures are calculated for each productivity measure, one valuing inputs and outputs in the domestic currency of the country in question and a second valuing inputs and outputs in terms of U.S. prices. (For a discussion of the problems of quantitative intercountry comparisons see the Appendix to this chapter.) The labor productivity index does not allow judgments on relative static efficiency because of the possible variation in capital per worker from one economy to another.

Table 9.6

Measures of Static Efficiency Adjusted for Labor Quality
(USA = 100 percent)

	National Income per Employed Worker	
	Based on foreign national price weights (1)	Based on U.S. price weights (2)
United States	100	100
Northwest Europe	47	60
France	47	60
Germany	47	61
United Kingdom	47	60

	National Income per Unit of Combined Factor Inputs	
	Based on foreign national price weights (1)	Based on U.S. price weights (2)
United States	100	100
Northwest Europe	53	67
France	53	66
Germany	53	69
United Kingdom	52	66

Source: Abram Bergson, Planning and Productivity, p. 26.

[1]Abram Bergson, Planning and Productivity under Soviet Socialism (New York: Columbia University Press, 1968), pp. 19-30.

Although the composite index reflects the amount of capital available, it too is still an imperfect measure of relative performance. The quantity of labor and quality and quantity of raw materials may also differ for each economy. An attempt is made to correct for difference in labor quality, and the resultant productivities are reported in table 9.6. All three economies are remarkably close to each other and the Northwest European average and considerably below the United States. Their relative performance is improved if adjustments are made for differences in the stock of capital and labor quality. Their performance vis-á-vis the United States would certainly be improved further if output per worker rather than employed worker were the measure of productivity. Although the United States appears to be more efficient, it has been much less successful than Northwest Europe in fully utilizing its labor force, as the unemployment rates in table 9.1 testify. Although there is little to contrast among the mixed economies of Northwest Europe, we will see in a later part of the book that they all perform very well when compared with the Soviet Union.

Dynamic Efficiency

Table 9.1 reports the growth rates of France, Germany, Britain, and the United States, but we must recall from chapter two that growth and dynamic efficiency are not synonymous. Dynamic efficiency reflects an economy's ability to increase its output per unit of input over time, called intensive growth. Growth rates are measures of increases in real GNP over time, due both to improvements in productivity and extensive growth, i.e., increases in the quantities of the factors of production themselves. In order to assess the relative dynamic efficiencies of the economies under consideration it is necessary to inquire into the sources of that growth and the relative importance of productivity advance in each case.

A study of the sources of growth of several European countries and the United States has been done and a portion of the results is presented in table 9.7. It appears that not only were Britain and the United States growing more slowly than France and Germany, but a larger percentage of their growth was due to increases in factor inputs—i.e., was extensive growth—rather than increases in factor productivity. This was the case despite the fact that France and Germany invested a significantly larger share of their GNP than did Britain and the United States. (See table 9.2) Table 9.8 reports the rate of increase of labor productivity for the four countries both in terms of number of workers employed and man-years. The two measures will diverge if the length of the work week is changing. This data corroborates the figures in table 9.7. Labor productivity has been increasing much more rapidly in France and Germany than in Britain or the United States.

It is extremely difficult and beyond the scope of this text to explain the relative performance of the four economies. However, we can point to some poli-

Table 9.7

Sources of Growth of Total National Income 1950-62

	FRANCE		GERMANY		UNITED KINGDOM		UNITED STATES	
	Total national income		Total national income		Total national income		Total national income	
	1950-55	1955-62	1950-55	1955-62	1950-55	1955-62	1950-55	1955-62
National Income	100	100	100	100	100	100	100	100
Total factor input	26	27	32	47	49	45	60	56
Labor	10	9	20	17	44	14	34	32
Capital	16	17	12	29	5	31	26	24
Land	0	0	0	0	0	0	0	0
Output per unit of input	74	73	68	53	51	55	40	44
Advances of knowledge	17	16	8	14	35	30	20	25
Changes in the lag in the application of knowledge, general efficiency, and errors and ommissions	16	17	19	2	-3	4	0	0
Improved allocation of resources	20	20	14	14	6	4	9	8
Economies of scale	22	21	21	23	12	17	10	10
Other	0	0	0	0	0	0	0	0

Source: Edward F. Denison, assisted by Jean-Pierre Poullier, Why Growth Rates Differ: Postwar Experience in Nine Western Countries, The Brookings Institution (Washington, D. C.: 1967), pp. 299, 307, 309, 315.

Table 9.8

The Growth of Labor Productivity 1956-1966
(Annual average percentage change)

	GNP	Employment	Output per worker	
			Employment	Man-years
France				
1956-61	4.9	.1	4.7	4.4
1962-66	5.4	.6	4.8	4.9
Germany				
1956-61	6.2	1.6	4.5	5.9
1962-66	4.3	.3	3.9	4.7
United Kingdom				
1956-61	2.9	.5	2.4	3.1
1962-66	3.0	.7	2.3	3.1
United States				
1956-61	2.1	1.0	1.1	1.6
1962-66	5.6	1.8	3.7	2.9

Source: U.S. Congress, Joint Economic Committee, Soviet Economic Perfor-mance: 1966-67, (Washington D.C.: U.S. Government Printing Office, 1960), p. 14.

cies and conditions of each economy that have influenced its performance. It is argued that Germany benefited from a rapidly growing labor supply that allowed firms to hold down wages and reinvest their profits.[2] Germany was able to pursue policies that increased aggregate supply, while maintaining a noninflationary level of aggregate demand through the use of a tight monetary policy. The output of exports, investment, and consumer goods rose without a substantial inflationary threat. The stop-go policies practiced in Britain were avoided. In the 1960s labor shortages rather than surpluses were the rule, wages did rise more rapidly, and the rate of inflation increased. Germany was successful, however, in promoting savings among middle and upper income groups and in maintaining a high rate of investment.

France faced labor shortages throughout the postwar period but was able to achieve high growth rates by allocating scarce resources to those sectors of the economy with a high growth potential. When inflation threatened, public consumption, rather than investment, was sacrificed. The French also devoted a considerable amount of resources to what they considered "high technology" areas. They also stressed the rationalization of industry, promoting mergers to take advantages of economies of scale. The preponderant share of their growth deriving from increases in factor productivity attests to their success. Germany and France have both been quite successful in sustaining high levels of invest-

[2]Charles Kindleberger, *Europe's Postwar Growth* (Cambridge: Harvard University Press, 1967), pp. 24-86.

ment despite the pressures of full employment, although they have often used quite different means to accomplish this task. Germany, through the promotion of savings and the control of credit and its flow into investment and export industries, has managed to grow rapidly while providing a comprehensive package of welfare services. France has tended to rely more heavily on direct controls and the use of budgetary policy to selectively cut spending in times of inflationary pressure. As a result growth rates have been high, but so has public discontent.

Britain also had a full if not over-full employment economy for most of the postwar period. Attempts to stimulate investment resulted in inflation, and policies were then put into effect that reduced investment rather than consumption. Although British taxes were a smaller percentage of GNP than in Germany, they were structured to encourage consumption rather than savings. Low interest rates designed to stimulate investment discouraged the small saver.

In summary, it would appear that intensive growth does not require any particular set of institutions or practices, whether of the planning or laissez-faire variety. Simply stated, a certain pattern of events must occur before sustained intensive growth can occur: new knowledge must be transformed into capital or new techniques, and these must be widely introduced into industry. The labor force must constantly upgrade its skills to match the ever-shifting requirements of industry. If institutions or past practices stand in the way of the progressive evolution of the economy, these institutions must be changed or eliminated. Whether this transformation occurs as a result of state prodding and incentives or whether it occurs spontaneously is irrelevant—men and machines must become more productive. Fiscal and monetary stimulation can only assure that increased productivity is fully utilized; it cannot of itself produce growth. It is the opinion of the authors that the concentration on long-run improved productivity (increasing aggregate supply) was the key to the success of postwar France and Germany. Their particular institutions were a matter of national tastes and preferences. Conversely, it was the concentration on short-run aggregate demand management and neglect of aggregate supply that became the critical failure of the British. The shuffling about of economic planning machinery might have been harmless enough if the British governments had realized they were not accomplishing anything. Instead they believed their own white papers and found later that industry and labor were ignoring their exhortations to invest and innovate, work and learn.

Our final point concerning dynamic efficiency is difficult to quantify or defend in detail. Our feeling is that overall macroeconomic stability, the avoidance of prolonged recessions or inflationary booms, is a positive factor in inducing labor and capital to make risky investments in improving themselves. France and Germany achieved macroeconomic stability through planning and controls in the former and through monetary policy in the latter. England was forced, usually because of its balance of payments, to restrict the economy—in

1947, 1949, 1951, 1955, 1957, 1960, 1961, 1964, 1968, and 1971—with stimulation in between. It does not make sense that labor or capital is going to be exuberantly progressive with that record. Rather, one would expect labor to be concerned with protecting its position rather than improving its skills and management to do the old, familiar things rather than new, daring ones. All in all, one would expect everyone to do what so many observers criticize the British for doing—standing pat.

Equity

The distribution of income in Britain, France, and Germany is determined in part by the individual's contribution as measured in the market place and in part by each government's vast system of social welfare programs. The intent of the government's social policies is not to promote an equal distribution of income but to provide a floor under the income of all families and protect them from the consequences of financial disasters beyond their control. A significantly larger share of the GNP of the three economies is devoted to government non-defense current expenditures and transfer payments than in the United States. Social welfare expenditures averaged over 10 percent of GNP in all three economies compared to under 5 percent in the United States.

The provision of family allowances, old age pensions, unemployment and disability compensation, rent subsidies, and low cost medical care have substantially raised the standard of living of the lower income groups. These government expenditures and transfers are paid for to a large extent by indirect taxes, usually payroll taxes rather than personal or corporate income taxes. They represent a transfer from one middle income group to another, rather than a transfer from the rich to the poor. Despite the relatively high level of welfare expenditures one does not find the "culture of poverty" or "generations of welfare" families in Western Europe as we do in the United States. Welfare payments are not considered as a transfer from the energetic, productive portion of the population to the lazy, unproductive portion, but as a source of services which all may dip into in times of need. Despite the high level of welfare expenditures, the percentage of the population in the labor force and the percentage of the labor force employed has been significantly higher in Britain, France, and Germany than in the United States.[3]

The Impact of Economic Integration on
Differences in National Economic Systems

In 1958 the continental heartlands of Europe—France, Italy, Germany, Belgium, the Netherlands, and Luxembourg—signed a treaty binding these nations to

[3]In 1960 40.5 percent of the population of the United States was in the labor force as compared to 43.2 percent in France, 47.8 percent in Germany and 47.6 percent in Britain.

a staged integration of their economies into a "common market." This attempt to create a "United States of Europe" was to have a far-reaching impact not only within the boundaries of this European Economic Community (EEC), but on the entire structure of the international trading and monetary system.

Efforts at binding together separate national economies, each retaining a good deal of economic and political sovereignty, is a tricky business in a climate of ancient enmities and recent conflagrations. However, perhaps the horrors of the World Wars have underscored the necessity of integrating the nations of Europe so tightly together that no one nation could ever again seek dominance over the whole. The United States of America together with Canada has demonstrated the advantages of a continental-size market for over a century, and the idea of one Europe has been the dream of several generations of European idealists.

The EEC has functioned as well as, and to a degree better than, its founders had conceived—certainly the fall of trade barriers proceeded more rapidly than anticipated. This resulted from the coming together of the unleashed energies of the separate economies at a very favorable moment, the completion of the reconstruction of most of their war damage. The logic and dynamics of this economic integration, once undertaken, has subtly—and sometimes not so subtly—altered the flavor and methods of national economic policy-making. For the remainder of this section we will examine in more detail the workings of a common market, noting that there are costs or disadvantages as well as benefits from the integration of only a portion of the world economy. We will conclude this survey of economic integration by noting how the institutions of national policy-making have been adjusted and adapted to the needs and demands of the larger community.

The Economics of a Common Market

Common markets are also called "customs unions" or areas in which tariffs and other trade barriers have been lowered between nations without simultaneous political union, such as occurred between the British ex-colonies in North America to form the United States. Almost all economists would agree that the lowering of trade barriers anywhere is a desirable thing, but the net effect of a customs union like the EEC is very ambiguous because a common market raises a common trade barrier against the rest of the world. On the one hand, the lowering of barriers between the member nations causes goods and resources to flow in rational patterns more in line with international comparative costs. This is a clear gain to the parties involved, and increased trade, income, and welfare are thereby created. The exchange of goods and factors of production between the Common Market countries burgeoned after 1958. On the other hand, economic relations with outside nations have been diverted and disrupted by the common barrier erected by the EEC.

This uprooting of established trade relations between an EEC nation and some outside country is termed the "trade diversion" effect of a customs union. For example, the United States and Britain had established positions in West Germany as a result of postwar occupation and reconstruction efforts. The American and British trade with France was considerably less because of France's long tradition of protectionism. With the establishment of a common EEC trade barrier, with tariffs standing somewhere between France's high ones and Germany's relatively low ones, the United States and Britain were scarcely better off in France, while their competitive positions in Germany were worsened a good deal. The result was that France could now enter the German market without hindrance. This muscling out of third parties, not on the basis of *real* cost differences but just because of a shifting of tariffs, constitutes the costs of trade diversion and runs counter to our concepts of economic efficiency. The question that remains is whether the benefits of trade creation outweigh the costs of trade diversion for the world as a whole rather than for just the EEC nations. After all, you can always make somebody better off by making someone worse off, but that is not the name of the game in economics.

The answer as to whether or not the EEC has been a net positive force in the world is not easy to determine. One argument defending the positive nature of the EEC has been the great acceleration in the growth rates of EEC countries. which has been attributed to the advantages of larger markets and the quickening of competitive forces as a result of increased exposure of firms to international suppliers and customers. This rapid growth had greatly increased the demand of EEC countries for the raw materials of the underdeveloped world and even for the manufactures of non-EEC industrial nations. In other words, prosperity has tended to spill over into outside markets, even over the trade barriers, leaving everyone better off. This argument is valid to a degree—the demand for imports from non-EEC sources grew faster than their demand for EEC goods. However, this fact serves only to emphasize the probability that *universal* trade-barrier dismantling could have accelerated everyone's growth rate and the spillover effects would have been mutually reinforcing rather than so one-sided. Economic rationality then requires either that the EEC lower its common barrier or the membership become more universal, which really amounts to the same thing in the long run. However, the EEC has developed supranational institutions and agencies of coordination that may be peculiar to the European context. Therefore the global optimum path of evolution for relations between EEC and non-EEC nations may be the negotiation of universal rounds of tariff reductions.

The common barrier of the EEC and the substantial number of important nations excluded from membership could only lead to some form of retaliation. Underdeveloped nations have talked of common markets such as LAFTA, Latin American Free Trade Association, but customs unions are weak devices for nations so dependent on the developed nations for markets. More significant has been the development of the European Free Trade Association (EFTA), a free trade union between the fringe or neutral nations of Europe—Austria, Britain, Denmark, Finland, Norway, Portugal, Sweden, and Switzerland. These nations were interested in lowering trade barriers and did so by 1967, but they were not as interested in submerging themselves ultimately in a political and economic union. Recent British entry into the EEC will probably result in the entry of several other nations from EFTA and lead to the formation of a special category of associated but independent nations.

To conclude this section on common markets, it is important to examine more fully the ambition of the EEC to conclude ultimately in some form of full political and economic union. This goal has been advanced fitfully because of the nationalist intransigence of the French under de Gaulle and his successors. Either the mellowing of France or its reduced importance within the EEC can lead to further advances toward this union. Institutions such as the European Parliament in Strasbourg, the Executive Commission of the EEC, the Council of Ministers, the EEC Assembly, and EEC Court of Justice, and an EEC bureaucracy in Brussels leave one with the strong feeling that the entire machinery of a European government is present in embryonic form, requiring the delegation of powers from the member nations.

The EEC nations already are a union in the sense that capital and labor are free to move wherever they obtain the best return. Though workers may not in fact move in large numbers between nations it is important that there be no legal barrier. If goods and factors of production are free to move, the only remaining areas of national sovereignty are fiscal and monetary policies.

National autonomy in fiscal and monetary policy is not really possible if full economic union or even a customs union is going to work. A nation could steal some marginal advantage by adopting a tax-subsidy structure designed to favor certain domestic industries. The logic of integration leads to increasing uniformity of tax structures and open subsidies logically derived rather than covertly slipped through.

Since differential rates of inflation can wreak havoc upon the pattern of payments surpluses and deficits, a common market cannot permit independent monetary policies in the long run. There is increasing evidence that it is the poorly managed money supply, rather than excessive government spending, that leads to prolonged inflation. If this is true, then it might be possible to permit national governments to determine their desired levels of government expenditure as long as the new expenditures were not financed by money creation.

It will be a number of years yet before it can be established what direction the EEC will take—whether it will continue to be a more or less loosely bound group of sovereign nations or forge ahead toward a United States of Europe confederation. Whatever the specific future of the Common Market, its existence has already altered the behavior of Britain, France, and Germany in a number of ways, each driven by the logic and momentum of economic integration.

The National Policy-Making Implications
of Economic Integration

As we have seen, French planning is nonimperative but nevertheless requires a substantial amount of subtle state intervention. The purpose and objectives of the European Economic Community were to eliminate government-business bargains involving the sheltering of national industry from domestic or international competition. Paternalistic French planning therefore had to be modified.

The opening up of competition from neighboring countries placed many small and medium-size French firms in dire straits. French monopolies and oligopolies found their power substantially diluted when confronted by foreign firms as large or larger. The implications of these trends for French-style planning is obvious—the state found it harder to arrange bargains with industries, firms, and special interests that could be meaningful or binding. An industry with a high plan priority could not be guaranteed that it would find markets for its products simply by following the plan projections. An industry or firm with low plan priorities or one being actively discriminated against could simply stage an end-run into foreign markets for supplies, sales, or even capital and labor. French planners could no longer rely on the cooperative instincts of businessmen due to the uncertainty of the pay-off from cooperation. The planners could no longer discipline industry with selective incentives. These facts, taken together with the entry of foreign firms into French industry, caused the French planners to alter their methods and their goals. Entry into the EEC certainly did not hamstring the planners, but they had to go back to the drawing-board and rethink their objectives.

By the late 1950s the advocates of German neoliberalism faced a number of internal problems that, when brought to a head by EEC discussions, pressured the authorities into considering some of the benefits of indicative planning. New economic forces and groups were asserting themselves in Germany. Early postwar growth had been rapid but was using up once-and-for-all favorable situations such as the migration of labor from the East and high return on large injections of capital into a capital-starved economy. By the sixties, West Germany had exhausted these "easy" sources of growth and had to do it the hard way by training existing workers in new skills, saving in order to invest, and hustling hard for new markets. The government was forced to turn its attention to areas of the economy that had been neglected to a degree in the reconstruction years when high priority was given to heavy industry. Small industry needed to be helped, agriculture needed restructuring, and social goods and investments had to be made in larger amounts.

After a long period of rather high unemployment following the war, the German economy reached full employment just as the need for enlarged government expenditures was beginning to be felt. It became obvious to the most devoted advocate of the free market that some sort of programming of public expenditures would be necessary to ensure that excessive claims on the national output were not permitted. The rising Social Democratic party was much more activist in its economic policy ideas, preferring the Keynesian methods of countercyclical budgetary policy-making to the monetary methods of Ludwig Erhard.

In EEC discussions the French and German positions with respect to planning were initially far apart. The French favored community-wide planning for the natural reason that if they wished to restore planning discipline internally, one way would be to impose planning on their competitors. The German negotiators were opposed to the French proposals because they naturally did not want to disturb the winning combination they had put together. For the reasons listed above, a compromise was reached to have medium-term or five-year projections at a very aggregated level to provide information to all the parties that felt they needed it, but for each of them to use the forecasts in whatever way they wanted—in France to implement the five-year plans and in Germany to program the level and structure of public expenditures.

Britain initially chose not to join the Common Market because of its substantial commitments economically and politically to the Commonwealth (most members of which have nothing in common and are not very wealthy), its ties to the United States, and a centuries-old reluctance to get deeply involved in continental politics. When the success of EEC and the costs of being excluded became obvious, Britain suggested that the membership be enlarged to include the rest of continental Europe and herself. This was rejected by the EEC, and thus the EFTA was born. A solo application for membership by Britain in 1961 was refused with a withering and humiliating veto by France under de Gaulle.

The British then faced an impossible task—to guard her reduced but still extensive international interests and outposts, to defend the pound sterling, to balance a weakened domestic economy, and to try not to offend the principal EEC countries of France and Germany in doing so.

Continued efforts by Britain to join the Common Market were capped by success in 1971 and a treaty was signed whereby Britain agreed to phase out its special ties with the Commonwealth and the United States, to change its "cheap food" policies at considerable expense to its consuming public, to make contributions to various EEC funds, and to gradually eliminate the pound sterling as an international reserve currency. Set against these sacrifices were the potential gains from entering the markets of the EEC and the stimulus of foreign competition in domestic markets.

The future success of the British venture into the Common Market depends upon whether the recent rounds of currency value changes and the future path of the domestic economy will leave Britain enough breathing space to export and improve the structure of her industries. The British record has been poor on this score to date, but there are signs she has learned a few lessons from her own experiences and those of the continental nations.

APPENDIX:
THE PROBLEMS OF MEASUREMENT

To compare the growth of the output of goods and services in one economy over time or the level of output in two different economies at a moment in time, it is necessary to express their outputs in terms of some common denominator, such as the money value of GNP. If prices and the physical chacteristics be a simple task. Unfortunately, however, this is seldom the case. Prices and qualities vary over time and among economies. Certain adjustments must be made to arrive at meaningful comparisons.

Table 9A.1

Output	1960		1970	
	Quantity (Tons)	Price/Unit	Quantity (Tons)	Price/Unit
steel	200	40	400	50
rice	500	5	600	15

Consider an economy which produces only two goods, steel and rice. The output and price of each commodity for two periods is represented in table 9A.1. How much has this economy grown? The output of steel has increased by 100 percent, while the output of rice has increased by only 20 percent. Our measure of the overall growth of GNP will depend upon the relative weight of steel and rice. We must weight the two by their relative values, but steel has a higher relative value using 1960 prices, while rice has a higher relative value using 1970 prices. An index of growth using first-period price weights is called a *Laspeyres index,* while one using second period price weights is called a *Paasche index.* The two are calculated below.

$$\text{Laspeyres} = \frac{\Sigma p_1 q_2}{\Sigma p_1 q_1} \ (100) = \frac{40(400) + 5(600)}{40(200) + 5(500)} = 230.3$$

$$\text{Paasche} = \frac{\Sigma p_2 q_2}{\Sigma p_2 q_1} \ (100) = \frac{50(400) + 15(600)}{50(200) + 15(500)} = 165.7$$

The Laspeyres index indicates a 230 percent increase over the ten-year span, while the Paasche indicates only a 165 percent increase. Whenever relative movements in prices and quantities diverge, indices calculated using different year price weights will also diverge; such divergence is one explanation for widely varying estimates of growth.

Additional measurement difficulties are posed by quality change as well as the introduction of new products. If in the example above rice in 1970 is a superior strain providing increased caloric value, the output figures for 1970 are really biased downward.

Suppose also that in 1970 a third product, television sets, appears in the national income statistics. If the output of television sets is weighted by the price at which it first appears, likely to be quite high, the growth index will be biased upward. All these problems require judgmental decisions in the construction of growth indices and are a legitimate source of variation among the estimates of various authors.

Comparisons between countries involve similar problems. The output of each economy is comprised of a unique mix of goods and services, which must be added together and thus weighted by their value in GNP. The measured size of output will depend upon whether the price weights reflect the relative price structure of one economy or another. When the output of the U.S.S.R. is weighted by U.S. prices it appears larger than when it is weighted by its own prices. This is due to the fact that many goods which are in short supply in the U.S.S.R. and consequently have relatively high prices—such as consumer goods—are plentiful in the U.S. and have relatively low prices. The reverse is true for products of heavy industry. Further problems of measurement are created by quality differences. Most researchers agree that a refrigerator in the U.S.S.R. is inferior to one produced in the U.S. and if some quality adjustment is not made the measurement of Soviet output will be biased upward.

QUESTIONS

1. What do you think are the most significant differences between the prewar and postwar economies of Britain, France, and Germany?

2. From your study of Britain, France, and Germany what do you think are the benefits of planning within the context of a market economy?

3. What measures can be computed to determine static efficiency, and how do the countries we have studied perform in this area?

4. What measures can be computed to determine dynamic efficiency, and how do the countries we have studied perform in this area?

5. What policies do Britain, France, and Germany use to achieve equity in the distribution of income?

6. What are the costs and benefits of the formation of the Common Market?

7. In what ways does a "common market" reduce national autonomy and promote uniform economic policies among nations?

10

The Marxist Critique
of Capitalism

Is Socialism Inevitable?

Introduction

In previous chapters we have pointed out that the capitalist market form of economic organization does possess serious flaws. These flaws are acknowledged by the most ardent defenders of capitalism, and a wide variety of social and governmental devices have been created to handle the worst of the failures. Research economists all over the world are continuously subjecting contemporary capitalism to searching criticism. Economists as far apart philosophically as John Kenneth Galbraith, Joan Robinson, and Milton Friedman can be counted on for stimulating attacks on complacency and the status quo at a moment's notice.

However, at the theoretical and practical level there can be no more searching criticism than the one that provides a total alternative. For over a century the most damning critique of capitalism has been that of Karl Marx and Friedrich Engels and their latter day interpreters such as Lenin, Mao Tse-Tung, Fidel Castro, and others. For half a century a practical demonstration of a thoroughgoing alternative to capitalism has been the socialist economy of the

Soviet Union, which has purportedly been constructed on Marxist principles, although that claim is subject to challenge.

A philosophical split developed early in the Marxist or socialist movement. One wing of the socialists felt that the economic triumph of the working class would come through the democratic political process, i.e., obtaining the vote and electing a socialist government. Another faction of the socialists, including Marx most of the time, felt that the resistance of the capitalists to expropriation would prevent a democratic triumph and that only the natural workings of history, discovered by Marx, would bring about the great revolution and the triumph of the working class. It is this massively documented and elaborately detailed theory of the inevitable demise of capitalism and the rise of socialism that stands as Marx's legacy to the twentieth century. The triumph of Marxist theories over other varieties of socialist thought was accomplished by sheer intellectual force—no other socialist thinker had constructed and defended a model of social, economic, and political development so all-encompassing. Using his method of dialectical materialism, Marx attempted to explain the rise of capitalism from a more primitive system. He predicted capitalism's rise to unprecedented power and productivity, and yet concluded that the complete revolutionary transformation of capitalism into socialism was its inescapable destiny.

MARX'S METHODOLOGY: DIALECTICAL MATERIALISM

The first thing to be noted in this section is that Marxist methodology and theory cut across several disciplines, including sociology, history, and philosophy as well as economics. In Marx's own time the boundaries between the social sciences were not as finely drawn as they have become in the twentieth century. In the intervening period each social science has developed its own jargon and methodology, and as a result each tends to view Marx from the perspective of its own bailiwick. Whole books have been devoted to just one aspect or another of Marxist thought. Since the purpose of this chapter is to summarize Marx's theory of the origin and fate of capitalism as an economic system, we will be forced to concentrate our attention on just the economic highlights of his thought. The bibliography at the end of this section will direct interested students to the enormous literature on Marx and Marxist thought.

To understand the unique flavor of Marx's thinking one must place him in the intellectual milieu of his times. Marx's earliest interest was philosophy, and he retained this interest throughout his life. German philosophy during Marx's youth was in a period of great ferment. A present day undergraduate student, usually exposed to little more than an introductory course in philosophy, probably cannot really comprehend the intense interest that young Europeans had in the study of philosophy in the first half of the nineteenth century. The term "philosophy" has, of course, been somewhat altered in meaning since then. Philosophy was once a study which covered virtually all systematic attempts to uncover the logic of and relationships between man and God, man and the universe, man and man, and man and his thought processes themselves. Since then, many of these explorations have been systematized and are now formal physical or social science disciplines.

Perhaps it is only hindsight that makes the extremely abstract philosophical theories and formulations of the period seem important. Some more contemporary commentators have alleged that twentieth century totalitarianism of one variety of another had its ideological foundations in this school or that of German philosophy. Whatever the merits of this view, it is certain that Marx at least derived two crucial cornerstones of his methodology and theory from his philosophical training, and Marxism is certainly the ideological foundation of Communist rule in the Soviet Union. First, Marx was a confirmed materialist. He rejected any notions that "good" or "evil" forces were at work behind the scenes and that men could trust in the workings of divine providence. He believed that this approach led to a rather fatalistic acceptance of the status quo; hence his often-quoted aphorism, "Religion is the opiate of the people." His view must be contrasted with rival philosophical schools which held that abstract ideas may be more "real" than the world we perceive—that some abstract essence of an object may exist even when the object itself has mouldered away. Clearly, this view is complementary to beliefs that abstract beings or forces may exist without benefit of physical existence as we understand it. Here philosophy blurs into theology. To repeat, Marx was a materialist, concerned only with the physical universe and actual living human beings in their brief span of mortality.

Secondly, Marx did not believe that the universe and man's place in it were random or predestined. His study of Hegelian philosophy had convinced him that the universe was not static, that the only universal truth was the fact of change. He believed that this process of change followed laws of regular behavior and that these regularities could be perceived by the intelligence of man. Hegelian philosophy pictured this useful notion of change as an evolutionary process, of something becoming something else, but in Marx's view Hegel was sidetracked into semi-mystical ideas. Hegel thought that a pure idea, a "thesis," could only have meaning through contrast with its exact opposite (good vs. evil; light vs. dark; etc.) or its "antithesis." From the struggle between the two opposing ideas a fusion of the two or a "synthesis" would result. This synthesis would have meaning only by contrast with, and would actually call into existence, a new antithesis. Marx found this concept of struggle between two opposites (the dialectic), the fusion into another form, and the rise of new tensions and opposites to be the vehicle he needed to analyze and explain the workings of the social and economic order. It is frequently said that Marx "stood Hegel on his head." Actually Marx took Hegel's truly useful analytical insight, stripped it of its "semi-mystical" notions about the struggle of abstractions, and substituted the clash of social classes and economic interests. This emphasis on objective reality is what is meant by the term "dialectic materialism"—the union of Hegel's dialectical concept with Marx's materialism. These ideas may not seem so striking or revolutionary today as they did then. But we have the advantage of having integrated most of what was useful in Marx, Darwin, Freud and other giants of the nineteenth century into our most basic assumptions about man's relationships with himself and the universe.

THE LABOR THEORY OF VALUE

Because of his political views and revolutionary activities, Marx spent over half his life in exile in England. While there, he studied the works of the great British economists as well as the growing literature on social and economic conditions under capitalist industrialization. He took these economic theories and masses of facts and wove them into a model of capitalism's origins, development, maturity, and eventual downfall, using the method of the dialectic. We will survey the outlines of Marx's model of capitalism in later sections of this chapter, but one last important intellectual debt of Marx must be indicated. The classical British economists spent a good deal of time trying to establish the objective basis for value, that is, why one good exchanges for another in certain proportions. Many of these economists held one form or another of a labor theory of value, which may be described as follows: all goods require labor to take raw materials from the ground, to process and shape them, to make the machines that assist the labor at all stages, and so forth. Therefore, it seemed to these non-socialist economists that labor was the universal ingredient or yardstick by which to establish exchange ratios between dissimilar goods. A good containing a given quantity of labor should exchange for other goods containing a similar quantity of labor. Other economists, in Marx's time and later, found the labor theory of value to be unsatisfactory in many ways, and they went on to develop the subjective or utility theory of value, which is familiar to students of economics today. Marx did not take part in this development of economic theory and instead made the labor theory of value a critical part of his own theory of capitalist development. Since orthodox Marxian theory became Holy Writ in Communist-run countries, the mainstream of economic theory passed them by until very recent years, when there have been some attempts by socialist economists to weave these disparate strands together.

Marx, of course, recognized that you couldn't just add up the hours spent producing a good to determine its value—the race would go to the tortoise in that case. Rather he formulated the idea that there was an *abstract* labor content embodied in each good, which represented the average amount of hours under current technology that would be required to produce the good. (One will notice that this conception is very much akin to the philosophical notion of abstract essences as more "real" than reality.) A tailor could take 20 hours to make a suit. If the suit contained 15 hours of "socially necessary" hours of labor, it would exchange for 15 hours' worth of food, shoes, etc. The fact that the tailor actually worked for 2 hours or 20 hours was irrelevant. That just meant that he was a better or worse tailor than average and obtained, therefore, more or less for his hour than the average.

THE THEORY OF SURPLUS VALUE

Marx saw the productive process under capitalism as a struggle of interests between two classes, the working class and the capitalists. Other groups, such as the military, clergy or middle classes, exist to serve the interests of the capitalists. The economic process involves the production of commodities by combining labor, capital, and materials. The capitalist controls the economic process because he controls access to the capital equipment without which nothing can be produced. Therefore, the capitalist dominates the terms of the two vital exchanges of capitalism—the exchange of a worker's labor time for cash or wages and the exchange of final goods and services for cash.

Let us look more closely at this process as Marx saw it. Marx recognized the importance of capital; that is, plant, equipment, and working funds, but he believed that the capitalist got out of a machine just the labor time that was put into it. Raw materials also contributed to the value of the good the amount of abstract labor time that had gone into their production. The capitalist hired labor for the final stage of production and then worked him for as many hours as he could get away with. Let us say that the raw materials contained 5 hours of labor time, the machinery depreciated or gave up another 5 hours of embodied labor time, and the worker labored for a 10-hour day to produce 100 yards of cloth. The cloth thus contained 20 hours of congealed labor effort and should be exchanged for 20 hours' worth of other products or their money equivalent. The capitalist had to pay for the ten hours of materials used and machinery wear-and-tear, but what did he have to pay for the ten-hour shift of labor effort? Marx applied the labor theory of value to the valuation of labor effort itself, and this yielded the devastating (to Marx and his followers) conclusion that the capitalist only had to pay labor subsistence wages. According to the theory, a commodity (labor effort) is worth only the labor effort embodied in it. The minimum abstract labor effort in reproducing the species is by definition subsistence. If wages fall below this level, the work force cannot reproduce itself. Wages cannot rise above this level because the capitalist certainly has no motive to raise wages needlessly, and the worker has no power to raise wages in the long run. Therefore, if only five hours' worth of inputs in food, clothing, and shelter per day are necessary to support a working family, the worker can expect no higher wages than that for his day's effort. Should the standard workday be in fact ten hours, the capitalist need pay the laborer for only five hours, and the remainder constitutes "exploitation" of the worker to the tune of five hours' worth of value. This residual between the value of the goods produced by labor's efforts and the value of the labor itself is the "surplus value," or the profits, of the capitalist.

Marx's Growth Model—The Accumulation of Capital

Marx discerned the two important social groupings, workers and capitalists, with the workers toiling at subsistence wages and the capitalists exploiting them, limited only by the physical endurance of the worker's human frame. Obviously the capitalists as a group had broken the bonds of a labor theory of value, since Marx felt that they contributed nothing yet reaped substantial rewards; they had also broken the bonds of subsistence. Marx now had to establish what they did with their incomes in excess of their consumption needs. Marx's observation, correct even to this day, was that society's saving is largely done by its better-off citizens. The capitalists of his day were proverbial for their reinvestment rate or the plough-back of profits into their businesses. Income and business taxes were virtually non-existent then, so the possibility of reinvesting profits in an expanding business was substantially greater than today. Marx viewed the capitalists with mixed feelings then. On the one hand he viewed with studied indignation the social costs of exploitation and industrialization. On the other hand he recognized that some social agent had to build the roads, railroads, factories, mills, and dams which would make progress to higher standards of living ultimately possible. Later socialists were to squabble over whether a stage of capitalist accumulation was *absolutely* necessary or whether some social agency like the government could step in and take over the role of capital accumulator (and exploiter?). The discussion of the Soviet economy which follows will touch on these points.

Marx did not believe that the capitalists put their money into more plant and equipment just because they didn't know what else to do with it. Actually more and more investments were needed because of the naturally aggressive tendencies of capitalists and capitalism. The more enterprising capitalists could make handsome temporary profits by adopting labor-saving machinery. The technologically displaced workers would become unemployed as a by-product of this process. In a comparatively short time span, the pressures of competition would force everyone to adopt the new equipment (more unemployment), and everyone would be back where they started—almost. Unemployment would be cranked up one more notch, and the capitalists would have more machinery but fewer workers around. It is well to remember that Marx believed that machinery added to production only what it cost to produce. Therefore, the capitalist was driven to reduce the proportion of workers to equipment, but *only workers* could be exploited to yield consistent profits. So the more aggressive or innovative capitalists deployed new investments as a way of creating new markets or expanding old ones at the expense of others. Less aggressive or imaginative capitalists had to follow the lead of those men either as imitators or to defend their interests against attack. Whether following an aggressive, imitative, or defensive strategy, the results were the same—invest, invest, invest or be swept aside.

The Falling Rate of Profit and Monopoly

The rising proportion of capital to labor in the productive process, as we have just observed, was squeezing out the sole source of steady profit, the exploitable and exploited worker. The resulting falling rate of profit in precisely the most dynamic industries (according to Marx's prediction) would create tremendous pressures for capitalists to seek combinations into cartels or monopolies of various sorts. This would effectively reduce competition, restrict output, and raise prices, hence restoring the rate of profit to prior levels.

Marx's Theory of the Business Cycle

Subsistence wages for the broad mass of working men and no wages for the growing pool of unemployed, displaced workers raised a serious problem for capitalism. Who was going to buy all the goods that the monopolies decided to produce? There were times when the sum total of demand for consumer goods and investment goods did not equal the amount produced. These periodic business cycles of recession and depression or "gluts" of unsold merchandise served two purposes in Marx's view. First, they threw large numbers of workers into the unemployed pool, accentuating the loss of purchasing power. Second, each depression would put the weakest firms through the wringer of bankruptcy. The ex-capitalists would join the working class or the unemployed, and the firms' assets would be gobbled up by larger, stronger firms. Thus, the already strong pressures for monopoly due to the declining rate of profit would be reinforced by the Darwinian force of the business cycle—survival of the strongest, largest, and most aggressive monopolists. Business cycles were not just squiggles on a graph of national income performance to Marx. They were part of the broad outlines of the capitalist crisis that Marx could detect emerging from his theories.

Unemployment

Marx was excited at the revolutionary implications of the "laws" of capitalism that he felt he was revealing. He believed, as we have shown, that capital accumulation would displace labor on balance and create a permanent pool of unemployed. He also predicted recessions and depressions which would periodically throw large numbers of other workers into this pool, thus reinforcing the solidarity of all workers and the commonality of their interests, even though most of the time most of the workers would be employed. He doubted the capacity of capitalist society to provide either work or adequate relief from misery for a growing proportion of the population.

Marx further predicted the squeezing out of the middle class. As capitalist society was going through its final convulsions, the independent commercial and professional middle classes would be caught between the growing misery and radicalization of the working class and the aggressive ruthless combines of monopoly capital. They would either be crushed by big business (small retail establishments pushed out by supermarkets, department stores, and franchise chains) or be taken on as hired lackeys of the monopolies. The concentration of wealth and power in the hands of ever fewer monopolists would increase the disparities between the haves and have-nots and heighten the revolutionary tensions inherent in capitalism.

Revolution

Drawing all these threads together Marx concluded that the climactic moment would at last arrive. The tempo and intensity of cyclical downturns would increase. Industry, finance, and commerce would be ruled by a small number of giant monopoly combines. The misery of the exploited working masses would be stretched to the limits of human capacity. The middle classes would be crushed by the monopolies and become sympathetically neutral to one side or the other. Finally, something would trigger a revolution, and the mass of the workers, led perhaps by professional revolutionaries like Marx himself, would rise and seize power.

The workers, or revolutionaries in the name of the workers, would take over control of the state apparatus—the police, judiciary, army, and fiscal powers. Marx believed that this state apparatus was a device used by the ruling class to enforce its will on the masses of the population. When the workers labored under socialism, there would be no superior and subordinate classes and so the chief functions of the state would become superfluous. The notion that the role of the state would be substantially reduced under socialism (the "withering away of the state" in Marx's terminology) is almost ludicrous in the light of what has developed in the Soviet Union under socialist central planning.

POST-REVOLUTIONARY SOCIALISM

Marx was not very clear about how the working class was to organize its economic affairs, allocate resources, provide for investment and progress, and distribute the fruit of its labors after the revolution under socialism. Marx, contrary to popular belief, did not believe in an equal distribution of income under socialism.. His famous slogan, "From each according to his ability, to each according to his need" should not be interpreted as everyone just grabbing whatever he "needs" out of a common warehouse. Even Marx would agree that the sum of human wants (needs) will always be greater than what can be produced even under socialism, but Marx and most socialists believed that a vast increase in productivity would be possible under socialism. Marx must be interpreted as suggesting that the element of need (medical services, adequate diet, education, etc.) must be emphasized above and beyond the reward for value of services rendered to the socialist economy. Marx was not so naive, as other and later reformers were and are, as to believe that human nature was likely to be so drastically altered, at least in the short run, as to permit significantly reduced demand for goods and services. However, Marx must be recorded in history as the prophet of the doom of capitalism and not as the architect of the new socialist order which would supplant capitalism.

There is no evidence in the countries that have adopted Marxism, or Marxism-Leninism (Maoism) as a basic ideology, that Marx gave them any sort of brilliant insight into how to become powerful, productive, peaceful, and democratic without making the same agonizing sacrifices that early capitalism made.

AN ANALYSIS OF MARX'S THEORY

Poverty

Marx's economic theory depended heavily on the labor theory of value, as we have seen. The mainstream of economic theory found the labor theory of value uninstructive and passed on to other formulations, many of which have appeared in the early chapters of this book. There is, in fact, no particular economic reason why the wages of the working class would be depressed to the subsistence level. Under the pressure of competition, capitalists are as likely to bid up the wages of labor as they are to bid up the price of coal or cotton if it is profitable to do so. So long as workers don't breed themselves back into poverty, a la Malthus, then wages can be permanently raised to indefinite levels, as we have in fact observed since Marx's time.

Of course, there may be considerable political, if not revolutionary, potential in pointing out that the rich are getting richer while the workers are only getting better off. The flames of social discontent may be fanned as much by a sense of inequitable *relative* poverty as by some absolute level of harsh, grinding deprivation. However, social irritability and political restiveness are a far cry from revolutionary passions. The strength of Marx's appeal lay in the idea that revolution—a major tearing down and rebuilding of social, economic, and political institutions—was inevitable. Take away the economic cornerstone of this inevitability, the "immiseration of the proletariat," and Marxism becomes just another political theory. Revolution may be possible, even probable in certain circumstances, but not inevitable due to the spontaneous immutable workings of economics and "history."

Unemployment, however, is a nagging worry in many capitalist countries, though not all. A fairly permanent pool of unemployed or unemployables has come into existence in the United States. The identity of these groups, the causes of their disadvantages, and some possible solutions are widely discussed in the economic literature today. Very few, but some, blame capitalism as an economic system for this failure. The problem is too complex for extensive analysis in this chapter. Most of the difficulties may be attributed to declining industries, declining regions, racial problems buried deep in American history, urbanization and suburbanization, and the rapid pace of technical obsolescence. The blame for the glacial pace of solving national problems must be placed at the door of the political system as much as the economic system. One need not be a Marxist to call wrath down upon the national and local authorities for their negligence.

The Business Cycle

At times depressions have been serious disturbances of capitalism. Marx claimed that purchasing power was leaking from the system because workers were exploited and not paid their full value. Actually Marx himself pointed out that this surplus value was taken by the capitalist and spent on machinery, so as a theoretical point, no purchasing power actually leaked from the system. However, if Marx had said that the capitalists or workers occasionally might not spend all their profits or wages and just sit on the money, he would have been making a truly prophetical statement and one with a very contemporary Keynesian flavor. Actually Marx was anticipating Keynes and amplifying Malthus in focusing his attention on under-consumption as a cause for recurrent crises and business cycles. What Marx could not see from his nineteenth century vantage point was the great variety of consumption-supporting and stimulating policies that are possible under capitalism. Marx's problem was that the evolutionary resiliency of capitalism had not been demonstrated in his time. Marx was in a position analogous to that of a naturalist observing a chameleon brown against a tree trunk and predicting that it would never survive in the grass.

As students of economics know, recessions and depressions have continued to plague capitalism from Marx's time to the present. A great deal of the institutional evolution of recent decades has been designed to solve the problem of business cycles in a competitive capitalist system. More recently the problem of preventing or minimizing the effects of recessions has been compounded by having to avoid over-full employment as a consequence. A modern capitalist democracy attempts to balance on a knife-edge of full employment, with inflation lurking on one side and unemployment looming on the other. The painful experience of the early 1970s is that past errors may whipsaw a nation's economy between unemployment and inflation with the result that in the transitional stages we may have both.

Monopoly

Marx's twin pressures which were to squeeze capitalism into the hands of monopoly capital were the falling rate of profit and intensifying business cycles. The falling rate of profit was a prediction based on the labor theory of value, which proved to be once again a weak reed on which to lean a revolutionary theory. The rise of new industries and the comparatively peaceful phase-out of declining industries served to maintain the profitability of industry, even though the proportion of capital to labor rose to enormous heights in many industries. Marx's formulas on the falling rate of profit are simply interesting exercises in obsolescent economics. Far more interesting are his thoughts on monopoly as a defense against the business cycle.

It is only natural for individuals and firms to want to protect themselves from uncertainty and risk. One way for individuals to do this is to pool risks through insurance. Firms may do something similar through diversifying their products or by combining and controlling their markets. Capitalist societies have felt that monopoly, except in a few cases of public utilities, is not in the public interest and have undertaken to prevent monopolies from occurring, have regulated natural monopolies or occasionally nationalized them.

Assisting public authorities in the control of monopoly are several tendencies inherent in the nature of capitalism. Where there are above-normal profits, competitors will press in with close substitutes and eventually erode a monopoly position. It seems today that it is more and more difficult to hold a monopoly position due to the rapid pace of technological change. A second trend is the increasing openness of the international economy. International trade offers the possibility of substantial competition in domestic markets even though domestic production may be highly concentrated in a few hands. The development and expansion of the European Common Market has seen some of the mightiest of German and French monopolies or cartels become swamped by the offerings of neighboring industrial nations.

It is easy to be too optimistic about the ability of capitalism to prevent monopoly abuse. Political lobbying can occasionally produce distressing and rather pointless protection of one industry or another, but the whole thrust of

Marx was that the system *as a whole* tended inexorably toward monopoly, and this is simply not supported by historical evidence or current trends.

Polarization and Revolution

The polarization of society between a small elite or class of enormously wealthy and powerful monopoly capitalists and a large mass of unemployed and/or impoverished workers did not work out as Marx anticipated. Immensely wealthy individuals, families, and great industrial combines do exist, but do not dominate the economy. A large middle class has developed with a substantial stake in the perpetuation of private enterprise. The industrial work force as Marx visualized it—horny-handed, sooty, day-laborers—is a declining proportion of the total work force and in attitudes and income are frequently indistinguishable from "white-collar" or office workers.

Summary

To sum up Marx's analysis of capitalism, it must be said that he was forced to utilize the data and trends of the capitalism of his own times. The elemental, brute energies of steam and coal and machine had created a transitional economy of great ugliness and callous indifference to workers' welfare. The alienation and boredom of routine machine-tending was a shattering blow to the then prevailing notions of man as a proud craftsman. Within Marx's own lifetime countervailing trends could be seen and exceptions to his model of capitalist development could be discerned at many points. However, exceptions to almost any notion can be found—it would have been extraordinarily difficult and prescient to have picked out precisely those portents of evolutionary capitalism that would ultimately triumph over the excesses of laissez-faire. Marx, least of all, would be inclined to be looking for rays of hope in the state of nineteenth century capitalism.

However flawed, incomplete, and preliminary Marx's model of capitalist development may seem from our vantage point, it was a tremendous intellectual achievement. A few latter-day analysts following Marxist traditions have made useful, critical observations of capitalist society concerning its not inconsiderable number of existing inequities and failures. These criticisms may be particularly useful since defenders of the status quo are rarely forced to defend their positions right down to the most fundamental assumptions.

Marx and the Twentieth Century

The impact of Marx on most of the twentieth century has not been through the accuracy of his analytical prophecies, but through the influence he had and has upon the minds of generations of revolutionary disciples. A Russian revolutionary Vladimir Ulianov (Lenin) was a brilliant and flexible Marxist who was willing to update and adapt Marx's ideas to new times and circumstances. Again, it is not so much the accuracy or analytical power of Marx's thoughts as transformed by Lenin that marks his impact on the twentieth century as the fact that he successfully seized power in Russia in 1917 in the confusion following the virtually spontaneous collapse of the Tsarist government. It is alleged that Marxist-Leninist socialism or communism is still the ideological, social, and economic creed of the bureaucrats who govern the industrialized super-power that the Soviet Union has become. Outside observers, including most non-communist socialists and even many foreign communists, search for evidence of idealism, democratic practices, and internationalism and are forced to conclude that the present Soviet leadership is more inclined to domestic repression, international intrigues, and mischief-making. These questions are political ones, of course, and therefore, would usually be only peripheral to economic problems, but in the case of the Soviet Union, politics and economics are inextricably bound together.

To return to Marx, if his model is inadequate to explain contemporary capitalism and nowhere does he present a blueprint of the present Soviet-type bureaucratized central planning system, what influence does Marx have today?

Marx's ideas today are reflected principally through the almost subconscious predispositions of Communist leaders throughout the world, from Mao to Brezhnev to Castro. An analogy might be to ask what influence Thomas Jefferson has on contemporary American society. Jefferson's notions of an ideal society sound incredibly quaint and disturbingly distant from our urbanized and depersonalized modern society. Yet Jefferson's beliefs about democracy and individual freedom are the ideological underpinnings of our attitudes and political postures despite the mass nature of many contemporary socio-political relationships. In brief, the myth of the individual is necessary despite its irrelevance, or perhaps even because of its irrelevance. It is just so in the Marxist command economies like the Soviet Union. Marxist leaders and thinkers are predisposed to permit or prescribe certain policies or actions depending on whether and how they fit into the Marxist-Leninist framework. Once a novel situation appears in which there are no Marxist guidelines, it is as if a chasm appeared beneath their feet. A number of the most important or significant predispositions will be discussed.

MARX'S IMPACT ON CONTEMPORARY COMMUNIST POLICY-MAKERS

The most important predisposition of the Marxist-Leninist leadership and planners has been a distaste for the market mechanism. The market is a device for allocating scarce goods according to effective demands *without conscious direction*. Therefore it is the very antithesis of the concept of social control of economic activity in the public interest, at least in the minds of Marxists and some other socialists. As we will see, the Soviet leaders have occasionally been willing to let markets function, but they have always felt *guilty* about it, as though they were permitting economic pollution of their society.

2) A second predisposition of Marxist economists and leaders has been opposition to the concept of charging interest for the use of capital. Since interest is a reward to capital owners for the loan of their money and this constitutes income without labor, Marxists are opposed to both the private ownership of capital and the earning or charging of interest. In a socialist society, capital is owned by the people and so why should interest be charged by the state to a state-owned firm that received investment funds from state sources? We will see that such interest charges are useful and needed in a socialist economy. Many centrally planned economies today, in fact, do charge interest on funds loaned to state-owned firms, and such loans must be repaid in a very capitalist fashion. This, however, is a comparatively recent development of centrally-planned economies.

3) A third major Marxist predisposition is the preference for social ownership over private ownership, even when such preferences are clearly counter-productive. Only when the economic consequences of total social ownership are so great as to approach crisis proportions will the Marxist leadership permit areas of private economic activity. The most costly ownership decision has been the perpetuation of the collective farm form of land ownership. This institution has long lost whatever utility it may have had since its built-in disincentives and low productivity now far outweigh its ability to produce forced surpluses for industry and export markets. The leadership's continued intransigence on this issue can only be ascribed to political and ideological rigidity. Some Communist states like Poland and Yugoslavia have returned to private farming without a collapse of their socialist societies.

A final predisposition of Communist leaders is a distrust of democratic political institutions. Marx was a strong-minded, disputatious fellow and experienced in the ways of conspiratorial revolutionary activity. Marxist revolutionaries tended to stress party discipline and adherence to Marxist precepts over democratic mass political activity. Marxists taking power through a revolution over considerable political opposition and with minority support could be expected to develop an elite of trustworthy party loyalists and then to put them in exclusive control over social, political, and economic institutions. In politics this situation evolves toward dictatorship and in economics the expression of this tendency is central planning.

QUESTIONS

1. What is dialectical materialism?
2. What is the labor theory of value?

3. Why did Marx believe that the worker would always be exploited in a capitalist system?

4. According to Marx, why is the downfall of capitalism inevitable?

5. What is Marx's concept of the socialist state?

6. What are the primary reasons for the failure of Marx's economic predictions?

7. What is the significance of Marxism for modern economic policy makers?

BIBLIOGRAPHY

France

Bauchet, Pierre. *Economic Planning, The French Experience.* New York: Frederick A. Praeger, Inc., 1964.

Cohen, Steven. *Modern Capitalist Planning: The French Model.* Cambridge, Mass.: Harvard University Press, 1969.

Hackett, John and Anne Marie. *Economic Planning in France.* London: Allen and Unwin, 1963.

Harlow, John S. *French Economic Planning: A Challenge to Reason.* Iowa City: Iowa University Press, 1966.

McArthur, John H., and Bruce R. Scott. *Industrial Planning in France.* Boston: Division of Research, Graduate School of Business Administration, Harvard University, 1969.

Sheahan, John. *Promotion and Control of Industry in Postwar France.* Cambridge, Mass.: Harvard University Press, 1963.

West Germany

Arndt, Hans. *West Germany: Politics of Non-Planning.* Syracuse: Syracuse University Press, 1966.

Erhard, Ludwig. *The Economics of Success.* London: Thames and Hudson, Ltd., 1963.

Pounds, N. J. G. *The Economic Pattern of Modern Germany.* London: John Murray Ltd., 1964.

Stolper, Gustav. *The German Economy 1870 to the Present.* New York: Harcourt, Brace & World, Inc., 1967.

Reuss, Frederick G. *Fiscal Policy for Growth without Inflation: The German Experiment.* Baltimore: Johns Hopkins University Press, 1963.

Britain

Bailey, Richard. *Managing the British Economy.* London: Hutchison and Co., 1968.

Beckerman, W., *et al. The British Economy in 1975.* Cambridge: Cambridge University Press, 1965.

Broadway, Frank. *State Intervention in British Industry 1964-68.* Teaneck, N.J.: Farleigh Dickinson University Press, 1970.

Department of Economic Affairs. *The Task Ahead: Economic Assessment to 1972.* London: Her Majesty's Stationary Office, 1969.

Dow, J.C.R. *The Management of the British Economy, 1945-60.* Cambridge: Cambridge University Press, 1964.

Hodgman, Donald R. "British Techniques of Monetary Policy," *Journal of Money, Credit, and Banking.* vol. 3, No. 4 (November 1971), pp. 760-779.

Marxism

Fusfeld, Daniel R. *The Age of the Economist.* Glenview: Scott, Foresman and Co., 1966, Chapter 5.

Hook, Sidney. *From Hegel to Marx: Studies in the Intellectual Development of Karl Marx.* Ann Arbor: The University of Michigan Press, 1962.

Robinson, Joan. *An Essay on Marxian Economics.* New York: St. Martin's Press, 1966.

Wolfson, Murray. *A Reappraisal of Marxian Economics.* Baltimore: Penguin Books, 1964.

General

Dennison, Edward, and Jean-Pierre Poullier. *Why Growth Rates Differ.* Washington, D.C.: The Brookings Institution, 1967.

Hansen, Bent. *Fiscal Policy in Seven Countries, 1955-1965.* Paris: OECD, March 1969.

Jewkes, John. *The New Ordeal by Planning.* London: Macmillan, 1968.

Kindleberger, Charles *Europe's Postwar Growth.* Cambridge, Mass.: Harvard University Press, 1967.

Lutz, Vera. *Central Planning for the Market Economy.* London: Longmans, Green, and Co., Ltd., 1969.

MacLennan, Malcolm, *et al. Economic Planning in Britain, France and Germany.* New York: Frederick A. Praeger, Inc., 1968.

Shonfield, Andrew. *Modern Capitalism.* London: Oxford University Press, 1969.

IV

THE SOCIALIST COMMAND ECONOMY

11

The Theory
of Central Planning

Introduction

If the socialist critics of the market system are successful in destroying it, they must install an alternative set of institutions to take its place. It is the premise of this book that all economic systems face similar problems and differ only with respect to the solutions adopted. If the market mechanism is to be abandoned, then something must take its place which will determine what goods are to be produced, what techniques are to be used in their production, and to whom these goods will be allocated. As we have observed in the preceding chapter, many socialists, including Marx, had some vague notions that central planning would replace market institutions. It is the task of this chapter to discuss the meaning of central planning—what it is and how it functions to solve the basic economic problems. In the following chapters we will examine central planning as it is actually practiced in the Soviet Union and other command economies.

THE PERFECTLY VISIBLE HAND

The essential concept in the definition of central planning is a hierarchic system of organization. One can imagine a centrally planned economy as a pyramid with a planning elite at the top issuing orders concerning output and production techniques, and a multitude of production units at the bottom carrying out these orders. The planning elite needs to obtain three types of information in order to formulate its commands, i.e., construct a plan to guide the behavior of production units in producing the optimal mix of goods and services. One, the planners must have knowledge of the physical capacity of the economy to produce, including the available supplies of labor and raw materials. Two, they must have knowledge of the production function of each commodity, i.e., the number and kinds of inputs necessary for the production of each output and the possibilities of substituting one input for another in production. Finally, the planners must have a preference function indicating the possibilities of substituting one output for another in order to maximize satisfaction. Armed with this information, essentially consisting of the supply and demand functions for all intermediate and final goods, the planners could construct an optimal plan, maximizing the welfare of that group whose preference functions were used in the calculations. In a frictionless world in which time and information costs are zero and the decision-making capacity of the planners unlimited, it would be possible to specify these orders in such detail that each production unit's task would be completely described and unambiguous. We will call this state of affairs the "perfectly visible hand."[1] It is analogous to the perfectly competitive case encountered in our discussion of the market system. The perfectly visible hand, like perfect competition, does not and has never existed in the real world. An understanding of its characteristics and implications, however, is quite useful in analyzing the imperfectly visible hand or the problems of actual command economies.

The existence of the perfectly visible hand is dependent upon the fulfillment of certain conditions.[2] These conditions include: 1) an omniscient government making all economic decisions—decisions which may theoretically reflect either the preferences of the population as a whole, as in a democratic system of government, or the wishes of the government leaders themselves, as in a totalitarian system; 2) the incorporation of these decisions into a detailed production plan and the transmittal of this plan to production units; 3) no free mobility of any factor of production, except by order of the government; 4) perfect knowledge of the orders embodied in the plan; 5) complete obedience to

---

[1] Adam Smith referred in the *Wealth of Nations,* written in 1776, to the "invisible hand" which directs the market system.

[2] These conditions are derived from the work of Oleg Zinam, "The Economics of Command Economies," in *Comparative Economic Systems,* ed. Jan S. Prybyla (New York: Appleton-Century-Crofts, 1969), pp. 19-46.

these orders by all production units; and 6) perfect fulfillment of the plan by all units.

The satisfaction of these conditions insures the construction and fulfillment of an optimal plan, comparable to the results obtained in a perfectly competitive economy. The planned solution would, in fact, even be superior to the competitive solution with respect to the three performance criteria—static efficiency, dynamic efficiency, and equity. The omniscient planners could include all externalities, such as environmental deterioration, in their calculations as well as plan for the optimal quantity of collective consumption and provide social goods such as education and health services, thereby eliminating two major sources of static inefficiency in a perfectly competitive market system. The planners, aware of all the benefits accruing to the economy from research, invention, and innovation, would not underinvest in these areas and could quickly disseminate information on and order the implementation of new techniques. Finally, goods and services could be distributed in any fashion whatsoever in accord with the leader's or the population's notions of equity.

Up to this point we have outlined an economic system that produces very appealing results. We seem to have achieved a combination of static efficiency, dynamic efficiency and equity unobtainable in even the most perfect of perfectly competitive economies. We have also pointed out, however, that the perfectly visible hand does not exist. What can we say about its real world counterparts? What are the real world frictions that prevent the conditions of perfect visibility from being fulfilled and make the actual workings of command or centrally planned economies far removed from the idealized system described above? We described the planning hierarchy or the pyramid as consisting of two parts, the planning elite at the top and the production units at the bottom. Huge quantities of information were to be costlessly obtained and analyzed, and costless calculations made, resulting in a plan which consisted of detailed specifications required for the production of all commodities. These plans were then to be transmitted to obedient production units which would follow the instructions to the letter, doing no less but also no more than they were told.

In all existing centrally planned economies there are layers, called the planning bureaucracy, between the planning elite and the production units. It is not mere chance but necessity that these bureaucracies are so prevalent, since planners are not omniscient and information is not costless. Production managers are not always blindly obedient. Real world frictions require intermediary layers to convey information about conditions where productive activity is actually going on to the planning elite at the top, to transmit orders in the reverse direction, and to check and report on plan fulfillment. The monitoring and information filtering functions of the bureaucracy are a source of countless problems and inefficiencies in centrally planned economies. We will now turn to some of the major problems involved in plan formulation and plan fulfillment.

THE IMPERFECTLY VISIBLE HAND

The process of planning involves plan construction, including data gathering and analyzing activities, and plan implementation, including supervision of production units and reporting on plan fulfillment. A functioning planning system must include: first, techniques of plan construction which will allow the planners to receive and digest large quantities of information, and then to issue specific production orders; and second, methods of assuring that these orders are carried out in practice. There are tremendous practical problems involved in both of these stages. These problems include the choice of plan construction techniques, the transmission of information, and the development of incentives and controls to insure that the activity of subordinate units is consistent with plan objectives. We will discuss these problems under the headings of plan construction and plan implementation.

The Process of Plan Construction

Ignoring for the moment the problems involved in information collection and assuming the bureaucracy is functioning effectively as a data transmitting service, the planners must still analyze the information they receive in order to construct a plan. The analysis of information takes time and computing capabilities, both mental and mechanical. What techniques are available to the planners to allow them to complete this task? There are two basic techniques available, econometric models and models involving direct economic calculation. Econometric models begin with the three types of data mentioned above, recognizing that the solution to the appropriate level of production of any one product is dependent upon the solution values for all other products. All outputs must be determined together in a system of simultaneous equations, specifying functional relationships for all goods and using electronic computers to perform the computations. Direct economic calculation techniques are iterative, i.e., repetitive trial-and-error, procedures in which an attempt is made to balance the supply and demand for all goods by equating production assignments with input requests.[3]

One might ask at this point why not use the most "sophisticated" technique available, the one which will produce the most sophisticated plan? By sophisticated we mean a plan which is both consistent and optimal—one in which the supply and demand for all goods and services are in balance and the maximum output is achieved with the minimum of inputs. Unfortunately, increased plan sophistication often requires more expensive methods of plan construction. Direct economic calculation techniques result in "cruder" plans

---

[3]For a discussion of methods of planning techniques by an economist engaged in planning, see J.G. Zielinski, *Lectures on the Theory of Socialist Planning* (London: Oxford University Press, 1968).

but, given available technology, are relatively cheap with respect to the costs of information gathering and processing. Econometric models produce more sophisticated plans but require complex and expensive electronic computing facilities, often not yet available, and large quantities of precise information. In this section of the chapter we will discuss two relatively simple techniques which do not involve the extensive use of computers; two advanced techniques requiring a significant amount of computer software and hardware will be examined in the appendix to this chapter.

A commonly used technique in plan construction is the "material balances" method. The planners begin with initial gross output targets for all commodities. These preliminary targets may be derived in several ways. Perhaps the crudest way is to take last year's production figure and add to it some percentage increase, representing an estimate of the expected growth in the industry, perhaps derived from a trend growth rate, for example last year plus 5 percent. More care may be taken in arriving at the initial targeted level of output by examining more closely the productive capacity of the industry involved and carefully estimating future gains in capacity resulting from the introduction of new capital equipment or the implementation of new technology. Once the initial targets are formulated they are presented to the production units, who then submit a bill of input requests which they feel is the minimum necessary to produce the targeted output. Production units are not completely free to determine their input requirements but are guided by a set of technical coefficients specifying maximum input/output ratios. It is the task of the planners then to reconcile input requests of enterprises using certain goods with output assignments of firms producing those goods, to insure that there is a balance between supply and demand. A simple material balance appears in table 11.1. The balancing task of the planners at this stage is extremely difficult, for it requires the juggling of thousands of commodities, given that the output of one production unit is the input of another. If one commodity—for example, steel—is out of balance, then many more will have to be readjusted, including

Table 11.1

Material Balance: Steel

Sources of Steel			*Uses of Steel*		
Current production		1000	Current consumption		1100
Steel mill 1	300		Automobile production	600	
Steel mill 2	500		Appliances	500	
Steel mill 3	200		Investment		200
Inventory reduction		100	Construction material	150	
Imports		200	Railroads	50	
			Inventory accumulation		0
			Exports		0
		1300			1300

inputs into the production of steel, such as iron and coking coal, and commodities using steel as an input into their own production, such as automobiles. The technique of material balances will be examined further in our discussion of its use in Soviet planning procedures.

A second technique we will call the iterative method.[4] The planners begin this procedure by developing a set of final output targets. Final targets are distinguished from gross targets by excluding the output of any good used as an intermediate good in the production of another commodity. Those targets are transmitted to each production sector, which then calculates its input requirements by multiplying the final targets by a set of technical coefficients. The input requirements are then transmitted to the planners, who add the input requests for a particular good to its final demand targets and then resubmit the new, higher targets to each sector. The process, an iterative procedure, continues until further additions are so small they can be ignored. Final demand targets have been transformed into gross output targets which now constitute ultimate plan targets and are assigned to each production unit.

Both of these methods do result in the solution of the problems of what and how much to produce and there is a rough correspondence between supply and demand. Neglecting the problem of information flows, however, both techniques can at best produce consistent plans but not optimal ones. Using either technique, the planners begin by setting quantity targets which are formulated independently of any precise knowledge of constraints imposed by capacity limitations. The planners do not know if the targets are achievable or what alternative bundles of goods can be produced with the same capacity. Unaware of the nature of the trade-off between one product and another, the planner is unaware of the true cost, in terms of alternatives foregone, of his initial targeted outputs. In an optimal planning procedure, preferences are combined with constraints, and output targets are the end result of the planning process.

A major problem involved in the use of both techniques is the elimination of the possibility of substituting one factor for another in production. The choice of production techniques and the proportion of total output assigned to each production unit are determined outside of the planning process itself and are represented by the technical coefficients and the original production assignments for each sector. Direct economic calculation techniques do not provide the planners with a method for choosing the least-cost method of production or for assigning production tasks to the lowest cost producers. The substitution of one input for another, the application of new technology, and the transfer of production assignments from high cost to low cost producers are all tasks beyond the capability of direct economic calculation techniques.

It has been argued that although both consistency and optimality are

[4]This technique is described in Benjamin Ward, *The Socialist Economy* (New York: Random House, 1967), pp. 44-49.

desirable, consistency is imperative for any economy.[5] An inconsistent plan will leave surpluses and deficits which can cripple an economy. Surpluses absorb useful resources and deficits throw other industries off balance. But if supply and demand are in balance, the economy can continue indefinitely at less than optimal levels of output. Thus, the major effort of centrally planned economies is to achieve the balance which is automatically attained via market adjustments in a capitalist system.

Both direct economic calculation techniques described above involve planning in physical terms. Although prices may be used as an accounting device to simplify aggregation problems, it is the physical quantities of commodities that matter in the balancing process. Each production unit is assigned a physical output target and is concerned with its gross output rather than with its net contribution to the welfare of society. Numerous examples of wasteful production have been cited as a result of the emphasis on gross output. Foundries pour as much metal as possible into castings to meet their weight quota, but the metal is just machined away at the next stage of production. Truckers run up as many miles as possible, resulting in wasteful cross-hauling. Marx claimed that in capitalist economies production is not for use but for profit. Critics of command economies allege that frequently production is for waste rather than for use.

Up to this point we have ignored the special problems of communication between planner and planned. Given the limitations of time and mental capacity, it is not possible for planners to plan in the detail necessary for the issuance of operational commands to the production sector. Nor is it possible for the planners to consider the detailed requirements and capacities of each production unit. The attempts to cope with these difficulties have traditionally resulted in the development of a bureaucracy.

The creation of a planning bureaucracy poses the problem of the appropriate degree of information or data aggregation. Because it is not possible for the planners to consider data in its raw form as it comes from individual production units it must be aggregated by a bureaucracy and presented to the planners in a compressed form. Further, the commands of the planners must be disaggregated so they are meaningful to the individual producer. The command to produce a certain quantity of building materials is meaningless to the steel, aluminum, lumber, and cement producers until it is disaggregated. The production reports of each of these sectors are beyond the limited comprehension of the planners until the reports are aggregated and presented to it by the bureaucracy. This process of aggregation and disaggregation, although necessary, results in distortions. Final plans may be out of balance, because while the aggregates may in fact balance, their components may not. The demand and supply of building materials may be equal, while the supply and demand of steel, aluminum,

[5]See Gregory Grossman, "Notes for a Theory of the Command Economy," *Soviet Studies* 15, No. 2 (October 1963), pp. 101-123.

lumber, and cement may not be; see table 11.2. Unless these products are perfect substitutes, the output targets of some goods using these products as inputs will not be reached. Although aggregation gives the planner an overview of the economy, it blurs the unique characteristics and capabilities of each sector.

Table 11.2

Material Balance: Construction Materials

		Sources		*Uses*			
		5000		5000			
Steel		*Aluminum*		*Lumber*		*Cement*	
Sources	*Uses*	*Sources*	*Uses*	*Sources*	*Uses*	*Sources*	*Uses*
2000	1800	1000	1100	1500	1700	500	400

The Process of Plan Implementation

In order for plan goals to be realized, production units must comply with plan directives. Given that the original plan will be imperfect—i.e., that inconsistencies between supply and demand will appear in practice—plan goals will never be completely achieved. Planners, aware of this problem, have designed a system of feedback, success or failure signals to inform them of the actual degree of plan fulfillment. These success or failure signals are linked with a reward-punishment system intended to encourage local managers to do the "proper" thing even though precise directives are not always available to meet every contingency. The planners must again rely on the bureaucracy to provide them with knowledge and to administer the incentive system. Let us turn to the question of gathering information regarding the behavior of production units. This problem is closely allied to the problem of attaining the appropriate degree of aggregation or disaggregation. Planners have a limited amount of time and capacity to supervise the operations of subordinates. Thus, they will group subordinates into administrative units, placing a supervisory agency over several production units. The supervisory agency is now responsible for the actions of its own subordinates, and the planners need deal with fewer units. One can imagine a three-tiered system consisting of 100 production units divided into ten groups, each controlled by a ministry. The planners need supervise only the ten ministries rather than 100 individual units. The capacity of superior units to control subordinate units determines the number of layers that are necessary in the hierarchy. In this example the span of control is ten. If the maximum number a superior can effectively control is only five, then the 100 production units ought to be divided into 20 groups of five firms each. These 20 groups would be further divided into four super-groups of five, the latter communicating directly with the planners. The number of layers in the bureaucracy has been increased from three to four. The total number of units to be controlled, together with the maximum effective span of control, will determine the number of layers in the bureaucracy necessary to oversee the plan implementation. In our example, there were one hundred production units. In the typical economy, there would be well over one hundred thousand.

The effective span of control depends on the degree of detailed supervision necessary to insure plan implementation. This brings us to the question of the appropriate degree of centralization or decentralization of decision-making. Granted that the plan will have to be altered in the course of its implementation, where will the power to make these changes reside? If the planners must authorize all changes, leaving the production units no autonomy, plan management will be completely centralized, and each superior unit will need to collect tremendous quantities of detailed information. If production units have greater autonomy, less of a superior agency's time will be taken up with detailed supervision, and the span of control may be larger. Decentralization of decision-making shortens information routes and thereby speeds decisions while reducing the costs of administering a large bureaucracy. Decentralization also allows those with the greatest information about local conditions to make decisions appropriate to those conditions. Planners in many command economies, however, have been reluctant to decentralize the decision process despite their recognition of the benefits just outlined. They are afraid that local units will act in ways which are inconsistent with overall plan objectives and thus will diminish the power of the planners to guide the economy.

Before production units can be given any autonomy, they must have a set of guidelines which will motivate them to make the "correct" decisions, decisions in accord with the preferences of the planners. The reward of the manager of a production unit must be tied to some success indicator so that he will make the correct decisions. A small number of success indicators must also be selected to ease the problem of communicating large volumes of information about every aspect of the production process. The manager of a textile enterprise may be directed by the plan to produce a large variety of designs, fabrics, and grades with a specified mix of inputs. The cost of information would prevent his reporting the progress made in all areas. A limited number of success indicators must be substituted. His material reward must be tied to these success indicators if he is to put forth more than the minimum effort to comply with the plan. A critical problem for all centrally planned economies is the number of success indicators and also their appropriateness.

Three types of general success indicators have commonly been used by centrally planned economies. The first is gross output, measured either in value terms or in some physical characteristic of the product. The success of the textile enterprise might be measured in terms of the dollar value of its output or in terms of yards of cloth. All measures of gross output distort manager behavior. In our example if the success indicator were the dollar value of output, the manager would be tempted to use high cost inputs and concentrate on quality items. If the success indicator were yards of cloth, he would be tempted to concentrate on lower quality materials which would allow him to produce the most yards with the least amount of inputs. The manager is not concerned with the cost of production in the first instance nor with the usefulness of the product to the consumer in the second.

A second category of success indicators motivates the manager to maximize the value-added (value of output minus value of material inputs) by his enterprise. Thus, he will no longer desire to use costly material inputs or concentrate solely on high priced goods. This success indicator, however, will cause distortions of its own. The manager will attempt to minimize the value transferred to him from earlier stages of production. There will be an incentive to use lavish amounts of labor, since any additional labor costs will add to value-added and increase the reward of the manager.

In an attempt to eliminate the distortions resulting from the use of gross output or value-added as measures of success, many command economies have recently adopted a system of incentives based upon profit. It is believed that the use of profit as a success indicator will result in fewer distortions because profit calculations simultaneously consider both the cost of production of an item and its contribution to the total value of output. In order for profit to accurately measure the performance of a producing unit, however, prices must reflect relative costs and values. If prices are distorted, profits will also give a distorted picture of performance. Managers will concentrate on high profit items, but if these items are profitable because their input prices are set too low or their output prices are set arbitrarily high, the planners will have to step in with additional directives to guide the managers.

The distortions caused by all three types of general success indicators will make it necessary for the planners to supplement them with specialized incentives. Specialized incentives, such as rewards for cost reduction, quality improvement, and the maintenance of the desired assortment of commodities, are designed to correct for the distortions resulting from the use of inadequate general success indicators. The existence of a multitude of success indicators, however, in practice leaves the enterprise free to comply with those most advantageous to him, while ignoring others. Taken to its logical conclusion, the addition of more and more success indicators to guide manager behavior ultimately results in complete centralization where superiors are attempting to oversee all of the detailed aspects of production.

We have described and contrasted the perfectly visible hand with its real world counterpart. The primary problems of adopting central planning involve the tremendous costs involved in gathering, analyzing, and transmitting information as well as supervising the behavior of a multitude of production units. As economies grow, these problems become more complex. As the number of specialized production units increases, and as limits to the span of control are reached, the layers of the bureaucracy must also increase. The number of interconnections between production units grows at a geometric rate. More data must be collected and processed through growing bureaucratic chains. There is resistance to new ideas which upset orderly communication processes. The growing complexity makes balance itself more difficult to obtain. The lack of local autonomy combined with the increasing inability of the planners to oversee all aspects of plan implementation not only results in larger inconsistencies but also makes the development and application of new techniques increasingly difficult. Balance, necessary for the smooth day-to-day operation of the economy, and growth, a measure of the long-run performance of the economy, are increasingly jeopardized. In our discussions of centrally planned economies in the following chapters we will examine the development and functioning of selected command economies and describe the achievements they have realized and the problems they have encountered.

APPENDIX:
INPUT-OUTPUT AND LINEAR PROGRAMMING AS PLANNING AIDS.

Input-Output

An input-output table presents in an extremely compact form an enormous amount of information about the allocation of goods and resources on the one hand and the input requirements of production on the other. In the preceding chapter material balancing, a method of planning and balancing input requirements with output demands, was introduced. Much of the information used in material balance planning may also be used to construct an input-output table. For example, the planning department charged with balancing the sources of production against the uses of a commodity such as steel naturally develop a list of steel consumers (see table 11.1.) These consumers may be consolidated into groups such as machinery, consumer goods, transportation (cars, trucks, railroad track, etc.), construction, and others. These groups of similar activities or industries can become the entries across the row of an input-output table. The steel planning department or ministry inevitably develops a list of sources of inputs to the various steel enterprises under its wing. These sources may also be grouped into similar industries and can become the entries down the column of the input-output table. If every industry is so represented, including consumers and government as a source of final demand, then the meshing of the input entries with output entries should be perfect. Industry sales to various other industries will read across Industry A's row as output items, but when read down another industry's column, the same number is interpreted as an input from Industry A. As a way of summarizing past flows of an economy, an input-output table is useful for a market economy as well as a planned one, however, it shows only what happened, not why it happened.

The number of rows and columns of an input-output table may be increased

Table 11A.1

A Hypothetical Input-Output Table

Inputs \ Outputs	Heavy Industrial Products	Light Industrial Products	Energy and Power	Raw Materials	Household Purchases	Government Purchases	Gross Output
Heavy industrial products	30	28	18	20	3	15	114
Light industrial products	8	5	3	5	68	5	94
Energy and power	18	16	2	12	13	7	68
Raw materials	25	15	30	2	6	1	79
Household services	26	20	8	34	1	22	111
Payments to government	7	10	7	6	12	—	42
Gross Outlays	114	94	68	79	103	50	508

to the limit of definition of an industry or product or to the limit of available information and computing facilities. The informational and computational complexity of input-output planning is a serious matter because the number of interconnections and interrelationships increases geometrically with the number of categories. Reducing the number of categories by lumping some industries or products together helps alleviate this problem of complexity but at the expense of planning precision—for example, the furniture, paper, and lumber industries could be designated the "wood-products industry."

An extremely simplified and aggregated input-output table is shown as table 11A.1. Productive activity is not shown for individual industries but for broad functional groupings. The outputs of a particular functional grouping are allocated to users or consumers of the product horizontally across the row of that industry. When the rows are ranged downward in the same order as the goods are allocated, a matrix is formed with equal numbers of rows and columns. Reading down a column so formed will indicate the sources and structure of inputs to each grouping from all others.

The categories shown are meant to reflect the first broad strategic decision that planners must make in a command economy. This decision is the choice between consumer-oriented products and investment-oriented products. More of one type of product must, in an immediate sense, spell less of the other, as productive inputs are transferred. We have seen in an earlier chapter, however, that the growth of consumption potential over time may require more investment in machinery and plants in the present. Such a longer-term perspective, of course, cannot be demonstrated in the confines of a one-year input-output table, so the implications of the following analysis are influenced by the very nature of its concentration on the short term.

The categories shown in table 11A.1 begin with heavy industrial products, which include basic metals, semifabricates, machinery, construction materials, etc. Light industrial products are basically consumer-type products, but many of them also have industrial uses and so feed back into the economic process as productive inputs to other sectors. Raw materials are the basic products of mine and farm which are the material basis for economic goods and also may be directly consumed by households. Energy and power may also be directly consumed by households, but most energy is consumed indirectly through its utilization in the industrial process. Households are the source of inputs of labor in a socialist context and also of capital and land services in a capitalist context. Government supplies a variety of productive services, but the row items under this category include tax payments also. Under socialist property arrangements, government row entries include returns on capital and land inputs, while under capitalist property institutions the same services are imputed to households, as we have just indicated. Two other important aspects of the productive process which have not been shown explicitly in table 11A.1 are inventories and the foreign sector. These categories are actually definitional catchall items. The term "import" or "inventory" does not inform you as to the nature of the originating source. An industry could as well be importing specialized machinery from abroad or the towelling for its restrooms, and the same goes for inventories. For our purposes, the foreign sector and inventories have been consolidated into other groupings or have been neglected.

The input-output table as shown in Table 11A.1 serves only a retrospective purpose—to show in a compact form the structure of past economic activity. The input-output table becomes a dynamic instrument for central planning by making a few heroic assumptions and plunging into the calculations these assumptions make possible. The assumptions that have to be made are that the relationships between inputs and outputs derived from immediate past experience are fixed in the short run and are optimal in an operational sense. The assumption that the ratios are fixed is a very conservative one—if the job were done that way once, obviously it can be done that way again. The optimality assumption is a weak one, since you really don't know if the performance could have been improved or if some alternative combination might have been better until you actually squeeze the ratios or do the job some other way. The input-output table is silent on this score.

Table 11A.2 shows a set of technical input-output production coefficients derived by dividing the input cells of an industry by the total gross output of that producing industry. If the input-output table were completely expressed in physical units, the result would be a vector of per-unit input requirements, such as X pounds of fertilizer per bushel of wheat or Y tons of iron ore per ton of steel. Since table 11A.1 is expressed in value terms, table 11A.2 represents vectors of costs of inputs in cents or kopeks per dollar or rubles' worth of output. For planning purposes, then, it would seem that all the planners have to do is to set the final demand for all outputs at the desired levels and the input requirements pop right out of the coefficient table. Unfortunately for practical planning, things are not that simple. For example, if the planners desire to produce $10 billion more machinery for investment purposes, more raw

Table 11A.2

A Table of Input Coefficients

	Heavy Industrial Products	Light Industrial Products	Energy and Power	Raw Materials
Heavy industrial products	$ .263	$ .298	$ .265	$ .253
Light industrial products	.070	.053	.044	.063
Energy and power	.158	.170	.029	.152
Raw materials	.219	.160	.441	.025

materials and energy will be required, and these will both require more machinery *and* more materials and energy themselves. These circles of consequences and interdependencies dwindle away more or less rapidly depending on the magnitude of the input-output coefficients, or put in another way, on how strongly other sectors feed back to produce changes in any originating sector.

From table 11A.2 it can be seen that the $10 billion worth of additional machinery output directly requires $700 million in Light Industrial products, $1.58 billion of Energy and Power, and $2.19 billion of Raw Materials, as well as the immediate feedback of $2.63 billion in Heavy Industrial products. These initial impact effects are shown as column 1 of table 11A.3. The induced expansion of the input sectors, of course, requires more of all inputs, including those of the Heavy Industrial sector. Considering Heavy Industry alone, the secondary feedback demands for Machinery/Metals are shown as column 2 of table 11A.3. So far the initial $10 billion expansion of machinery output has induced $4.5 billion in additional demands for products of that sector itself.

Further calculations get cumbersome because the number of interactions becomes very large very fast. For example, the expansion of the Light Industrial Sector by $700 million (col. 1, table 11A.3) requires $209 million in Heavy Industrial Products (col. 2, table 11A.3) and also $37 million in inputs from its own sector, $119 million of Energy and Power, and $112 million of Raw Materials. These third round or tertiary induced demands can be calculated for the Energy and Power and Raw Materials sectors as well, and the demands for any or all sectors can be derived and summed. The process does not stop but can go on for an infinite number of rounds, trailing off in size more or less quickly,

Table 11A.3

Direct and First Round Induced Consequences of a $10 Billion
Increase in Output of the Heavy Industrial Sector
(Machine-building)

	Column 1 Direct Demands	Column 2 Induced Demand for Heavy Industrial Products Only (From Col. 1)
Heavy industry	$2.630 Billion (= $10 B.x.263)	$ .692 Billion (= $2.63x.263)
Light industry	.700 Billion	.209 Billion (= $.700x.298)
Energy power	1.580 Billion	.419 Billion
Raw materials	2.190 Billion	.554 Billion
		Total $1.874 Billion
		Col. 1 2.630 Billion
	Direct and	$4.504 Billion
	First Round	
	Induced Demand	

depending on the strength of the feedback effects between sectors. The reader who wishes to be driven mad is invited to calculate and sum the effects of four or five rounds.

It is the magnitude and variability of the circuits of induced demands for inputs and outputs that illustrate the critical flaw of materials balances as a planning technique. Using materials balances, the planners must communicate up and down channels with firms and industries and laterally between industries, sectors, and ministries a large number of times to ensure that they haven't overlooked some important feedback effects. Each round of consultations and queries takes valuable time and large amounts of bureaucratic resources. As a practical matter the planners cannot go through this process enough times and so quit too soon or just arbitrarily add a "fudge factor," an amount which optimistically may be equal to the uncalculated additional rounds of feedback effects. It would be remarkable indeed if the amounts so added were not too large for some industries (waste) and too small for other industries (shortage).

There are mathematical techniques which permit planners possessing the input-output information shown here to directly calculate the solution for the economy *as if* endless rounds of calculations like the above had been done and added up. The method is expressed mathematically as inverting a Leontief matrix, derived by subtracting a matrix of input coefficients such as is found in table 11A.2 from an identity matrix. The inversion process, not shown in this appendix, can be done by hand for extremely small matrices such as we have here, but are best left for the computer for large matrices such as those that would be used by planners. Short presentations of the process of matrix inversion can be found in any number of mathematical texts or economic studies of input-output techniques.[1],

An inverted Leontief matrix derived from the coefficients of table 11A.2 is shown as table 11A.4. The full consequence of a $10 billion expansion of machinery production is an expanded output of Heavy Industrial prod-

Table 11A.4

Direct and Induced Demand for Inputs

	Heavy Industrial Products	Light Industrial Products	Energy and Power	Raw Materials
Heavy industrial products	$1.826	$ .847	$ .613	$ .667
Light industrial products	.200	1.179	.190	.158
Energy and power	.459	.462	1.422	.371
Raw materials	.650	.593	.874	1.369

[1]William H. Miernyk, *Input-Output Analysis* (New York: Random House, 1965); Heinz Kohler, *Welfare and Planning* (New York: John Wiley, 1971).

ucts by $18.260 billion, $10 billion of which is the initial expansion and $8.260 billion is the induced production to meet the needs of input sectors and the Heavy Industry sector itself. Reading down the Heavy Industry column, the numbers represent the cents per dollar of inputs/outputs generated by a dollar's increase in initial demand. The same is true for the other three columns associated with the other producing sectors. A $1 billion increase in Energy and Power will induce a full $422 million additional demand for energy for its own use and to service its own suppliers.

Armed with *this* information, the planners may draw up a list of final net outputs for household consumption and state or society's purposes and determine how much aggregate total expansion will be necessary to achieve these goals. What might seem to be reasonable net goals may be infeasibly ambitious when account is taken of the gross input requirements of intermediate products. Should this occur, the planners must prune back some of their goals until the resources available will fill the demands. The problem is that since the planners can cut back anywhere to ultimately produce a feasible plan, what should in fact be cut back? No amount of matrix inversion will settle this problem, which is essentially one of tastes and priorities.

Interestingly enough, input-output techniques were developed in the capitalist West in connection with the rationalization of indicative planning in Western Europe and as the result of the career interests of particular economists like Vassily Leontief. The centrally planned countries of Eastern Europe and Asia have been very slow to do work in this area. There are several reasons that might explain the lag. Such methods have been tainted as "capitalistic" devices and thus have been politically unacceptable until practical need has recently forced their use. Soviet data has also not been of the quality needed to produce satisfactory coefficients—the Soviet planners prefer to plan with a broad stroke and then juggle things around when trouble crops up. Finally, the Soviets have been sluggish in the development of computer capacity and software. This is a critical bottleneck for the development of input-output planning, but input-output has other difficulties which reach beyond such matters.

First, technical coefficients which are at the heart of input-output calculations must inevitably be industry-wide averages. As any student knows, there is a tremendous variance in productive capacities and efficiencies in any industry at any particular time. Thus economies of scale, technological change, and differences between firms are ignored. Directives to firms based on industry averages are likely to be inappropriate to almost all firms—too ambitious for some and too conservative for others.

Second, coefficients are assumed constant for the planning period. This assumption may not be all that serious for a one-year period, but the essence of planning, West or East, is to make projections up to five years and beyond. Clearly this is unacceptable in the light of the tremendous technical advances of the last several decades.

Finally, input-output calculations and analysis do not contain any meaningful notions of the opportunity costs of policy objectives. Planners have no way of determining what alternatives are foregone when a particular production pattern is chosen; hence, they have no objective basis for detecting errors or preventing errors from being perpetuated and compounded. Several variants of final demand vectors may be quickly run through the computer, but all the planners will get back is that each is feasible or infeasible. The real question as to which is better—or even what the objective trade-offs are—is not available from input-output calculations. *Linear programming* techniques have been developed to circumvent precisely these weaknesses of input-output.

LINEAR PROGRAMMING

We have seen that planners can construct a balanced or consistent plan using the technique of input-output, but there are many final output mixes which satisfy the consistency requirement. Which particular mix should the planners choose? Rather than starting out with an arbitrary mix of final goods and services and then determining the needed amounts of inputs, linear programming allows the planner to derive that particular mix which will maximize the value of output. In order to solve a linear programming problem the planner must possess three types of information: 1) the total amounts of inputs available, 2) the relationship between product output and factor inputs for each product, and 3) a set of preferences indicating the subjective rate of trade between products (the MRS).

Consider a simple economy with two final products, wheat and cloth, and three primary factors of production, land, labor, and machinery. To simplify our analysis we will assume that there are no intermediate products. The task facing the planner is to determine the optimum mix of wheat and cloth, the mix that will maximize the value of output. To solve the problem the planner has collected the three types of information listed above. Table 11A.5 indicates the amount of the resources available.

Table 11A.5

Inputs	
Land	1000 acres
Labor	500 man hours
Machinery	100 machine hours

Table 11A.6 describes the relationship between factor inputs and product output for the two types of final goods. To produce each bushel of wheat requires five acres of land, two man hours, and no machinery. To produce one yard of cloth requires no land, four man hours, and two machine hours.

Table 11A.6

Inputs	Outputs	
	one bushel of wheat	one yard of cloth
Land (acres)	5	0
Labor (man hours)	2	4
Machinery (machine hours)	0	2

Finally, let us suppose that the planners are willing to give up one bushel of wheat if they can get three yards of cloth in return. They value each yard of cloth three times as much as each bushel of wheat. We can now pick a set of prices which reflects these relative values by setting the price of wheat at $1 per bushel and the price of cloth at $3 per yard.

The objective of the planners is to maximize the value of output subject to the constraints on resource availability. The function to be maximized is Y = $1 (No. of bushels of wheat) + $3 (No. of yds. of cloth). The constraints are expressed in the following three equations:

1) Land constraint

$$5(\text{no. of bu. of wheat}) + 0(\text{no. of yds. of cloth}) \leqslant 1000 \text{ acres}$$

2) Labor constraint

$$2(\text{no. of bu. of wheat}) + 4(\text{no. of yds. of cloth}) \leqslant 500 \text{ man hours}$$

3) Machinery constraint

$$0(\text{no. of bu. of wheat}) + 2(\text{no. of yds. of cloth}) \leqslant 100 \text{ machine hours}$$

Consider the land constraint. We see from table 11A.6 that it takes five acres of land to produce one bushel of wheat and no land to produce cloth. The constraint tells us that we cannot produce more wheat than the amount which uses up 1000 acres of land. Both wheat and cloth require labor, but we cannot produce a combination greater than that which uses up 500 man hours, and each bushel of wheat uses up two while each yard of cloth uses up four. Finally, we cannot produce more cloth than that quantity which uses up 100 machine hours.

We can represent our problem graphically, by considering the constraint imposed on each product by each factor separately. If we devote all our machinery to cloth production, we can produce a maximum of 50 yards of cloth, ignoring the labor constraint. If we devote all our land to wheat production, we can produce a maximum of 200 bushels of wheat. If we devote all

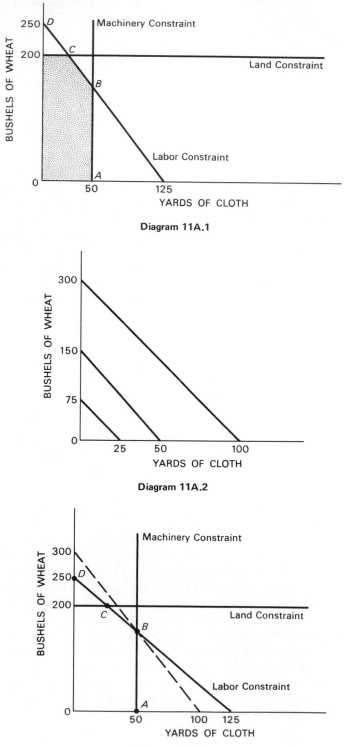

Diagram 11A.1

Diagram 11A.2

Diagram 11A.3

labor to cloth production, we can produce 125 yards of cloth; or if we devote it instead to wheat production, we can produce 250 bushels of wheat, ignoring the labor constraint. When all three constraints are operating, we are limited to the shaded area and the boundary described by the dark lines in diagram 11A.1. The boundary represents the production possibilities open to the economy. The planners can choose any point within the boundary. A point within the boundary represents a waste of resources, so the problem is to choose the point on the boundary that maximizes the value of output. The slope of the production possibilities boundary represents the relative costs of the two goods. Recall from chapter two that to produce the optimum output mix requires that relative costs be set equal to relative values, and we have a measure of relative values. It is expressed by the ratio of the prices of wheat and cloth. The slope of the preference line in diagram 11A.2 is the reciprocal of the price ratio of wheat to cloth and measures the rate at which the planners are willing to trade wheat for cloth. Any point on the preference line provides an equal value mix of cloth and wheat. Lines to the right represent higher levels of output and value. If we superimpose diagram 11A.2 on diagram 11A.1, we can find the mix that maximizes the value of output.

At point B (150 bushels of wheat and 50 yards of cloth) the preference line is tangent to the production possibilities boundary, and therefore the slopes of the two are equal. Thus, at point B relative values are equal to relative costs and the value of output is maximized at $300.

$$Y = \$1\ (150) + \$3\ (50) = \$300$$

Any point on the production boundary represents a feasible, consistent plan, but only point B represents a consistent and efficient or optimal plan. Observe that at point C (200 bushels of wheat and 25 yards of cloth):

$$Y = \$1\ (200) + \$3\ (25) = \$275$$

We have thus constructed a plan specifying the production of 150 bushels of wheat and 50 yards of cloth. In this simple example we assumed that each product was produced using only one technique. In fact linear programming, unlike the input-output method of plan construction, does not limit the planners to a single production technique for each commodity. Consider the example above with the addition of a second, more labor intensive method of wheat production using four acres of land and three machine hours for each bushel of wheat. We can label wheat produced using the old method as W_1 and wheat produced by the second method W_2. We now have a problem involving three products, although we know W_1 and W_2 are identical in value. The solution to this problem will specify the amount of each product to produce, but now the amount of W_1 and W_2 indicated tells us not only how much wheat to produce but which combination of techniques to use.

From our brief discussion of linear programming, we can see that it is a superior technique when contrasted with input-output, for we are enabled to pick that particular output which maximizes value and simultaneously that set of production techniques which minimizes costs. The practical problems of using linear programming in the process of plan construction, however, are enormous. In any economy involving more than two goods we must use an algebraic rather than a graphical solution technique. Although such techniques are available and can be computerized, the computing capacity required to construct a realistic plan for a modern economy is enormous and presently beyond the capacity available in any economy. The data necessary for the solution of a linear programming problem requires that the planners have knowledge of the quantities of the huge variety of factors of production and all technical alternatives. Information systems, such as those operating in the Soviet Union, do not provide the planners with information in this form. The planners must also be able to translate the priorities of the leadership into relative values. Those relative values may or may not reflect consumer preferences.

Finally, the assumption of linearity poses some problems. Linear programming assumes all production processes are linear—i.e., that they have constant returns to scale—and that relative values are constant, regardless of the amounts of each product produced. We know in fact that some production processes display economies of scale while others show diseconomies. The assumption of constant relative values ignores the principle of diminishing marginal utility. Those problems can be corrected through the use of non-linear programming, but the practical, computational problems are even greater.

If these practical problems can be surmounted, a plan can be constructed which will provide the enterprise manager with specific instructions on what to produce and what production techniques to use. An alternative to the allocation of resources by the command mechanism is available when the linear programming technique is used. The algebraic solution of a linear programming problem provides information on the marginal products of factors and the marginal opportunity cost of final products. Prices, called shadow prices, can be set for all factors and final goods, which reflect relative scarcities, and thus can perform the same function as prices in a perfectly competitive market economy. These prices can then be used to guide managers who are instructed to maximize profits. Researchers in the Soviet Union are experimenting with the possibility of constructing shadow prices for a few basic commodities and then using these as levers to influence enterprise behavior in a more decentralized economy.

QUESTIONS

1. What are the characteristics of the "perfectly visible hand," and why is it unlikely to exist in the real world?

2. What are the functions of the bureaucracy in a planned economy?

3. What are the major problems facing the planners in their attempt to construct a plan?

4. What is the method of material balances, and how is it used in constructing a plan?

5. What are the major problems facing the planners as they implement the plan?

6. What are the advantages and disadvantages of centralizing all economic decisions?

7. What functions do success indicators serve in a planned economy, and why does their use often produce economic distortions?

12

The Modernization
of the Soviet Economy
1880–1928

Introduction

In 1928 the Soviet Union was the first nation to embark upon central planning. In order to understand the Soviet planning experience it is important to examine the development of the economy in the period prior to 1928. The problems encountered in the early phases of Russian development will enable us to understand the events leading up to the 1928 planning decision and the circumstances surrounding that decision. Although we will examine the Soviet economy as a prototype of a centrally planned economy, its own unique historical development influenced the nature of its economic institutions. Just as the study of each market economy illustrates certain features common to all market economies, so too does the study of the Soviet economy illustrate features common to all centrally planned economies. Yet each market and planned economy is also a unique blend of economic institutions, tempered by its own historical development. We will divide Russian development prior to 1928 into three parts. The first is concerned with the development of the Russian economy prior to the Bolshevik takeover in 1917. The second part deals with the pre-plan Bolshevik experience from 1917 to 1926, while the third examines the events leading up to the 1928 decision to plan. In the following chapter we will examine the institutions adopted to centrally manage the economy.

Russian Development Prior to 1914

Russian Backwardness

According to the limited evidence available, Russian industry in the middle of the eighteenth century—the eve of the industrial revolution—was comparable to Western European industry, although Russian agricultural productivity was below that of the West and trade was not as developed. At the end of the eighteenth century Russia was the leading producer of iron and copper. The government played an important role in the economy in the early phases of industrial development. It subsidized investment in industry and financed this investment with taxes on salt and tobacco. A recurrent theme and continuing problem in the process of Russian and Soviet development has been the task of generating sufficient savings from the mass of the population, the peasants, and transferring these surpluses to the industrial sector. Periods of rapid economic growth have usually reflected a concerted government effort to force industrialization by transferring resources from the peasant to the urban sector.

Despite the promising beginning in the eighteenth century, urbanization and industrialization in Russia slowed down, particularly when compared to the growth of its Western European counterparts. By the late nineteenth century 13 percent of the population of Russia lived in urban areas compared to 40 percent in France and Germany, and 70 percent in Britain.[1] In 1880 Russia was predominantly an agricultural country with only the barest beginnings of industry. The use of primitive agricultural techniques combined with an incentive-stifling land tenure system resulted in low yields per acre and per man. The limited railroad network was inadequate for connecting raw materials with markets in a country with vast distances between population centers and ore deposits. There was no banking system or corporate form of business structure to aid in the concentration of capital necessary for the establishment of large, modern firms.

Many economic historians have speculated on the causes of the retardation of Russian industrial development. A variety of reasons have been advanced and we shall briefly outline three prominent ones. The first deals with the despotic government and its stifling influence on the economy. It is extremely difficult to

---

[1]For a discussion of the early phases of Russian development see Alexander Baykov, "The Economic Development of Russia," *The Economic History Review,* 2nd series, 7, No. 2, (December 1954), pp. 137-149.

untangle political and economic factors in Russian development both before and after the Revolution of 1917. Russia was an autocratic state in both periods. Prior to the Revolution political power was tightly held by the monarchy and the large estate owners. Although the autocratic power of the Tsar was often a driving force behind economic change, it also stifled change by protecting the privileges of a feudal nobility well into the nineteenth century and fostering non-competitive industrial monopolies through the imposition of high tariffs on imports. The rise of a middle class, often associated with the growth of repre-sentative government as well as industrial development in Western Europe, had not proceeded very far in Russia by the end of the nineteenth century.

A second argument advanced to explain Russian backwardness deals with the natural factors of geography and climate.[2] It has been suggested that the slow development of Russian industry was due primarily to the poor location of her natural resources, the lack of a river transport system, and poor quality of her agricultural land, whose productivity was even further reduced by harsh climatic conditions. Iron ore and coking coal were key elements in the industrial development of Western Europe in the late eighteenth and nineteenth centuries. With the technology available at the time iron ore deposits near the populated centers of Russia were exhausted by the mid-nineteenth centruy, and ore had to be mined in the Urals—a thousand miles from population centers. Further, Russian rivers, flowing north and south, were useless in connecting the three areas. Railroads had yet to be built.

The natural factors of poor soil, cold climate, and deficient rainfall made about two-thirds of Russian land unarable. Thus, even with the use of modern techniques it is reasonable to believe that Russian yields per acre would be lower than in Western Europe. But effects of the poor quality of Russian soil on agricultural productivity were compounded by the land tenure system, which has been claimed by many economic historians to be the chief reason for Russian economic backwardness. Russia developed the institution of serfdom quite late by Western European standards and maintained it long after it had been abandoned in much of the rest of Europe. Serfdom was formally abolished in Russia in 1861, but was replaced by a traditional village communal form of agricultural organization rather than by the individual private farms familiar in the West.

Both before and after the abolition of serfdom Russian peasants lived together in villages called *mirs*. The peasants owned the land collectively, al-though individual peasants tilled certain specified areas. The land was periodi-cally redistributed on grounds of equity to insure that each family had roughly comparable pieces of land, the size of its holdings corresponding to the number of adult males in the family. When the peasants were serfs, they tilled the land of

[2]*Ibid.*

the nobility as well as that of the *mir*. When serfdom was ended by a government decree in 1861, the nobility was compensated for the loss of the services of their serfs by interest-bearing, forty-nine-year bonds. The former serfs were in fact to provide the funds to make the interest payments, as well as the funds for the ultimate redemption of the bonds, by a series of annual money payments extending over forty-nine years.

After 1860 Russian agriculture was a peculiar mixture of private and communal ownership. Peasants farmed their own land, located in widely scattered strips, but the *mir* collectively determined sowing and harvesting times and was collectively responsible for the redemption payments and taxes as well as for the periodic redistribution of land. Agriculture remained backward due to the disincentive effects of the land tenure system, the burden of the redemption payments, and the lack of funds for investment in new techniques to increase productivity. The individual peasant had little incentive to make improvements in land which he would not be farming in the future. The peasant was restricted from selling his land and leaving the village without the permission of the *mir* because of its collective responsibility for redemption payments and taxes. If one family left, the remainder would be responsible for its share of the burden. The burden, in fact, kept growing due to the inadequacy of the revenue obtained from the sale of peasant crops to meet the redemption payments. By the end of the nineteenth century, the peasants owed more than they did in 1861, since they were not even able to meet the interest payments on the debt. Due to the poverty of the peasants themselves, the lack of government aid, and the unavailability of credit in the private sector, investment in agriculture remained very low throughout the nineteenth century.

Despite this dismal picture, some progress was made in increasing agricultural output, particularly after 1880. The most enterprising peasants, those with better quality land and larger holdings, were able to purchase the land of poorer peasants. Increasing differentiation among the peasantry resulted in a few wealthier peasants, called *kulaks,* along with the larger landowners producing crops for sale, while the great bulk of the peasants were engaged in subsistence agriculture, producing primarily for their own consumption. All peasants were forced to sell some of their produce on the market, however, to meet their taxes and redemption payments. The commercialized sector grew more rapidly than the subsistence sector, food grains increasing at a 2 percent annual rate between 1860 and 1914, and industrial crops increasing at 3 percent. Export crops, wheat and barley, increased more rapidly than rye, the staple of the peasant diet. The overall growth rate of agriculture is estimated to be less than 2 percent per year during this period.[3]

[3]The statistics on the growth of agricultural output were taken from Raymond Goldsmith, "The Economic Growth of Tsarist Russia 1860-1913," *Economic Development and Cultural Change,* 9, 1 (April 1961), p. 442.

Russian Progress

Russian industrial development proceeded much more rapidly in the latter part of the nineteenth and early part of the twentieth centuries than did agricultural development. Table 12.1 indicates the fairly rapid progress made in increasing industrial output over this span. It is difficult to formulate a precise explanation of the quickened pace of industrial development prior to World War I. Savings originating in the peasant sector were captured and used to finance investment in industry. The government played a central role in this process. By collecting taxes and redemption payments in money, rather than in kind, at harvest time, it forced the peasants to sell their crops, driving the price down,

Table 12.1

The Growth of Manufacturing
and Mining

Period	Average annual Percentage increase
1860 - 1913	5.3
1860 - 1887	5.1
1888 - 1900	7.3
1901 - 1913	3.8

Source: Raymond Goldsmith, "Economic Growth of Tsarist Russia," p. 465.

and supplying the government with cheap grain. The cheap grain lowered the cost of living for urban factory workers and fostered the expansion of industry. The government also used its revenues to invest directly in railroads and factories. A second major source of financing Russian industrial development was foreign loans. The cheap grain provided Russia with a low cost export commodity which could be used to service the interest payments on foreign loans and to pay for imported machinery. Despite the low productivity of agriculture, the tax policies of the government, together with the increasing commercialization of the kulaks, made a substantial agricultural surplus available for export. Between 1860 and 1913 Russia had a positive balance of trade for forty-three years. Over the entire period the value of exports exceeded that of imports by 6½ billion rubles.[4] Russia was known to the world as "the granary of Europe," in spite of its low standard of living and its technically backward agricultural sector. In addition to aiding in the financing of industry, the government also encouraged and protected the private sector by setting high tariffs on import-competing commodities, particularly consumer goods, while setting low tariffs on needed imports of machinery.

[4]Alexander Baykov, "Economic Development of Russia", p. 145.

Although the growth of industry speeded up substantially in the nineteenth century, it does not represent a smooth upward trend, shared equally by all sectors of industry. Growth was uneven with respect to time, geography, and sector of industry. Large-scale modern industries developed in the major cities, comparable to the best in Western Europe and the United States at the time. But these industries were islands of modernization in a sea of traditional handicraft industries. As late as 1915 small-scale handicraft industry still employed two-thirds of all industrial workers and produced 33 percent of industrial output.[5] Although industrial output grew at an annual rate of between 5 and 6 percent from 1885 to 1913, the growth of total output was much slower due to the poor performance of the large agricultural sector. The growth of total output was only 3 percent per year during this period. Population was increasing at an annual rate of 1½ percent, reducing the growth of per capita real output to approximately 1½ percent per year.

Table 12.2

Comparative Growth Rates 1860 - 1913

	Average Annual % Increase of Total Output	Average Annual % Increase of Total Output per Capita	Average Annual % Increase of Industrial Output per Capita
United States	4½	2½	2¾
Japan	4	3	—
Germany	3	2	2¾
Russia	2½	1½	3½
United Kingdom	3¼	—	1
France	1¾	—	—
Italy	1½	—	—
Near and Far East	0	—	—

Source: Raymond Goldsmith, "Economic Growth of Tsarist Russia", p. 474.

Table 12.3

Comparative Levels of National Income

	1894	1913	Growth
	(Given in Rubles per Capita)		(Percent)
United Kingdom	273	463	70
France	233	355	52
Italy	104	230	121
Germany	184	292	58
Austria-Hungary	127	227	79
Russia (European)	67	101	50

Source: Cited in Alec Nove, Economic History of the USSR.

[5]Alec Nove, An Economic History of the USSR (London: The Penguin Press, 1969), p. 17.

It is difficult to comprehend growth rates in the abstract. Is a 5 percent industrial growth rate low or high? What about a 1½ percent increase in per capita total output? Some calculations have been made comparing Russia's growth rate and absolute standard of living to other developed and developing nations. These data are presented in Tables 12.2 and 12.3. Increases in per capita output as well as the absolute level of national income in Russia were far below her Western European counterparts, although probably considerably above the so-called underdeveloped world.

Russia on the Eve of Revolution

At the end of the Tsarist period Russia stood midway between the developed industrial economies of the West and the underdeveloped nations which were still basically subsistence agricultural economies. Much evidence can be cited by those who wish to show that the Soviets inherited a backward agricultural economy. At the turn of the century, less than 15 percent of the population lived in towns, medium and large scale industry employed less than 10 percent of the labor force and contributed less than 20 percent of national income. Industrial workers were still tied to their villages, often returning home at harvest time. Industry remained dependent upon government assistance, foreign capital, and high tariffs. Agriculture was characterized by a high population density resulting in significant amounts of underemployment in the villages. Yields per acre were still very low by Western standards due to the use of primitive techniques and the lack of investment capital.[6] The industrial growth rates and the increasing commercialization of agriculture, aided by governmental reforms designed to consolidate peasant holdings, have been cited by others as evidence of Russia's increasing modernization. Some progress was made in the consolidation of peasant holdings. By the end of 1915 one-tenth of the holdings in European Russia had been consolidated. Funds were made available to peasants to help them buy land. But despite this limited progress, it must be concluded that the backwardness of Russian agriculture was a major stumbling block to continued industrial development. Fifty-five years after the abolition of serfdom, the bulk of Russian peasants were subsistence farmers cultivating widely scattered strips with wooden ploughs. The rapid increase in population growth created an agricultural employment surplus, which could not be absorbed by the growth of industry.[7]

---

[6]This pessimistic view of Russian pre war development is presented in Maurice Dobb, *Soviet Economic Development Since 1917* (New York: International Publishers, 1948), pp. 34-80

[7]This more optimistic but still somewhat dismal portrayal of Russian development is presented in Hugh Seton-Watson, *The Decline of Imperial Russia 1855-1914* (New York: Frederick A. Praeger, 1952), pp. 272-292.

THE COMMUNIST TAKEOVER:
SOVIET ECONOMIC DEVELOPMENT 1917 to 1928

The period from November 1917, the Bolshevik takeover, to the end of the Civil War in 1921 is a truly remarkable period in Soviet history. Economic policies were promulgated under the shadow of war and civil war in an atmosphere close to total anarchy. It is beyond the scope of this text to analyze the complex political, social, and military events taking place at the time. Rather, we shall limit ourselves to a brief description of some of the major economic events and policies of the time.[8]

The Bolsheviks were in power for eight months before the outbreak of Civil War in 1918. During this period several important decrees were announced, which gave the government greater formal control of the economy. Formal and actual control did not always coincide, however, because of the lack of a bureaucratic structure to carry out the instructions of the political leadership. The decrees of the Fall of 1917 included a system of land reform, the establishment of "workers control" through the strengthening of factory committees, the nationalization of the banking system and the railways, and the setting up of the VSNKH, the Supreme Council of National Economy, charged with the organization of the national economy and state finance. Some have argued that these measures represented a cautious economic policy in which the state wanted to avoid precipitously nationalizing all industry.

Despite the intentions of the government, growing economic as well as political and military problems resulted in the adoption of an economic program called War Communism. Although private trade in grain had been illegal even under the Provisional Government, much of Russian agricultural output was still finding its way into illegal channels. With the outbreak of the Civil War, the already acute problem of the grain shortage became more severe. Due to the decreased level of agricultural output and the small share of manufactured goods allotted to the rural areas, the peasants were unwilling to market their produce, particularly at the low official prices available in the state grain market. Thus, faced with a crisis in the procurement of agricultural produce to feed the industrial population, the Soviet government procured grain from the peasants by force. In May 1918, the government declared a state grain monopoly. All grain except that needed for maintenance of peasant families and sowing reserves was to be delivered to the state at fixed prices. The state estimated the total quantity of each product and divided it proportionately among districts, villages, and ultimately individual farmers. Despite these drastic measures, a large share of agricultural output entered the market via the illegal private traders.

[8]We recommend to the reader who is interested in a fuller account of this period, Alan Nove, *Economic History of the USSR,* pp. 29-83.

In addition to its compulsory agricultural procurement policies the state attempted to nationalize all industry and abolish all private trade. Prices were frozen, rationing was introduced, and workers were paid in kind rather than in money wages. Illegal private trade in manufactured commodities flourished, however. Side by side with the state distribution system there existed a large black market that sold the same goods at substantially higher prices. The growth of a barter economy was facilitated by the decreasing value of money. The State Bank was essentially a branch of the Treasury. The chief function of the bank was to provide the government with revenue to finance the Civil War. Note issue became the single most important source of revenue, since pecuniary taxes and the sale of bonds provided little or no government revenue. The money supply increased so rapidly that it became practically worthless through inflation.

Thus, the period of War Communism was characterized by a complex program of nationalization, requisitioning, rationing, and payment of income in kind. The consequences of these policies, together with dislocations of war and civil war, were disastrous for the economy. Agricultural output had already begun to decline in 1914, and it is estimated that by 1917 the output of grain had fallen to approximately 59 percent of the level of 1913. It continued to decline, reaching 39 percent of its 1913 level by 1921. By 1918 industrial production had fallen to approximately 43 percent of the level of 1913, and it reached its lowest point in 1920, at about 19 percent of the 1913 level.

The New Economic Policy

By 1921 Russian industry was paralyzed by a shortage of food and raw materials. The population was exhausted by war and famine. Many Soviet leaders, including Lenin, recognized the necessity for a drastic change in economic policy. The New Economic Policy (NEP) was adopted in 1921 in an attempt to salvage the economy from the disasters of War Communism. The beginning of NEP marked the beginning of the recovery of agricultural and industrial production. After 1921 private trade was legalized, money transactions replaced the widespread barter system, and the requisitioning of agricultural supplies was abolished. After 1923 the rate of inflation was greatly reduced.

One of the most important steps taken by the Soviet authorities at the beginning of NEP was a substitution of a tax in kind for the distributive quota procurement scheme. The peasant was now allowed to sell all his surpluses in the open market after a fixed tax to the state. Cooperative and private trade developed alongside state trading organizations. The collection of goods for distribution among enterprises, or between enterprises and consumers, was carried out at free market prices.

Although private trade flourished, NEP cannot be characterized as a pure market economy. Nearly all large- and medium-scale industry remained nation-alized. The nationalized enterprises, however, functioned independently of the central government, producing to maximize profits in response to market signals. The state did influence the distribution of investment funds, thereby deter-mining the direction of industrial developments.

NEP was quite successful in achieving its immediate objectives. From its low point of 1920, industrial production rose steadily, regaining its 1913 level between 1927 and 1928. The recovery of industry, however, was uneven, with light and consumer goods sectors growing more rapidly than heavy industry. Agricultural production recovered more slowly than industrial production, recovering to 54 percent of the 1913 level by 1922 and 61 percent by 1923. This rise was halted in 1924 as the result of a partial crop failure. From 1925 to 1928, agricultural output continued to rise, nearly reaching its 1913 level by 1928.

The Industrialization Debate

Although the economy was recovering under the policy of NEP, most Soviet leaders felt that the NEP represented a transition phase rather than a permanent economic system. What road was the Soviet economy to travel once the immediate task of restoring industry and agriculture had been completed? All agreed on the long-run necessity of industrialization but differed as to the methods to be used in achieving it. The basic problems hindering industrializa-tion were the shortages of raw materials, fuel and power, and a supply of foodstuffs to maintain industrial workers employed in the factory. How were these goods to be transferred from the peasants to the urban sector? These were the key economic questions in the industrialization debates. Many of the arguments advanced much later in the West in the studies of economic develop-ment were made in Russia in the 1920s. In order to completely understand the nature and significance of those debates one must understand the political events of the time. Politicians allied themselves with economists and, thus, with particu-lar economic viewpoints, for strategic political reasons as well as for purely economic convictions. In the limited space available we can attempt to sketch only the economic arguments of the participants. Many fascinating works are available to the reader interested in a broader coverage of the period.[9]

The economic debate centered on the appropriate path to industrialization and socialism. Three basic positions were put forward. The first to be discussed, identified with the economist Bukharin, we will call the balanced growth view. Bukharin, supported by Stalin at the outset of the debates, believed that the

[9]See Alec Nove, *Economic History of the USSR*, also Alexander Erlich, *The Soviet Industrialization Debates 1924-1928,* Columbia University Press (New York: 1960).

market link between the agricultural and industrial sectors had to be preserved for some time to come. Industry was dependent upon agriculture for supplies and so must offer the peasants something in return for their output. Until the nationalized sector was strong enough to supplant private enterprise, Bukharin argued that it was necessary to foster the private sector to ensure an adequate supply of consumer goods and provide investment capital for the expansion of the state sector. As the state sector grew and supplied the market with cheap goods, private trade would shrink. In the interim, part of the profits of the private sector could be used to provide investment capital for the development of state industry. Thus, Bukharin and his supporters supported the use of the market system and market incentives to provide industry with the supplies necessary for its expansion. This policy implied, however, that a substantial portion of industrial investment, at least initially, must be in the consumer goods industry rather than in heavy industry. If industrial workers produced machines instead of shoes, textiles, or agricultural implements, there would be nothing to offer the peasant sector in return for their production. A market link between agriculture and industry required an offer of exchange. The peasants had to be motivated to part voluntarily with their crop by the possibility of buying manufactured commodities with their earnings.

Bukharin's views were attacked from the right and from the left. A group on the right argued that the rate of return on investment in industry was much lower than in agriculture. Thus, investment should be channeled into agriculture and light industry, such as food processing, because of the shorter pay-off period. Once agricultural output had expanded as a result of the introduction of new techniques, the extra production could be used to pay for the imported machinery necessary to set up heavy industry. This view was politically unpopular both because of the long, apparently circuitous route to industrialization and because it made the Soviets dependent upon the outside world for imports of machinery. The political views of the leadership closed off one of the most important sources of industrial capital in the Tsarist period—foreign loans and investments.

A more serious attack on Bukharin's views came from the economist Preobrazhenski, who was supported by Trotsky. He argued for the necessity of rapid industrialization with an emphasis on heavy industry. He believed that the growth of the 1920s was the result of repairing and reorganizing the industrial structure inherited from the Tsarist period. If massive amounts of investment were not quickly made in heavy industry, not only would growth be slowed down, but the economy would collapse as the old, worn out equipment was not replaced. Preobrazhenski asserted that it was impossible to collect the necessary supplies from agriculture voluntarily. The peasants would not part with their output except in exchange for manufactured consumer goods, and the economy was incapable of providing adequate amounts of these goods with its present industrial facilities. It was argued that more drastic measures would have to be taken to force the peasants to part with their output. Preobrazhenski proposed that a policy of relatively low agricultural prices, combined with high prices for manufactured goods and heavy taxes, be adopted. The opposition quickly pointed out that the peasants could refuse to cooperate with this policy as they did during War Communism, reverting back to a subsistence economy. Industry was dependent upon agriculture, but agriculture was not dependent upon industry. But if the bulk of industrial development were dependent upon the rate at which agricultural production and light industry could expand, perhaps it would be a case of too little, too late.

The Close of the Debate and the Decision to Industrialize

In 1928 the first five-year plan was announced. Its targets were extremely ambitious, beyond the wildest imaginings of Preobrazhenski and the other advocates of rapid industrialization. The plan proposed an annual growth rate for industry of between 22 percent and 25 percent. The level of investment was to result in a doubling of the fixed capital stock within five years. The output of consumer goods, agricultural goods, education, health care, and housing were also to expand, though not at the pace of heavy industry. Had the underlying problems of the debate been solved? Where was the agricultural surplus, so vital to the growth of industry, to come from?

These questions had certainly not been resolved. In fact the announcement of the first five-year plan closely followed the grain crisis of 1927-28, in which the government was unable to collect adequate grain supplies to feed urban workers. The traditional explanation of the government's failure was that not only was grain production lower than before the war, but the share of marketed output was lower. The government thus was not able to provide the supplies necessary for the increased pace of industrialization.

This view has been challenged as the result of a further, intensive study of this period. According to an expert in Soviet agriculture, the dimensions of the grain crisis of 1927-28 were exaggerated by Stalin, and the agricultural problem itself was due in large part to the improper policies of the government.[10] The government based its assertions on data which purported to show that gross output in 1926-27 was sharply below that of 1913, while the marketed share in 1926-27 was less than half the level in 1913. These figures were chosen in such a way as to exaggerate the grain problem. First, 1913 was an extremely good year for agriculture. Second, marketed share in 1913 refers to gross marketings, while for 1926-27 it refers to net marketing. The difference between gross marketing and net marketing reflects the quantity of grain repurchased on the market by the agricultural sector, and thus not available for the urban areas.

[10]Jerry F. Karcz, "Thoughts on the Grain Problem," *Soviet Studies,* 18, No. 4 (April 1967), pp. 399-434.

If one compares the period 1909-1913 with that of 1926-27, gross marketings of grain were almost identical.[11] Net marketings were significantly lower, however, in the latter period. The grain procurement crisis was not due primarily to reduced levels of output or even the unwillingness of the peasant to sell his grain, but rather to the peculiarly inept economic policies of the government. In an attempt to secure grain for the urban areas, the government tried to lower the price of manufactured consumer goods which were in short supply in order to offer the peasants cheaper goods in return for their grain. The government also tried to lower grain procurement prices to provide cheap grain for industry. The results were disastrous. Manufactured goods were quickly bought up at bargain prices by urban workers and speculators and resold in villages at much higher prices. The peasant marketed less grain to the government, sold more to private speculators and repurchased at low official prices some of what he had marketed to feed his livestock, and switched to the production of other products. Net marketings in 1928 were below the level of 1927, but other agricultural products such as meat and eggs were substantially above the level of 1927. The private price of grain rose to over twice that of the official price. There is little wonder that peasants attempted to evade the government and sell their grain in illegal channels. Instead of altering its pricing policies the government resorted to force, prohibiting private trade, increasing compulsory deliveries, and instituting harsh penalties for those failing to comply. Private trade was abolished at a time when the government had not made the preparations for public institutions to replace it. Collection, transportation, and storage facilities were inadequate to handle the task of grain procurement. The mass collectivization of agriculture followed in 1929-30.

It was believed that the collectivization of agriculture would permit grain to be extracted from the peasants at artificially low prices, for the government would no longer need to rely on the market link between agriculture and industry. The tragic drama of collectivization is impossible to relate here. The evidence indicates that there was little planning and little understanding of exactly what collectivization meant. Despite the confusion and abrupt changes of policies in the early 1930s, 70 percent of peasant families had pooled their land, livestock, and equipment and entered collective farms by 1935. The market link between the rural and urban sectors was replaced by administrative control over the output of the new collectives. The managers of the collective farms, responsible to the government, were told what to produce and directed to deliver obligatory quotas of their output to the state.

The peasants reacted to forced collectivization and the high obligatory quotas by attempting to sabotage the program. They burned their barns, killed their livestock, and reduced their output. There was widespread famine in rural areas. Despite all of this, the government was successful in procuring the agricultural supplies necessary for rapid industrialization. The government was able to secure increased agricultural supplies and raw materials for the industrial

[11]*Ibid.*, p. 409.

sector in the face of declining levels of total output. Rural living standards could be depressed by the use of physical controls to divert agricultural output to urban areas.

The Stalinist formula for industrialization can be described as the collectivization of agriculture, a high rate of investment in heavy industry, and the rapid upgrading of labor skills, together with the adoption of Western technology. This formula was applied to the Soviet economy by the use of central command planning. The abandonment of the market mechanism and the institution of direct physical controls over production were begun in the management of industry. Nearly all private production and trade were illegal. Nationalized industries produced in response to government directives. Thus, during the period of the first five-year plan the economy was transformed from a market to a centrally planned system. By destroying the private economic institutions which characterized NEP, assuming direct control over the entire economy through the adoption of central planning combined with the use of force, the government pushed for the achievement of rapid industrialization as embodied in the first five-year plan. This pattern of industrialization is in sharp contrast to that followed in the West. Industrialization in Western Europe and the United States was accompanied by the expansion of the decentralized market economy with a reduction of governments' role in the determination of the direction of the economy. These differences have been attributed to the "logic of haste" required when a backward nation desires to industrialize rapidly.[12]

QUESTIONS

1. Why did Russia trail the nations of Western Europe in the industrial revolution?
2. What was the Tsarist strategy for economic development in the latter part of the nineteenth century?
3. Was Russia a developed, developing, or underdeveloped economy on the eve of World War I?
4. Into what category (capitalist, mixed, planned) did the Soviet economy of the 1920s fit?
5. What were the basic differences among the participants in the Soviet industrialization debates?
6. How did Stalin transform the Soviet Union from a market into a planned economy?
7. What is collectivization, and what function did it perform in the development process?

[12]For a fuller exposition of the argument of the "logic of haste" see Gregory Grossman, "The Structure and Organization of the Soviet Economy," *The Slavic Review,* 21, No. 2 (June 1962), pp. 203-220.

13

Planning the Soviet Economy

Introduction

A discussion of the process of economic decision-making in the Soviet Union cannot begin without reference to the political institutions. The popular image of Soviet politics is of a government headed by a supreme leader to whom all Soviet society defers. The Stalinist era of apparent one-man dictatorship went far to consolidate this view. The flamboyant Khruschev demonstrated, on the one hand, that power tends to drift into a single man's hand, but his dramatic ouster and "retirement" indicates that the "supreme leader" is subject to some checks ultimately. Even Stalin had to mark time occasionally when he had overstepped certain bounds. While a full discussion of the Soviet political process is not appropriate here, examination of its salient features can provide a basis for study of the economic decision-making process.

THE POLITICAL INSTITUTIONS

The Communist Party

The ultimate repository of power in the Soviet Union is the Communist party. The Communist party must not be conceptually compared by the reader to a typical political party in a Western democracy. The C.P.S.U. is actually much closer in concept to a military reserve unit. Individual C.P. members may be farmers, factory workers, managers, technicians, professional people, or government officials. The vast majority earn a living pursuing nonpolitical careers. However, their party membership places them under strict discipline— they may be assigned to any task at the pleasure of the full-time party Secretariat. The Secretariat is an administrative apparatus that oversees the recruitment of new members, periodically purges the party rolls of slackers or dissidents, and assigns loyal party members to positions suited to their talents or the party's need to have dependable people in key positions. The position of General Secretary of the C.P.S.U. was originally assigned to Stalin because the work was considered too mundane or dull for the more spirited revolutionary intellectuals of the time. The position's potential for accumulating political I.O.U.s and placing loyal supporters in influential positions was not appreciated at the time but is quite well known at this juncture.

To return to the party grass roots, members are organized into party cells (again like military units) which periodically elect representatives to a national Party Congress. These representatives, not too surprisingly, are most noted for their fierce loyalty to the current C.P.S.U. leadership. Issues of vital national policy are occasionally put to the Party Congresses, but approval is a foregone conclusion; such action is for the record books rather than for demonstrating any sort of democratic political action. The Party Congress elects a Central Committee which serves as a decision-making body in the interim between Congresses, which may be several years.

The hundred or so members of the Central Committee constitute an inner circle of influential party officials from all over the Soviet Union, but even this body meets only a few times a year. Meetings of the Central Committee are not quite as pro-forma as the Party Congresses, but these meetings serve mainly to provide a sounding board for decisions made by the Politburo and/or the General Secretary. In recent history there are alleged to have been Central Committee actions that overturned or modified Politburo policies. Given the secrecy of Politburo and Central Committee deliberations, it is difficult to verify these assertions. It is known that an early attempt to oust Khruschev by the Politburo was overturned by the full Central Committee. Khruschev's downfall was a result of having alienated too many factions within the Central Committee with his "harebrained" schemes of reorganization.

The Politburo is a small circle of high party personalities, noted in the past for their devotion to the General Secretary and dependent on him for their advancement. In recent years, promotion to this group has been on the basis of recognized achievement and outstanding abilities as well as general adherence to the party line. Strong personalities and conflicting institutional loyalties may provide fireworks at Politburo meetings, but little of the sound or fury reaches the outside world.

The General Secretary, or just Secretary, of the C.P.S.U. holds a very powerful position, probably the most powerful position in a hierarchy of powerful institutions. An ambitious man in this position can attain dominance in the party by placing a few proteges in key positions and grasping or creating opportunities to gather reins of power whenever they become available.

The Leninist principle of party organization was defined as "Democratic Centralism." Party members would elect successively higher circles of party officials whose policies would be debatable until the final decisions were made and then became binding on all party members. In practice there has been more emphasis on "centralism" than "democracy." The Secretary and the Politburo ensure that the Central Committee membership is reliable by ensuring that delegates to Party Congresses are "sound" party people—unsound party members are purged or disciplined. The end product is a party organization in which authority devolves directly down from the top rather than deriving from the consent of the governed.

The Government of the Soviet Union

The Soviet Union is a federation of national and regional units based on historical, racial, or national boundaries. A Soviet citizen is considered first a citizen of the Union and then a member of one or another national or racial groupings such as the Kazakhas, Ukrainians, Cossacks, Lithuanians, Jews or one of many other "nationalities." There are the familiar local governments, including city governments, which function as do local governments everywhere—providing services such as education programs, police protection, medical services, sanitation and fire protection. Officials may be elected, but alternatives to the official slate are usually lacking. In the future the Soviet government may extend to local governments the option of competing candidates for a single office. The possibilities for significant strategic economic decision-making at this level are quite limited.

Regional governments exist and at times have had significant responsibilities. Their economic function is principally to oversee and coordinate the development of projects too small for direct consideration by the central planners but too large or widespread for local governments to handle. Stepping up to the Union level (the equivalent of our Federal government level) the political authority is formally vested in the Supreme Soviet.

The Supreme Soviet meets only several times a year; hence, it is patently obvious that serious deliberation does not take place at its sessions. Elections for the Supreme Soviet, however, produce a good deal of ballyhoo. Prominent local leaders may be nominated, popular (publicized) workers, stars of stage or screen, Olympics-level athletes, chess champions, novelists, physicists—all may be nominated and elected. A session of the Supreme Soviet may be likened to a national convention of Who's Who in the Soviet Union. The delegates listen to long-winded speeches on the economy and world affairs and applaud dutifully in all the right places. The one business item of importance—the election of the Executive Committee—is, of course, a foregone conclusion because the slate has been selected in advance.

The Executive Committee meets more frequently and probably has more true political functions than the Supreme Soviet. However, its size (several hundred) does not suggest that substantive decisions are made here either. The Executive Committee of the Supreme Soviet, in turn, elects the Council of Ministers, which is an executive body with substantial economic decision-making responsibilities. The Council of Ministers functions much like an expanded British Cabinet: individual members have executive responsibilities over various governmental departments and agencies; collectively their decisions determine the direction the Soviet government and economy will take in the future. Two governmental positions are determined by elections in the Executive Committee—the President and the Premier of the Soviet Union. These two offices may be compared to the American Presidency as some have suggested it be modified. The ceremonial functions of the Chief of State have been delegated to the President of the Soviet Union, while the administrative and executive powers have been vested in the post of Premier. The Premier directs the on-going and regular affairs of the state, such as foreign policy, through the Ministry of Foreign Affairs and the execution of governmental responsibilities in ensuring fulfillment of the State Plan. The Premier interacts with the Council of Ministers to propose and evaluate various economic policies.

It is not possible, however, to stop here and say we have found where economic decision-making power rests because of the lateral responsibility of the Premier and high government officials to the Communist party. The Premier is also a member of the Politburo of the C.P.S.U. and holds this post at the pleasure of the party because he was elected by the Executive Committee of the Supreme Soviet, whose members are usually also party members. The Premier need not be a cowed, spineless sycophant of the Party Secretary. He may be a power in his own right through having a personal following in the Central Committee or the Politburo of the party. However, ultimately the power of the Party Secretary must overwhelm the authority of the government chief, no matter how much authority he may have over countless legions of government bureaucrats. The logic of power politics has tended to pressure the Party Secretary into aspiring to the position of Premier of the government as well. The combined authority of party and state under Stalin and Khrushchev led, however, to autocratic practices which later leaders have felt to be inconsistent with rational decision-making. See table 13.1 for an overview of Soviet political and government institutions.

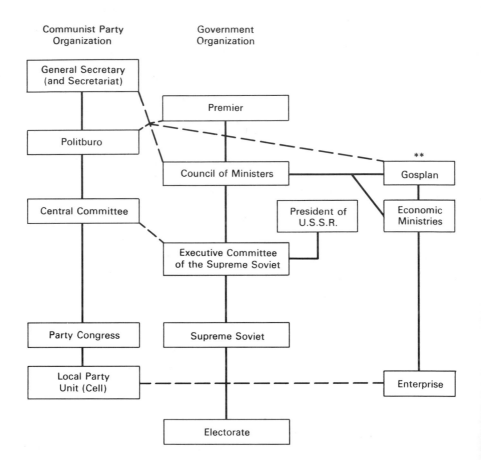

TABLE 13.1   Political and Governmental Organization of the Soviet Union.

*Note: Solid lines indicate formal lines of authority. Broken lines represent probable informal lines of authority or communication between party and government.
**Note: See table 13.2 for a schematic diagram of the economic planning apparatus.

A DECISION SCENARIO

Let us consider a decision to adopt a proposal which requires large expenditures of resources for the further development of agriculture. At this point we are concerned with the interaction of economic and political institutions and will reserve for chapter fourteen our discussion of the more technical aspects of the formulation of specific investment proposals. Suppose a research organization proposes diverting the waters of the north-flowing Siberian rivers into the arid regions of Central Asia. The sums of investments and time involved would be astronomical, but the agricultural payoff might be equally large. The proposal would reach the Premier through Gosplan, the central planning agency, and the Ministry of Land Amelioration and Water Management. The Premier would send it to the Council of Ministers for an independent feasibility study. If this study were favorable, the proposal would go back to Gosplan, whose task it would be to determine where the resources would come from. The party would have been routinely notified of any significant activity in the ministries involved and would have been informed of the Council of Ministers' action. The referral to Gosplan would probably trigger action in some section of the Party Secretariat when the dimensions and implications of the resource shift became evident. As soon as Gosplan began to have some rough notions as to where the resources would be diverted from (the opportunity cost of the project), the party Politburo would probably agendize the project. Some opposition might appear here—members might allege that the project would be too costly and risky or that the investment might be put to better use in industry and the agricultural products the project would have made available ought to be imported. If the project were deemed impractical or dangerous or inappropriate at this point, it would die. If favorably recommended, it would go the Central Committee for approval. Gosplan, having received a go-ahead from the party, would complete a report on the project and refer it to the Council of Ministers, where debate would cover the same ground as in the Politburo of the party. It is conceivable that the Council of Ministers could reject the proposal over the recommendation of the party and that dickering would take place between the party and government. It is possible that the government would be sustained and the project rejected as the party admitted that it had judged prematurely or not considered all factors. Needless to say, the government Council of Ministers would have to have a good case to achieve such a reversal. In most cases, the party imprimatur would be sufficient, the Council of Ministers would formally approve the project, and Gosplan would be instructed to incorporate the project into the State Plan.

Now that we have briefly reviewed the political and governmental decision-making processes in the Soviet Union, we will turn to an analysis of the economic institutions which are responsible for the formulation of plans and the day-to-day functioning of the economy.

THE ECONOMIC INSTITUTIONS

Gosplan

Since 1928 there has been a great deal of bureaucratic reshuffling of the economic institutions responsible for planning. Although planning responsibilities have been grouped and regrouped among various agencies, we shall refer to *Gosplan,* which is now responsible for both short and long-term planning, as *the* central planning agency. It is the responsibility of Gosplan to construct plans to implement the broad economic goals formulated by the political leadership. Two basic types of plans are constructed for this purpose—longer, usually five-year, plans, which map the future development of the economy, and one-year plans, which serve as operational guides to production units. The one-year plans, subsequently broken down into quarterly and monthly plans, specify physical output targets for the most important industrial and agricultural commodities as well as the distribution of important raw materials and equipment and the level of investment. The plan is concerned basically with the production of output and the allocation of inputs in physical terms; it is the aim of the planners to secure a balance between the supply and demand of all commodities. A financial plan which seeks to maintain a balance between the disposable money income of the population and the value of goods and services available in the consumer sector is drawn up to accompany the physical plan. We will discuss financial planning separately in a later section of the chapter.

When the physical plan prepared by Gosplan reaches the enterprise, it provides the managers with detailed instructions on the volume of output to produce and in what assortment, what inputs to use, and what prices to charge, as well as specifying the introduction of new techniques and new products. In order to carry out this tremendous task Gosplan is organized into two types of subunits, one responsible for output plans for key commodities and the second responsible for supply plans of key inputs. The former group of subunits is divided along sectoral lines, with one agency responsible for planning the production of a particular branch of the economy such as machine building, consumer goods, or steel. The latter group of subunits is responsible for the supply and distribution of essential raw materials. Once production targets are set, the success of the plan depends upon the arrival of needed supplies.

Below the All Union Gosplan are Republican Gosplans, which are responsible for the construction of plans for less critical industries located in their region. The All Union Gosplan is responsible for planning approximately 2000 commodities, considered to be the most important for the achievement of plan goals, while plans for the remaining commodities are under the control of the Republican Gosplan and local planning agencies.

The Ministries

In order for an enterprise to receive operational plans specified in enough detail to be meaningful to it, a tremendous amount of information must be collected from the enterprise, transmitted to Gosplan, analyzed and processed, and sent back down to the enterprise in the form of production directives for the new plan period. As discussed in chapter ten, no central planning agency has the time, the manpower, or the computing facilities to process all the needed information. Rather, an institutional structure must be developed for the purpose of data collection, processing, and dissemination, as well as for the supervision of enterprise performance to ensure the fulfillment of plan targets. Two basic types of bureaucratic structures have been developed in the Soviet Union for handling these tasks: a ministerial system organized along functional lines, which has been the dominant form of organization from 1932 to 1957 and 1965 to the present; and a territorial system organized along geographical lines, which existed from 1959 to 1965.

The ministerial system consists of ministries which are responsible for overseeing the performance of enterprises grouped together according to branch or industry. Anywhere from three to thirty or forty functional ministries, based in Moscow, have performed the disaggregative and aggregative tasks necessary for plan construction and implementation. The exact number of ministries has depended upon the number of industries deemed sufficiently important to warrant their own ministry. When the number of ministries has become too large to coordinate effectively, industries have been consolidated into a single ministry. Each ministry has control over all the enterprises in its sector throughout the Soviet Union. The ministry has regional subdivisions which carry out the work of the ministry in republic or local areas. The ministry itself is divided into departments of planning, supplies, and deliveries and is responsible for drafting and submitting to Gosplan the output and supply plans of enterprises under its control.

In the past the ministerial system has been attacked by the government for promoting inefficiency in the economy through the creation of self-sufficient empires. To limit their dependence on supplies from other ministries, the ministries had encouraged vertical integration which tended to make industries self-sufficient. Ministries perferred to buy inputs produced by other firms in their own jurisdiction rather than depend upon outside sources, and long, wasteful cross-hauling of supplies often resulted. The advantages of specialization were ignored in the attempt to achieve ministerial autonomy. The territorial system, established in 1957 under Khrushchev's leadership, was substituted for the ministerial system in an attempt to eliminate some of the major problems discussed above. Rather than organize information flows along functional lines, it was decided to organize them along regional lines. One hundred regional councils (Sovnarkhoz) were established to supervise and control the industries in a given region. These regions, in turn, were divided into smaller territorial administrative units, each unit being responsible for all types of production carried on within its boundaries. Problems similar to those associated with the ministerial system soon developed. Instead of striving for ministerial autonomy, the new Regional Councils strove for regional autonomy, so that they would not be dependent upon supplies from enterprises in regions not under their control. Regional self-sufficiency replaced ministerial self-sufficiency with the result of wasteful cross-hauling and the duplication of enterprises in each region. Again the advantages of specialization were ignored. In response to these problems the ministerial system was restored in 1965. See table 13.2 for an overview of the two types of organization.

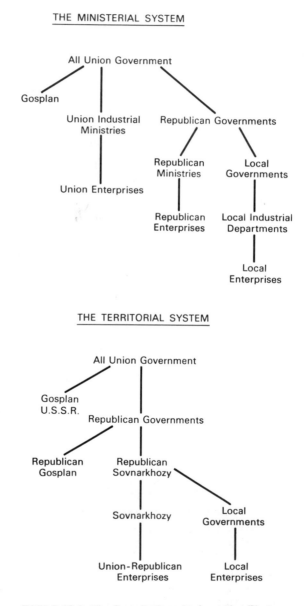

TABLE 13.2 The Organization of Information Flows

Under each system, administrative units, whether functional ministries or Regional Councils, tended to be large bureaucracies, concerned with their own welfare rather than with the overall interest of the economy. The primary explanation of this behavior lies in the nature of the planning process itself. As we shall see in the next section of this chapter on Plan Construction, plan targets are set so high relative to capacity and available supplies of materials that shortages are endemic to the system. The arrival of needed supplies is unreliable, particularly when they come from other regions or other ministries. Thus, from each agency's point of view it is better to rely on supplies from enterprises over which it has some control.

The Enterprise

Plan directives are ultimately forwarded to enterprises to guide them in their production activities. The great preponderance of industrial output, over 95 percent, is produced in state-owned enterprises. The remainder, a small and shrinking portion, is produced in cooperatives and the private sector. No Soviet citizen is allowed to employ or sell the output of another. Thus, the only citizens who are engaged in private economic activity in the Soviet Union are artisans, craftsmen, and those who produce a service, such as tailors, lawyers, and priests. Private activity of this type, although legal, is discouraged by the imposition of heavy income taxes. The state has preferred cooperatives to private activity, but cooperatives in the manufacturing sector were nationalized in 1960. These latter two types of organization are inconsequential in industrial production today, but we shall see that they still play a significant role in the agricultural sector.

State enterprises are owned and managed by a representative of the government and are considered financially independent units, operating under the principle of *khosraschet,* which translates as economic accountability. This form of enterprise has traditionally received its initial plan and equipment from the government in the form of a non-repayable grant. Since 1965 the enterprise must pay 6 percent interest on its fixed and working capital. Once an enterprise is established it is expected to be financially independent to cover its current expenditures for wages, raw materials, and depreciation out of the revenue received from the sale of its output. In the past many enterprises made continuous losses and were subsidized by the state.

The task of the manager, who is responsible for the performance of his enterprise, is to fulfill the plan targets. Prior to 1965, his behavior was circumscribed by a bewildering variety of targets, specifying such things as gross output, assortment, labor productivity, costs, taxes, profits, and material inputs. See table 13.3 for a more complete listing of the major plan indexes. After 1965 the number of plan directives was reduced from 35 or 40 to 8 key indicators. These targets include the physical output of key commodities produced by the

Table 13.3

Schematic Listing of Major Plan Indexes

Assignments	Assignments	Resources
Output gross output marketable output output composition assortments new products improvement of products subcontracted output	Profit contributions to budget contributions to economic council share remaining in firm distribution among various funds percentage of profit (to cost)	Fixed assets new machinery and equipment construction work
Labor Productivity	Depreciation and its apportionment	Labor wage fund (total and by categories) number of employees (total and by categories) average wages
Costs production costs of marketable output expenditures per ruble of marketable output percentage cost reduction unit costs of major goods	Technical progress installation of equipment starting up new processes improving of processes new product design prototype building	Materials from specific sources for specific uses
Accumulation turnover tax	Capital and current repairs	Working capital normatives balance at end of plan period rate of turnover

Source: Reported in George Feiwel, The Soviet Quest for Economic Efficiency (New York: Frederick A. Praeger, 1967), p. 111.

enterprise, overall sales, overall profits, profitability calculated as a percent of fixed and working capital, the wage fund, payments into the state budget, capital investment from centralized funds, the introduction of new products and new technology, and the use of material supplies. Within these constraints the manager's task is to hire labor and combine it with material allocated to him by the plan to produce the planned output. Although it would appear from the all-encompassing nature of even the reduced number of targets that the manager has little flexibility or room to maneuver, we shall see that he must exercise some discretion and make important decisions, particularly when it is necessary to sacrifice one target to achieve another.

The Worker

One area of activity in which the manager is relatively free is the employment of labor. The manager cannot freely buy raw materials or capital, but he can hire workers, being limited only by his total wage fund. Although the demand for labor is centrally planned, the supply is not. With a few exceptions, workers are free to choose their occupation and their place of employment. The state certainly attempts to induce labor into certain occupations through educational subsidies and differential wage rates, but the worker is free to respond to these material incentives, as is his counterpart in capitalist economies. All Soviet citizens, however, are expected to work, and labor force participation rates are among the highest in the world.

With the passage of the 1958 "School Law," all Soviet citizens are provided with a free education, which is compulsory through the eighth grade. Various forms of technical training and higher education at secondary schools and universities are available at no charge for students wishing to go beyond the eighth grade. In the late 1950s there was a serious labor shortage due to the low birthrate of the World War II period. Students were encouraged to work at least two years before continuing their education and to combine work and study as much as possible. This policy was changed in 1964, and brighter students are now encouraged to continue directly to institutions of higher education. Although competition for admittance to these institutions is extremely fierce, given the limited number of slots available, the vast majority of Soviet students receive additional training in extension, correspondence, or night courses, or on the job itself. The government is able to plan the supplies of different skills by the number of positions available at various training institutions. The study of engineering is encouraged by the admittance of a relatively large number of students, while the study of law or the humanities is discouraged.

Once a student has finished a vocational school he will be aided in finding a job by the school itself. Graduates of secondary schools and institutions of higher education are obliged to work in a job assigned to them for three years. Graduates of the eighth grade find jobs for themselves.

Institutions for the formal recruitment of labor in the Soviet Union have not been well developed in the past, although increasing efforts have been made in this area since 1968, when labor exchanges were opened in the major cities. There has been a persistent ideological bias against labor exchanges or employment offices because of the Soviet belief that in a planned economy there is no unemployment. Except for the planned placement of new entrants in the labor force and the relocation of workers in the East, the matching of jobs with workers has been a very unorganized process. Enterprises in need of labor recruit locally, and most people find their own jobs through reading notices and newspaper ads. The Soviets have been concerned with excessive labor turnover since the 1930s, when the average worker changed jobs 1.5 times a year, usually in the hopes of attaining higher wages and better working conditions in an alternative place of employment. In 1938 workers were issued permanent labor books which were presented to and held by employers upon employment. The books were not to be relinquished unless the worker was given permission to leave. These rules were not strictly enforced after the war and were abolished in 1956. Labor turnover increased slightly and now averages 2 to 3 percent a month in most industries and regions. A recent Soviet survey indicated that most workers changed jobs because of poor working and living conditions.

Although there is no formal unemployment in the Soviet Union there is a significant amount of what we would call seasonal and structural unemployment. Workers are displaced as industries or regions decline and some time may elapse before they are retrained or relocated. Others are displaced by mechanization and also require retraining. The Soviets have been quite remiss in developing institutions to retrain and relocate labor, which has added to the problem of labor shortages in developing industries and areas.

Most workers, seeking their own jobs, are induced into various industries and locales by wage differentials. Wage scales are centrally determined, with base rates and steps for skill level determined by the government. Wage differentials are used to recruit labor for difficult, skilled, and high priority jobs. Prior to the wage reform of 1956 differentials between the lowest and highest workers ranged from two to four hundred percent. After 1956, the wages of lower paid workers were raised, and differentials narrowed. In the following chapter we will discuss the growth of real wages and the standard of living of the Soviet worker.

CONSTRUCTION AND IMPLEMENTATION OF THE ONE-YEAR PLAN

Stages of Plan Construction

Now that we have reviewed the primary institutions responsible for the conduct of the economy, let us turn to the process of plan construction itself. The essence of the planning process is the transformation of the broad goals of

STAGES OF PLAN CONSTRUCTION

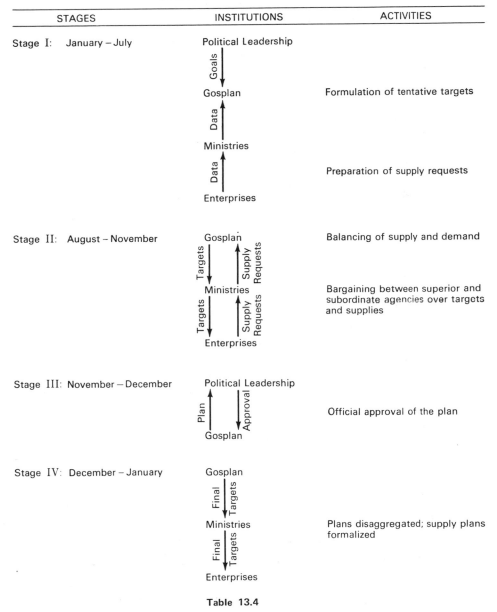

STAGES	INSTITUTIONS	ACTIVITIES
Stage I: January – July	Political Leadership ↓ Goals Gosplan ↑ Data Ministries ↑ Data Enterprises	Formulation of tentative targets Preparation of supply requests
Stage II: August – November	Gosplan Targets ↓ ↑ Supply Requests Ministries Targets ↓ ↑ Supply Requests Enterprises	Balancing of supply and demand Bargaining between superior and subordinate agencies over targets and supplies
Stage III: November – December	Political Leadership Plan ↑ ↓ Approval Gosplan	Official approval of the plan
Stage IV: December – January	Gosplan Final Targets ↓ Ministries Final Targets ↓ Enterprises	Plans disaggregated; supply plans formalized

Table 13.4

the political leadership into meaningful production directives for the enterprise manager. This process takes a considerable amount of time and involves all layers of the economic bureaucracy. The construction of the plan can be divided into four stages. The selection of stages is arbitrary and some are bound to overlap, but it is a convenient way of analyzing plan construction. See table 13.4 for a schematic diagram illustrating these stages. Let us consider the preparation of a one-year national plan to be operative in 1975.

The first stage consists of three different activities conducted by three distinct groups in the Soviet Union and runs from January through July of 1974. Planners at Gosplan are gathering statistics on the past performance of the economy to enable them to estimate the capacity of the economy in 1975 and thus to derive production targets for 1975. It is unlikely that complete information on the performance of enterprises in 1974 will be collected, aggregated, and forwarded to Gosplan by the Ministries as of January 1974. In all likelihood, Gosplan will be evaluating economic capacity on the basis of 1973 data. Toward the end of Stage I, in June and July, the political leadership will make their goals and objectives for 1975 known to Gosplan, which will then incorporate them into output targets. At the same time that economic planners at Gosplan and politicians in the Politburo are making their decisions, the Ministries and their subordinate units are drawing up tentative supply requests on the basis of their estimates of probable output targets. These lower units will thus be in a position to respond quickly to the directives received from Gosplan.

Stage II, running from August through November, involves the receipt of Gosplan's aggregate output targets by the Ministries, their disaggregation into output targets by industry, and the transmittal of supply requests from lower echelons through the ministries to Gosplan. This stage involves a considerable amount of bargaining between different layers of the bureaucracy. Gosplan is concerned with achieving maximum output through the assignment of high production targets coupled with low material input allocations. The enterprise, preferring easier to more difficult plans, has traditionally tried to secure lower production targets coupled with higher levels of material inputs. Enterprise managers are constrained in their supply requests, however, by technical coefficients specifying the required input of a particular resource per unit of output. The manager may still be able to overstate his input needs by understating the capacity of his physical plant, not reporting inventories of raw materials, or semi-finished goods, and attempting to secure a "favorable" assortment of final products. This tendency on the part of the enterprise manager may not be as strong today as it has been in the past, since the reforms of 1965 have elevated profits as a key measure of success. We will discuss the effect of the reforms on planning in a later section of this chapter and again in the next chapter.

A key planning process that occurs in Stage II is the balancing of input requests with output targets. One must remember that one enterprise's inputs are another's output. Thus, when final production targets are established, the supply and demand for each product must balance. In chapter eleven we discussed some alternative procedures for arriving at balance, and in the next section of this chapter we will discuss the techniques used in the Soviet context.

Stage III begins when the balancing process is completed and formal targets have been arrived at, normally in November and December. The third stage consists of the submission of these targets to the political leaders for their approval. Changes in the plan may take place at this stage, and approval is not a formal routine, as was the case when the French planners submitted their plan to Parliament. There may be changes of fortune in the factional struggles occuring among the political leadership, which will dictate a change of emphasis in economic goals. Investment in agriculture, consumer goods, or defense may move up or down in the priority list, requiring alterations in the output targets and input needs of these industries. These changes tend to be incorporated in a rather ad hoc fashion by the planners since they have little time this late in the year to work out fully the repercussions of target changes. Thus, the apparent balancing of supply and demand in the final plan is likely to be quite unrealistic.

Once the plan is formally adopted, the targets are disaggregated as they pass down the bureaucratic hierarchy. Stage IV typically occurs in December and January, although it is not unusual to find enterprises operating without a plan well into the new plan year. The timing of plan construction is so tight that the discovery of errors, changes in goals, the necessity of incorporation of new technology, etc., may delay the transmittal of the final plan.

Balancing Techniques

As we stated above, a major activity during Stage II is the balancing of the supply and demand of key commodities by Gosplan. Balances of approximately two thousand commodities are constructed centrally, while those for other, less critical commodities are drawn up at a lower level of the planning bureaucracy. The technique used for attaining balance in Soviet planning is the material balances method discussed in chapter ten. Sources of a product are listed and compared with the planned distribution or uses of the good. The distinguishing feature of the use of the material balances technique in the Soviet context is the method typically used to eliminate discrepancies between supply and demand. Given the emphasis on high rates of economic growth, high targets are set for many commodities, usually resulting in large input requests. Often the supply of a product will fall short of the demand. Several approaches to the solution of this problem are possible. Let's consider the case of iron, steel, and the production of tractors, whose initial tally of sources and uses are illustrated in table 13.5. Given the planned distribution of steel, there is a deficit of 200 million rubles. This deficit may be eliminated in a variety of ways. The easiest solution, with the fewest repercussions involves a decrease in inventories of steel. This solution, however, is limited by the necessity of keeping minimal inventories to cope with unforseen contingencies. Significant increases in supply must realis-

Table 13.5

A Hypothetical Set of Material Balances

Iron

Sources		Uses	
1. Imports	100 million rubles	1. Exports	25 million rubles
2. Inventory reduction	50 million rubles	2. Inventory increases	none
3. Current production	1600 million rubles	3. Current uses	1650 million rubles
a. Iron plant A	600	a. Steel plant A	600
b. Iron plant B	300	b. Steel plant B	400
c. Iron plant C	700	c. Steel plant C	350
		d. Pipe plant A	200
TOTAL	1750 million rubles	e. Nail plant A	100
		4. Investment	75 million rubles
		Total	1750 million rubles

TECHNICAL NORM: 1 million rubles Iron = 2 million rubles steel

Steel

Sources		Uses	
1. Imports	150 million rubles	1. Exports	none
2. Inventory reduction	25 million rubles	2. Inventory increase	50 million rubles
3. Current production	2700 million rubles	3. Current uses	3025 million rubles
a. Steel plant A	1200	a. Tractor plant A	300
b. Steel plant B	800	b. Tractor plant B	200
c. Steel plant C	700	c. Auto plant A	1525
		d. Machine Tool	
Total	2875 million rubles	plant A	1000
		Total	1050 million rubles

TECHNICAL NORM: 1 million rubles of steel = 5 million rubles tractors

Tractors

Sources		Uses	
1. Imports	200 million rubles	1. Exports	none
2. Inventory reduction	none	2. Inventory increases	200 million rubles
3. Current production	2500 million rubles	3. Current uses	2000 million rubles
a. Tractor plant A	1500	a. Collectives	1500
b. Tractor plant B	1000	b. State farms	500
		4. Investment	500 million rubles
Total	2700 million rubles	Total	2700 million rubles

tically come from increases in planned production. These production increases may originate in one of two ways. Supplies of raw materials, iron for instance, may be diverted from other industries, enabling the steel industry to increase its output while remaining within the constraints of its technical coefficients. This solution naturally involves repercussions for those industries that lose their inputs to the steel industry. Second, the planned output of the steel industry may be increased by increasing the efficiency of its operation. In other words, its input-output coefficients are lowered. It may be told to use its equipment more intensively or speed up the introduction of new capacity or a new process. Although this solution may eliminate the planned deficit, it often does not eliminate the actual deficit, since firms are already working near maximum capacity.

An alternative set of solutions to the problem involves a planned decrease in the distribution of the product. A planned reduction in the distribution to the consumer sector, where applicable, results in few repercussions on the production of other commodities. If the product is an intermediate good, the targets of industries using it may be lowered, i.e., planned tractor output may be reduced. This will have an effect on agricultural production. More likely, the distribution of the intermediate good will be reduced without a corresponding reduction in output targets. Again the planners choose a solution which involves an apparent increase in productive efficiency or decrease in input-output coefficients. When balances for very high priority items are constructed, deficits will more often be eliminated by increasing production through planned increase of inputs. Rather than reduce the output targets of industries from whom supplies were borrowed, however, the planners will lower the input-output coefficients of the lower priority industries.

Any solution other than increases in efficiency involves repercussions for others. It has been estimated that approximately twelve or thirteen iterations are necessary to take into account the consequences of an initial change in planned output. The Director of Economic Research at Gosplan has been quoted as saying that three or four iterations are rare, and the calculation of indirect effects are limited to conspicuous changes. Planners prefer instead to use techniques which minimize second round effects.

An alternative technique for achieving balance is input-output, discussed in the Appendix to chapter ten. The Soviets have been experimenting with input-output techniques and have constructed several tables reflecting economic activity in the national economy. Up to now, however, these tables have been used to check the consistency of plans which have been constructed using the older techniques. The Soviets have been reluctant to use input-output as a technique of plan construction for a variety of reasons. One of the primary problems is that this technique involves the collection and processing of massive amounts of data, in a form quite different from what is now flowing through bureaucratic channels. Data is now grouped by industry and branch as it is transmitted to Gosplan. Input-output techniques require data grouped instead by product. Data for enterprises producing a variety of goods would have to be separated. A second major problem in constructing ex-ante input-output tables for planning purposes is the lack of computer facilities to handle the solution of the necessary size matrix. The largest tables constructed in the Soviet Union so far have been 400 by 400. Yet this size table involves a tremendous amount of aggregation and, thus, loss of detailed information. Before the use of input-output techniques can reduce the planning burden, information and computer systems will have to be significantly upgraded.

Plan Implementation: Controls and Incentives

Prior to the reforms of 1965 the Soviet enterprise manager received a plan which specified his performance in thirty to forty different indices (refer back to table 13.3). A major problem connected with supervising plan implementation is the evaluation of the manager's performance in so wide a variety of areas. Given the nature of the plan, with its high targets and low input-output coefficients, it is extremely unlikely that the manager will be able to complete successfully all of the tasks assigned to him. Rather, he will have to use discretion in determining which indices to follow and which to sacrifice. Since Soviet planners recognize that the plan will not be perfectly consistent and local decisions will have to be made, a system of priorities has been developed to guide the behavior of an enterprise manager. An ideal incentive system is one which would result in the manager making those decisions which the planners would have made if they could have been apprised of all the information relevant to the case in question. The system which did develop tied the material reward of the manager to the fulfillment of the key indices.

Throughout the early stages of Soviet development, from 1930 to the middle 1950s, the managers' bonuses were tied to gross value of output. Bonuses for overfulfilling the gross value of output targets ranged from twenty to fifty percent of a manager's yearly salary. This singleminded devotion to increasing output resulted in many distortions in the Soviet economy, and the waste and inefficiency which resulted have been widely reported both in Soviet and Western literature.

The overriding concern with gross value of output resulted in poor quality, few styles, and a disregard for costs of production. It was in the interest of the enterprise manager to use any and all materials and labor which would increase gross value of output. Expensive materials were particularly favored. Products which required few raw materials and a considerable amount of processing were avoided. Unnecessary quantities of expensive steel were used in the production of machine tools only to be machined away at the next stage of production.

The combination of high targets, uncertain supplies, and a sharp line of demarcation between success and failure resulted in obvious waste and inefficiency. The manager, considering inputs of any type, materials, labor, or capital, as essentially free, paid little attention to cost. Operating in a seller's market, in which the disposal of his output was guaranteed, he paid little attention to quality, assortment, or the requirements of the users of his products. Since success depended upon meeting this year's output targets, the manager's time horizon was very short. The introduction of new techniques or new products which had the potential of disrupting current production, even though they would bring great long-run benefits, were shunned.

To correct for quality distortions specific output targets were substituted for gross value of output in many instances. But each of these led to distortions of its own, many often quite humorous. Targets for window glass measured in tons resulted in extra thick glass, while targets specified in square meters resulted in glass which was extremely thin. A metal works is reported to have increased its output of roofing iron by twenty percent when output was measured in tons, but only ten percent when output was measured by area. Boiler manufacturers, whose output target was measured in terms of heating surface, resisted the introduction of new, more efficient boilers because they had smaller heating surfaces. Numerous additional examples of wasteful and inefficient behavior resulting from the imperfection of narrowly defined targets could be given.[1]

Toward the end of the 1950s the key measure of success was shifted from output to cost reduction, given that minimum output targets were reached. This led to use of lower cost inputs, resulting in lower quality output and fewer styles. Managers attempted to reduce cost without regard to the attendant effects on the usefulness of the product. When book publishers tried to minimize cost per page they printed fewer words per page, naturally increasing the overall costs of book production.[2]

Reform of the Incentive System

One of the major features of the reforms of 1965 was a rationalization of the incentive scheme. Evsei Liberman, an economist at Kharkov University, sparked an extended debate on the need for reform with a series of publications analyzing the problems of Soviet planning and suggesting certain reforms. Liberman set forth a series of reform proposals concerning the incentive system designed to eliminate some of the problems outlined above. He wanted to stimulate Soviet enterprises to work at peak efficiency and thus refrain from concealing capacity and overstating input requirements. He also wanted to stimulate enterprise managers to introduce new technology and new products, improve the quality of their output, and develop a greater concern for the needs of the buyer. These objectives were to be accomplished by drastically reducing the number of planned targets, introducing a capital charge, and replacing previous success indicators with one based on planned profitability of sales. Once the stated output goal had been achieved, the manager's bonus was to depend entirely on the achieved rate of planned profitability, profitability to be

[1]For further examples see Alec Nove, *The Soviet Economy*, pp. 163-166.

[2]Robert Campbell, *Soviet Economic Power,* 2nd ed. (Boston: Houghton-Mifflin Company, 1967), p. 79.

measured as profits as a percentage of total capital. The exact bonus would depend upon the relationship of the profitability rate achieved and some norm established by branch of industry.

Liberman explained that the new bonus system would result in the conservation of capital and materials; an increased emphasis on quality, since sales rather than output would determine bonuses; and in more truthful reporting of capacity and material requirements. The reforms announced by Kosygin in 1965 and gradually extended throughout the economy embodied many of Liberman's ideas. Planned targets were reduced to the eight discussed earlier. Bonuses were to be paid for the fulfillment of planned targets for sales, profits, or profitability, depending upon the industry in question. Further, the enterprise was to retain a portion of its profits, which were to be deposited in three separate funds. A complex set of formulas was developed for determining the size of the funds.

As it stands now, the "Fund for Material Stimulation" is based upon the enterprise's planned payroll in addition to the rate of profit and the increase in profits on sales over the previous year: for each percentage increase in profits or sales, an amount equal to X percent of the wage fund is put into the incentive fund. For each percentage point of profitability an amount equal to Y percent of the wage fund is also added to the incentive fund.[3] The incentive fund is used for the payment of bonuses to managerial personnel. A similar formula is used for additions to the "Fund for Social-Cultural Measures and Housing Construction." Additions to the third and final "Fund for the Development of Production" are based upon a firm's capital rather than wage fund. It is to be used for financing decentralized investment.

We will evaluate the effect of these reforms on Soviet performance in the following chapter. It is important to emphasize at this point, however, that the reforms really leave the basic system of central planning intact. To the extent that they are effective in increasing economic efficiency it will primarily be as a result of the behavior of the manager in a changed environment. As we mentioned in chapter ten, the substitution of profits for output or cost reduction as success indicators may not result in significant improvements if the manager does not have the correct information regarding the cost of alternatives on which to base his decisions.

FINANCIAL PLANNING

As we mentioned earlier, all Soviet enterprises are expected to be financially independent. They receive revenue from the sale of their products, which they use to purchase their allotted supplies. Individual workers receive

---

[3]For a discussion of the operation of the new incentive system see Robert Campbell, "Economic Reform in the USSR," *American Economic Review* 58, No. 2 (May 1968), pp. 547-48; and Gertrude Schroeder, "Soviet Economic Reforms: A Study in Contradictions," *Soviet Studies* 20, no. 1 (July 1968), pp. 1-22.

income in the form of money wages, which they use to purchase goods and services. Money does exist in the Soviet economy; it consists of bank deposits held by firms and collective farms and currency held by individual consumers. It serves the function of a medium of exchange and a store of value. Soviet financial institutions perform two major functions in the economy: one, they oversee the spending of the enterprises' revenue to ensure that only planned expenditures take place; and two, they attempt to regulate the total quantity of money in existence to assure a rough correspondence between aggregate demand and aggregate supply in order to avoid both inflation and the piling up of unsold goods. We shall consider each of these functions separately.

Control by Ruble

Although the enterprise receives revenue from the sale of its products and the revenue is held in the form of bank deposits in *Gosbank*, the state bank, the enterprise cannot freely determine its mix of cash, materials, capital, or labor, since this mix is specified in its plan. It cannot freely convert its deposits into supplies unless the state bank approves the purchase. Thus, all expenditures are checked against the plan, which gives the planners greater control over the behavior of the enterprise. Since all enterprises must hold their deposits in Gosbank, it can supervise all inter-enterprise transactions. Because of the necessity of converting deposits into currency to pay wages, the State Bank has traditionally had less control over the enterprise's expenditures on wages. Enterprises have traditionally overspent their planned wage bill only to request additional money in the form of loans. Until the late 1940s the Bank freely granted the enterprise the needed loans, with the result that actual wages exceeded planned wages. After the Currency Reform of 1947, additional loans for payments were granted only in the case of overfulfillment of the output plan.

Financial Equilibrium

In addition to its control over inter-enterprise transactions, Gosbank prepares credit and cash plans for the entire economy to attain financial equilibrium or balance. The objective of financial planning is to insure that enterprises have an adequate supply of money to purchase all planned inputs at planned prices, and that consumers have an adequate income to purchase the available supply of consumer goods at planned prices. In equilibrium the supply and demand for goods and money must be equal. Let us examine briefly the conditions for financial equilibrium. Consumers and enterprises are demanders of money, which they hold to facilitate transactions. The major source of money is Gosbank, which has control over the issue of currency and is the predominant supplier of credit. When the bank makes a loan, a deposit is entered in the enterprise's account. Thus, money is created in the same way as in capitalist economies, wherein banks create money through the loan process. A key question in obtaining financial equilibrium is the optimal quantity of money.

The enterprise requires funds for the purchase of raw materials, semi-finished goods, and wages. In addition, it must have some additional funds for planned profits. By the end of the plan period, total revenue will equal planned expenditures plus planned profits. Revenues and expenditures will not be perfectly synchronized, however, and it will be necessary for Gosbank to make short-term loans to the enterprise. A variety of credit plans are possible. Gosplan can make one large loan at the beginning of the plan period to be repaid at the end, or several smaller loans for shorter duration. The larger the loan and the longer the loan period, the greater the quantity of money in existence. Large holdings of cash balances may tempt the enterprise and result in unplanned behavior such as the hiring of additional workers, discussed above. Gosplan has been well aware of this problem and has made every attempt to both police expenditures carefully and to limit the amount of cash balances needed by the enterprise at any one time. For example, inter-enterprise debts are settled monthly, so an enterprise's account is credited with only net receipts after all revenues due and payments owed have been cancelled.

The Soviet consumer can allocate his wages for the purchase of commodities, and he can add to his cash holdings. In equilibrium the demand and supply for consumer goods must be equal, and households must be adding to their cash balances at the desired rate. It is the task of Gosplan to formulate a cash plan to achieve this result.

If the cash and credit plans are incorrect, i.e., financial balance is not achieved, serious repercussions may result. If the quantity of money created is too great, inflationary pressures will result. If it is insufficient, the planned level of consumption or production, or both, will not be achieved.

The State Budget can be used to mop up excess purchasing power, since it collects money from enterprises and consumers in the form of taxes and recirculates it as it finances State expenditures. A budget surplus takes money out of circulation, while a deficit adds money to circulation. The State Budget is a powerful weapon for controlling the level of purchasing power, since approximately half of the national income flows through it. The planned budget for the year 1970 is shown in table 13.6. The bulk of the revenue is derived from a tax on enterprise profits and the turnover tax, which is a sales tax on all consumer goods and some producer goods. The tax is levied at the wholesale level and ranges as high as 100 percent of the cost of production but varies from commodity to commodity. The turnover tax serves two purposes: it provides revenue for the government, and it allows the government to vary its level to equate the supply and demand for individual consumer goods. The budget as a whole is both a tool for the attainment of financial equilibrium as well as a device for reallocating resources from one sector of the economy to another.

Table 13.6

Planned Revenues and Expenditures
Soviet State Budget 1970
(Billions of Rubles)

Revenues		Expenditures		
Turnover tax	46.4	Financing state enterprises		63.48
		Industry and construction	23.9	
Enterprise profits tax	50.4	Agriculture and		
		procurement	9.5	
State taxes on the		Trade	6.1	
population	12.7	Transportation and		
		communication	2.8	
State loans	—	Municipal economy	21.2	
		Housing and residual		
Local taxes and lotteries	.9			
		Social-cultural measures		54.85
Other	34.3	Education, science and		
Income Tax on Organizations		culture	24.5	
Social Insurance Receipts		Health and Physical		
Residual		culture	9.2	
TOTAL	144.93	Social welfare	21.1	
BUDGET SURPLUS	.27	Defense		17.85
		Administration		1.71
		Loan Service		.2
		Residual		6.56
		TOTAL		144.66

Source: *U.S. Congress, Joint Economic Committee, Economic Performance and The Military Burden in the Soviet Union (Washington, D.C.: Government Printing Office, 1970), p. 58, 59.*

Prior to 1948 the government ran budget deficits, putting more money back into the economy than it took out, resulting in inflation. After 1948 government surpluses increased, and this, together with a more conservative lending policy on the part of Gosbank, resulted in a lower rate of inflation.

Prices

Throughout most of the history of Soviet planning, prices have been used primarily as an accounting device to aid planners in specifying targets and evaluating success in ruble terms, which can be more easily aggregated than can physical units of commodities. In contrast, in a market system prices provide decision-makers with information on relative costs. Prices in the Soviet Union have traditionally been a control device rather than a source of information for decision-makers. Given this primary objective of control, the major requirement of a price system has been that individual prices be stable, giving the planners a constant yardstick with which to measure changes in output.

Four different sets of prices are in existence—industrial wholesale prices, state retail prices, agriculture procurement prices, and collective farm market prices.[4] We will limit our discussion at this point to the first two, leaving a discussion of the latter to the next section of the chapter. Industrial wholesale prices are the prices at which Soviet enterprises buy and sell from each other. Prior to 1967 they were calculated on the basis of planned average cost of production, transportation costs, and a small profit of approximately 5 percent. Cost of production included the cost of raw materials, power, labor, administrative overhead, depreciation, and interest on state bank loans. Retail prices, relevant only for commodities sold to the consumer, included the above plus a turnover tax, the cost of wholesale and retail distribution facilities, and a planned profit for the distribution agencies.

Prices thus reflected average cost of production, where costs were defined to exclude charges on capital and rent. Further, prices represented costs which prevailed in 1955, the last major price revision prior to 1967. Since prices were based on average cost, high cost industries had to be continually subsidized. The need for price reform was recognized by many Soviet planners and economists in the late 1950s and early 1960s. Conservatives felt that although the basic pricing system was sound, it had to be revised so that prices more accurately reflected current costs. More radical reformers felt that the whole system needed to be scrapped, and a new method of calculating prices which would make them more reflective of opportunity costs be substituted. They argued that although the primary function of the price system had been control and evaluation, prices had played a role in resource allocation decisions, and were inadequate for the task. The pricing of substitutes influenced decisions on inputs assigned to enterprises. The price of outputs influenced the manager's decision on output mix. Yet the mere fact that the price of one input was higher than another did not really indicate that it was more scarce. The reformers further argued that the economic reforms of 1965, which proposed to increase the autonomy of the enterprise manager and substitute profits for output as a measure of success, required a new system of prices to function successfully. For managers to make rational economic decisions prices had to reflect relative scarcities.

If we look at the price reform, which was introduced in 1967, the results are quite disappointing for the reformers, although a few improvements were made.[5] The general level of prices was raised so that all enterprises would be nominally profitable. There was some attempt to make the prices of substitutes comparable. Prices were still calculated, however, on the basis of average cost of production plus a profit markup, although the definition of costs was broadened

[4] This section draws from the work of Morris Bornstein, "Soviet Price Theory and Policy," U.S. Congress, Joint Economic Committee, *New Directions in the Soviet Economy,* part 1 (Washington, D.C.: U.S. Government Printing Office, 1966), pp.63-94.

[5] For an excellent discussion of the price reform, see Gertrude Schroeder, "The 1966-67 Soviet Industrial Price Reforms: A Study in Contradictions," *Soviet Studies* 20, no. 4 (April 1969), pp. 462-477.

to include a 6 percent charge on the value of fixed and working capital. The concepts of marginal cost pricing and rent were introduced in the iron ore, oil, and gas industries. A system of price markups was instituted for products of above-average quality in the ferrous metals and parts of the machinery industries.

In addition to the change in the method of calculating prices made in 1967, there was also a major reorganization of the price fixing bureaucracy. Before the reform the task of setting prices was scattered among a large number of government departments, with little or no communication among them. After the reform a State Price Committee was established to develop a unified pricing policy which would be compatible with the goals discussed in relation to the reform of the incentive system. Presently the State Price Committee has the power to determine wholesale prices on key producer and consumer goods, while the Ministries are responsible for setting the prices of other commodities. Prices under the new system, although by and large still determined centrally, are to be more flexible and reflect costs more currently than under the old system. Prices still reflect average cost, however, and are not therefore reliable guides to opportunity cost in making resource allocation decisions. Further, it is difficult to see how the State Price Committee will be able to adjust so many prices frequently enough to reflect current costs or equate supply and demand.

Planning and the Agricultural Sector

The Collective Farm

After the collectivization drive of the early 1930s the predominant form of agricultural organization in the Soviet Union was the collective farm. In theory, the collective was a cooperative venture wherein peasants voluntarily pooled their land, equipment, and livestock, and shared the profits resulting from their efforts. As mentioned earlier, the voluntary element in collectivization was minimal. Peasants were forced to join collectives and pool their resources. The basic organizational structure of the collectives was outlined in the Collective Farm Statute of 1935 and remained in force with minor changes until 1958.

Each collective was composed of a group of families, often two or three hundred. In theory, the members of each collective selected a manager, although, in fact, the manager was selected by local party officials for his political reliability, rather than by the members of the collective. Each collective received a plan which specified acreage to be sown, output quotas for each crop, and the raising of livestock. A certain portion of each crop was to be delivered to the state and comprised the compulsory delivery quota. The remainder could be sold to the state or on the private market.

The income of the collective depended upon the difference between its revenues and expenditures. Its revenue was derived from sales to the state and the private market and from handicrafts and small-scale industry. Its expenditures included normal production expenses plus payments into a capital fund, insurance fund, and cultural fund, taxes, and payments to the Machine Tractor Station for the rental of heavy farm equipment. Thus, the income of the members of the collective was the residual after all other obligations had been met. Each member's share of the residual depended upon the number and "quality" of labor days he contributed during the year. An hour worked by a skilled worker, such as a tractor operator, entitled him to a greater share of the output than an hour contributed by a field hand. Each member's income was uncertain until the end of the agricultural year, and no minimum income was guaranteed.

Typically, procurement prices for compulsory delivery quotas were so low and delivery quotas so high that very little remained for the peasant at the end of the year. The high and rising prices of manufactured commodities further reduced the purchasing power of the peasant. State agricultural procurement prices were nearly constant from 1935 to 1953, while the price of manufactured commodities increased several-fold. In many cases procurement prices did not even cover the cost of production. Poorly situated farms suffered severely, and all farms suffered during periods of bad harvests. Needless to say, incentives for increasing production were poor, and this, together with the low level of investment in agriculture, resulted in the virtual stagnation of output in the 1930s and 1940s.

The Private Plot

Many collective farm members could not have survived this period without the income derived from the cultivation of their private plots. As a concession to the plight of the peasant in the 1930s the state allowed farmers to retain from one-half to one acre of land which they could farm privately after completing their responsibilities on the collective. The peasant sold the output of his private plot on a free collective farm market. Although the state recognized the necessity of the private plot, it constantly discriminated against all activity undertaken by the peasant on his plot. Compulsory delivery quotas were established for the output of the private plot as well as the collective, and heavy taxes were levied on the basis of the area sown and the amount of livestock. Despite this treatment by the state, the private plot often provided the peasant with his only source of income, and peasants preferred to work on their private plots rather than on the collective land. Even today private plots account for less than 3 percent of the land under cultivation but contribute almost one-third of the gross value of agricultural output.

The State Farm

An alternative form of agricultural organization is the state farm. Although fairly unimportant in terms of total production in the 1930s and 1940s, its importance has been growing in recent years, and today state farms comprise approximately 50 percent of the land under cultivation and contribute 25 percent of the gross agricultural output. The low productivity of the state farms is partly attributable to the fact that many are located on inferior or marginal land. The organizational structure of the state farm is similar to that of an industrial factory. It is owned and operated by the state, which appoints a manager, who in turn hires labor at a wage set by the state. The planners centrally determine the output and input plans of each farm, and until the reforms of 1965, the goal of the manager was to fill his output quota, which was then sold to the state at prices predetermined by the state.

Although state farms have been preferred to collectives by the political leadership on ideological grounds, their growth has not been encouraged for practical economic reasons, since most state farms ran chronic deficits and had to be continually subsidized from the State budget. Unlike the workers on collective farms the state farm workers were paid wages on a monthly basis and had an equal claim on state farm revenues along with other production expenses. Thus state farm workers were not forced to bear the burden of low productivity combined with low procurement prices. Collectives were a far more efficient form of organization for the transfer of resources from the agricultural to the industrial sector.

Agricultural Prices and Reforms

As mentioned above, compulsory delivery prices for many crops, grain in particular, were nearly constant from 1935 to 1953. The prices of all crops were very low, and the prices of food crops often did not cover costs of production. Furthermore, relative prices reflected neither relative costs nor national requirements. Given the two-tier price system, the average price of crops rose in years of good harvests and fell in years of bad harvests, since the peasants had more to sell at above-quota prices on the free market in good times and less to sell in bad times. The irrational pricing system, combined with the uncertainty of the collective peasant's annual income, resulted in low productivity and a diversion of the peasant's attention to his private plot.

Throughout the 1950s various agricultural reforms were initiated in an effort to increase agricultural output. Prices paid by the state to collective farms were increased in 1953 and 1956, although the pricing system itself was unchanged. In 1958, the two-tier pricing system was eliminated and a single higher price set for sales to the state by collective farms within a given region. Regional variations in prices represented an attempt by government to account for cost differentials due to favorable climate and soil conditions in certain locations. At the same time the government announced that compulsory deliveries would be eliminated and the output delivered by the collective to the state would be on a contract basis. Further, the new uniform state prices were to be long-term averages to be raised in bad harvest years and lowered in good years. Relative prices still had little meaning, however, and did not represent relative scarcities. The rate of growth of agricultural output increased significantly during the middle 1950s but fell off again in the late 1950s and 1960s.

A series of more far-reaching reforms was instituted in 1965.[6] Procurement prices for nearly all products have been significantly increased, and the two-tier pricing system has been reinstated. Output above the state procurement target is sold to the state at prices 50 percent above the basic procurement price. In an attempt to improve the incentive system, collective farm members are now guaranteed a monthly income equivalent to the rates paid on state farms, and poorer farms are granted five-year loans to enable them to meet this new expense. Members are also entitled to additional income at the end of the year depending upon the level of total production. These reforms have resulted in a 20 percent increase in the income of collective farmers.

The industrial reforms of 1965 were applied to the state farms, which are now to be financially independent. The manger is to be given increased flexibility, and profit rather than output has become the primary success indicator. Incentive funds have been established which are similar to those for industry. The major source of new investment funds is to be the farm's own profits and long-term loans. Farms have been given additional freedom to establish subsidiary enterprises, so that their labor force can be used more effectively during periods of slack employment.

The Future of Soviet Agriculture

It is too early to tell what the long-run effects of these 1965 reforms will be, but recent statistics do not show any improvement in performance. Many problems remain. The new price system still does not reflect relative scarcities and thus cannot be used as a decision-making device to guide the behavior of farm management.

Centralized planning of agricultural activity has been the least successful application of the command principle of economic organization in the Soviet Union and East Europe, and several East European states have abandoned the collective and returned to some form of individual family farming. The poor

[6]For a more complete discussion see Roger Clarke, "Agricultural Reform Since Khrushchev," *Soviet Studies* 20, no. 4 (April 1969), pp. 159-178.

performance of Soviet agriculture can be attributed to the irrational price and incentive system as well as a low level of investment, but there appear to be other, more fundamental, difficulties involved in the centralized planning of the agricultural sector.[7] The management of a farm requires a large number of activities which cannot be standardized to the extent possible in a factory. Workers must perform a variety of tasks over a wide geographical distance and are difficult to supervise closely. Management must respond quickly to local changes in weather and pest conditions. Further, each farm is a unique combination of natural resources, and uniform production patterns and regulations are particularly poorly suited to the attainment of efficiency in a given locale. If one recognizes these management problems inherent in agriculture, one must conclude that improved pricing and incentive schemes can only be partial solutions to the problems of slow growth and that decentralization is a key element in a productive agricultural sector.

QUESTIONS

1. Compare and contrast the decision to undertake a large investment project in the USSR and in the mixed economies we have studied.

2. Why is there a tendency for ministerial or regional autonomy in the Soviet planning hierarchy?

3. How do the Soviets achieve a balance between the supply and demand for a commodity?

4. In what ways did Liberman's proposed incentive system represent an improvement over the incentive system in use prior to 1965?

5. Compare and contrast the use of monetary and fiscal policy in the USSR and in the mixed economies.

6. What functions do prices serve in the Soviet economy? How have these functions changed since the 1965 industrial reform?

7. Why do you think that the performance of the agricultural sector in the USSR has been so poor? Do you think the recent reforms will improve the performance of this sector?

[7]For a discussion of the problems of planning the agricultural sector see Michael E. Bradley and M. Gardner Clark, "Supervision and Efficiency in Socialized Agriculture," *Soviet Studies* 23, no. 3 (January 1972), pp. 465-473.

14

The Performance
of the Soviet Economy

Introduction

In judging the performance of the Soviet economic system, we shall return to the criteria against which other systems have been evaluated—static efficiency, dynamic efficiency, and equity of income distribution. Often our discussion will be in terms of the comparative performance of the Soviet Union because it is difficult to measure performance against some absolute standard. Both past performance of the Soviet economy and the probable impact of reforms on future performance will comprise this evaluation of the Soviet system.

STATIC EFFICIENCY

As one will recall from chapter two, static efficiency involves both the full use of an economy's resources and the optimal allocation of those resources among competing uses, as summarized by the six efficiency conditions. The Soviets have pointed with pride to their superiority over the West in maintaining full employment and avoiding the waste and human suffering associated with recessions and depressions. They claim to have done away with unemployment. Although no data is available, there seems to be little or no unemployment caused by insufficient aggregate demand. In fact the Soviets have traditionally been troubled by labor shortages rather than surpluses. In the last chapter, it was noted, however, that the Soviets have had a significant amount of frictional and structural unemployment due to changing skill requirements. A more concerted effort to retrain and relocate displaced labor would certainly be a source of increased efficiency, particularly in a labor-short economy. Seasonal and disguised unemployment in agriculture are problems which the Soviets themselves have long recognized and which the recent provisions for small-scale industries in rural areas are designed to correct. Up to this point we have restricted our discussion to the employment of labor, but full employment also implies full utilization of the capital stock, although, admittedly, what constitutes full employment in this case is more difficult to define because of the existence at any time of high cost, obsolete equipment. Reports have persisted in Soviet literature of the under-utilization of capital. Fifty percent of the equipment of an enterprise may sit idle due to a shortage of raw materials or the absence of spare parts. Given the tendency of the manager to provide himself with a safety margin, new capital may be requested and accepted even if it stands idle for a year or two. Perhaps the reforms will modify the manager's behavior in this respect, although a six percent capital charge seems too low to effectively ration the demand for capital.

The second requirement for the achievement of static efficiency—optimal allocation of resources—can be examined using two types of evidence: (1) qualitative evidence of instances of inefficient resource use and, (2) quantitative evidence on the relative productivity of Soviet factors of production. We find the latter type of evidence used to study static efficiency in the Bergson study[1] first reported in chapter nine. Attempting to measure relative static efficiency, the study compares national income per worker and per composite unit of labor and capital among several countries, including the Soviet Union (see table 14.1). Two measures of efficiency are reported for each country, one in terms of the value of inputs and outputs in the domestic prices of the country and the other in terms of United States prices. Regardless of the price weights chosen, national income per employed worker, (reported in columns 1 and 2, table 14.1) is considerably lower in the U.S.S.R. than in all Western economies except Italy. Can one conclude, then, that the Soviets are less efficient because Soviet workers produce less than their Western counterparts? The answer is no. Soviet workers may produce less for a variety of reasons not connected with our concept of static efficiency. If capital is relatively scarce in the U.S.S.R., the capital-labor

---

[1]The results of his investigations are reported in Abram Bergson, *Planning and Productivity Under Soviet Socialism* (New York: Columbia University Press, 1968).

Table 14.1

Real National Income Per Employed Worker and Per Unit of Factor Inputs, Selected Countries 1960

	NATIONAL INCOME PER EMPLOYED WORKER				NATIONAL INCOME PER UNIT OF FACTOR (LABOR AND REPRODUCIBLE CAPITAL) INPUTS			
	Unadjusted for Labor Quality		Adjusted for Labor Quality		Unadjusted for Labor Quality		Adjusted for Labor Quality	
	1	2	3	4	5	6	7	8
	Domestic Price Weights	U.S. Price Weights	Domestic Price Weights	U.S. Price Weights	Domestic Price Weights	U.S. Price Weights	Domestic Price Weights	U.S. Price Weights
United States	100	100	100	100	100	100	100	100
Northwest Europe	44	56	47	60	50	63	53	67
France	43	55	47	60	49	62	53	66
Germany	43	55	47	61	52	63	56	69
United Kingdom	44	56	47	60	50	63	52	66
Italy	22	37	26	44	28	45	32	32
U.S.S.R.	22	38	29	48	28	45	34	56

Source: Abram Bergson, Planning and Productivity Under Soviet Socialism (New York: Columbia University Press, 1960), pp. 22, 26.

ratio will be lower as well as output per worker. The quality of labor may be different in different economies, or workers may have inferior raw materials. Additional measures of efficiency, attempting to correct for variations in the quality of labor and for variation in capital-labor ratios are reported in columns 3 through 8 of table 14.1. Although these adjustments improve the measured performance of the Soviet economy, it retains its relative position vis-a-vis the other advanced, industrial economies. Given the problems of measurement, these figures can only be taken as rough indicators of the comparative efficiency with which the Soviets use their inputs. This evidence is corroborated, however, by the view of the leading Soviet economist-mathematician, Kantorovich, who estimated in 1960 that the U.S.S.R. could increase its national income by 30 to 50 percent by adopting techniques to allocate existing resources more efficiently. It is interesting to speculate why the Soviets appear to use their resources inefficiently; we turn now to qualitative evidence concerning the sources of Soviet inefficiency.

Three major sources of static inefficiency stand out in any study of the functioning of Soviet economic institutions—the method of plan construction, the incentive system, and the price system. As we saw in the last chapter, planners must make a tremendous number of decisions in a limited amount of time using highly aggregated data. Their traditional concern has been the achievement of technical efficiency and internal consistency, but they have not had the necessary information to assure that resources are being combined using the least-cost method of production, that resources are allocated to firms such that the marginal product of all factors are equal in all uses, and that firms are producing the output mix to maximize planners' or consumers' preferences.

The taut nature of the plan itself has produced bottlenecks, resulting in the under-utilization of capital and labor. The size of the bureaucracy and the resources expended in continual supervision of subordinate units is a serious source of inefficiency. Bergson reports that requisitions for ball bearings by one automobile manufacturer had to be processed by fourteen separate agencies and required 430 pounds of documentation. A metal works enterprise was inspected 445 times within a six-month period.[2]

The traditional measures of an enterprise manager's performance, together with the continual uncertainty of material supplies, produce still further inefficiency. The tendencies to hoard and to sacrifice quality for quantity are traditional. Bergson reports that 33 percent of clothing articles, 25 percent of knitwear, and 33 percent of leather shoes inspected by the Ministry of Trade had to be rejected or classified in a lower category.[3] Further evidence of obvious waste stemming from poor quality and lack of assortment are the reported large stocks of unsold consumer goods on retail shelves in the 1960s. Nor is in-

[2]*Ibid.*, p. 48.
[3]*Ibid.*, p. 42.

efficiency limited to consumer goods industries—one-third of the output of a machinery plant was reported to be defective.[4]

A third major cause of inefficiency is lack of a reliable guide for planners in achieving optimal allocation of resources. Prices do not measure relative scarcities nor do they reflect marginal rates of transformation in production or marginal rates of substitution in consumption. Rather, prices are a weighted average of enterprise costs plus a profit markup; until recently they did not include interest or rent charges. Planners do not know what is the least-cost method of production, nor do they have the information necessary to cause resources to flow from low productivity to high productivity areas.

We have observed that static inefficiency results whenever private costs diverge from social costs. The effects of this type of static inefficiency are evidenced in the pollution of air and water and the destruction of the natural environment. It is often thought that this problem is unique to capitalist economies, where greedy businessmen pursue their private profits with disregard for the effect of their activities on the public welfare. Recent reports, however, suggest that this behavior is not unique to capitalism but results whenever the prices used for decision-making purposes do not reflect the total resource costs of that decision. Soviet plant managers, like their Western counterparts, will attempt to achieve their goals, whether they be output or profit maximization, without regard for the larger social consequences of their behavior, unless effective regulations can be developed and enforced to force them to make decisions which are optimal from society's point of view. If a plant manager does not have to pay to dump his wastes into a lake or river, it will appear to him that this is the cheapest form of waste disposal and that its use will contribute to the fulfillment of his objectives. We have observed that in their great zeal to expand production, the Soviets have often ignored costs. The disregard of the total social costs of increasing production have resulted in serious pollution problems.

An interesting case in point is the continuing destruction of Lake Baikal, the deepest freshwater lake in the world.[5] Lake Baikal is famous for its purity as well as its unique wildlife, but in recent years it has been seriously threatened by the growth of industry along its shore as well as the shores of its tributaries. In recent years fifty enterprises, including meatpacking plants and lumber mills, have begun dumping their wastes into the lake, and only ten of these treated their wastes before discharging them. Concern for the preservation of Lake Baikal increased at the end of the 1950s, when the Ministry of Timber, Paper, and Woodworking revealed plans to build two cellulose plants on the shores of the lake. At the same time pollution control laws affecting the use of the lake were passed by the Council of Ministers of the Russian Republics. The Ministry of Timber, Paper, and Woodworking argued that the lake was the most desirable

[4]*Ibid.,* p. 42.

[5]Marshall T. Goldman, "The Pollution of Lake Baikal," *The New Yorker,* 15 June 1971, pp. 58-66.

site for the new plants because of the purity of the lake water, which would allow the production of low cost, high quality cellulose and paper products. Several reports were issued by investigating commissions warning of the dangers of pollution if the plants were built and charging the Ministry with understating the true costs of producing at the new sites. The success of both the Ministry and higher administrative agencies, however, depends on the fulfillment of production targets, and there is no reward for the preservation of clean air or water. The construction of the new plant sites proceeded, and one plant went into operation in the middle of 1966, even though its waste treatment techniques had never been tested. In 1967 and 1968, 383 tons of toxic substances were discharged into the Lake, resulting in floating islands of alkaline sewage. It was estimated that animal life was reduced by one-third to one-half around the plant site. New, tougher pollution control legislation was passed in 1969, but it remains to be seen if it will be enforced or ignored, as was the earlier legislation.

Static inefficiency, leading to a reduction in real output, can also occur when decision-makers receive false price signals. An extremely interesting study appeared recently which attempts to quantify the amount of output lost annually due to the distortions caused by another misleading price indicator—the interest rate charged to enterprises for new capital.[6] The Soviets have traditionally used different interest rates to determine the allocation of capital among different sectors of the economy, with high-priority industries charged lower interest rates than low-priority industries. The study indicates that for the period 1960-64 if capital and labor had been reallocated among industries, holding the level and mix of output constant so that the rates of return were equalized, annual output could have been increased approximately 3 or 4 percent. Initially,

$$\frac{MPP_K}{MPP_L} \text{ Industry A} > \frac{MPP_K}{MPP_L} \text{ Industry B.}$$

A substitution of capital for labor in industry A and of labor for capital in industry B will result in a freeing of resources for some other productive use, if the output of the two industries is held constant.

The Investment Decision: A Digression

In the last chapter we focused our attention on short-run planning procedures. A discussion of the investment decision, however, is important to our analysis of the static and dynamic performance of the Soviet economy. We have seen in the last section that the proper allocation of new investments among sectors of the economy is important for maximizing factor productivity. The level and direction of investment is also a key factor in determining the economic

[6]Judith Thornton, "Differential Capital Changes and Resource Allocation in Soviet Industry," *Journal of Political Economy*, 79, no. 3 (May/June, 1971), pp. 545-561.

growth of an economy. Investment planning must be coordinated with yearly production plans, but the time horizon of investment planning normally exceeds one year. Investment planning involves three primary decisions: (1) the overall level of investment, (2) the allocation of investment funds among sectors, and (3) the choice of technologies to expand production facilities in any one sector.

The first decision is primarily a political one, determined by top party and government leaders and dependent upon the desired overall growth rate. Given the projected incremental capital-output ratio—in turn dependent upon projected increases in labor, raw materials, and technological change—the planners can calculate the necessary amount of new capital to achieve the targeted growth rate. The second decision depends on output priorities, larger shares of investment being needed in those industries with large targeted increases in output. Enterprises estimating their input and capacity requirements to achieve future production targets request investment funds. These requests are forwarded to superior agencies and, if approved, form part of the State Plan for Capital Investment. It is the task of Gosplan to insure a balance between requests and available supplies of capital. The request for new investment is prepared for the enterprise by specialized project organizations, and includes information on capacity, costs, and expected starting and completion dates. Once approved, the investment is financed by budget grants or bank credit; the latter has been the predominant method since 1965.

Prior to the reform of 1965 no interest charge was included in cost calculations, and there was a widespread tendency to underestimate the costs of new projects. As a result, scarce resources were scattered in a wide variety of projects, many often sitting in a semifinished state.

The preparation of the investment request leads to to the third basic decision—the choice of technologies. Production capacity can be expanded in a variety of ways. Techniques involving labor- or capital-intensive methods of production may be selected. The more capital-intensive are the variants selected, the greater will be the pressure on the nation's resources devoted to new investments. What is the optimal degree of capital intensity? In market economies the interest rate or the price of capital is a measure of the scarcity of capital and represents the cost to the firm of any increase in its capital stock. If the return on a new piece of capital equipment exceeds the interest rate, the firm will find it profitable to invest. Thus, the interest rate acts as a capital rationing device in a market system.

The Soviets have traditionally been opposed to the use of an interest-rate concept for ideological reasons and have tended to favor capital-intensive production techniques, even though capital may have been in short supply. In the 1930s and 1940s the project-maker considered only savings in annual operating costs when choosing production techniques. A classic example of the problem is illustrated in the decision of whether to expand electricity production using a steam, hydroelectric, or nuclear power station. Suppose the Soviets desire to increase their generating capacity by 20 million KWH. Table 14.2 illustrates the three possible methods. Each successive method requires higher levels of investment but results in lower annual operating costs. If the cost of capital is not considered, the third variant will be chosen. If this method is applied to all investment decisions, the demand for capital will in all probability exceed the supply, and low-priority sectors will have to forgo their expansion plans.

Table 14.2
Alternative Methods of Producing Electricity

	(1) Steam	(2) Hydroelectric	(3) Nuclear
Capacity	20 m KWH	20 m KWH	20 m KWH
Initial investment	30 m rubles	50 m rubles	80 m rubles
Annual operating costs	15	10	5
Labor	10	7	3
Fuel	3	2	1
Depreciation	1	1	1

During the 1950s investment planners developed a technique called the "payoff period" to help them make a more rational choice among production techniques. The payoff period is a measure of the length of time necessary to pay off the initial added investment outlay by the annual savings in operating costs. The pay off period equals

$$\frac{K_2 - K_1}{O_1 - O_2},$$

where K_1 and K_2 are the initial investment outlays in the two projects under consideration, and O_1 and O_2 are their respective annual operating costs. Applying this procedure to our example in Table 14.2:

$$\frac{50 - 30}{15 - 10} = 4$$

$$\frac{80 - 30}{15 - 5} = 5$$

It will take four years to recover the additional 20 million rubles required for the hydroelectric station and five years to recover the additional outlay required for the nuclear station. The Soviets call the reciprocal of the payoff period the coefficient of relative effectiveness (CRE) and it can be interpreted as an interest rate. In fact, it is the rate of return on the additional investment involved in variants two and three. One must be careful, however, not to interpret the CRE as the rate of return on investment in electric generating capacity. It measures only the return on marginal investment expenditures once the decision to expand electric generating capacity by 20 million KWH has been made.

The use of the payoff period represents a marked advance in Soviet economic thought, for it brings in the consideration of cost and yield of capital. The question remains, however, as to where to draw the line in the spectrum of payoff periods. Should projects with payoff periods of four, five, or ten years be approved? Ideally, one would centrally set the maximum payoff period to balance the supply and demand for capital and then let project-makers use the official payoff period to guide their selections. The Soviets have not been willing to set one payoff period and apply it universally. Rather, lower payoff periods have been applied to lower-priority industries and higher periods to higher-priority industries. The average payoff period has usually been set too low, so that additional rationing techniques have had to be applied. The use of a variety of periods has resulted in the misallocation of resources reported in the Thornton study cited above. The 1965 reforms introduced an interest charge into the calculation of annual operating costs, thus making them more representative of the real costs of each technique and thereby reducing the demand for capital. As stated earlier, however, the charge is too low to effectively ration capital, and a uniform payoff period is still not being applied in all industries.

THE DYNAMIC EFFICIENCY OF THE SOVIET ECONOMY

The Record of Growth

Table 14.3 reports Western and official Soviet growth rates of gross national product and its two major components, industry and agriculture, for selected years from 1928 to 1972. The data for the years 1928-1937, the period of the first two five-year plans, indicates extremely rapid progress in industry and extremely poor performance in agriculture, which was suffering from the dislocations caused by the mass collectivization campaign. Growth of industrial output was not even, with the output of heavy industry—including machinery, electric power, and chemicals—far exceeding that of light industry (the sector producing most of the consumer goods). Table 14.4 indicates that per capita consumption was nearly stagnant during the period. If the figures are adjusted for the declining output of small handicraft industry and the deteriorating quality of manufactured consumer goods, most Western experts agree that output per capita fell during this period, particularly in the rural areas.

The period 1937-1950 covers the war and its aftermath. During this time, Soviet industrial efforts were shifted to the production of weapons and then the reconstruction of the plant and equipment destroyed during the war. The reconstruction effort placed high priority on heavy industry, so that the prewar level of output was regained in 1948. The output of consumer goods lagged behind and did not reach the prewar level until 1951. The period 1950 to 1958

Table 14.3

Soviet Economic Growth, 1928-1972
(Average Annual Rates)
in constant prices

Year	Western Estimates			Official Soviet Estimates		
	GNP	Industrial Output	Agricultural Output	GNP	Industrial Output	Agricultural Output
1928-32	4.8	10.6	-5.5	14.9	19.2	
1932-37	11.9	10.1	1.0		17.1	
1937-40	3.6	1.9	-1.4		9.4	
1950-55	6.9	11.7	4.7	10.5	13.0	4.4
1955-58	7.4	9.5	7.2		11.3	9.3
1959	4.9	10.2	-3.9	8.0	11.0	0.0
1960	5.2	7.8	1.0	8.0	10.0	2.0
1961	7.0	7.2	8.7	7.0	9.0	3.0
1962	4.2	8.3	-1.2	6.0	10.0	2.0
1963	2.8	6.8	-5.0	5.0	8.0	-10.0
1964	7.9	7.6	11.1	8.0	7.0	14.0
1965	6.2	8.2	.6	6.0	8.6	1.0
1966	7.1	7.2	10.3	7.5	8.6	10.0
1967	4.3	7.7	-3.1	6.7	10.0	1.0
1968	5.8	6.1	5.4	7.2	8.1	3.5
1969	2.3	5.2	-4.4	6.0	7.0	-3.0
1970	8.5	7.1	14.5	8.5	8.3	8.7
1971	3.9	6.5	-1.4	6.0	7.8	0.0
1972	1.6	5.2	-11.1	4.0	6.5	-4.6

Source: Western Estimates: 1928-58. Cited in Stanley Cohn, Economic Development in the Soviet Union (Lexington, Massachusetts: D.C. Heath and Co. 1970) p. 28; 1959-1972 reported in U.S. Congress, Joint Economic Committee, New Directions in the Soviet Economy (Washington, D.C.: 1966), Soviet Economic Performance, 1966-67 (Washington, D.C.: 1958), Economic Performance and the Military Defense Burden in the Soviet Union (Washington, D.C.: 1970), and Soviet Economic Prospects for the Seventies (Washington, D.C.: 1973). Soviet Estimates: 1928-1950. Central Statistical Agency of the USSR, National Economy of the USSR (Moscow, Foreign Languages Publishing House, 1957); 1950-60, Central Statistical Agency of the USSR, National Economy of the USSR in 1960, translated by the U.S. Joint Publication Research Service (Washington, D.C.: U.S. Government Printing Office, 1962) p. 105, 235; 1960-1964, Central Statistical Agency of the USSR, Narodnoe Khoziastvo, (Moscow: 1965) p. 65; 1965-67, Soviet News, Nos. 5242, 5369, 5423; 1967-71, Current Digest of the Soviet Press vols. 21, no. 4; 22, no. 4; 23, no. 5; 24, no. 3, 25, no. 5.

Table 14.4

Average Annual Rates of Growth in Soviet Per Capita Consumption by
Major Component, 1928-72 (percent)

	1928-37	1937-40	1951-55	1955-60	1961-65	1965-72
Total Consumption	1.0	-1.4	6.0	4.0	3.0	5.0
Food products			4.9	2.8	2.3	3.9
Nonfood products						
soft goods				4.8	1.4	7.9
consumer durables			10.9	13.5	8.0	5.8
Services, excluding health and education			5.3	5.9	5.5	6.3
Health and education services			3.3	3.8	5.4	5.1

Sources: 1928-40, Cited in Stanley Cohn, Economic Development in the Soviet Union, p. 28; 1951-55, U.S. Congress, Joint Economic Committee, Soviet Economic Performance: 1966-67 (Washington, D.C.: U.S. Government Printing Office, 1968), p. 89; 1956-69, U.S. Congress, Joint Economic Committee, Economic Performance and the Military Burden in the Soviet Union (Washington, D.C.: U.S. Government Printing Office, 1970), p. 94; 1965-72, U.S. Congress, Joint Economic Committee, Soviet Economic Prospects for the Seventies (Washington, D.C.: U.S. Government Printing Office, 1973), p. 382.

witnessed a rapid growth of industry and agriculture as well as output of consumer goods. Growth rates in all sectors tapered off considerably after 1958, with agriculture being particularly hard-hit.

The Sources of Growth

In order to assess the dynamic efficiency of the Soviet economy, we must examine the sources of growth over the entire period. We will be particularly interested in possible explanations for the slowdown of the 1960s. As you will recall from chapter two, we classified growth as extensive when due to the increases in the quantity of the factors of production and intensive when due to increases in factor productivity. The results of two studies on the sources of Soviet growth are reported in tables 14.5 and 14.6. Table 14.5 measures the average annual increase in the productivity of labor and capital over the period 1928 to 1965. The results of labor productivity measures depend upon whether labor inputs are measured in terms of employed persons or man-hours. In the late 1950s and 1960s hours worked in the Soviet Union were declining, so labor productivity measures using man-hours give considerably more favorable results. The negative figures reported for the growth of capital productivity indicate a decline in the marginal product of capital. One would expect the tendency of the marginal-product of capital to decline in an economy undertaking large

Table 14.5

Growth of GNP Per Employed Person and Per Capital Unit
(Average Annual Rates)

	Aggregate	Per Employed Person		Per Capital Unit
		Annual Average Employment	Man-hour	
1928-37	4.8-11.9	1.7-7.9	1.8-8.0	−0.7-1.0
1937-40	3.6	.8	−.4	5.8
1940-50	1.8-2.2	1.0-1.3	1.3-2.4	0
1950-55	6.9	4.3	4.9	−2.6
1955-58	7.4	6.0	7.4	−1.6
1958-61	5.4	4.1	5.9	−3.5
1961-67	5.4	3.3	3.3	−3.0(1961-65)

Source: GNP—Aggregate and Per Employed Person
1928-1950: Abram Bergson, The Real National Income of Soviet Russia Since 1928, Harvard University Press, 1961, pp. 210, 217, 226, 232. 1950-1961: Stanley Cohn, Economic Development in the Soviet Union, p. 59. 1961-1967: U.S. Congress Joint Economic Committee, Economic Performance and the Military Burden in the Soviet Union, p. 11.
GNP—Per Capital Unit
1928-1950: Richard Moorsteen and Raymond Powell, The Soviet Capital Stock, 1928-1952, Irwin, 1966, pp. 315, 322-323 for capital stock estimates which are then divided by GNP index. 1950-1961: Stanley Cohn, Economic Development in the Soviet Union, p. 59. 1961-1967: U.S. Congress Joint Economic Committee, Economic Performance and the Military Burden in the Soviet Union, p. 11.

Table 14.6

Comparative Growth of GNP, GNP Per Employed Worker, and GNP
Per Unit of Factor Inputs 1950-1965
(Average Annual Percentage Increase)

	GNP		GNP per Employed Worker		GNP per Unit of Factor (Labor and Capital) Inputs
	1950-58	1958-65	1950-58	1958-65	1950-62
United States	2.9	4.4	1.9	2.6	2.0
France	4.4	5.4	3.9	5.0	4.1
Germany	7.6	5.8	5.1	4.6	4.6
United Kingdom	2.4	3.9	2.0	2.9	1.4
Italy	5.6	6.1	3.9	6.5	4.7
U.S.S.R.	7.1	5.3	5.3	3.5	2.8

Source: *1950-62 Abram Bergson, Planning and Productivity, p. 53; and 1950-65 Stanley
Cohn, Economic Development in the Soviet Union, p. 61.*

amounts of investment. The decline has been offset in all other developed
economies, however, by improvements in technology and the addition of
complementary human capital. The Soviet Union's record of the declining
marginal-product of capital is unique.

Table 14.6 provides data comparing increases in Soviet labor productivity
and combined factor productivity with that achieved in Western Europe and the
United States. During the early 1950s, Soviet growth of output per man-hour
exceeded that achieved by Western Europe, but dropped below France,
Germany, and Italy after 1958. The increases in labor productivity can be
attributed to the increased skills of the newly educated workers, the increased
capital-labor ratios, and the structural transformation of the economy occuring
during this time. Productivity gains are registered whenever labor is transferred
from low-productivity to high-productivity employment. Output per worker
increased significantly as labor moved from agricultural to industrial employment. When capital is added to labor in the measurement of combined-factor
productivity, the Soviets rank above only the United States and the United
Kingdom. The declining marginal productivity of capital pulls the combined
measures down.

In order to account for the high, long-run growth rates of Soviet output it
is necessary to go beyond the measures of the growth of factor productivity in
tables 14.5 and 14.6 to consider the increases in the quantities of the factors
themselves. In his study of the sources of Soviet growth Stanley Cohn finds that
increases in inputs are more important than increases in factor productivity in
explaining Soviet growth rates in all periods except 1950-1958.[7] Tables 14.7 and
14.8 summarize the contribution of increased inputs to Soviet growth rates.

The Soviets have been able to mobilize large quantities of labor and capital
resources. Their labor-force participation rate is the highest in the developed

[7]Stanley Cohn, *Economic Development in the Soviet Union.*

Table 14.7

Trends in the Labor Participation Ratios

Year	Participation Ratio (Percentage)
1928	56.8
1937	70.1
1950	71.7
1958	70.8
1964	76.1
1968	72.4

Source: 1928-64, in Stanley Cohn, Economic Development in the Soviet Union, p. 66; and 1968, in U.S. Congress Joint Economic Committee, Economic Performance and the Military Burden in the Soviet Union, p. 75.

Table 14.8

Rates of Growth of GNP, Employment, Fixed Capital, and the Incremental Capital-Labor Ratio
(Average Annual Rates)

Period	GNP	Employment Annual Increase	Man-Hours	Fixed Capital	Incremental Capital-Labor Ratio[a]
1928-37	4.8-11.9	3.7	3.6	8.8-10.8	2.4-3.0[b]
1937-40	3.6	3.0	3.8	10.3	2.7
1940-50	1.8-2.2	.3	.6	−1.7-2.2	2.8-3.7
1950-55	6.9	2.5	1.9	9.8 ⎱	6.9
1955-58	7.4	1.4	nil	9.0 ⎰	
1958-61	5.4	1.2	−0.5	9.2 ⎱	15.7[c]
1961-65	5.2	2.4	2.0	8.5 ⎰	

[a]Increase in fixed capital, net of retirements, divided by increase in man-hours of employment.
[b]Data for 1929-37.
[c]Data for 1958-64.

Source: Stanley Cohn, Economic Development in the Soviet Union, p. 69.

Table 14.9

Trends in Allocation of Soviet GNP
(Percentage of Total)

End Use	1928	1937	1940	1950	1955	1965	1970
Private consumption	64.7	52.5	51.0	51.0	50.6	46.2	55.3
Communal consumption[a]	5.1	10.5	9.9	8.0	8.2	9.9	
Investment	25.0	25.9	19.2	23.0	25.3	30.4	31.2
Defense	2.5	7.9	16.1	13.3	13.0	11.3	13.5
Other	2.7	3.2	3.8	4.7	2.9	2.4	—

[a]Includes public education, health, and science.

Source: 1928-1965, Stanley Cohn, Economic Development in the Soviet Union, p. 71; 1970, Abram Bergson, "Future Growth Strategy for the Soviet Economy," ACES Bulletin 14, no. 1 (Spring 1972), p. 9.

Table 14.10

Comparative Trends in Allocation of GNP

(Percentage of Total)

Country	1950		1955		1965	
	Private Consumption	*Investment*	*Private Consumption*	*Investment*	*Private Consumption*	*Investment*
France	63.8	16.6	65.1	16.7	61.0	24.3
Germany	57.2	19.7	55.4	22.8	56.6	26.8
United Kingdom	66.9	12.2	65.1	13.7	63.7	17.9
U.S.S.R.	51.0	23.0	50.6	25.3	46.2	30.4

Source: National Accounts of OECD Countries, 1950-68, pp. 350, 351, 363.

world, Among the adult female population 53.7 percent were employed in 1960 compared to 32.8 percent in the United States and approximately 37 percent in France and Germany.[8] Fixed capital has been increased at a very rapid rate despite the fact that the marginal product of capital is declining. The rapidly increasing incremental capital-labor ratio indicates the increasing capital intensity of Soviet production. Table 14.9 and 14.10 illustrate the large share of total output the Soviets have devoted to investment and the consequently small share devoted to consumption. If investment in human capital is included, the total share of output going to investment is even larger.

In summary, the Soviets have succeeded in transforming a basically peasant, agricultural society into an advanced industrial power. They have achieved their objective through an ability to mobilize huge quantities of inputs, as witnessed by their high rates of physical and human capital formation and labor participation. Certainly productivity gains have contributed to Soviet growth but cannot by themselves account for the success of the Soviets. The system of planning instituted by Stalin allowed the leadership to implement their growth objectives despite the high cost in terms of deferred consumption. Planners were able to capture resources in the agricultural sector and concentrate them in the high-priority area of heavy industry to an extent achieved in the West only during wartime. Taut planning with a heavy infusion of inputs into a few key sectors produced a series of leaps forward. These advances created bottlenecks in lower-priority areas. When the bottleneck areas became too troublesome, they in turn could receive priority attention. The bottleneck strategy appears to have been quite successful until the late 1950s when the continued infusion of inputs did not have the same results, and growth rates declined. The prospect of additional growth of the extensive type appears to be limited.

EQUITY AND THE SOVIET CONSUMER

Table 14.4 illustrates the growth of consumption per capita in the Soviet Union between 1928 and 1972. As mentioned earlier, there was little, if any, gain in real per capita consumption in the period prior to World War II. It is estimated that real per capita private consumption rose 85 percent between 1928 and 1958, and total per capita consumption, including communal goods and services, rose 100 percent.[9] The growth of per capita consumption slowed down in the late 1950s and early 1960s but picked up again after 1964. Table 14.11 compares the Soviet standard of living with that of the United States. The Soviets fare better when the consumption of food, health, and education is considered but do considerably worse in the areas of consumer durables and

---

[8]*Ibid.,* p. 67.

[9]J. Chapman, "Consumption," in *Economic Trends in the Soviet Union,* eds. Abram Bergson and Simon Kuznets (Cambridge, Mass.: Harvard University Press 1963), pp. 238-39.

other services. The availability of housing is particularly acute. In 1967 the per capita living space was seven square meters, half of that available in West Germany.

Table 14.11

Comparison of U.S.S.R. and United States
Consumption per Capita (U.S.S.R. as a Percentage of United States)

	1955	1958	1960	1962	1963	1964	1965	1966	1967	1968
Total Consumption	27	30	31	31	31	30	31	31	32	33
Food Products	43	47	48	49	50	49	51	53	56	57
Soft goods	15	17	18	18	18	17	17	17	18	18
Durable goods	4	6	7	8	8	8	8	8	9	9
Personal services	17	19	20	23	23	23	24	24	26	27
Health and Education service	57	55	55	56	57	56	60	58	56	57

Note: Comparisons are based on indices of consumption in the two countries calculated in value terms using comparable price weights.
Source: U.S. Congress, Joint Economic Committee, Economic Performance and the Military Burden in the Soviet Union, p.97

Equity is concerned, however, not with the absolute amounts of goods and services but with their distribution among consumers. Marx outlined two theories of distribution which would prevail in the two stages following the revolution. During the stage of socialism the slogan was "from each according to his ability, to each according to his contribution." Upon achieving the stage of communism, output was to be distributed according to need. The Soviets have followed the first principle, and wages have been tied to skill level and difficulty of work. Extremely large differentials have resulted between the lowest-paid factory worker and the highest-paid manager. Even greater differentials are observed if one considers the meager income of the collective farm worker. The widespread use of the piecework system has contributed to the spread. If one abstracts from the dividend and interest income received in capitalist economies, the distribution of income in the Soviet Union is about on a par with that of the United States and Western Europe.

Measures have been taken to reduce income inequality resulting from large wage differentials. The continuing policy of overfull employment planning has benefited the lower-paid workers, often the victims of unemployment in the United States. The income of lower groups has also been raised by the Soviet policy of subsidizing the prices of essential goods and services such as housing, medical care, and urban transportation. Reforms initiated in 1964 have increased wages of the lowest-paid workers by 20 percent. The recent provision of a guaranteed income and social security coverage for collective farmers is helping to raise their relative position. Although the Soviets still adhere to the policy of remuneration according to contribution, they appear to be showing increasing concern for the welfare of the lowest-income groups.

THE RECENT DECLINE OF ECONOMIC GROWTH

Regardless of whether one looks at official Soviet statistics or Western estimates, it is clear that Soviet growth rates in the late 1950s and 1960s are distinctly lower than those achieved earlier. The reduction in growth rates occurred despite continued high levels of investment. The growth of labor inputs declined from 1955 to 1961 due to the reduced number of new entrants into the labor force, resulting from the low wartime birthrate and the decline in the length of the work week. This measure picked up again, however, after 1961.

A major cause of the slowdown is illustrated in the rising capital-output ratio, another way of measuring the declining marginal productivity of capital. Table 14.12 illustrates this trend and compares the Soviet experience with that of other developed economies. The figures indicate a sharp increase in the incremental capital-output ratio. Thus, more investment is required in the period 1960 to 1965 to obtain the same increase in output achieved in 1954 to 1960. The figures in Table 14.12 are marginal figures. Soviet data indicates that the average gross capital-output ratio increased from approximately 2.2 to 3.5 and the net from 1.5 to 2.4 during this same period.[10] If the share of net investment were 15 percent, this would generate a growth of 10 percent per year in the period 1950 to 1958 but only 6 percent per year after 1958.

One would expect the capital-output ratio to be low in a developing economy with capital in short supply. As productive investment possibilities were exploited, this ratio would tend to rise. As we mentioned earlier, however, this rise may be—and normally has been—offset by the productivity gains of technological change. According to modern growth theory, the level of investment is not the key to growth. In fact, the long-run growth rate is independent of the level of investment but is dependent on the rate of growth of the labor force and the rate of technological advance. It can be argued that the tremendous increase in investment achieved by the Soviets after 1928 resulted in a movement from one long-run growth path to another. Growth rates increased during the transition phase but may again be returning to their long-run path. Further increases in investment could push the growth rate up again, at least temporarily, but would necessitate even greater pressure on the consumer sector, which could have a disincentive effect, reducing labor productivity.

Two studies of the recent slower growth phenomenon point out that there

[10]Judith Thornton, "Factors in the Recent Decline in Soviet Growth," *Slavic Review* 25, no. 1 (March 1968), pp. 101-119.

Table 14.12

U.S.S.R. and Selected Market Economies: Comparative Incremental Capital-Output Ratios

Country	Aggregate[a]				Output Per Employee			
	I O 1954-1960 1955-1961		I O 1960-1965 1961-1966		I O 1954-1960 1955-1961		I O 1960-1965 1961-1966	
U.S.S.R.	2.6		3.6		2.5		6.0	
France	2.8		2.8		2.9		3.1	
Germany	2.9		4.5		3.0		4.7	
Italy	2.4		3.3		2.4		2.3	
United Kingdom	4.1		5.6		6.9		3.6	
Japan	1.6		2.8		1.9		3.1	
United States	6.3		2.1		11.5		4.1	

[a] "Aggregate" refers to the increase in fixed nonhousing investment required to obtain a unit increase in gross national product. A lag of a year between a unit of investment (I) and of output (O) has been assumed. The ratio is increased to the extent that unutilized productive capacity exists. Thus, the high United States ratio in the earlier period and German ratio in the later period reflect idle capacity in the depressed years of 1961 and 1966 respectively.

Source: U.S. Congress, Joint Economic Committee, New Directions in the Soviet Economy, (Washington, D.C.: U.S. Government Printing Office, 1966), p. 120.

has been a decrease in the rate of increase of factor productivity beginning in the 1950s and continuing into the 1960s.[11] Growth due to productivity increase has never been as important in the Soviet economy as in the developed market economies. If the possibilities of further extensive growth are limited by labor shortages and a already-high level of investment, however, the rate of productivity change must increase if the Soviets desire to repeat the experience of the 1950s. A major question raised by Soviet, as well as Western, economists is whether the Stalinist model of central planning is capable of allowing sustained high rates of productivity increase.

The Economic Reforms

It is practically a truism recognized by all observers that the Soviet economy today is much more complex than when the basic model of centralized planning was developed. Today there are 20 million products in the Soviet industrial classification system, produced in 200,000 separate industrial enterprises. It is well-known that the task of planning becomes more and more difficult as the complexity of the economy increases. The number of interrelationships among products grows in proportion to the square of the number of products themselves. Errors are consequently more frequent and more serious, affecting a wide variety of enterprises. Economic growth has resulted in an increasing variety of outputs and inputs and thus a wide range of possible production processes. The highly centralized bureaucratic structure is unable to cope with the volume of decisions which must be made. It is unsuited to making the complex judgments necessary to maximize output and minimize cost under a variety of special circumstances and local conditions. Lacking a rational price system, planners must make decisions without reliable information on the cost of alternatives. The old bottleneck strategy is becoming inappropriate. Major imbalances in the consumer and agricultural sectors are serious problems and can no longer be treated as slack variables in the planning process. The rising cost of increased industrial production is a threat to future progress.

The key to future growth is productivity increase, which is in turn dependent upon the rate of technological change. The Stalinist planning model has been most successful in mobilizing vast quantities of resources and least successful in creating the conditions for discovery, invention, and innovation. Although large amounts of resources may be diverted for basic research with often spectacular results, as evidenced by Soviet space technology, the system is not conducive to the application of new knowledge on the enterprise level. The

---

[11]Norman Kaplan, "Retardation in Soviet Growth," *Review of Economic Studies* 50, no. 3 (August 1968), pp. 293-303; and Judith Thornton, "Value Added and Factor Productivity in Soviet Industry," *American Economic Review* LX, 55 no. 5 (December 1970), pp. 863-871.

bureaucracy is unable to disseminate the type of detailed knowledge appropriate for use in the enterprise, and the incentive system has traditionally guided the manager into concentrating on increased output in the short-run without regard to long-run quality or cost considerations.

The reforms beginning in 1965 have been an attempt to deal with the basic sources of static and dynamic inefficiency in the Soviet economy. We have described the basic institutional and behavioral changes inherent in the reform measures in the previous chapter and will now assess their effectiveness in increasing economic efficiency.

THE CONTRIBUTION OF THE REFORMS TO ECONOMIC EFFICIENCY

What were the principal benefits of the reforms of industry and prices? According to a Soviet economist the reforms resulted in a variety of improvements in the planning procedure and increased economic efficiency. First, the reforms brought about a more optimal combination of centralized government planning and local enterprise initiative as enterprise managers gained increased decision-making power. Second, the substitution of profits and sales for gross value of output as the primary success indicators resulted in an increase in quality and a reduction in costs as enterprises became more conscious of the needs of their customers and more attuned to the relationship between cost reduction and profits.[12] Numerous instances of increased efficiency were reported in the Soviet press. Delays in shipments were reduced since sales, not production, determined the manager's success. Due to the introduction of the 6 percent charge on capital, surplus capital was sold and the turnover of working capital speeded up. Hidden reserves of raw materials were discovered as enterprises increased their profits by making fuller use of their internal reserves.

The objective of the price reform, according to another Soviet economist, was to actively promote technical progress, the improvement of quality, and the rational use of raw materials and supplies. Further, the new price system had to guarantee that each normally functioning enterprise obtain a profit.[13] In fact, as a result of the reforms, prices came to reflect costs of production more closely, and all major branches of industry were nominally profitable. At the same time the spread of profit rates was reduced. The inclusion of interest on capital and rent on land in the calculation of prices was a major advance. Administrative machinery was also established for a continual review of prices.

How significant are these reforms? How far do they go in solving the basic

[12]A. Bachurin, "The Economic Reform," *Problems of Economics* 11, no. 12 (April 1969), pp. 11-25.

[13]A. Kamin, "Economic Reform and Tasks in Further Improving Price Formation," *Problems of Economics* 11, no. 8 (December 1968), pp. 39-46.

problems faced by the Soviets, particularly those problems of central planning responsible for the slowdown in economic growth. Most Western writers and some Soviet writers are quite critical of the reforms and feel they do not represent any basic change in the system of centralized planning and allocation of supplies. We will first consider some specific criticisms of the reforms themselves and then concentrate on some broader problems still remaining in the system.

A CRITIQUE OF THE REFORMS

It appears that one of the major stated objectives of the reform, shifting decision-making power to the enterprise manager, has not been achieved. Although the number of targets circumscribing the manager's behavior has been greatly reduced, the key targets—including inputs, outputs, and the assortment mix—have been retained. The manager is extremely limited in his ability to adjust his input or output mix to improve his profits. The Soviets have complained already, however, that managers have violated their assortment mix in order to concentrate on the most profitable items. It is extremely difficult for the manager to respond quickly to changes in consumer demand when his supplies are still allocated centrally. He still lacks the independence to innovate, a task so vital to long-run growth in productivity. Discoveries of hidden reserves and the reduction of waste in the production process indicate that the manager is responsive to new incentives, but these are one-time gains, not continuous sources of increased efficiency. One major source of increased managerial independence was to be his control over the investment fund. Evidence indicates, however, that managers have had very little success in spending these funds independent of the approval of higher authorities. Because supplies are allocated centrally, a manager may accumulate profits in his investment fund but be powerless to obtain materials on which to spend them.

The behavior of the bureaucracy has been a major stumbling block in increasing enterprise autonomy. The ministries have been extremely reluctant to allow the manager to exercise the limited autonomy formally granted him by the reforms. Ministries have reportedly set additional targets and specified additional tasks for enterprises. They have frequently changed enterprises' plans and confiscated investment funds of profitable firms and transferred them to unprofitable ones.

The new incentive system, although it contains many features superior to the old, is extremely complex and even contradictory. The manager must now weigh profits, profitability, sales, the wage fund, and fixed and working capital in an attempt to maximize revenues channeled into the various funds. He may find that costs can be reduced by firing workers, but the incentive fund is tied to the size of the wage bill. He may also find that it is profitable to reduce his expenditures on capital, but the development fund is tied to the value of his capital stock. Because his bonus depends not only upon profits and sales but on increases in profitability, the manager may become discouraged as it becomes more difficult every year to increase profit rates further. Although the substitution of sales for output was designed to improve quality, it is not a potent force in a seller's market. Finally, the maximization of profits will not lead to economic efficiency when prices are not rational.

Let us now turn to the problems inherent in the new price system, considered by the Soviets to be an integral and crucial part of the total reform package. First, the new price system is not radically different from the old. Prices still reflect average cost of production, now including capital and rent charges, and are still set centrally. They do not reflect relative scarcities and are not responsive to changes in supply and demand conditions. To the extent that managers have an influence on price formation they inflate cost estimates and quality characteristics to obtain higher prices and secure higher profits. Although planners intend to set prices which will encourage the development of new products, promote the use of substitutes for scarce resources, and improve quality, they have no methodology for achieving these objectives. As a result, scarce resources may be used lavishly because their price is set too low, while abundant resources may be rationed because their price is set too high. If prices cannot be used as guides to rational behavior, decentralization of decision-making is impossible. Prices cannot be used as economic levers to influence managerial behavior, and the central determination of the allocation of resources must continue.

CONTINUING PROBLEMS

By now the reader has gained an impression of the overall functioning of the Soviet economic system—its achievements and its deficiencies. A summary of what we believe to be the major continuing problems blocking the way to increased economic efficiency follows:

1. Centralized physical planning and allocation of supplies.

The basic process of plan construction described in chapter thirteen continues. Despite the increasing complexity of the economy, planners still plan for the production of over 20,000 commodities centrally, using the materials balance method to achieve consistency. Although advances have been made in the application of input-output and linear programming techniques, most Soviet economists and mathematicians are extremely skeptical of their practicality in achieving efficient allocation of resources even in the long run.

2. The role of the bureaucracy.

The layers of burearcracy between Gosplan and the enterprises have not been reduced by the reforms. They continue to perform the function of data gatherers, data disseminators and watchdogs over enterprises. They continue to stifle local initiative.

3. The incentive system.

Although the new incentive system may correct some of the more obvious irrationalities inherent in the old system, they introduce new ones of their own. Managers now juggle costs, assortments, and profit norms to secure larger bonuses. Two major problems in this area remain. The manager still has a yearly time horizon and no incentive to risk short-run profits for long-run gains. Further, his markets continue to be assured, and few channels of communication between buyer and seller have been opened.

4. The price system.

As we have stressed repeatedly, prices do not serve the planner or the enterprise manager as rational guides for economic decision-making.

5. Taut planning.

The Soviets have continuously employed taut or pressure planning to promote rapid economic growth and still do so. Although one can argue the merits of such a strategy in a backward economy with vast untapped resources, it is increasingly inappropriate in a mature, industrial economy. Continuous pressure leads to uneconomic, shortsighted behavior on the part of the manager. A continuous seller's market results in resistance to innovation and quality deterioration. The absence of reserves causes bottlenecks to have widespread repercussions in a highly interdependent economy.

There is a great deal of controversy, both in the Soviet Union and the West, as to whether the reforms, imperfect as they are, represent a first step in the direction of decentralization, to be followed by other more meaningful measures, or are just one more round in the continuing struggle to achieve the appropriate degree of decentralization, already being followed by recentralization. One thing is clear—the new system is not stable. The reform measures do not have a firm theoretical base and are full of contradictions leading to inconsistent behavior. They must be gradually extended and modified, or there will be increasing pressure to return to more centralized planning techniques with the hope that the use of new mathematical techniques and computers will make centralization and efficiency compatible.

The Soviet Union has not been the only centrally planned economy to undergo reforms in its planning system. All the countries of the East European bloc, with the exception of Albania, have undergone some degree of decentralization in the last few years. Many have adopted measures much more far-reaching than those implemented in the Soviet economy. To shed some light on the possible future course of the Soviet economy it is worthwhile to conclude with a brief look at the reforms undertaken in Eastern Europe.

THE REFORMS OF THE EASTERN EUROPEAN ECONOMIES

After the war the countries of the Communist bloc instituted planning systems along the lines of the Stalinist central planning model of the Soviet Union. Although considerable progress was made under this system, particularly

Table 14.13

Average Annual Growth Rates of Industrial Output and Index of Industrial Slowdown
(U.S.S.R. and East European Socialist Countries)

| | AVERAGE ANNUAL RATES OF INDUSTRIAL GROWTH | | | | | | INDEX OF INDUSTRIAL SLOWDOWN | | | |
| | 1951-1955 | | 1956-1960 | | 1961-1965 | | First to second five-year period (column 1 and 2 as percentage of column 3 and 4) | | Second to third five-year period (column 3 and 4 as percentage of column 5 and 6) | |
Country	Soviet Estimate	Western Estimate	Soviet Estimate	Western Estimate	Soviet Estimate	Western Estimate[a]	From Soviet Estimate	From Western Estimate	From Soviet Estimate	From Western Estimate
U.S.S.R.	13.2	11.2	10.4	9.0[b]	8.5	7.3[c]	126.9	124.4	122.4	123.3
Albania	17.8	N.A.	21.6	N.A.	6.9[d]	N.A.	82.4		313.0	
Bulgaria	13.7	8.4	15.9	12.7	11.2	8.2	86.2	66.1	142.0	154.9
Czechoslovakia	10.9	4.6	10.5	9.1	5.2	1.9	103.8	50.5	201.9	478.9
GDR	13.8	11.2	9.2	7.2	5.7	4.1	150.0	155.6	161.4	175.6
Hungary	13.7	9.0	7.5	5.5	7.7	8.2	182.7	163.6	97.4	67.1
Poland	16.2	9.6	9.9	8.1	8.3	7.3	163.6	118.5	119.3	111.0
Rumania	15.1	7.6	10.9	9.4	13.8	11.7	138.5	80.9	79.0	80.3

[a]Unless otherwise stated, 1961-64.
[b]1956-61.
[c]1962-65.
[d]1961-64.

Source: Harry G. Shaffer, "Economic Reforms in the Soviet Union and East Europe: A Comparative Study," Association of Comparative Economics, Proceedings of Joint Meeting (April 1970), p. 11.

in the less industrialized nations, growth rates began to decline in the late 1950s (see Table 14.13). Declining rates of growth of factor productivity appeared to be a major factor in the East European, as well as the Soviet, economic slow-down. The response of the leadership of these economies was to reform the planning system. East Germany and Czechoslovakia instituted reform measures as early as 1963 and 1964. Although the nature of the reform measures varied from one economy to another, they shared common characteristics.[14] All expressed the desire to limit the authority of the central planners and increase the autonomy of the enterprise manager. This was to be achieved by reducing the number of targets specified in the annual plan and increasing the importance of economic incentives in preference to administrative orders as guides for manager behavior. All considered it essential to substitute profit for the gross value of output as the major success indicator. All recognized the need for price reforms and the adoption of prices more reflective of opportunity cost. All these objectives are similar to those expressed by the Soviet leadership.

Czechoslovakia and Hungary adopted the most far-reaching reforms, moving the farthest away from the centralized allocation of supplies and centralized control of the enterprise. Czechoslovakia's reform program was interrupted in the spring of 1969 with the Soviet invasion of the country and recentralization measures. We have chosen to discuss Hungary's "New Economic Mechanism" not as representative of the reform programs of the Communist countries but as indicative of the extent of decentralization possible in a country where major economic and political policies must be approved by the Soviet Union.

The reforms implemented in Hungary in 1968 were discussed and developed over a period of years beginning in 1964. The model called the New Economic Mechanism had the backing and support of the Party leaders.[15] Its adoption implies a basic change in the economic structure and institutions of the country, described as a transformation from a command to a socialist market economy. Although ownership of the means of production remains public, the government no longer issues a binding national plan. Enterprises prepare their own production plans, which need not be submitted to higher agencies for approval. Centralized allocation of supplies, the major component of the national plan, has been eliminated. Enterprises deal with each other directly; they order from suppliers and make contracts with buyers.

The reward of the managers is tied to profits, with the government leaving the enterprise to divide after-tax profits between the development and sharing

---

[14]For a discussion of the reforms in East Europe see Harry Shaffer, "Varieties of Economic Management in East Europe," *East Europe,* 19, nos. 2 and 3, (November and December 1970).

[15]For a more complete discussion of the Hungarian reform, see Richard D. Portes, "Economic Reforms in Hungary," *American Economic Review* 60, no. 1 (May 1970), pp. 307-313.

funds. All wage increases must be paid out of the sharing fund before it is distributed to managerial personnel as bonuses. This measure was intended to moderate the manager's tendency to grant wage increases and thereby prevent inflation.

Decentralized investment financed from internal sources or from bank loans became increasingly important. Seventy-five percent of an enterprise's working capital is to be financed from its own funds and twenty-five percent from bank credit.[16] Longer-term investment is to be financed by the enterprise's development fund, long-term loans from the Investment Bank, or in certain instances, from the national budget.

Some degree of price flexibility has been introduced. Prices fall into four categories: centrally fixed, maximum, limit and free, with the latter accounting for approximately 20 percent of the total. The goal is to move more and more prices into this category.

Although the planners have relinquished many microeconomic controls, they still have a powerful influence on the direction of the economy. Industrial ministries can appoint and dismiss enterprise managers. The Hungarians have firmly rejected the concept of worker control of an enterprise. The state can levy fines on enterprises for undesirable behavior such as quality reduction or illegal price increases. Further, the government controls the level of investment by limiting the amount of long-term credit granted by the Investment Bank.

It is too early to tell whether these measures will increase productivity and help solve many problems; conflicting rules need to be worked out. It does appear, however, that the Hungarians are committed to decentralization and are moving forward in that direction rather than back. In chapter 16 we will consider the experience and performance of a Communist country which has had a considerably longer period of experience with decentralization.

QUESTIONS

1. What factors contribute to the relatively low productivity of labor and capital in the Soviet Union?
2. Why can environmental pollution be a problem in a planned as well as in a capitalist economy.
3. Compare and contrast the decision to invest in a new cement manufacturing plant in the Soviet Union and in a market economy?
4. What were the major causes of the high Soviet growth rates achieved in the period prior to 1960?
5. What were the major causes of the slowdown in the Soviet growth after 1960?

[16]*Ibid.,* p. 310.

6. Do you think the industrial reforms will be successful in increasing the static and dynamic efficiency of the Soviet economy?

7. Compare and contrast the Hungarian and Soviet economic reforms.

BIBLIOGRAPHY

The Theory of Central Planning

Grossman, Gregory. "Notes for a Theory of the Command Economy," *Soviet Studies,* vol. 15, no. 2 (October 1963), pp. 101-123.

Kohler, Heinz. *Welfare and Planning: An Analysis of Capitalism versus Socialism.* New York: John Wiley & Sons, Inc., 1966.

Solo Robert. *Economic Organizations and Social Systems.* New York: The Bobbs-Merrill Company, Inc., 1967.

Ward, Benjamin. *The Socialist Economy.* New York: Random House, 1967.

Wilczynski, J. *The Economics of Socialism.* Chicago: Aldine Publishing Company, 1970.

Zielinski, J. *On the Theory of Socialist Planning.* London: Oxford University Press, 1968.

The Soviet Union

Bergson, Abram. *Planning and Productivity under Soviet Socialism.* New York: Columbia University Press, 1968.

———. *The Economics of Soviet Planning.* New Haven: Yale University Press, 1964.

Campbell, Robert. *Soviet Economic Power* 2nd ed. Boston: Houghton-Mifflin Company, 1966.

Cohn, Stanley, *Economic Development in the Soviet Union.* Massachusetts: Heath Lexington Books, 1970.

Ellman, Michael. *Soviet Planning Today.* Cambridge: Cambridge University Press, 1971.

Feiwel, George. *The Soviet Quest for Economic Efficiency.* New York: Frederick A. Praeger, 1967.

Goldman, Marshall. *The Spoils of Progress: Environmental Pollution in the Soviet Union.* Boston: MIT Press, 1972.

Joint Economic Committee, *New Directions in the Soviet Economy,* 89th Congress of the United States, 2nd session, 1966. Washington, D.C.: U.S. Government Printing Office.

Nove, Alec. *The Soviet Economy* 2nd ed. rev. New York: Frederick A. Praeger, 1969.

———, *An Economic History of the USSR.* London: The Penguin Press, 1969.

Subcommittee on Foreign Economic Policy, *Economic Performance and the Military Burden in the Soviet Union,* Joint Economic Committee, 91st Congress of the United States, 2nd session, 1970. Washington, D.C.: U.S. Government Printing Office.

Subcommittee on Foreign Economic Policy, *Soviet Economic Performance: 1966-67,* Joint Economic Committee, 90th Congress of the United States, 2nd session, 1968. Washington, D.C.: U.S. Government Printing Office.

Zaleski, Eugene. *Planning Reforms in the Soviet Union, 1962-1966.* Chapel Hill: University of North Carolina Press, 1967.

Eastern Europe

Balassa, Bela and Trent J. Bertrand. "Growth and Performance of Eastern European Economies and Comparable Western European Countries," *American Economic Review,* 60 , no. 2 (May 1970), pp. 314-320.

Gamarnikow, Michael. *Economic Reforms in Eastern Europe.* Detroit: Wayne State University Press, 1968.

Ljubo, Sirc. *Economic Revolution in Eastern Europe.* New York: Frederick A. Praeger, 1969.

Shaffer, Harry. "Varieties of Economic Reform in East Europe," *East Europe,* 19, nos. 2 and 3 (Nov. and Dec. 1970).

U.S. Congress, Joint Economic Committee. *Economic Developments in Countries of Eastern Europe.* Washington, D.C.: U.S. Government Printing Office, 1970.

V

MARKET SOCIALISM

15

The Theory
of Market Socialism

Introduction

The "scientific" socialism of Karl Marx quickly fractionated into warring philosophical and political schools of thought based on the particular needs of the social movements that adopted socialism as an ideological base. Revisionist or evolutionary Marxists associated themselves with European labor or trade union movements and formed Socialist or Social Democratic parties. These parties took part in parliamentary elections, established mass political bases, and occasionally came to power. However, once in power, Social Democratic parties appeared to be more concerned with smoothing the rough edges of capitalism than with promoting a socialist alternative.

Revolutionary or orthodox Marxists were more concerned with the ultimate revolutionary overthrow of capitalism and the substitution of socialism as an economic form of political and economic organization. It is only natural that those socialists least likely to come to power democratically would adopt the most revolutionary of Marxist variants. Such a group was the Bolshevik faction of Russian Marxists. Forces of unpredecented magnitude and complexity brought this faction to power with the passing of the Tsarist regime and several weak successors. Thus, in a sense, the "blueprint" of socialist organization that has evolved in the Soviet Union is the product of one of the least representative strands of socialist thought—a dogmatic, nationalistic, undemocratic, and messianic orthodox Marxism.

Many radicals, socialists, and even communists have concluded that, whatever the purported virtues of central planning in the early stages of economic development and industrialization, a point of diminishing returns has long since been reached, and that some alternative organizational form is required. It is recognized that input-output and linear programming are not true alternatives to central planning so much as techniques to improve the efficiency and performance of a centrally planned system. Ultimately these mathematical tools can serve only to stave off the day of reckoning for a few more years.

There is, however, a socialist alternative to central planning—market socialism—whose variants have attracted interest among academics, socialist theoreticians, and most importantly, in policy-making circles of the centrally planned economies in Eastern Europe.

A THEORY OF MARKET SOCIALISM

In the late 1930s many economists in the United States contributed elements of what has become known as the Lange-Lerner model of market socialism. Oscar Lange's purpose, as a socialist and a first-rank economist, was to devise an economic system based on socialist property relations, consumer sovereignty, and decentralized decision-making. This was not just an academic exercise because of the intense political passions and advocacies of the times. Democratic socialists were disturbed by the authoritarian tendencies of Soviet planning, communists were upset at any criticism of the Soviet system, and defenders of capitalism were eager to demonstrate that any form of socialist organization was not only impractical but logically improbable. Lange and others demonstrated that the point concerning the logical or theoretical impossibility of a socialist market economy was incorrect.

Having more or less silenced the criticism from the right, Lange then had to contend with critics on the left. There was, and is, a distressing tendency among socialist-oriented economists or theoreticians to gloss over the hard choices between alternatives imposed by scarcity of resources. A major accomplishment of Lange was that he forced socialists with any claims to serious thoughts on the subject to recognize the conditions of static and dynamic efficiency. Let us turn now to Lange's very important blending of standard microeconomic theory with socialist property relations.

Lange makes several assumptions in his socialist model that strike right to the heart of the economic problem. First, he assumes that individuals and households have freedom to allocate their labor services and skills to the highest bidder. Absolutely no state direction of the labor force or wage or work conditions must be permitted. Second, the household, once its income is established, should be free to spend its income on whatever goods or services it pleases. In other words, consumer choice should not be subject to state direction other than the usual proscriptions for health and hazard reasons. It will be further shown that resources will flow ultimately to those sectors where the intensity of household demand is greatest and vice versa. This means that the condition of consumer sovereignty is met, a stronger condition than just consumer choice. Consumer choice is a case of the Egyptians being offered the choice between one tall and two short or three middle-sized pyramids. Consumer sovereignty is a case of their being able to choose between pyramids and housing or anything else they might want.

So far the assumptions of the Lange-Lerner model are the familiar ones of the capitalist market economy. Next, however, Lange assumes that all capital, plant, equipment, and inventories are owned by the state. The firm is an organization with a civil servant for a manager that is charged with the responsibility of producing goods that consumers want at minimum social opportunity cost. The state is not concerned with what the firm produces, how it produces it, or to whom it sells the resulting product. The state's sole concern is that total social satisfaction be maximized over time. The state does not play a passive role, however; it is active and has a presence in every market. This seeming contradiction works out, at least on paper, to produce a close approximation to a capitalist market economy.

The state's presence in the economy is expressed through professional managers assigned to direct the affairs of firms, a Socialist Industry Manager assigned to conduct certain activities at the industry-wide level, and a Central Planning Board (CPB) responsible for those functions best discharged at the national level.

Starting at the top of the structure, the Central Planning Board sets the prices for all inputs and outputs, goods and services, except for the wages of labor. These prices are neither arbitrary nor eternal, just fixed for a period of time and subject to revision according to certain rules. The Central Planning Board is also responsible for determining the level and structure of collective consumption, education, defense, and cultural affairs. Whether the CPB is totally responsible for the saving necessary for future consumption is a matter for some debate.

The firm manager must take the price fixed by the CPB for all inputs and for the firm's output. The behavior of a firm in a market socialist economy is similar to the behavior of the competitive firm whose market position is so small that he cannot alter market price. However, the manager of a socialist firm may actually command a substantial fraction of any given market and have considerable latent market power. But so long as the manager behaves *as if* the CPB price were a competitive price, the latent market power never is exercised. The firm manager takes and combines all resources, including labor, to produce the product; and he must obey one rule—to produce that quantity of output at which the additional or marginal cost of the last unit produced is equal to the price assigned by the CPB. Obviously, then, the manager must utilize the firm's resources so that the marginal product of the last dollar's (ruble's) worth of every resource is the same. Otherwise, the manager could produce the same output at lower cost by substituting one resource for another. For a socialist firm in an industry which approximates the competitive model in numbers anyway, the rule "marginal cost equals price" is the same as the familiar "marginal cost equals marginal revenue" profit-maximizing rule of the capitalist firm. For a socialist firm in an oligopolistic or monopolistic situation, the rule MC=P produces a much different solution than the MC=MR rule. Output will be higher and price will be lower than under unregulated capitalist monopoly conditions. In sum, the activity of a socialist firm manager will be similar to that of a capitalist manager or entrepreneur. He may not be explicitly maximizing profits by minimizing costs, but he behaves by the rule *as if* he were. The resulting output, combination of resources, and revenues in excess of costs (profit) will be the same as for a capitalist firm.

Socialist firms producing a similar product constitute an industry in which each, equating marginal cost with price, is contributing to a "market" supply schedule, such that a higher CPB-set price will call forth more total industry output and a lower price, less output. Consumers will react in the usual fashion to the CPB-set price—they will determine the utility-maximizing amount they want at that price and will buy less if the price rises or more if the CPB should lower the set price. Putting the two together, only three possibilities are possible: (1) the CPB sets the price too high, and firms supply more of the product than consumers are willing to absorb; (2) the CPB price is too low and consumers demand more than firms are supplying; (3) the CPB happens to set the price where the output of the firms is equal to the combined demand of consumers. In the first case, surplus supplies are left unsold; in the second shortages develop; and in the third a balance exists. No simpler signalling system to the Central Planning Board can be devised—it is the same one that signals changes to a competitive capitalist market. Should surpluses develop, the CPB ought to lower the price; shortages should cause the CPB-set price to be raised. In real world conditions of shifting demands and imperfect information, the CPB price will probably always be pursuing balance without ever achieving it, but the same may be said of prices under capitalist competition.

The Socialist Industry Manager is charged with a function often neglected by socialist writers—creating a new firm or liquidating an old one. The capitalist entrepreneur will seek profits by entering an expanding, profitable industry or will leave an old one when profits evaporate. The personal drive of self-interest is absent under socialist property relations but the entrepreneurial function cannot be dispensed with. Therefore, Lange proposed an industry-wide manager. The Industry Manager compares the marginal cost of the last unit of output produced by any existing firm with the cost of producing the marginal output with a new firm. If the costs of producing additional output with new firms is less than the current set price, the industry manager should start up new firms. Old firms will be shut down when average costs exceed the CPB-set price. This arrangement ensures that shifts of demand will be matched by flows of resources and that the ultimate production of output will be at the lowest possible social opportunity cost.

Savings for capital accumulation may be derived from three sources. First, savings of households may be channeled through state banks to firms. The state banking system thus serves the same role as the commercial banking and financial intermediary system of capitalism. It accumulates the liquid savings of society and channels it to the highest bidder for investment purposes. Second, some of the state-owned firms are going to make a profit as likely a state of affairs as under capitalism, since the Industry Manager works to weed out unprofitable firms. These profits may be reinvested. Third, the state receives use-revenues from the firms who use state-owned property and normal taxes from households. The state may choose to run a budgetary surplus, taxes and receipts exceeding revenues, and to allocate the funds to firms for investment purposes.

Research and invention will be carried out by state-run laboratories and the results made available to all firms in society, thus assuring the most rapid spread of technical improvements possible.

Since the labor market is the only really "free" market, wages are determined basically by the forces of supply and demand. Rising industries will be able to pay higher wages and can expect to attract more and better workers. Declining industries will not be able to pay prevailing wages and will lose workers. No obviously "socialist" principle of income distribution is involved since the market will produce higher incomes for higher skills, more education, or the luck of having a scarce skill when demand shifts unexpectedly. These differentials are probably necessary to induce people to obtain skills or to retrain for positions in new areas of demand. The socialists will have to content themselves with the knowledge that at least no property incomes are being earned and that labor incomes earned are "deserved." The distribution of market incomes may always be altered by using the tax system to meet whatever redistributional needs a society desires, as even capitalist societies do. However, there are no really compelling socialist principles involved, and society could well accept the market's judgment.

Once the state determines the optimal amount of reinvestment for future consumption needs, it may find that funds are left over. The state may then declare a Social Dividend, much as an enterprise enjoying unusually good profits may declare a special dividend to its stockholders. The precise structure of the Social Dividend should be something left to the tastes and needs of the particular society at a moment in time. However, the Social Dividend clearly can serve to rejuggle the distribution of incomes, without having to take anything away from a particular group. It could be divided equally on a per capita basis, which would move incomes in an equalitarian direction. It could be given out as an income supplement to bring lower-income households up to some specified level. This is even more equalitarian in effect. No one method is, in theory, superior to another; it is a matter of value judgments.

A Critique of Lange's Market Socialist Model

This market-socialist model so faithfully reproduces the static efficiency conditions dear to the hearts of economists and so admirably achieved by competitive capitalism that one is tempted to ask, Why bother switching from one system to another? The socialist would respond that capitalist profits and rents are too much compensation for the simple task of allocating resources efficiently. The state can do the job just as well using the devices just outlined above and at considerably lower resource cost. The difference may be invested for even greater growth potential or given out for all to enhance their present consumption. The class of individuals who otherwise would have made a substantial living from the use of their property can still live as well as their skills can earn in a free labor market.

A substantive criticism of the model should begin by granting that the system may indeed work as well in blueprint form as does competitive capitalism: but like capitalism, in practice there are all sorts of problems. First, motivating the firm manager to do the right thing may be tricky. Such men cannot be expected to be automatons—they will want and deserve rewards for success. But what will measure success? Equating marginal cost with price is a technical exercise, and it is rather difficult to establish whether or not you have accomplished it. If the reward is in proportion to the output of the firm, the manager may respond by reducing quality, as we have seen in the Soviet case. If the reward is in proportion to profits earned, then the manager is properly motivated but may choose to exercise any latent market power the firm may possess. Singly or collectively, firm managers in concentrated industries could cut back production. The Central Planning Board would observe the resulting shortage and raise the price of the product. The firm or firms would thus have achieved the same results as a capitalist monopoly or cartel arrangement.

Second, there are problems with the role of the Socialist Industry Manager. In bureaucratic structures men are frequently rewarded materially and with prestige in proportion to the size of the establishment they manage. This may work to prevent the desired contraction of a declining industry as well as to prompt unnecessary expansion in progressive industries. Moreover, the Industry Manager may strike up a "cozy" relationship with the firms under his jurisdiction and restrict entry so as to assure the profitability of existing firms. Again, we observe results analogous to European cartels or some "regulated" industries in the United States.

Finally, the Central Planning Board cannot really remain just an information collection agency. The number of prices it must manage will run into the hundreds of thousands, perhaps millions. The more prices the CPB must manage, the slower the inevitable price changes will come. The longer between price changes, the greater will be the shortages and surpluses resulting from dynamic shifts of supply and demand conditions. Firms will be under tremendous pressure to switch to products with the most recent or most favorable price change even though society may need their present product as much or more. Firms may also artificially differentiate their old products so as to get a quick "new product" CPB price ruling. Under these sorts of pressures the system of pricing can rapidly explode in complexity. The CPB can respond to complexity by ordering firms to produce a limited line of products to minimize the number of prices it has to manage. This line of development clearly violates the condition of consumer sovereignty and is evolving toward central planning.

Whatever the problems with the static efficiency conditions in the Lange-Lerner model, there is some reason for concern about the conditions for dynamic efficiency as well. It is one thing to state that research and development will take place in state research labs and quite another thing to assure that technical improvements will become incorporated into the productive process. Unless there is some drive or push as impelling as the profit motive, the manager of the state-owned firm will find it much easier and safer to continue to do things the old way than to take risks without possibility of reward. There is much evidence that a great deal of productivity change takes place through a myriad of tiny, almost imperceptible, improvements. No one of these may be notable in isolation, but collectively they can spell the difference between progress and business-as-usual. It is hard to believe that a state-appointed manager would have the incentive to constantly probe the nooks and crannies of the production process in search of little savings and improvements. The burden of proof rests on those who state that this could occur—too much evidence exists of managerial lethargy in large capitalist profit-oriented firms for "practical" socialists to accept this claim at face value.

Once the level of the Social Investment Fund is established, it is reasonably likely that a Lange-Lerner economy will allocate the funds efficiently; that is, the funds will go to the highest bidder and that bid will reflect the strength of consumer demand. However, the determination of the overall or global level of the society's Social Investment Fund is another problem. Potential sources of investment funds are profits, use-revenues, household savings, and if necessary, taxes on households. It is possible that state planners could have a collective savings-investment function which, when exercised through state intervention, might conflict with the preferences of households.

Too little state-managed savings means that consumers have lost some possibility of greater consumption in the future. Too high a social savings rate means that consumers have been denied some present consumption in return for future goods that they would just as soon have enjoyed earlier rather than later. Lange's model assumes that the Central Planning Board will decide the global savings rate for the society—it will tax to make up any shortfall of funds or give back any excess of revenues in the Social Dividend.

For those socialists who have become suspicious of bureaucratized decision-making processes, there is an interesting alternative to Lange's assumption. The state could give back in the Social Dividend *all* use-revenues and profits which have accured in its management of the economy. Households could then freely determine how much of their income they wish to consume now and how much they wish to set aside for the future. These private savings would be deposited at set interest rates in state banks which would extend loans to firms at market interest rates. A great demand for investment funds would raise savings interest rates to attract deposits. The burden would then rest on the state planners to make a case for a savings rate higher than that which households have freely determined. A case could indeed be made, but the state planners should have to make it before the court of public opinion. A capitalist democracy usually arrives at collective investment decisions like roads, schools, and defense through the political process—no less should be expected of a socialist democracy.

While this latter proposal would assure maximum exposure of the saving decision to a market test, one side effect would be to open up the possibility of the accumulation of wealth in private hands. If interest were paid on private savings deposits and some households had high savings rates, and if inheritance or gifts of savings were permitted, then it would theoretically be possible for some households to subsist on interest income without current labor effort. If interest is not paid on deposits, households would lose the incentive to place their funds in state banks and the state would lose track of household savings. If no inheritance or gifts were permitted, then the state would have violated consumer sovereignty in the disposition of earned income. Either way, socialist "purity" would be bought at the price of economic efficiency and freedom—a choice that is perfectly proper as long as the tradeoff is recognized. Capitalist societies have circumscribed gifts or the inheritance of wealth through the tax system—a socialist society could well choose the same route with a minimum loss of freedom.

In summary, a Lange-Lerner market-socialist economy would have problems of monopoly and oligopoly similar to those of capitalism when the pure assumptions of competition are dropped, *as well as* the probability of bureaucratic paralysis due to the overloading of the information system of the Central Planning Board. A Lange-Lerner economy in practice would probably be an unstable organizational form and would evolve one way or the other—toward a system of truly independent competitive socialist firms or a centrally planned system with no enterprise autonomy.

Lange's formulation of a market socialist economy was flawed by a desire to have his cake and eat it too—to satisfy the marginal efficiency conditions, to decentralize the managerial function, but also to keep the central planners and give them authority over several critical economic functions. Sympathetic students of Lange's model have concluded that this schizophrenic approach is interesting as a theoretical exercise but not good enough for practical implementation.

AN ALTERNATIVE FORMULATION OF MARKET SOCIALISM—
THE LABOR-MANAGED ECONOMY

In the preceding summary statement, reference was made to implementation of a market-socialist model. Theoretically a market-socialist economy can be established either by converting a market-capitalist economy to socialist property relations or by converting a centrally planned socialist economy to a decentralized market-oriented system of socialist firms. In point of fact, no capitalist economy in recent history has felt the need to so completely transform the fabric of its property relations. Reforms of the so-called "welfare state" variety have been found to be compatible with a strong progressive capitalist economy. However, should some capitalist economy so seriously falter (Britain might be a candidate) that doubt was cast on its continued viability as a nation, then market-socialism stands as an alternative form.

The more likely candidate for transformation is the centrally planned economy. An advanced capitalist economy seems to suffer crises of "abundance"—an abundance of pollution from an ever-larger flow of industrial goods, the crisis of equitably distributing the wealth of society, the crisis of agricultural overproduction, the crisis of leisure time. On the other hand, advanced, centrally planned economies have tensions of the opposite sort—declining growth rates and declines in productivity advance, unsatisfied consumer demand, a poor industrial structure, lagging agriculture, and heavy-handed bureaucracies stifling local initiative.

Several East European Communist nations have flirted with one aspect or another of a market-socialist model and can be expected to press for further reforms to the limit of the political possibilities peculiar to this region. (Czechoslovakia in 1967 is an example of the political constraints imposed on economic and political decision-making in East Europe). As we shall see in chapter sixteen, Yugoslavia, through the workings of historical forces, was ejected from the Soviet bloc in 1949. Having achieved political independence at considerable economic cost, the Yugoslav Communist leadership had the imagination and courage to experiment with new organizational forms and to turn their small nation into a political and economic laboratory. The Yugoslav decision was to adopt a variety of market socialism which differs to a degree from the Lange-Lerner model. The chief innovation was the introduction of Workers' Councils, a form of management in which the affairs of the firm are the responsibility of the firm's employees, those most directly concerned with the fate of the firm. This version of market socialism will be termed "Labor-Managed Market Socialism."[1]

The Model

The assumptions of labor-managed market socialism are subtly different from those of the Lange formulation. There is no private ownership of industrial capital, but neither is "ownership," i.e., working authority, vested in an agency of the state. Ownership or title to the firm is vested in "society," everyone in general but no one in particular. Management responsibility, however, is the joint concern of the Workers' Council—the firm's laboring force, staff, and professional management working together as a democratic miniature society. Provision of capital to the firm is on a contractual basis and implies no control over the firm. Such debts must be serviced, and the firm may be held legally accountable; but creditors cannot alienate the authority of the Workers' Council. The firm is thus autonomous—totally independent of the state and of "absentee" owners. It is important to remember, however, that the workers do not "own" the firm. In effect, they are the trustees of society.

Firms so managed must purchase all inputs, including labor, in free competitive markets, combine these resources in an optimal manner, and sell their output in a free competitive market. Consumers are free to allocate their incomes as they wish. Successful firms can bid for and obtain additional resources; unsuccessful firms cannot maintain their position and must release resources. Consumer sovereignty is thus assured, and it only remains to be seen if the efficiency conditions are met.

The theory of labor-managed market socialism is not fully developed, but the broad tendencies of the system appear to contain reasonable approximations

---

[1] Yaroslav Vanek, *The General Theory of Labor-Managed Market Economies* (Ithaca, N.Y.: Cornell University Press, 1970).

of the static efficiency criteria. Labor will be hired until the marginal contribution of the last worker is equal to the prevailing wage. This assures that the optimum quantity of labor will be used in combination with resources and capital. The prices of resources, labor, and goods will correspond to relative scarcities and will alter with changing market conditions. Firms will bid for credit in capital markets, and the banking system may be composed of independent worker-managed financial intermediaries which bid for deposits and relend them at interest. The state may determine the level and structure of collective goods consumption and may tax firms or households to obtain the revenues. Research and development may take place in departments of firms or in specialized research firms which would license commercial applications to firms. Basic research would be a state-financed activity contracted out to the research firms. Workers' Councils would have all the required incentive to innovate and economize, because such activities would directly benefit the innovators.

The problem of market power would persist, but the state could intervene as always with price ceilings, regulation, or promoting entry of new firms. An interesting countertrend would be pressure toward smaller-size firms rather than larger. The more heterogeneous the activities of a firm, the more workers might object to having decisions affecting them made by workers in remote shops or different departments. This tendency to split into small homogeneous work units could be accommodated by setting up intra-firm "Shop Councils" to handle those matters best dealt with "locally," without undermining the authority of the enterprise-wide Workers' Council.

Capital accumulation would take place along the lines of the suggestion at the close of the previous section. Funds would come from voluntary savings of households, from reinvestment by firms (to improve labor productivity and thus wages), and from any surplus the state might run and allocate to the capital market. The first two sources would be based on satisfaction—maximizing behavior, whereas the state savings function would be based on the usual political test for collective investments or to compensate for market oversights and externalities.

In summary, the theory of labor-managed market socialism is incomplete and perhaps will never give precise answers because of the imponderables introduced by collective decision-making at the firm level. The Workers' Council may consider a number of other factors beyond income maximization, such as improved work conditions, more stable employment patterns, investments in worker amenities like brass bands and beauty contests. Nevertheless, a powerful theme runs throughout the model—the major economic agents are in control of their destiny, will benefit or fail depending on the wisdom of their decisions, and rewards and punishments are in direct proportion to the ability to satisfy consumer demand. The discipline of the market can be as sobering to an errant Workers' Council as it is to a lazy or feckless capitalist entrepreneur.

Summary

The Lange-Lerner market socialist model was developed to pose a socialist alternative to both capitalism and communist central planning. It was the intention of the developers to meet the static efficiency conditions posed by Western economists and simultaneously avoid the "ills" of private property, as well as the inefficiency of planning bureaucracies. The system of pseudo-markets coordinated by a Central Planning Board was a theoretical tour de force that did indeed demonstrate all that a democratic socialist economist could wish. When model is pitted against model, market socialism performs as well as market capitalism. However, as the Defense Department has discovered, models that fly in the computer may not be able to get off the ground in fact. Instead of avoiding the pitfalls of capitalism and planning, the Lange-Lerner model is as prey to monopoly abuse as capitalism and as prone to develop bureaucratic arthritis as communism.

A worker-managed version of market socialism has been formulated with more emphasis on "market" than the previous model. The force of the Yugoslav reforms was the precipitating element in constructing this model. The tentative nature of the model precludes hard and fast conclusions, but no flagrant violations of the efficiency conditions are obvious in the model. In practice, the Yugoslav economy has accommodated to the new organizational forms very well, as we shall see in the next chapter.

QUESTIONS

1. Who determines what goods and services will be produced in Lange's model of market socialism?
2. What role does the state play in this model?
3. Compare and contrast the methods by which economic information is transmitted in a market model and in a market socialism model?
4. How is the decision to invest in a new plant made under market socialism?
5. Who determines the overall level of savings and investment in this model?
6. Do you think market socialism is conducive to the process of research, invention, and innovation?
7. What is a labor managed economy?

16

The Yugoslav Economy

Introduction

Yugoslavia is one of the least-known European nations to most Americans. Although its rich history and fascinating people have long captivated writers and in recent years many tourists have gone to Yugoslavia, it remains obscure, distant, and seemingly insignificant. Yugoslavia appears in this study, however, on account of the unique evolution of its national economic institutions in the last two decades. The only nation in the world to organize its economic system along the lines of market socialism, Yugoslavia was propelled toward this revolutionary turn of events by a succession of social, political, and economic upheavals almost without precedent in the history of nations.

Yugoslavia Between the Wars: 1919-1941

Yugoslavia as a state was created out of bits and pieces of the collapsed empires of Turkey and Austria-Hungary. As an attempt to unify all the Balkan or South Slavs under one roof it was a valiant effort but one doomed to founder on the shoals of petty Slav nationalism, intense religious antagonisms, and the pressures of German and Italian imperialism. Frequently, one searching for an adjective to describe underdevelopment, abject poverty, and general backwardness has used the term "Balkan."

In the interwar years Yugoslavia was the model Balkan state, literally and figuratively. Agriculture, which was the principal source of livelihood for most of the population, was particularly poorly organized and equipped. The average farm was minute in size; equipment, working capital, draft animals, and fertilizers were in very short supply or lacking altogether. Farmers were debt-ridden and ignorant, having only recently been freed from the heavy hand of feudalism but not yet freed from its consequences. There was little industry and what existed was concentrated in the North—largely inherited from close contact with the pre-war Austro-Hungarian economy. Industrial expansion was fostered to a degree by a high protective tariff, but the limited size of the domestic market placed a ceiling on the growth potential of such a barrier. Ownership of property was largely private with the exception of primitive cooperatives in agriculture.

Following many examples in East Europe and pre-war Tsarist Russia, state intervention in the economy became increasingly extensive during the interwar years. State ownership in railroads and extractive industries was traditional. Various regulatory measures and price controls were instituted in the late 1930s, as successive governments of Yugoslavia drifted into the orbit of the Third Reich. In the wealthier areas adjacent to Austria-Hungary, Yugoslavia had inherited investments in railroads made by the Austro-Hungarian government. Many other Austro-Hungarian state investments had also been inherited by the new state of Yugoslavia.

State entrepreneurship may be an important stimulus to economic development in the absence of any other impulse. However, a sustained growth trend has never been generated in a capitalist economy solely by state entrepreneurship. At some point private capital and entrepreneurs must step in to fill the gaps left by the state or even to displace the state. Without this private effort the economy becomes rigid, inflexible, and biased toward those goods the government wants, which may or may not be the best thing for society as a whole. Private risk-takers must be convinced of the overall stability of the economy and the society-at-large for them to risk career and capital in long-lived projects.

Through the 1930s, Yugoslavia drifted toward political, and ultimately, physical civil war, while all Europe moved inexorably toward what has been called its own "civil war," the second in the twentieth century. Needless to say, the impulse of private risk-takers in this period was to avoid risk wherever possible and to invest only in easily or quickly liquidated projects or in foreign money markets.

By 1941 Yugoslavia was in most ways no better off than in 1919. Industrialization had not gotten underway, overpopulation in the agricultural regions was greater than ever, and productivity had not been improved. Yugoslavia's foreign trade was tightly bound to nations like Austria and Czechoslovakia, who were being overwhelmed by the Nazi war machine. Its own defeat and occupation was just a matter of time.

Yugoslavia: 1941-45

In April 1941 the Yugoslav army and nation were defeated and occupied by Germany and its allies. The Yugoslav state was dismembered and its major regions converted into an "independent" state of Croatia and an occupied state of Serbia, while the border areas were parcelled out as annexations to Italy, Germany, Hungary, Bulgaria, and Albania. A partisan movement drawing from all constituent nationalities grew to such proportions during the course of the war that Yugoslavia was largely liberated by its own armies in the field.

The Yugoslav economy suffered grievously as a consequence of the crushing defeat in 1941, the years of occupation and struggle, and the frenzy of destruction and death as the Germans were forced into a retreat. After liberation, industry after industry was found to have been reduced to 30 to 50 percent of prewar capacity. Metal industries, critical for the task of reconstruction, were especially hard-hit: they had been reduced to 15 to 20 percent of prewar levels. Rail transportation had been all but obliterated by the retreating Germans. The population and, naturally, the cream of the industrial labor force had been literally decimated by the war—10.8 percent of the population had been killed.

Postwar Yugoslavia: 1945-1946

In 1945 Yugoslavia was a nation in ruins, surrounded by nations in ruins. Many of the interregional, interwar bickerings had been made irrelevant by this incredible purging of a society. The old politics of petty nationalisms was discredited, at least in the old forms. A new "Yugoslav" nationalism based on Communist or socialist doctrines was to take its place.

Nationalization of industry and trade proceeded at a rapid pace with virtually no effective domestic opposition. This important event was made possible by several unusual circumstances:

1. The new Communist leadership had a popular mandate.
2. Existing industry was heavily damaged and there was little private capital to rehabilitate these firms.
3. Foreign capital had owned half of Yugoslav industry; much of this had been forfeited by the defeated nations and their nationals.
4. The royal government had had considerable holdings in industry and resources.

Taken together, these elements permitted the new government to virtually completely nationalize industry and trade without the political and economic disruptions which usually attend such a revolutionary turnabout. The Soviet Union, for example, had been forced to retreat to a partial capitalist economy for a number of years because of the internal resistance to complete socialization. Remember that the leaders under Marshal Tito for some years after the war were fervent believers in the Soviet Stalinist model of economic development through socialist centrally planned industrialization. They took pride in having achieved a degree of control reached by the Soviets only after eleven years of revolution, civil war, and the NEP.

Through 1946, the nationalization and repair of industry, the reconstruction of the ravaged transportation system, and the consolidation of Communist political power proceeded apace. By early 1947, the economic and political scene indeed closely resembled that of the Soviet Union on the eve of its First Five-Year Plan in 1928. Agriculture was mostly in private hands; the state had a dominant position in industry and trade; the Communist party was in exclusive power; the economy had reached a plateau and was poised for new undertakings to be decided by the national leadership. A decision was reached, and the Yugoslav society was plunged into a headlong drive for industrialization which would absorb virtually the entire energies of the society.

The First Five-Year Plan: 1947-1951

The adoption of the First Five-Year Plan took place in a psychological climate of national optimism and enthusiasm. It was an act of national naivete, on the part of both leaders and people. The leaders believed in Stalin, the Soviet Union, and central planning, while the people had great trust in the leaders who had extricated them from national humiliation and defeat. One might term this early experience with central planning as the "exuberant phase" of Soviet-style socialism. There was an exciting air of great things happening, great ideals being shaped into concrete and steel, boundless opportunities for advancement for ambitious men and women. In such an atmosphere tremendous energies may be unleashed and extraordinary sacrifices can be borne for a time.

Yugoslav planning authorities delivered their First Five-Year Plan in 1947 as a very model of how to plan an entire economy. They had indeed "out-Stalined" Stalin in the completeness of coverage, detail of regulation, and rigidity of structure. Their plan was actually almost a parody of planning, with hundreds of reports due to higher authority every year; the plan document itself was reported to have weighted close to 3000 pounds. Any Soviet planner could have told them, and some did, that many elements of the plan would have to be adjusted in practice and that overly ambitious goals left no reserves to meet unexpected contingencies.

The goals of the First Five-Year Plan 1947-1951 amounted to no less than a complete restructuring of the economy. National income was to double, industrial output to quadruple, and heavy industry to quintuple, all in five years. Ambitious housing, social and cultural, and transportation investment plans were also announced. Industry and transportation together were to get two-thirds of all investments allocated during the period, while agriculture was to receive 7 percent. It must be remembered in this context that agriculture employed well over half the population and was the largest single source of national income. A detailed examination of the structure of the First Plan is interesting but not particularly illuminating. Unachievable, overly ambitious goals appear throughout every sector of the plan. Had the Plan run its full course, nothing but collapse could have resulted as failure after failure to meet planned outputs mushroomed through the economy. Unfortunately, or perhaps fortunately in the long run, the Plan ran into political difficulties in the early years and had to be virtually abandoned before it really had a chance to fall of its own weight.

Agriculture was prominently featured for substantial expansion in the First Plan but received no resources to implement goals. The aftermath of the war had dealt a body blow to an already shaky agricultural picture. The authorities wanted expanded output but feared a capitalist peasantry and so harassed successful peasants—biting the hand that fed them, so to speak. The most productive northern agricultural areas had been tilled by German minorities, which were expelled, killed, or otherwise uprooted after the war. Their lands and farms remained, but the Slav peasant farmers who replaced them had lower skill levels and a smaller stock of capital and equipment. In other regions the typical peasant farm was too small and ill-equipped to be efficient. The breakup of large estates in the postwar land reforms resulted in more peasant households rather than larger farms. These large estates had supplied the lion's share of marketable surpluses and so the reforms actually lowered the overall productivity of agriculture.

The Collapse of the First Five Year Plan: 1948-1949

Through 1947 and 1948, the early symptoms of economic trouble loomed. Construction costs of the multitude of new projects exceeded all estimates and absorbed funds which should have been used to re-equip existing facilities. Exports were nowhere near planned targets at a time when import financing needs were unprecedented. Overly optimistic resource availability projections had been stretched into the projections for the output of industrial metals and materials, which were in turn strained into the input needs of machinery, equipment, and consumer goods. At no juncture had the possibility of error, miscalculation, or breakdown been admitted.

Political tensions with the Soviet Union blossomed into a full-scale crisis, with

Yugoslavia being expelled from the Cominform in June 1948.[1] All Soviet-bloc countries severed economic relations with Yugoslavia and withdrew aid, technicians, and delivery of supplies against contracts. Trade with such natural partners as Hungary, Rumania, Bulgaria, and Albania was severely disrupted. The economic consequences of the boycott were everything that one would have predicted would happen to the plan over time, but it occurred all at once. Foreign aid pledges had been inserted at critical points in the Plan, sometimes even before the aid had been offered. These sectors failed, and their customers were without supplies, and they in turn failed. The economy simply came unglued.

In the immediate postwar years of reconstruction, the socialization of agriculture did not have as high a priority as that of industry. Land reforms had gained a measure of popularity for the regime in the countryside without contributing to productivity. By 1949 Tito found himself in a situation similar to that of Stalin in 1928—he needed vast quantities of resources to fuel an ambitious central plan and he found that there is only one substantial pool of resources in an agrarian nation, the peasantry. The Yugoslav leadership made a decision to press for collectivization of agriculture in 1949. The impact on output duplicated Stalin's experience in Russia—the output of grain fell dramatically by over a millions tons compared to 1939's output. Vital foodstuffs and raw materials had to be imported, which used up foreign exchange earmarked for machinery imports. Clearly the agricultural shortfall alone was putting pressure on the integrity of the Plan.

The Soviet-bloc boycott, collapsing agricultural production, an infeasible original Plan, a strained balance of payments all led to the extension of the Plan's goals to 1952. The *coup de grace* was the drought of 1950 and the resulting harvest failure. The Plan was totally abandoned in 1950 and replaced with a Key Investment Program. In effect, the Yugoslav regime put its First Five-Year Plan through bankruptcy and concentrated resources on a few critical industries such as fuel, transportation, and electrical power. This was an eminently sensible policy, given the political and economic uncertainties of the Yugoslav situation.

The Development of the New Economic System: 1950-1957

From 1950 to 1952 a succession of laws developed the broad outlines of a new socialist organizational form in Yugoslavia which was termed the New Economic System (N.E.S.). There is some controversy over how seriously reform-minded the leadership of the League of Communists actually was at this time. There may indeed have been a good deal of political rhetoric to the loudly trumpeted "freeing" of the economy from the shackles of central planning.

[1] For a history of the causes of the tensions leading to the break in relations with the Soviet bloc see M. George Zaninovich, *The Development of Socialist Yugoslavia* (Baltimore: Johns Hopkins Press, 1968).

Certainly collectivization of the nation's small peasant households continued for another two years after the reforms of industry were instituted. It is possible also that the political leaders simply had not thought through to the ultimate conclusion the implications of what they were doing in industry and wanted to hedge their bets a bit. The progress toward decentralization was uneven, occasionally falling into retreat. The test of a policy is its long-run durability, and today we find the Yugoslav economy decentralized, socialist, and with a pace of development matched by few nations in the world.

In 1950 ownership of state enterprises was vested in "society," and control was passed to the working collective of the enterprise. The actual working out of this concept involved the election of "Workers' Councils" or a representative body with the responsibility for the managerial integrity of the enterprise. This principle of self-management was carried to its logical conclusion as an organizational form and introduced into government agencies and other organizations in which the self-interest of workers did not conflict with the interests of those they served.

Decentralization and self-management would be seriously compromised unless the central system of controls was scrapped simultaneously. From 1952 on, the functions of the Federal Planning Commission were removed and personnel transferred or released. By 1955 the number of Federal employees fell to one-fifth of the level of the central planning period. A Federal Planning Institute took the place of the defunct Commission and is still charged with the responsibility for drafting national economic plans. However, these plans no longer have the force of law and no machinery of controls exists to enforce the details of the plan. The status of the Yugoslav published plans is now analogous to that of the French plans.

YUGOSLAV SELF-MANAGED MARKET SOCIALISM—AN OUTLINE

Property Relations

The first separation here is, of course, between socialist property and capitalist property. With the collapse of the planned system and the decision to decentralize, the question naturally arose as to whether and how much private economic activity was to be permitted. The logic of decentralization in agriculture pointed to the private family farm or voluntary cooperatives if the forced system of collectives were to be abandoned. The government accepted private property in agriculture as the price of increased productivity and social tranquility. Naturally, it has tried to encourage cooperatives by channelling agricultural resources to them and has been successful to a degree. Acreage ceilings on the private farm may be set too low for efficient agriculture, so the residual socialist bias in agriculture may result in some lost productivity. The socialist leadership may have some fears of a well-to-do, conservative, capitalist-oriented peasantry as a political threat.

Another area of tolerated private capital is small service-oriented shops or firms. Cafes and restaurants of limited size, small *pensions* or hotels, family retail shops like tobacconists, news dealers, repair shops, makers of souvenirs or household items, are legally sanctioned as long as the number of hired employees is restricted to set levels.

In particular, the Yugoslav government has encouraged private provision of services to tourists in the knowledge that the state is notoriously cold and heavy-handed in its provision of merriment and a good meal. A not inconsiderable further factor is that all tourist services provided by private entrepreneurs are that much less of a drain on state funds, which may be heavily committed in other areas such as the provision of roads for tourists and natives.

Labor Relations

In contemporary Yugoslavia the labor market is free in the sense that workers may work where they please, and also free in the sense that wage rates are determined by the interaction of the economic situation of the firm and the willingness of labor to work at the combined wage and bonus rate the firm is productive enough to provide.

Wage and Labor Policy

Wage policy in Yugoslavia has seen considerable flux and institutional change over time. With the advent of worker committees as a management device, it has become difficult to conceptually work out which policies are management policies and which are labor or wage policies. From the considerable number of financial restraints which were imposed on firms in the early days of the worker-management experiment, it was clear that the government feared a breakdown in the financial management of the firm. It was felt that workers' committees would tend to disburse the funds of the firm in wage bonuses, hence leading to under-investing and over-consumption. The fears were justified but not for the reasons indicated. Firms were not under unusual internal pressure to squander their "seed-corn"—rather they were faced with the problem of recruiting, training, and then retaining a skilled work force. Given the tight conditions in the market for skilled labor and the rapid rate of expansion of the economy, Yugoslav firms were simply bidding against each other for the limited pool of skilled workers.

The solution was not to set limits on the amount of the wage fund or to tax the wage bill at high rates or to force the firm to reinvest a fixed and high proportion of its net income, although all these were tried. The solution would have been to take some of the aggregate pressure off the labor market by reducing the rate of economic expansion and to increase the input of skilled workers by investing in human capital or skills rather than in so much physical capital. Another anomalous result of this pressure on the labor market was that skilled workers were well-paid while a large percentage of unskilled workers were unemployed. Firms could not afford to hire an unskilled worker because once the worker acquired some skills (at considerable expense to the firm), someone else would hire him away and their investment in him would be lost. Large numbers of Yugoslav workers were permitted to leave the country to seek work in Common Market nations, where jobs were plentiful for unskilled labor. Remittances from these workers to their families in Yugoslavia ultimately become a very important source of foreign exchange for the country. While it may seem a strange arrangement, the labor situation just outlined is a rational one. Workers may obtain skills through formal education or on-the-job training (O.J.T.). For a poor society, a system of formal education is an expensive proposition and cannot be built overnight. At the same time the small core of expanding industry does not provide the quantity of O.J.T. exposure necessary to build the skills of the work force. The rate of increase of industry will outstrip the rate of skills formation, and the shortages of skilled labor we have described are inevitable. Permitting workers to go to West Germany, for example, permits workers to be exposed to training programs and to acquire skills at the expense of another country—one which certainly can afford it better than the Yugoslavs can. The other country reaps the anti-inflationary benefits of indefinitely large supplies of less-skilled labor inputs into their expanding industry. As a long-run solution to Yugoslavia's development, it is clearly a transitional phase. Over time Yugoslavia will develop an educational system and sufficient industry to provide skills for its own work force and at its own expense.

Foreign Trade

Foreign trade with and among the centrally planned economies has always been a difficult matter. Because the internal prices of products usually do not reflect their true value to the domestic economy, planners are reluctant to use internal prices as an index of value for trade with other countries. Therefore, trade with the Soviet Union or between planned economies actually amounts to gigantic barter swaps with everybody wheeling and dealing, the intent of the planners being to have a trade balance with *each* partner.

Yugoslavia was no different from any of the other planned economies until the decentralization and break with Stalin. At this point the logic of the market intruded on the Yugoslav leadership's assessment of their relations with the world economy. This logic dictates that, given the exchange rate of your currency with other currencies, you sell in the highest markets and buy in the lowest markets and hope that the surplus of exchange with one market will be sufficient to offset the deficits in another. If the deficits in some markets outweigh the surpluses in others, then the exchange rate must be moved or internal adjustments must be made. The changeover from one way of thinking to another must have been a wrenching experience for the economic leadership, but they made the transition and have not retreated since then.

A consistent trend has been to liberalize the relations of Yugoslav firms with the outside world. Firms are free to sell to whomever they will and largely free to purchase foreign goods and equipment if the price and terms are right, and foreign exchange is available. Those firms that export are permitted to retain a fraction of their foreign exchange earnings for importing their needs or goods for resale.

An extensive debate on whether or not to make the dinar convertible or to have a fluctuating exchange rate has taken place in recent years. The debate has not been resolved because hard decisions involving a degree of risk are involved. A convertible dinar is only as good as the confidence in the exchange rate at which it is pegged. The experience of the last twenty years with a number of devaluations and continuing inflation is not such as to inspire confidence in the notion of a convertible dinar.

CREDIT AND BANKING INSTITUTIONS

The Banking system as constituted under the regime of the central planning period was highly centralized. Ultimately almost all cash flows were channelled through an office of the National Bank. Marxist economists felt that money was a "veil" or merely a reflection of real economic activity—but it was a useful veil for planners. Control over the financial flows of an enterprise was considered to be an indispensable check on performance and an important disciplinary device. If a firm misbehaved, the financial system would probably pick up evidence of this behavior and discipline the firm by cutting off its credits until it corrected itself and returned to the prescribed planned activities. The method for determining the level of credit which each firm would need was, on paper, elementary. The physical volume of output of a firm was planned, and the price of this output was fixed. Therefore the total value of turnover, costs of production, and the payment patterns were pre-determined. These facts established how much cash the firm would need to meet the moments when more money was being paid out than being received. By subtracting from this the cash reserves of the firm, planners found the amount of credit the firm would need to carry on its everyday activities. These credits were self-liquidating since the payments patterns reversed themselves, sometimes more receipts coming in than payments going out and at other times the reverse being true.

The centralized banking system could thus collect all the flows of funds from private and enterprise savings, from the budget surpluses of all levels of government, and then parcel it out to credit-worthy firms according to the priorities of the planners.

The transition to a decentralized economy after 1951 was not accompanied immediately by a decentralization of the banking system. In fact, the system formally became more centralized than ever, into one gigantic National Bank with a large number of branch offices. An important change that took place at this time was the introduction of an interest charge on credits to the working capital of a firm to induce it to economize on those borrowing. By 1954 the logic of decentralization and the failure of the central banking system to control the volume and direction of credit necessitated a reform of the financial system. The communal banks were restored and granted fairly free rein to carry on a number of banking activities, subject to reserve requirements imposed by the National Bank. Specialized investment and service banks were created to serve agriculture, industry, and foreign trade; these functions were removed from the National Bank, which became more like a normal central bank.

By 1961 the outlines of a rational banking system had appeared—a National Bank with central bank functions and powers, local and regional banks to extend credit on a commercial basis, interest charges subject to supply and demand forces, and independent profit-oriented firms. This does not mean, of course, that the monetary system has functioned properly since then; it has not. But the Yugoslav record does not compare unfavorably with other, more advanced market economies. The fact remains that, market system or planned, capitalist system or socialist, political forces will intrude upon economic decision-making, occasionally in a destabilizing fashion.

Capital Auctions as a Credit or Capital-Rationing Device

A good deal of interest was generated in the West and in socialist circles over an early (1954) measure devised by the National Bank to ration credit. Firms were asked to submit bids for loans and state the interest they were willing to pay—on the assumption that this would reflect their marginal productivity. The National Bank could then run down the list of submitted bids, granting funds to the highest bidders successively until the funds ran out. The interest rate charged to all would be that quoted by the last bidder to receive funds. As an alternative to administrative grants of interest-free capital funds, the capital auction concept is interesting but extremely unsatisfactory. The problems in brief are:

1. The high bidders would have asked for more funds if they had known beforehand what the marginal-bid interest rate would be. This rise in demand, in turn, would probably cut off that marginal bidder, and the rate would edge up.
2. The interest rate submitted by the firm was frequently in fact unrelated to the productivity of the firm. Desperate firms near bankruptcy would offer the moon for a last chance at solvency.
3. The process was clumsy and inflexible because it forced a large number of decisions into a short period of time rather than spreading them out to suit the needs of the moment.

The capital auction quickly collapsed into a system whereby a rate was quoted, a demander of credit had to submit a request for funds and establish his credit-worthiness before receiving funds, and finally the funds were granted and repaid continuously rather than once or twice a year. A discerning eye can detect little difference between this state of affairs and a normal capital market. The capital auction scheme, then, was an interesting interlude between the central capital allocation period and a decentralized financial system, containing too many flaws to be sustained very long.

MANAGEMENT OF THE FIRM

Opinions on the feasibility of the self-management system of Yugoslav enterprises has varied depending on the political views and experience of the analyst. One early school of thought alleged that self-management was just another delusion of the workers—that in fact the management of a firm would remain firmly in the control of central planners or of the Communist party, or both. When the Yugoslavs dismantled the vast bulk of the central planning bureaucracy, these analysts felt that the party would still have the determining voice in management policy. It was not clear how this voice would make itself felt at the enterprise level because the market was to determine the critical variables of price and cost.

Other observers of Yugoslav decentralization felt that the ideals of socialism would at last find expression in Workers' Councils and the working-man's control of his own destiny. This school of thought was quite optimistic about the workers' ability to perceive their true, long-run interests (hence would be as willing to invest in the firm as any capitalist). The possibility that workers might squander all the firm's profits on wage increases or bonuses and not reinvest at all was not considered seriously.

Neither of these extreme views of self-management was completely correct in its initial evaluation. Strict central planning was discontinued, and the role of the political authority was substantially diminished. The League of Communists is still the dominant political force in the country, and Communist party membership is an important but not the only route to a successful career. The party has, by and large, left the microeconomic workings of the economy to the market and does not interfere in the intimate details of enterprise management. However, the political authorities retain the substantial macroeconomic powers of monetary and fiscal policies and occasionally favor or discriminate against some sectors of the economy through tariffs, quotas, subsidies, or tax relief measures. No government, capitalist or socialist, is innocent of such manipulations—those areas we have pointed out above are ones in which government may legitimately intervene. A socialist-oriented government might be expected to be more activist in its interventions than a capitalist one, but Yugoslavian socialism has frequently deferred more reverently to the free market than have conservative governments in the United States, Britain, and continental Europe.

The workers, at least initially, did not prove to be the farsighted entrepreneurs visualized by the socialist idealists either. Many Workers' Councils indulged in an orgy of wage bonuses and frittered away the firm's liquidity. It has become clear since the early period of workers self-management that this self-indulgence was a problem of transition and workers' unfamiliarity with responsibility. Living standards were low; workers had been under tight discipline; and many were ex-peasants, only lately subject to industrial rhythms. Only time and a painful, costly period of experimentation could provide the experience necessary to do the right things most of the time. Sometimes a forceful manager could browbeat his Management Board or Workers' Council and do things his way. Other times a stubborn Workers' Council could overrule expert advice and get the firm into hot water, hiring and firing managers until they found a complaisant individual. Occasionally, a Workers' Council would hire a manager, and the two would respect each other's authority and reconcile their differences in the common interest of the firm, letting profit be the final arbiter. These different possibilities are still to be found in Yugoslav firms and depend on the personal qualities of the individuals and the psychological and economic climate of the firm. The same could probably be said of firms in the United States. To this extent, then, the organization of the firm in Yugoslavia is probably on as sound a basis as most in the capitalist West. Only the performance of the system remains to be evaluated.

STATIC EFFICIENCY OF THE SELF-MANAGEMENT OR DECENTRALIZED SYSTEM

There is considerable evidence that violations of static efficiency are prevalent in the Yugoslav economy. We have mentioned political factory-building, putting up industrial plants to placate some political group or nationality. Much investment of this sort is justified under the rubric of "regional development." It is true that the economic development of some regions lags substantially behind that of others. The developed regions allege that the payoff from new investment in their industry is greater than investment in less developed regions. No doubt this is true. Many complementary investments have not been made in social overhead capital (transportation, communication, and human capital) in the less developed regions. It is difficult to judge the static efficiency of industrial investment in a context of rapid economic growth and large investments in social overhead capital. In general, if one observes an investment project that is markedly different from the general pattern of economic activity in a region, and if a subsidy is required to maintain its competitive position, and if no overall emphasis on comprehensive economic change is observable, then we may say with some confidence that the project is a boondoggle. The number of firms requiring such support is not inconsiderable, and the tendency for local governments to start up firms is well-established. The working of impersonal market forces does two things: first, it weeds out the worst of these irrationalities; second, it usually makes the costs of static inefficiency explicit, so that those authorities responsible for the problem must decide whether the costs are worth it.

Another source of static inefficiency is monopoly. Yugoslav firms have all the natural inclination to maximize profits by restricting output and raising prices if they can make it stick. In many lines of industrial activity, the optimum capacity for the firm may make natural monopoly likely for a small country like Yugoslavia. Competition would lead to destructive price cutting or inefficient-sized firms. An important substitution for competing local firms would be complete exposure to the world market. The Yugoslav government has been courageous in its general tendency to expose Yugoslav industry to international competition. The price of such a policy is balance of payments difficulties and occasional embarrassing bankruptcies. Some protection still exists; however, the great degree of openness of the economy makes apparent in even greater contrast those areas of the economy that enjoy the favors that only a protective government can offer. What politics can do, politics can undo, and so even the threat of loss of privilege protection may cause a local monopolist to temper his behavior.

Overall, it would be hard to state that Yugoslavia is any more statically inefficient than a country like the United States, where we have made Tulsa, Oklahoma a deep-sea port, made Wichita, Kansas an aerospace production center, subsidized shipbuilding fifty cents on the dollar, landed men on the moon at astronomical expense, and yet have cities that are scarcely livable.

DYNAMIC EFFICIENCY OF SELF-MANAGEMENT SOCIALISM

A primary objective of the Yugoslavs has been rapid economic growth, and they have invested a high percentage of their output to achieve this goal. We have observed that industrial growth under central planning was rapid until the

Table 16.1

Growth of the Gross Domestic Product in Yugoslavia
1953-1971

Year	Annual Percentage Change	Gross Investment as a Percentage of GDP
1948	20.0	32
1949	9.2	32
1950	−10.1	33
1951	9.2	33
1952	16.1	30
1953	17.9	32
1954	3.7	33
1955	14.0	29
1956	−3.6	29
1957	22.7	28
1958	3.2	30
1959	16.4	31
1960	6.4	32
1961	5.6	35
1962	4.3	35
1963	12.3	35
1964	12.0	33
1965	1.4	27
1966	6.6	27
1967	0.9	29
1968	3.6	31
1969	9.8	—
1970	6.0	—
1971	8.5	—

Source: Saveani Zavod za Statistiku, Jugoslavia 1945-1964 (Belgrade: 1965),
p. 80; Organization for Economic Cooperation and Development, Yugoslavia,
Nov. 1970, pp. 23, 53.

boycott of other Communist countries slowed the economy down. Agriculture was in particularly bad shape because of the collectivization campaign. The collapse of central planning and the turn to decentralization resulted in slow growth until the new system had a chance to shake down, but economic activity picked up substantially by the mid 1950s. See table 16.1. Agricultural production recovered from collectivization and grew at a 9 percent pace from 1952 to 1960. A real achievement was the fact that exports grew faster than imports for this same period.

The period from 1960 on saw somewhat reduced rates of performance but also a pull-back from forced-draft pressures to industrialize. Macroeconomic gyrations—rapid inflation followed by deflationary policies—actually destabilized the economy and reduced the rate of growth as well. Note the similarity of macroeconomic experience in Britain and Yugoslavia: "stagflation" is a term which is neutral between economic systems. The foreign sector has not performed as well due to currency problems associated with the rapid inflation and the creation of large trading blocs in Western Europe, which put up barriers against outsiders such as Yugoslavia. The instability just mentioned would naturally tend to upset export industries, and periodic surges of demand for imports would further destabilize the balance of payments. Therefore, on the basis of reduced growth and continued macroeconomic instability, the Yugoslav economy's dynamic efficiency has been impaired in recent years.

On the other hand, Yugoslavia under market socialism has retained a clear advantage in dynamic efficiency when compared to the period of central planning. One study has indicated that, accounting for the increased inputs of labor and capital under central planning, output did not rise by as much as it should have, even assuming zero productivity gain. However, when the same study was extended to the reform years after 1955, there remained some growth, which could not be attributed to labor and capital inputs and must therefore be positive productivity gains. Over 40 percent of the growth experience from 1956 to 1967 can be attributed to this increased efficiency.[2]

Summary

A complete and up-to-date view of progress and change in a society as volatile as Yugoslavia is impossible in this limited space. It is particularly difficult to evaluate a system like market socialism because there are so few parallels, and the historical record is so short and varied. In general, the Yugoslav economy was and is underdeveloped; it must trade with the world to survive and is finding it harder to do so. Its economic system is fragile and subject to distressingly frequent institutional overhauls. The lack of economic and political stability is a severe test of its unique system of self-managed, socially-owned enterprises. The fact that the system continues to function, to grow, and to innovate is an indication that market socialism is a viable alternative to centrally planned socialism, a fact that curries no favor in Moscow and accounts for the extreme sensitivity to Balkan affairs in those quarters.

QUESTIONS

1. Why did the Yugoslavs abandon central planning?
2. Under what circumstances was market socialism introduced in Yugoslavia?
3. How has the export of unskilled labor aided Yugoslav economic development?

[2]Branko Horvat, "Yugoslav Economic Policy in the Post-war Period," *American Economic Review* 61, supp. 3, (June 1971), p. 92.

4. How was the capital auction used to ration capital in Yugoslavia?
5. Do Yugoslav workers control the enterprises in which they work?
6. What are the major sources of static inefficiency in the Yugoslav economy?
7. How does the dynamic efficiency of the Yugoslav economy compare with the mixed economies of Western Europe?

BIBLIOGRAPHY

Adizes, Ichak. *Industrial Democracy: Yugoslavia*. New York: The Free Press, 1971.

Bombelles, Joseph T. *Economic Development of Communist Yugoslavia*. Stanford, Calif.: Hoover Institution, 1968.

Horvat, Branco. "Yugoslav Economic Policy in the Post-war Period: Problems, Ideas, Institutional Developments," *American Economic Review* 61, no. 3, Suppl (June, 1971), pp. 69-169.

Lange, Oskar and Fred M. Taylor. *On the Economic Theory of Socialism*. New York: McGraw-Hill, 1966.

Macesich, George. *Yugoslavia. The Theory and Practice of Development Planning*. Charlottesville, Va.: The University Press of Virginia, 1964.

Marshak, T. A. "Centralized versus Decentralized Resource Allocation: The Yugoslav Laboratory," *Quarterly Journal of Economics* 82, no. 4 (November 1968), pp. 561-587.

Pejovic, S. *The Market Planned Economy of Yugoslavia*. Minneapolis: University of Minnesota Press, 1966.

Sturmthal, Adolf. *Workers Councils*. Cambridge, Mass.: Harvard University Press, 1964.

Vuckovic, M. "The Recent Development of the Money and Banking System of Yugoslavia," *Journal of Political Economy* 71, no. 4 (August 1963), pp. 363-377.

Ward, Benjamin. "The Firm in Illyria: Market Syndicalism," *American Economic Review* 48, no. 4 (September 1968), pp. 566-589.

VI

ECONOMIC SYSTEMS

AND

INDIVIDUAL VALUES

17

The Evaluation of Systems

The Convergence Hypothesis

Up to this point we have examined the differences in institutions and performances among market, mixed, and planned economies. There is a significant body of opinion, however, that these differences are becoming less important and that the developed economies of East and West are growing more similar as they face and attempt to solve common problems. Let us examine the arguments supporting this convergence hypothesis, and the view of its critics.

Proponents of the hypothesis argue that all modern, developed nations share common experiences and problems and that this commonality leads to the adoption of similar economic institutions and policies. First, most developed nations, East and West, are highly industrialized. They have all experienced mass movements of their populations from rural to urban areas and thus share the values and problems of a concentrated urban society. Industrialization has been closely linked with education and increased consumer welfare, and educated, mass-consumption populations tend to share a common view of the world and use similar reasoning processes in coping with the problems and challenges of the modern world. All live in highly technological societies, and it is argued that the development of new techniques, so important to the achievement of rapid growth, is a process not linked to any particular set of economic institutions but common to all. It has been argued that the behavior of managers of Soviet and German chemical or machine tool plants is determined as much by the dictates of common technical processes as by their different economic settings.

Postwar developments in both East and West have led many observers to argue that extreme versions of both market and centrally planned economies are inappropriate for managing the complex modern industrial economies. It is pointed out that the leadership of both systems has been forced to adopt an eclectic mix of economic policies and institutions. Central planning and command have proved inadequate in directing vast quantities of resources to produce the fantastic variety of modern industrial products and to cater to the preferences of sophisticated consumers. Some amount of decentralization and the use of certain market techniques have been considered necessary to cope with the tasks. Market economies, on the other hand, have suffered from instability, unemployment, and inflation, and their governments have found it increasingly necessary to guide, if not control, economic life.

Before we consider more specific evidence supporting the hypothesis of the convergence of the economic institutions of market or mixed and planned economies, let us first consider the first group separately. The growing similarity of the developed, capitalist nations of the West is quite apparent.[1] All have been called "post-modern," a term used to describe high mass-consumption societies in which the service sector is growing most rapidly, and a highly educated, urbanized population is enjoying increased leisure as well as greater material abundance. There has been a dramatic change in the role of governments in the postwar period as they have felt it incumbent upon themselves to promote growth and stability and protect the individual from the risks of illness and unemployment, as well as engage in practices to redistribute income from the rich to the poor. Despite the fear of many opponents of "big government" and the welfare state, the growth of government has appeared to level off and the size of government to stabilize in most advanced market economies. Britain, France, Germany, the United States, and many others have retained their capitalist institutions and are less enchanted with the promised benefits of greater control of the economy through some type of planning. Although capitalist institutions are not under serious attack in any of the mixed economies we have studied, it can be argued that the nature of capitalism has changed. Firms are no longer of the perfectly competitive variety with little market power but are vast corporations responsible to a variety of groups and possessing considerable amounts of both economic and political power. Labor has combined together in powerful groups to promote their interests, and consumers

---

[1] For an analysis of this view see Benjamin Ward, "What is Distinctive About Contemporary Capitalism," *Journal of Economic Issues* 3, no. 1 (March 1969), pp. 32-48.

are finding it increasingly necessary to band together to protect their own interests, because they can no longer rely solely on the discipline of competition to reward and punish producers. The advantages of specialization and economies of scale have made most European governments reluctant to adopt or enforce antitrust measures for fear of losing markets to low-cost producers in other countries. Detailed planning to influence the behavior of corporate giants is not favored either. Rather, it is hoped that continued economic integration will permit both the advantages of large-scale production and competition.

In addition to economic institutions, the mixed economies of the West also share certain noneconomic values and attitudes. They all have some form of representative democracy and value individual freedom. Their societies are flexible, responding quickly to changing patterns of demand and changing technology. Their willingness to adapt to new conditions and their ability to innovate are keys to their performance in the postwar period.

If it is true that modern mixed economies are growing more alike, is it also true that mixed and planned economies are growing more similar? We have examined some general arguments favoring convergence; let us now look at some specific evidence purporting to show that this has actually been happening. The announcement and implementation of reforms embodying some amount of decentralization and the adoption of certain techniques associated with market economies in the economies of Eastern Europe and the Soviet Union have been cited as evidence of convergence. The use of the interest rate, the introduction of profit as a measure of performance, the development of market links between user and supplier, all support the view that the Stalinist model of central command planning is not appropriate to the solution of the economic problems of the second half of the twentieth century and that new techniques must be employed. Advocates of the convergence hypothesis often take an evolutionary view of command planning, arguing that it is useful in the early stages of modernization and industrialization but must be modified in the later stages. Evidence can also be cited to show that market economies are developing many of the characteristics of command economies. The growth of the nationalized sector, the large share of the GNP collected in taxes and spent by government, the adoption of indicative planning, and the use of price and wage controls are all examples of the increased centralization of economic decisions. It is argued that Yugoslavia and France represent the outermost fringes of command and market systems, respectively, and the probable direction of the future development of their neighbors.

Before we can accept the convergence hypothesis, we must examine the arguments of its critics. It is extremely difficult to determine the extent and significance of convergence by looking at the development of a myriad of separate economic institutions in each economy. If one does not take the view that economic systems can be characterized by a single property, such as the degree of centralization of decision-making, it is impossible to put systems on a continuum and then see if they are moving toward the middle. To determine the extent of convergence in a multidimensional classification system it is necessary to weight the importance of different characteristics, all of which are changing, but not necessarily at the same speed or even in the same direction. Germany may be experimenting with a form of budget planning at the same time it is removing restrictions on the flow of capital. France may be backing off from detailed sectoral planning and at the same time attempting to implement an incomes policy in order to control prices and wages. The extension of Soviet reforms throughout the economy has resulted in the use of profitability as a success indicator in all of industry, but direct contracting has not formed a part of the reform package as it has been extended beyond the initial experiments. The evolution of economic institutions is not unidirectional, and it is difficult to assess how basic are the changes which do occur. Do they alter the fundamental nature of the initial system?

It can certainly be argued that many fundamental differences remain between the mixed and planned economies. The most basic are the role of consumer sovereignty, the freedom of the firm's manager, the extent of private property, the size of the public sector, and the role of prices and competition. The Soviets themselves have attacked the convergence hypothesis as a bourgeois myth designed to hide the true superiority of the planned economies.[2] A prominent Soviet economist has stated that although the superficial appearance of certain economic institutions may be similar, their basic natures are very different. He argues that profit in the Soviet Union serves a very different purpose from in the West, being used in the former for the social good, while in the latter as a reward for the capitalist. The final outcome of market processes will be very different in a socialist state from in a capitalist one because different groups of people are making the decisions. Finally he argues that the economic reforms of the 1960s are designed not to replace central planning but to make it function more effectively.

Our analysis of Soviet institutions and reforms supports the view that the central allocation of resources and central determination of the direction of the economy have not been challenged in the Soviet Union and that the power of the consumer and enterprise manager have not meaningfully increased. One may challenge this conclusion by pointing to reforms in certain East European countries, such as Hungary, as the vanguard of future economic developments. Certainly the extent of decentralization and the enhanced role of the market in Hungary are impressive. That these developments can be used to prophesy convergence in the near future is another question. We argued earlier that there was a great deal of similarity in the objectives and structure of the mixed economies of the West. The same cannot be said for the planned economies of Eastern Europe. There appears to be a much greater variety in planning systems

---

[2]See L. Leontiev, "Myth About 'Rapprochement' of the Two Systems" *Comparative Economic Systems,* ed. Jan S. Prybyla (New York: Appleton- Century-Crofts, 1969), p. 477-485.

in the East than in market systems in the West. The reform packages adopted by nearly all Eastern European economies in the 1960s showed a great deal of diversity. The reforms themselves have been implemented in fits and starts, with Czechoslovakia as the outstanding example of the dismantling of reforms and a return to older methods.

The convergence of economic institutions is an appealing idea, particularly because it implies to many that political differences and the dangers of war may be reduced at the same time. But an unequivocal case cannot be made for convergence at the present time and a reduction of international tensions need not follow from, nor depend upon, the convergence of economic institutions. There is a popular belief that new economic institutions will result in the development of new political patterns. Decentralization of economic decision-making and the increased freedom of the manager will spill over into the political sphere, resulting in the development of democratic institutions and the growth of individual liberties. The relationship between economic and non-economic values and institutions is a tenuous one, and has often been left to the speculation of philosophers rather than the examination of social scientists. This relationship, although extremely difficult to understand, is fundamental! Can one choose an economic system independently of political and social systems? Can two nations which appear to have similar economic systems be judged equal in their ability to satisfy human wants? In this final section we will make some tentative statements on this complex issue.

THE RECONCILIATION OF ECONOMIC VALUES AND OTHER VALUE SYSTEMS WITHIN AN ECONOMIC SYSTEM

It is a common fallacy to suppose that economics is a rather dessicated, mechanical, valueless social science concerned only with the means for promoting the material welfare of mankind. Historically this could not be further from the truth. Great economists of the past—Adam Smith, Ricardo, Malthus, Mill, Marx, Keynes, etc.—have been deemed great precisely because they met the challenges of their times head on, frequently profoundly altering the thinking of later generations. The historical problems, themes, and theories of these men are amply dealt with elsewhere.[3] For the remainder of this chapter, we would like to consider in the modern context the interaction between the economic systems described in this text and ethical and political value systems.

The concept of freedom is subject to subtle nuances and honest men strongly differ as to precisely what freedom is and how to achieve it. Some might even dispute whether freedom is a desirable goal. Their case might run

---

[3]Robert Heilbroner, *The Wordly Philosophers,* 2nd Ed. (New York: Clarion Books,1970).

thusly: "Man is a social animal, deriving as much satisfaction from his social life, contact, and associations as he does from satisfying his individual wants and needs. Contemporary world society is too complex and variegated to make any generalizations about values. Most men derive much of their self identity from their allegiance to class, caste, race, nation, religion, family, party, or profession. These allegiances may be so strong as to make the term "freedom" almost meaningless. Men may even have a positive instinct to submerge their individuality in some broader cause—the very antithesis of "freedom."

This is a strong argument with ample historical and contemporary precedents. However, it is possible to grant even the core of this argument and still conclude that more freedom is better than less.

Whatever values men hold dear, and however completely they submerge their individualities in some larger cause, the fact remains that there will always be other values and other causes. Freedom from constraint does not imply that the individual must "free" himself from all value or bonds, but that he must be left free to impose on himself any values he finds useful and agreeable. Freedom must be seen then not as a goal in itself, but as a process or state of affairs wherein the totality of human experience is accessible and it remains only for the individual to choose. The prospect of unlimited choice and the implicit toleration of others' values may be unnerving to many individuals. Once having made their choice, they may want to close down the unselected options. The genius of the founders of the American political system was their recognition that freedom is a process from which all other values ultimately derive. In this section we will further amplify some aspects of freedom and discuss them as a component of or complement to an economic system.

Freedom is sometimes separated into freedom "from" and freedom "for" categories. "A person is free to the extent that he has the capacity, the opportunity and the incentive to give expression to what is in him and to develop his potentialities." For ages, men were "free" to conform to certain standards, practices, beliefs, and patterns or to accept unpleasant consequences. This asymmetrical "freedom" is of course not freedom at all but conformity—a conformity to high standards and high ideals perhaps, but nevertheless conformity. In religion this tradition has been typified by "true faiths" and state religions in which the concepts of state, ruler, and the divine were inextricably linked; the Pharaohs were thought of as gods. In politics, this has usually meant absolute fealty to a wealthy monarch or an elite in power. In the realm of ideas it has meant conformity to a tradition such as the Aristotelian system in the Middle Ages. In economics, it has spelled enforced common practices such as the Guild system, also of the Middle Ages, and resistance to innovations. Even in our own time, freedom of conscience, freedom of thought and political practice, and freedom of enterprise and association are hardly universal. Freedom of conscience or belief involves the free choice or denial of religious persuasion, and puts limits on the way your view may be impressed on others. Freedom of thought involves the right to have access to the full range of thought, past and present, and the right to produce and disseminate new thought.

There should also be limits on the manner in which past and present ideas can be impressed on others. As in the case of religious ideas, your right to individual belief and thought does not extend to forcing your ideas on others. They should have the right to say "No thanks, not interested," and thus end the contact. One should be able to join or quit any political grouping or social association as it suits his purpose or ideals. These groups or associations should have strictly limited spheres of influence, designed to check the encroachment of one group's ideas, views or interests on some other group's. When one group holds public office, the right to dissent, to register opposing views, and to seek a change of administrations must be ensured.

Freedom of economic enterprise and association involves the right to choose an occupation, to obtain skills, to offer these freely to employers, and to change employment. This concept is reasonably universal. However, the ownership of capital, the right to establish, manage, and liquidate an economic enterprise, and to enjoy its fruits are a matter of debate. Some maintain that the rights of one man to own and manage capital must inevitably conflict with the rights of other men to the fruits of their labor. This debate may never be resolved because economic theory in this case collides with deep-seated political, social, and cultural values.

However, to pull back from these thorny issues, one may define freedom of economic enterprise as the right of an individual to manage his affairs so as to promote his own welfare, with limits on the extent that his welfare may be advanced at the expense of others. Examining these general definitions of freedom, one pattern is clear—the individual should be free to extract from his environment only those factors that suit his tastes, preferences, and interest. He should be free to neglect those elements that do not suit his needs. Since all men are bound to each other in societies, the freedom *not to accept* a portion of the environment requires positive checks on an individual's freedom to impose a life-style on his neighbor.

It is this symmetrical responsibility of freedom that is the hardest thing to communicate in a free society. The freedom to choose selectively your beliefs and ideals, politics, associates, and occupation should be valued highly. The high value men place on such matters makes the temptation to impose these ideals and interests on others almost irresistible—"for their own good," naturally. Therefore, how much one values freedom of choice can be measured by his defense of others' freedom to choose values differing from his own. The individual who demands conformity values only his own set of beliefs, not the freedom to hold, express, or create values.

Having developed this concept of freedom, it may be possible to examine the economic systems we have studied to determine how compatible each is with respect to the broader goals of individual freedom.

Freedom and Central Planning

It is obvious that the purpose of social organization is to produce results superior to those of individual efforts. There is very little rationale, particularly economic, for social organizations in which the results of collective effort are actually inferior to separate individual efforts. It is difficult to weigh the advantages and costs of a centrally planned economic system to determine whether it is indeed superior to another organizational form. It is accepted that the individual worker, firm, resource owner or user, or consumer will have to sacrifice a greater or lesser degree of autonomy or sovereignty to the central authorities in the management of his affairs. If the planners issue directives that duplicate what the individual would have done himself, the planners are not needed. If the planners give orders that diverge from this pattern, the individual is forced away from the position he perceives as optimum. A heavy burden of evidence is placed upon defenders of central planning to show where the extra payoffs are going to come from to compensate individuals and society for the loss of freedom to manage one's own affairs.

The inner logic of centralization is standardization and conformity. Standardization has an economic and an organizational basis—first, to reduce direct production costs and second, to reduce the information required to make and transmit decisions and orders and to check up on performance and obedience. Such standardization may indeed deliver a product which is cheaper, but one that is also "inferior" in the sense that it may be fully appropriate or useful to no one. Henry Ford is quoted as having said that his customers could have any color Model T that they wanted as long as it was black. The military offers universal jumpsuits to its recruits—too long for short men, too short for tall, too tight for fat, too baggy for thin men—it fits only the statistically average recruit. Procurement planning and production costs are enormously simplified and reduced. The typical university building has elevator capacity to meet the statistical flows of students—unfortunately, students tend to flow in one hour spurts, a fact that has never gotten through to state architectural committees.

To people concerned with the overall trend toward conformity in modern mass industrialized, urbanized society, it is the absence of alternatives that is the most offensive aspect of central planning. The worker faces one employer, the resource owner faces one purchaser, the consumer buys what the system makes available. It is not necessary to pick examples from the planned economies of the Soviet bloc to grasp, at an intuitive level, the implications of reduced alternatives. What American has not experienced the frustrations of some "locked-in" situation? Who has not stood in line in some government or business office, experienced rudeness, indifference, carelessness, or even intimidation at the hands of some flunkey? In such a situation nothing is so psychically liberating as to be able to say, "You are not the only (fill in the blank) in the world. I'm taking my business elsewhere!" To have no alternative is to lose leverage or control over some facet of your environment. To prevent *you* from abusing your position, others should have an alternative to you.

Conformity to centrally determined standards and directives is also inimical to what most of us would recognize as democratic processes. Great economic power centralized in a bureaucracy is comfortably associated only with a similar political structure. It is almost impossible to conceive of a natural relationship between great central economic power and decentralized political democracy. Such an arrangement would leave society with no effective check on decisions made by the central planners in the name of society. Democratic political authorities would have a grasp on the tail of the tiger—they would go only where the tiger went, holding tighter wouldn't help, and letting go might be disastrous.

Freedom and Market Socialism

When Yugoslavia beat a retreat from central planning, they fell back on the "natural" alternative, the market, as a form of economic organization. As has been suggested, a centralized political or economic apparatus does not fit well with a decentralized counterpart. In this case, a centralized political apparatus surrendered the power to command in detail the structure and pace of economic development. The Communist party found itself in the position of a jockey with whip and spurs but no horse to ride. They had unchallenged political dominance and essentially nothing to do but hold meetings and make speeches—pretty boring stuff for revolutionaries. Ambitious men were left to scramble for a declining number of influential government posts or to get a job in industry.

The logic of self-management in industry—the existence of the market, of alternatives, of competition—was bound to have an impact on political ideas. Alternative employment, managers, customers, suppliers, ideas, and parties must inevitably get intermingled in mens' minds.

The socialism of Yugoslavia is an artificial construction—laws determine what may be privately owned and what publicly and who exercises managerial prerogatives. Change the law and you may change the mix of socialist-capitalist ownership. A democratic society changes laws to suit the needs of its people. These needs change. The record of market socialism is too short to know whether it is a viable system in and of itself or an artificially maintained hybrid.

Freedom and the Competitive Mixed-Economy

It is a measure of the intellectual climate of times past and present that is sometimes embarrassing to defend capitalism too vigorously. Many progressive intellectuals find it difficult to accept the notion that it is possible to defend the market system and still be a respectable humanitarian. A defense of capitalism is not a defense of "capital" or of the dominance of business over labor or consumer interests. Rather it is the defense of a system which ensures, when working properly, that no interest can ever assume a position of dominance over another. Liberal attacks on monopolies, collusion, and undesirable business practices are ignoring the fact that these are aspects of a malfunctioning market system. All too often it can be shown that the existence of private restrictions on the competitive market mechanism is not a natural product of capitalism but a direct result of governmental interference. For example, government regulation of railroads began as an attempt to prevent abuse of a transportation monopoly. When trucking and air transport opened up the possibility of a return to competition in the field of transportation, the government then held all in the embrace of regulatory agencies.

It does not require an extended analysis to demonstrate that the market system is the economic expression of the concept of freedom through free choice among alternatives. This is the historical strength of the ideas and theories of competitive capitalism. These doctrines have complemented the development of political democracy in Britain, the United States, and other English-speaking nations. When the finest aspirations of idealistic men are matched by those of "practical" men, and both together produce social stability in a context of evolving political freedom and economic progress—the combination is virtually unassailable. It took the collective insanities of two world wars and a protracted world-wide depression to discredit capitalism and democracy. Alternatives to capitalism exist, and all too many alternatives to democracy exist. We have enough evidence to form reasoned opinions.

Competitive capitalism has been reconstituted with a substantial degree of vigor in Europe and most of the British Commonwealth. Substantial expansions of the social welfare systems of these countries have not materially undermined the workings of the economic system. Political democracy is at its high water mark in virtually all of the developed capitalist countries of the world. Enormously difficult problems remain but it would be hard to defend the notion that a radical upheaval of society and the economic structure would resolve them.

Some people may have a deep distaste for capitalism. The crass hustle of the market is offensive to delicate souls and properly may be avoided by them. The groves of academe are filled with men and women who could earn more in the "real world" but who are quite content to pursue other goals. That certainly is their business and plenty of alternatives to commercial careers exist in modern capitalist democracies. However, it is interesting to note that the keenest critics of competitive capitalism and advocates of statist planning are also professed defenders of individual freedom. One is naturally almost as bemused by staunch Chamber of Commerce speeches in defense of laissez faire, made by businessmen who are lined up first and longest at the public trough. Actually the point is that people are people—they have ideals and motives that may not be fully consistent with each other. The economic system that assures us that individual greed, ignorance, or chicanery will have natural checks or redound to the discredit of the individuals involved is the best. Any system which does not have these checks is not as desirable as one that does.

QUESTIONS

1. What arguments support the view that the economies of the developed nations of the East and West are converging on a common pattern?
2. What major differences do you believe still exist between the planned and mixed economies?
3. What is freedom? Do you agree with the definition given in this chapter?
4. What is economic freedom? Is the right to own property a necessary aspect of economic freedom?
5. Is central planning compatible with freedom?
6. Is capitalism compatible with freedom?
7. Is market socialism compatible with democratic political institutions?

BIBLIOGRAPHY

Friedman, Milton. *Capitalism and Freedom.* Chicago: University of Chicago Press, 1962.

Hayek, Frederick A. *The Road to Serfdom.* Chicago: University of Chicago Press, 1944.

Mishan, Ezra. *The Costs of Economic Growth.* New York: Frederick A. Praeger Publishers, 1967.

Schumpeter, Joseph, A. *Capitalism, Socialism, and Democracy,* 3rd edition. New York: Harper and Row, 1947.

Solo, Robert. *Economic Organizations and Social Systems.* New York: The Bobbs-Merrill Company, Inc., 1967.

Index